YĀDAVENDRAMAHODAYA

OF

NĪLAKAṆṬHA

WITH THE COMMENTARY OF V.S. RANADE — A CRITICAL EDITION AND STUDY

by

Dr. Siddharth Yeshwant Wakankar
Research Officer,
Oriental Institute,
M. S. University of Baroda,
Opposite Palace Gata Palace Road,
Vadodara-390001
(Gujarat)

BKP

BHARATIYA KALA PRAKASHAN
DELHI—INDIA

Published by:
C.P. Gautam
Bharatiya Kala Prakashan
3421-A, 2nd Floor, Narang Colony,
Tri Nagar, Delhi-110035
Ph. 7153083

First Published : 2000

ISBN : 81-86050-41-8

Laser Typesetting by
Ishan Comprint
G 16/14, Qutab Enclave-I, (DLF)
Gurgaon (H.R.), Ph. 91-352412

Printed at
Santosh Offset Press
40, Anand Nagar, Inder Lok, Delhi-110035

PREFACE

In the Sanskrit Language there are a number of works which are still in the form of manuscripts. Their authors have so to say remained into oblivion because of the non-currency of their works. Some works were fortunate enough to be printed. But, the unpublished material outnumbers the published one. The majority of such unpublished works is stored in manuscript-collections throughout this land.

Here is an attempt to publish one such unknown and rare *mahākāvya* dealing with the life of Kṛṣṇa from his birth upto his marriage with Rukmiṇī. It is composed in the middle of the nineteenth century by Nīlakaṇṭha, a Kannadiga Brahmin, who was domiciled in Maharashtra and immediately, a small commentary was written on it, that too in Pune by Viṣṇu Śāmarāya Rānaḍe-a versatile scholar, scribe and collector of manuscripts. Both these works are edited together in this Book.

Their manuscripts are available in only two libraries, viz. the Bombay University Library and the Bharat Itihasa Samshodhaka Mandal Library in Pune. The present work is based on these three manuscripts as no other manuscript of any of these two works is available anywhere else, neither are they mentioned to be in existence in any of the catalogues of manuscripts. Authorities of both these Institutes were very kind to supply the xerox-copies of their manuscripts. The active co-operation of those authorities is acknowledged with gratitude.

During the course of my study, I received guidance and assistance from many scholars and well-wishers, to whom I am deeply obliged. It is difficult to mention all of them here.

First of all, I express my deep sense of gratefulness to the authorities of the Bombay University Library, especially, the Librarian, Shri A.C. Tikekar, for promptly supplying the xerox-copy of the manuscript. Secondly, it is my duty to thank the authorities of the Bharat Itihasa Samshodhaka Mandal, Pune, for supplying the xerox-copies of their two manuscripts, one each of the original poem and its commentary.

Amongst the scholars who helped me in all respects, I must mention my *Gurus*, in fact, the *Gurutraya*, viz. Prof. Dr. (late) Govind Keshav Bhat, Prof. Dr. M.D. Paradkar and Prof. (late) M.V. Mahashabde - all of the Bombay University, for their active encouragement and guidance in all respects.

Next, I must put on record that the entire staff of the Oriental Institute was very co-operative with me and always ready to render any kind of help. It is my fortune that everyone helped me in all possible ways. I must mention the debt which I owe to three scholars from this Institute - who are experts in manuscript-reading. They are : Shri P.H. Joshi, the senior-most Research Officer, Sau. Vijaya S. Lele, formerly a Research Assistant in the Institute and Prof. Dr. M.L. Wadekar, my young and energetic colleague and presently the General Editor in the Oriental Institute. All these three have helped me in various ways by giving guidance and tips for the improvement of the work. I am deeply grateful to them.

Last, but not the least, I must put on record my deep sense of gratitude to the authorities of the Maharaja Sayajirao University of Baroda, for not only granting me nine-month study-leave to complete my Thesis, but, also for granting permission to get the thesis printed.

I will be failing in my duty if I do not put on record my appreciation of the staff of the Library of the Oriental Institute - who was ever-ready to help me by issuing books whenever asked for and bearing with my delay in returning the books. Other libraries like the Asiatic Society, Bombay, Bombay University Library etc. were also of much help in procuring required books. I express my gratitude to all of them.

August 1999 **(S.Y. Wakankar)**
Baroda

CONTENTS

PART - I

INTRODUCTION

CHAPTER-I

PREFATORY REMARKS/ OBSERVATIONS

Sanskrit is the only Classical Language in the world which has the longest and continuous history of poetic compositions-dating back from the hoary past and extending till the present day. In this long span of time, many works were composed. Some were very lucky to be known, studied, appreciated and consequently, printed, while others lacked that fortune. The unpublished mass of literature outnumbers the published one. In course of time, some authors and their family-members were relegated to subordinate status, mainly due to the non-publicity and non- currency of their works. There are many causes for this like lack of patronage (royal as well as academic), social and political situation not conducive to academic and intellectual excellence or poetic taste, indifferent attitude of the elite, mutual professional rivalry et al. It is, however, a fact that the general/usual tendency of a majority of Sanskrit scholars of not blowing their own trumpet - their disinterest in or indifference towards publicity/propaganda, not giving much importance to themselves - must have been the root-cause of their silence about themselves and their own works, their propagation and publication - thus leading to their non-popularity with the masses. This peculiar self-denying tendency must have sent them as well as their works/compositions into oblivion, for a long time. Our author is no exception to this traditional approach of a majority of Sanskrit scholars.

Our poet Nīlakaṇṭha belongs to a very educated and cultured Kannadiga family of poets of eminent standing. Fortunately, his works as well as of his two near relatives, viz. his father and younger brother, are extant and furnish us with very valuable biographical account which enables us to have a fairly clear picture of their family background, their intellectual pursuits and the heights they reached.

It is a matter of great surprise that this family of sound scholars and good poets could not attract due attention of scholars towards their creative and genius members and consequently, remained in the dark till the present century as far as the publication of their poetic compositions is concerned. In fact, only the two works of Trivikrama, the father of Nīlakaṇṭha, saw the light of the day. Neither any work of Nīlakaṇṭha nor of his younger brother Mukunda has been seen to have been printed. Here is, therefore, an humble attempt *to bring to light for the first time* a *Mahākāvya*, viz. *Yādavendramahodaya* of Nīlakaṇṭha, describing in ten cantos, the life of Lord Kṛṣṇa from his birth upto his marriage with Rukmiṇī. Nīlakaṇṭha is a chip of the old block in the sense that his father Trivikrama has two poetic compositions to his credit. Nīlakaṇṭha's younger brother, Mukunda, also has two works to his credit, which are still unpublished, as against those of his father which have been printed.

With these prefatory remarks, we turn to the actual data about our author-poet, his father and brother and their works and possible dates, as gleaned from their compositions or commentaries thereon.

CHAPTER - 2

AUTHOR, HIS RELATIVES, WORKS AND DATE

A: NĪLAKAṆṬHA: BIOGRAPHICAL ACCOUNT:

In the second last and the last verses of all the ten cantos, Nīlakaṇṭha gives the names of his father, mother, his own as well as of his poem and its canto number. Towards the end of *Yādavendramahodaya* (and of *Śaṅkaramandārasaurabha*. and *Śaṅkarābhyudayakāvyam*), Nīlakaṇṭha furnishes the important details about his parentage, preceptors, grand-parents etc. which are summarised as follows: Trivikrama and Pārvatī were his parents, Cidghanānandanātha and Anasūyā alias V/Keṅkammā were his grand parents, Tryambaka was his uncle, he studied Nyāya and Vyākaraṇa from (Trivikrama and) Gaṅgādhara and his spiritual preceptor was Nṛsinha Bhāratī Svāmī, of the Śṛṅgeri Mutt. From these details, the approximate date of Nīlakaṇṭha could be reasonably fixed, as he specifically does not give any kind of information about his times. In this respect, the date of the commentary on YM. is also of paramount importance. We turn to that :

Trivikrama, the father of Nīlakaṇṭha, composed his famous *Pañcāyudhaprapañcabhāṇa* in Śaka 1727 (corresponding to A.D. 1805), as is clear from the second-last verse of the *bhāṇa*, which reads as under:

Ṛṣinayanācalaśaśimitaśakavarṣe (1727) krodhanābhidhe śukre/
Yātassitadvitīyāsuragurudina eṣa pūrṇatām bhāṇaḥ//

(Verse no. 344)

Shri V.S. Ranade, the commentator of the Y.M. specifically states the date of the completion of his *Ṭippaṇa* in the following words:

Śake 1771 *phālgunāsitadvādaśyām ravivāsare ṭippaṇam samāptam//*

Śake 1771 corresponds to 1849 A.D.

Shri V.S. Ranade was a well-known scribe, in addition to being a *Ṭippaṇakāra* also. He wrote down two Mss. of the *Śaṅkaramandārasaurabha* of Nīlakaṇṭha and at the end of each, he gives the dates of the writing down of those two Mss. as under: (Mss. Nos. 27147 and 27148 deposited in the Oriental Institute, Baroda).

[Idam pustakam rānaḍe-ityupanāmakaśāmarāyāṅgajena viṣṇunā puṇyākhyapattane kaṣṭena sampāditam/ Śake 1771 saumyābde Pauṣamāsyasite dale daśamyām bhaumavāsare samāptim paphāṇa// and *Idam pustakam rānaḍe-ityupanāmnaḥ śāmarāyāṅgajasya viṣṇorasti/Śake 1771 pauṣe māsi kṛṣṇapakṣe trayodaśyāmasya granthasya lekhanam samāptam//*] It means that Nīlakaṇṭha must have definitely composed his Y.M. and SMS. before *Śaka* 1771, that is 1848/ 49 A.D. Thus, he must have flourished in the middle of the 19th century.

Prof. Dr. W.R. Antarkar, in his edition of the *Śrīśaṅkarābhyudayakāvyam* of Nīlakaṇṭha, "based on a Devanāgarī copy of a solitary copy of the same printed in the Telugu characters in the South" and published in "*The Journal of the University of Bombay*, September, 1964, Vol. XXXIII (New Series), Part 2, Arts Number, No. 29, p.129 - adduces another important evidence for this date (time) as under:

"At the end of the *Śaṅkaramandārasaurabha* and also at the end of the *Yādavendramahodaya* - (addition mine-SYW), the author (i.e. Nīlakaṇṭha) salutes Deśikas called Śrīman Nṛsiṁhabhāratī and others, by which are now to be understood Nṛsiṁha Bhāratī Svāmī and/or Saccidānanda Śiva Abhinava Nṛsimha Bhāratī, for, after 1805 A.D., these two *Ācāryas* only of the Śṛṅgerī Mutt bear the title Nṛsiṁha Bhāratī. According to the Śṛṅgerī Guru Paramparal, these two *Ācāryas* reigned between 1817 A.D. and 1879 A.D. and 1879 A.D. and 1912 A.D. resp."

The fact that both the commentaries (on Y.M. and SMS) were composed/copied down in *Śaka* 1771 (i.e. 1848-49 A.D.) confirms this date of our author and suggests that both these works (as well as the *Śrīśaṅkarābhyudayakāvyam* - in the absence of any contradictory evidence) must have been composed by the forties of the 19th century, much before the outbreak of the First War of Independence fought in 1857 A.D.

B. WORKS OF NĪLAKAṆṬHA:

Nīlakaṇṭha is supposed to have composed three works in Sanskrit, resorting to three forms of composition, as stated under:

(i) *Yādavendramahodaya* - a *mahākāvya* in ten cantos describing the life of Lord Kṛṣṇa from his birth upto his marriage with Rukmiṇī.

(ii) *Śaṅkaramandārasaurabha* - a *campū* in six *taraṅgas*, describing the life of the Great Ādi Śaṅkarācārya and

(iii) *Śriśaṅkarābhyudayakāvya* - a *khaṇḍa/laghukāvya* in six *sargas* - again describing the life of Ādi Śaṅkarācārya.

About the 2nd and 3rd compositions, a strange fact has come to light. One and the same author treats of one and the same subject-matter/theme in two different poetical forms, viz. *Campū-kāvya* and *laghukāvya*. It is still more baffling that neither of these two works refers to the other one, even remotely, although the ending portions (that is the last 17-18 verses) of the last chapters (*taraṅga* and *sarga* respectively) of both the works mention the antecedents (parentage, *gurus* etc.) of both these Nīlakaṇṭhas, which are exactly identical. It is really curious that no one, even indirectly, refers to the other one or the other work composed by him. Is it a case of not disclosing one's identity, due to some inexplicable reason - best known to the author himself? Not only that the last stanzas of these two works on Śaṅkarācārya are similar, but, some phrases and stanzas from *Śrīśaṅkarābhyudayakāvyam* are to be actually found in the *Yādavendramahodya* too - suggesting that both the authors were/are one and the same, as is clear from the genealogical account available from all these three works - as given at the end of the last chapter of each of the work.

After the discussion about our author, his date and works, we turn to a brief discussion of two of his near relatives - father and younger brother - each one of whom composed two works.

C. FATHER (TRIVIKRAMA) : BIOGRAPHICAL ACCOUNT:

Trivikrama (wife Pārvatī) of Puṇyagrāma (i.e. modern Pune in Maharashtra), son of Cidghanānandanātha and Anasūyā (or Veṅkammā/Keṅkammā) and father of Nīlakaṇṭha (author of *Yādavendramahodya*) has composed two works, viz. *Kuvalayāśvavilāsacaṁpū* alias *Mahālasācaṁpū*, in six chapters, called *ullāsas*, dealing with the life of Nala. It is printed in the *Grantharatnamālā*, No. 4, Bombay 1890.

The second work of Trivikrama is the famous and the longest *bhāṇa* in Sanskrit, viz. *Pañcāyudhaprapañcabhāṇa* which was composed in 1805 A.D. Both these works begin and end with the same verse as follows :

Beg: *Granthasya likhyamānasyāsyāntarā patatām muhuḥ/*
Śāntyarthamantarāyāṇām Śivām pañcamayīm numaḥ//

End: *Trivikramakṛtāmetām śītāṁśusahajāsakhaḥ/*
Trivikramaḥ kṛtim pāyādapāyādaghasaṁbhavāt//

In two verses (8 and 9) of the *Ppbhāṇa*, Trivikrama gives some details about the scholarship of his brother as well as his own as follows :

Nyāyāmbhonidhimandaraḥ śrutiśiraḥ kāsārapāṭhīnarāṭ
Mīmāṁsātrimuniśruta-prakaṭitānalpātmadhīvaibhavaḥ/
Yaḥ sāhityakalāvilolanayanāmāṅgalyasūtram dṛḍham
So'yam tryambakapaṇḍito vijayate yasyāgrajaḥ sodaraḥ//8//
Na kevalamagrajo vidyāpradaśca.
Kim brūtha ?

Kimayamanavadyasakalavidyānidhesstryambakavidvanmaṇer-aṇujanmanā trivikrameṇa praṇīto bhāṅḥ? Tarhi vidita evāyamasmākam/

Yatkāruṇyātkavayituramuṣyāgrajaḥ khyātakīrtiḥ
Loke sārasvatajalanidheḥ pāradṛśvā babhūva/

So'yam vidyāguṇamaṇikhaniḥ sarvamantrātmamūrtiḥ
Tāto yasya tridaśadṛśaścidghanānandanāthaḥ//9//

From these verses it is very clear that both the brothers were well-versed in different sciences in Sanskrit.

The author specifically states in the beginning of this *bhāṇa* that it is being staged in Puṇyapura, i.e. modern Pune in Maharashtra. cf: *Bhagavataḥ śaṁbarariporvasantapūjāmahotsavaḥ parisarodyāne samārabdhaḥ puṇyapuravilāsibhiriti/ Tadahamapi tatra gatvā kañcit samayam mano vinodayāmi/*

At the end of this *bhāṇa*, the date and place where this *bhāṇa* was staged are given in the following verses :

Ṛṣinayanācalaśaśimitaśakavarṣe (1727) *krodhanābhidhe śukre/*
Yātaḥ sitadvitīyāsuradina eṣa pūrṇatām bhāṇaḥ//
Jayati dhṛtapuṇḍracāpaścaraṇasarojanatākhilāśāpaḥ/
Puraharapuṇyavivartastrivikramāghaughajantusaṁvartaḥ//

It means that it was composed in *Śaka* 1727, corresponding to 1805 A.D., in Puṇyapura, i.e. modern Pune in Maharashtra.

Since both these works are already printed, I need not dilate on them here.

This Trivikrama had another son, besides our present author Nīlakaṇṭha. His name is Mukunda, the author of *Caṇḍīdaṇḍaka*, a *stotra* in praise of Caṇḍī in the *Daṇḍaka* metre and *Śaṅkaramandārasaurabhasamīra*, a commentary on the *Śaṅkaramandārasaurabhacaṁpū* composed by Nīlakaṇṭha.

D. BROTHER (MUKUNDA): BIOGRAPHICAL ACCOUNT:

Mukunda, the younger brother of Nīlakaṇṭha, composed two Sanskrit works, viz. *Caṇḍīdaṇḍaka* - a praise in the *Daṇḍaka* metre of the Goddess Caṇḍī and a commentary, *Samīra*, on his elder brother's (Nīlakaṇṭha's) *Śaṅkaramandārasaurabha*.

In the last verse as well in the colophons to both these works, he gives some biographical information, but, does not give any clue to his date. The scribe, one Rāma, gives the date of the copying down of the *Daṇḍaka* as *Śalivāhana Śaka* 1765, i.e. 1843

A.D. The relevant portions are reproduced here from the unpublished manuscripts of both the works :

Bālājīti ca yam prāhurmukunda iti yam jaguḥ/
Caṇḍapuṣṭiprayāsākhyo daṇḍakastena nirmitaḥ//

Colophon: Iti śrītrivikramasūrisūnoḥ pārvatigarbhasaṁbhavasya mukundasya kṛtau caṇḍidaṇḍakassamāptaḥ/

The scribe adds: Śrīśālivāhanaśake 1765 śobhakṛdvatsarajyeṣṭhavadya (śubha) pratipadi likhito'yam rāmeṇa daṇḍakaḥ/

The end of the *Śaṅkaramanda rasaurabhasamīra* runs like this:

Jātāttrivikramaguroḥ saṁbhūto yo mukundaśabdaguṇāt/
Ākalpāntam caratāt śaṅkaramandārasaurabhasamīraḥ//

The colophon runs like this :

Iti śrīmattrivikramavidvanmaṇisūnoḥ pārvatyambātanayasya nīlakaṇṭhānujasya mukundasya kṛtau śaṅkaramandārasaurabhesamīre ṣaṣṭhastaraṅgaḥ/Sampūrṇaścāyam granthaḥ//

As pointed out earlier, though the dates of compositions of these two works are not given by the author, in the case of these two works, the scribes, fortunately furnish the dates when the works were copied down by them. In the case of the *Sms samīra*, the scribe, V.S. Ranade, gives clearly the dates when he completed the writing down as *Śaka* 1771 (A.D. 1849 - as already mentioned while discussing the date of Nīlakaṇṭha). Thus, it is clear from the dates (that is the age) of the manuscripts that Y.M. and S.M.S. were composed by Nīlakaṇṭha in the early forties of the 19th century and immediately the commentaries were written on them - suggesting thereby that the works must have been very popular at his time or at least they had some recognition as far as their poetic compositions were concerned. It is just possible that they were popular in limited circle or the *pāṭhaśālā* - inducing some one to write a *Ṭippaṇa* or a commentary to keep them in currency.

After the works and date of our author and his near relatives - who were definitely Karnataka Brahmins, as the names of some members such as V/Keṅkammā, Cidghanānandanātha and their adherence to Śaṅkarācāryaparaṁparā would make us believe-, we turn to the treatment of the date and works of our commentator, Viṣṇu Śāmarāya Rānaḍe - a prolific *Ṭippaṇakāra*, scribe and owner of many manuscripts of classical Sanskrit works and a traditionally sound scholar.

CHAPTER - 3

THE COMMENTATOR (ṬIPPAṆAKĀRA)

VIṢṆU ŚĀ(ŚYĀ)MARĀYA RĀNAḌE - HIS DATE AND WORKS:

In some of the colophons at the end of the works, it is clearly stated by our Commentator that he was a resident of Puṇyapattana, i.e. modern Poona (Pune) in Maharashtra. From the *ṭippaṇas*, it can be easily surmised that he had a family background of Sanskrit learning, esp. the traditional method of the *Pāṭhaśālā*. It is also a fact that he belonged to a very well-known family of educated and cultured scholars, who possessed a treasure of Mss. as a family heritage. This is borne by the fact that many Mss. copied down and owned by V.S. Ranade - our *ṭippaṇakāra*/ scribe - are deposited in the Bharat Itihas Samshodhaka Mandal, Pune.

It is my conjecture that V.S. Ranade must have started his career as a scribe for some distinguished Sanskrit Paṇḍita, either his teacher, a relative or a friend - as a number of Mss. written or copied down by him would make as believe. This statement can be verified by a glance at the *Catalogue of Mss.* in the BISM., edited by Prof. G.H. Khare - wherein, there are many Mss. that are specifically mentioned as written by V.S. Ranade. In course of time, he must have ventured to write down notes - either independently or with the help of some existing scholarly commentary of other scholar - as is specifically mentioned by Ranade himself in the colophon of his *Ṭippaṇikā* on the *Kādambarī* (*Pūrvārdha*) Cf.

Iti Śrīmatpaṇḍitasārvabhaumaśrībhānudīkṣitaviracita-kādambarīṭīkānusāreṇa kādambarīṭippaṇikā rānade-ityupanāmaka-śāmarāyaṅgajena viṣṇuśarmaṇā mahatā prayāsena granthāśayajñānārtham nirmitā/Śake 1769 plavaṅgābde māghe māsi navamyām ravivāsare puṇyākhyapattane samāptam//

This essay of his was either meant for himself as a ready reference while teaching his private students or for others. The nature of his *ṭippaṇas/ṭippaṇīs/ṭippaṇikās* makes it clear that they were class-room notes, like guides, since, he briefly discusses *samāsavigrahas*, gives the meanings of only some words and not of all words and gives quotations, mainly from *Amarakośa* and rarely from *Haima* (*Anekārthasaṅgraha* of Hemacandra) in support. He knew the limitations of his notes and hence, he has purposely termed them as *ṭippaṇa, ṭippaṇikā* etc. and not *vyākhyā, ṭīkā* etc. As a result of this brief or sketchy nature of his treatment, sometimes, he is very much ambiguous and misses the exact mark and purport of the verse. At times, he has to offer some explanation that seems to be far-fetched. When he realized his capacity to prepare notes, he made it a habit to study a particular work and immediately jot down his points/notes for further reference. It is just possible that due to heavy workload of teaching etc., he might not have been able to write down a detailed commentary on any work and was obliged to remain content with this service of preparing only notes, whenever he found leisure. Thus, his leisurely hours have proved to be a great help/boon for the readers to comprehend the meanings of some difficult words. In due course, he started writing gloss after gloss on various works of his choice/liking - thus, the bulk of his Mss. increased - some of them were his own *ṭippaṇas* and others the works he copied down. Though, majority of his *ṭippaṇas* are very short - sometimes to the extent of becoming very vague/ambiguous - his *ṭippaṇi* on the *Yādavendramahodaya* is the longest in view of the fact that it is on a *māhākāvya* consisting of ten cantos and having a continuity of events and narration. Of course, in this *ṭippaṇī* also, at times, he is extremely miserly in his treatment and explanation. One thing must be said to the credit of our *ṭippaṇakāra* that he has meticulously mentioned the day and date of the completion of a particular *ṭippaṇa* in its colophon. Only this piece of information has helped us in fixing the period of his commentatorial activity. A look at such colophons of some of his works suggests the approximate duration/period of his activity. A detailed alphabetical list of the works on which he has written his *ṭippaṇas* is furnished below - in support of this statement. It may be further noted that all these works with his glosses are available only at the Bharat Itihas Samshodhaka Mandal, Pune - as per the present state of our knowledge.

Name of the work:	Date of composition in *Śaka*
(1) *Uttararāmacarita-ṭippaṇikā*	1768
(2) *Kādambarī-ṭippaṇikā (Pūrvārdha)*	1769
(3) *Kuvalayāśvacaṁpū-ṭippaṇikā*	1772
(4) *Nalacaṁpū - ṭippaṇī*	1771
(5) *Pañcāyudhaprapañcabhāṇaḥ, saṭippaṇaḥ*	1771
(6) *Mālatimādhava-ṭippaṇī*	1772
(7) *Muktāvaliḥ, saṭīkā*	1766
(8) *Yādavendramahodaya-ṭippaṇī*	1771
(9) *Rāmacarita-ṭippaṇī*	1777
(10) *Rāmāyaṇacaṁpū-ṭippaṇikā*	1768
(11) *Lakṣmīsahasram (Yamakastabaka-ṭippaṇī)*	-
(12) *Lakṣmīsahasra-ṭippaṇī*	1769
(13) *Viśvaguṇādarśacaṁpū-ṭippaṇikā*	1768
(14) *Veṇīsaṁhāra-ṭippaṇikā*	1768
(15) *Śākuntala-ṭippaṇikā*	1768
(16) *Śrinivāsacaṁpūḥ-saṭīkā*	1763

There is a doubt regarding the authorship of the following works/*ṭippaṇī*/*ṭippaṇikā*, as the authors thereof are not specifically mentioned:

(1) *Kuvalayānanda-ṭippaṇikā*

(2) *Tattvasaṁkhyāna-ṭippaṇī*

(3) *Nīlakaṇṭhacaṁpūḥ*

The details are based on the information contained in the *Catalogue of Manuscripts* at BISM, edited by Prof. G.H. Khare.

I am very much constrained to mention here that as nearly six trips in the last ten years of mine failed to even have a look at many of these Mss. I am obliged to rely solely on the information given in the catalogue. In view of this genuine difficulty, it is extremely difficult to say with precision whether a particular com. is penned by V.S. Ranade or is actually composed by him - unless it is specifically stated at the end of the work (in the colophon) to be a work of V.S. Ranade.

From the dates given above, we may roughly say that the peak years of activity of our *ṭippaṇakāra* are from *Śaka* 1763 to *Śaka* 1772, the most fruitful years in this span being S. 1768, 1769, 1771 and 1772, as most of the *ṭippaṇas* are completed during these four years.

It seems very likely that Pune was not only the birth-place of our *ṭippaṇakāra*, but, his place of literary activity too. It is indeed very interesting to know that only at one place, at BISM, and that too in Pune, we find the Mss. of the works of our *ṭippaṇakāra*. Hence, probably, he has remained unknown till this date. Thus, *this happens to be the first ever attempt to bring to light a little-known treasure.* It is needless to add that I am fully aware/conscious of my limitations - personal as well as circumstantial - in this venture. I can only assure the discerning readers of having spared no pains in not only locating or spotting, but, in collecting the material for this work in an atmosphere that can hardly be said to be conducive to solid research.

CHAPTER - 4

MANUSCRIPT MATERIAL

The present poetical work is available in only three manuscripts - two of the original text and one of the commentary. The Bombay University Library has only one ms. of the original *kāvya,* while, Bharat Itihas Samshodhaka Mandal, Pune, has one ms. each of the *kāvya* as well as its *ṭippaṇa.* I furnish below the necessary details of all the three Mss.

(1) The BUL has a ms. of this work, Accession No. 2211 - designated in this study as B. The physical description is:

Folios: 74; Size: 9.25" x 4.25". Material: Thick blue, green and yellow paper; Condition: good; Characters: distinctly good and clear Devanāgarī; 8 lines in a page and 41 letters per line.

The ms. begins on f. lb. and ends on f.74a. Folios la and 74b have the title. The ms. does not look very old and is almost accurately written. At times, there are some lacunae and orthographical errors. It may be that this ms. was copied down from a source different from that of the Pune text, although, it is observed that there is a complete agreement between this and the Pune ms. Barring some cases to be counted on finger-tips, there are no marginal notes - matter- suggestive of second thought, revision or correction etc. On a closer comparison/collation, it is observed that B is a copy, almost *verbatim,* of the Pune (P) ms., as except at some places - which are microscopically minor - there seems to be complete agreement between the B and P as far as readings, carrying out of marginal corrections (with a few exceptions) are concerned. Of course, at times, we get the impression that B has some different reading from that of P, possibly because of some other source to be copied down from.

The Bharat Itihas Samshodhaka Mandal, Pune, has one ms. each of the original work and its commentary, designated herein as P and P (1), respectively.

(2) P. Acc. No. 53.26 ka. F. 40; Size: 12.8" X 5.5". Material: thick yellow paper; Condition : good; Characters: very clear, distinctly good and beautiful Devanāgarī; 10 lines per page and 48-56 letters per line.

The ms. begins on f. 1b and ends of f. 40a. Folios la and 40b are blank. The ms. does not seem to be very old and is almost very accurately written and no lacunae are found. Hence, it is used as a *Vulgate*. One important feature of this ms. is: marginal additions in the form of gloss, quotations, corrections and insertion of a new verse after II. 48, suggesting the after - thought. The meticulous additions suggest the diligence and carefulness of the scribe, due to his sincerity and integration of character. On the strength of this piece of evidence, it may be conjectured that P. is a revised first copy of the original ms. which is now very difficult to trace, as nowhere in any of the catalogues, any mss. apart from these two (of the text) are mentioned to be in existence - although its record and mention - in any hand-list cannot be gainsaid. It may be said to the credit of the scribe of P that there is hardly any orthographical error - indicative of the conscientious nature and scholarship of the scribe. It makes an impression on our mind that he is a trained or seasoned scribe and hence there are no scribal mistakes/aberrations in his writings.

(3) P. (1) Acc. No. 53.26 kha; F. 28, Size : 12.8" x 5.5". Material: Thick yellow paper; Condition: good; Character: very clear and distinct Devanāgarī. The lines per page vary from 10-16 and letters per line vary

from 56-60. The text is represented by only the *pratīkas* (*lemmax*) - which are not always carefully and rightly taken. There are additions on all the four sides in the margins on almost every folio with the sign of *kākapadas* - many times rendering it very difficult to exactly decide the place where a particular line is to be inserted. These passages in the margins are not at all clear in the xerox-copy supplied to me by the authorities of the BISM, resulting into extreme difficulty in deciphering the letters. This has its adverse effect on the understanding of the text at a few places. My repeated trips to BISM failed to yield any tangible results, since these two Mss. are reported to be misplaced or lost. Consequently, I am obliged to be content with the existing situation. The special feature of this ms. is the date of composition of this commentary specifically written as *Śaka* 1771 *Phālguna-sitadvādaśyām revivāsare ṭippaṇam samāptam*. This is the only internal evidence to corroborate our statement that the poem must have been composed before *Śaka* 1770, i.e. 1849 A.D. Some orthographical lapses to be found in this ms. are pointed out at the necessary places in the Thesis and some are silently corrected.

PECULIARITIES OF THE SCRIBES:

(B) The Bombay University Library Ms. (B) is from a scribe having a very good, in fact, excellent, hand-writing, the character or way of writing being basically Maharashtrian. This ms. shows a variety of cases of Marathi (local or vernacular) impact e.g.

ऊ written as ऊ

ह्व written as -ह्व

Other peculiarities of the scribe could be mentioned as under:

B. starts with *Śrīgaṇeśāya namaḥ* at the beginning of every *sarga*. There are nearly five cases of lacunae.

He at times fails to understand and hence carry out the

corrections made in P., such instances are pointed out at their relevant places. He hardly makes any distinction between *sta/stha, va/ba* etc.

He invariably writes *dhdha* for *ddha, scha* for *stha, cha* for *ccha, kha* for *ṣa, jhjha* for *jjha* etc. Such instances are silently corrected.

At places, he hurriedly writes/spells the words, giving rise to metathesis.

He omits/drops unknowingly some letters, *mātrās, repha, visarga, anusvāra* etc. and then many times joins the two words and creates difficulties/confusion in comprehending.

At some places he rubs or erases some letters and writes over them - making the words illegible.

The most glaring peculiarity is writing *gni* for *ti* or *ni*. At a couple of places, he has omitted certain verses that are found in P.

Sometimes, he retains both the *anusvāra* as well as the *anunāsika*, writes *anusvāra* for *n* and *vice-versa*.

From all these, we get the general impression that B. scribe is not a careful, expert and seasoned scribe, which is further supported by the huge number of variants to be found in it.

(P) The Bharat Itihas Samshodhaka Mandal Ms. of the Text (P).

It is crystal clear from the excellent calligraphy of the P. that the scribe must have been a Maharashtrian, as some peculiar traits of Marathi orthography have inadvertently crept in, e.g.

ऊ is written as ३ू or उ॑

हृ is written as ह्रु

hra (ह्र) is invariable written as *rha* (-र्ह)

Since the work deals with Lord Kṛṣṇa's life, the P. starts with *Śrīkṛṣṇāya namaḥ* at the beginning of each *sarga*.

There are not much scribal errors in this ms., no spelling mistakes peep in and its a sheer joy to read the text characterised by excellent calligraphy and absence of orthographical errors.

(P-1)

The Bharat Itihas Samshodhak Mandal Ms. of the Commentary (P-1)

The P-1 is a *sui generis* ms. of the *Ṭippaṇa* and is the only source to comprehend the nuances of the original text/poetic composition. The beautiful and neat Devanāgarī hand-writing indicates its Maharashtrian leanings. There are some cases of mis-spelling of certain words - which are the general traits of almost every scribe, e.g. *dhdha* for *ddha*, *scha* for *stha*, *ca* for *cha*, *va* for *ba* and *vice-versa*, *jhjhi* for *jhi*, उी for ū, अै for ऐ. It seems that he is either not so keen and careful while writing down (or shall we say copying down) from other ms. or he is not so seasoned and careful writer, as the writing in all the four margins of folios would make us believe. He uses almost on all the folios the *kākapada* to insert some matter in the margins, making full use of the blank spaces at his disposal. It may be a case of diligent and conscientious writing, so that nothing should be left out. Despite this congested way of writing, his neat and clear handwriting is a joy and poses hardly any problems in deciphering the letters. The influence of Marathi orthography unknowingly/inadvertently peeps in such cases of spelling उी/अू instead of ऊ, अै for ऐ, -ह for ह्र etc. Other peculiarities are the usual ones such as :

No distinction between *va/ba*, *sta/stha*

Omission of *mātrā*, *repha*, *visarga*, *anusvāra* and joining the words etc.

Use of both - the *anusvāra* as well as the *anunāsika* in the same word.

Orthographical lapses like, *utgīrṇa* for *udgīrṇa*, etc. which are either silently corrected or shown at their proper places.

The present Thesis is based on the xerox-copies of these three manuscripts. It may be noted here that in the xerox-copies the marginal notes are not clear and hence, sometimes, the portions cannot be easily read or deciphered. The Bombay University authorities promptly supplied the xerox-copy of their ms. The BISM also was quite quick in supplying the xerox-copies of their two mss., but, after that, the original mss. could not be seen by the present researcher, despite his 5/6 trips to Pune. The authorities of BISM report that the mss. are lost/misplaced. Hence, the present researcher craves the indulgence of the scholars. On this background, it is heartening to note that the BUL Ms. was always available for referring to, whenever the present researcher went there. But, the B. ms. is so nicely written - with neat, clear and beautiful handwriting - that there was no scope for any doubt or confusion, except at a couple of places of overwriting.

At the end, it may be noted that except these three mss. - two of the original poem and one of its commentary -, there is no mention of any other copy of any of these mss. existing or reported to be existing or recorded in any of the catalogues, as per the knowledge of the present researcher. Even the authorities of the *New Catalogues Catalogorum* could not supply more information about these three, except the one, so painstakingly collected by the present scholar.

PEDIGREE OF THE MANUSCRIPTS :

It seems that there were more manuscripts of this original poem than the ones that are extant now. As is already stated, the P considered by us to be the *Vulgate* - seems to be revised copy of an untraceable ms. - which is proved by the marginal insertions. The original from which it could have been copied is lost to us. The same is the case with B. Though mostly the readings of B. make us believe that it follows the P., at a couple of places, the readings in B. seem to have been based on some other source - which also seems to have been lost. Another source of its being later than P is - at a few places, there are erasions and corrections, resulting into illegibility due to overwriting; some marginal corrections done in P. are not to be found in B, probably because B had a different source than P. The case with P-1 is quite different. Despite hectic efforts to procure another ms/copy of this commentary, the present researcher could not lay his hands on any other ms., thus - compelling him to solely rely on only one ms. without a second for comparison. This has diminished the value due to insufficient means for collation. The present researcher may be excused for this factor beyond his reach or control.

STEMMA CODICUM

Supposed Original

Ur Text

P B

P P-1

CHAPTER - 5

THE WORK PROPER-
CANTO-WISE SUMMARY OF THE YĀDAVENDRAMAHODAYA

The *Yādavendramahodaya* is a *Mahākāvya* in ten cantos, dealing with the life of Śrīkṛṣṇa from his birth upto his marriage with Rukmiṇī. The "Great Rise or Appearance of the Best of the Yādavas" as the title would literally mean, is so named because the poem primarily describes only those incidents from the life of Śrīkṛṣṇa which brought him glory, due to his bravery, prowess, as also some other very popular incidents from his life, such as his childhood, butter-stealing, sports, adventures, *Rāsalīlā* etc. The poet describes these as they are handed down by tradition, adding poetic flavour to it and not much bothering about the inner meaning of some of these incidents nor thinking about the propriety of the Highest God having amours with the *gopīs*. His seems to be an attitude perpetuated by tradition and relished by the poets and masses alike.

I furnish below the summary of each *sarga* as per the order of the incidents narrated therein.

Canto - I :

The canto opens with the praise of Śrīkṛṣṇa, who is talking to a *gopa* by disrespecting Lord Indra - whose pride was removed by Kṛṣṇa himself by uplifting the Govardhan mountain.

The second verse just describes the kings in the Dvāparayuga. The third vs. describes the Earth distressed due to the tyranny of Kaṁsa etc. who had unleashed a reign of terror and injustice, the plight of the Earth, her going to Lord Brahmadeva and describing her pitiable condition to him (vs.4).

Then Brahmā along with her and other gods goes to Lord Viṣṇu who was reclining on the Śeṣa- serpent in the Milky ocean (vs. 4/5) Viṣṇu's statement agreeable to the gods (vs.6), consoling the gods accordingly by Brahmā and dispatching the gods and the Earth to their respective places (7- 10), description of the Śūrasena country (11-13), description of Mathura, ruled over by Śūrasena (14-15), the news of the marriage of Vasudeva and Devakī (16-17), Kaṁsa's driving their chariot (18), the Aerial Speech, announcing the death of Kaṁsa at the hands of the eighth son of Devakī (19), the cruel Kaṁsa desirous of killing Devakī (20), the promise of Vasudeva to hand over the children to Kaṁsa and saving the life of Devakī (21-22), the birth of the six sons of Devakī and their killing by Kaṁsa (23- 25), Nārada going to Kaṁsa and instigating him (26-29), imprisonment of Devakī and Vasudeva (30), dethroning of Ugrasena and usurping his throne by Kaṁsa (31), the transfer of the seventh *garbha from* the womb of Devakī to that of Rohiṇī (32-34), Viṣṇu's desire to enter the womb of Devakī (35), the *dohadas* of Devakī (36-37), graphic description of the pregnant Devakī (38- 40), the praise of Viṣṇu by the Gods, headed by Brahmā, Śiva etc. (41-53), the birth of Śrīkṛṣṇa and the pleasant conditions at that time, the joy expressed by the gods, the dances of the *Apsarasas* and the showering of flowers by the gods etc. (54-58). The last two verses in every *sarga* mention the name of the poet with the names of his parents (59) and the name of the poem and number of the *sarga* (60). It is the peculiarity of the poet that he invariably mentions the name of his parents and himself in the penultimate verse of every *sarga* and the number of the *sarga* and the name of the poem in the last verse.

Canto - II :

The first verse describes the birth-rites of Kṛṣṇa.

The second verse mentions the sixteen-year old form of Kṛṣṇa.

The third verse describes the wonderment of the parents, their praising their son and his commencing his pleasant speech.

The vs. 4-10 describe Kṛṣṇa narrating the previous lives of his parents.

The vs. 11-18 - Kṛṣṇa's advice for the exchange of the daughter of Nanda for him and his placement at the house of Nanda and Vasudeva executing his orders, opening of the gates of the prison, the watchmen not hindering the path of Vasudeva, the taking place of the exchange of the two children and Vasudeva's return to the prison.

The vs. 19-25 describe the birth of the seventh child and its flying to the sky after warning Kaṁsa that his death is living elsewhere.

The vs. 26-34 describe the consultations Kaṁsa has had with his counsellors and his plans for the killing of the eighth son of Devakī. (Mention of Pūtanā wandering here and there for killing the young ones-newly-born-children.).

The vs. 35-41 describe the birth celebrations of the son at the house of Nanda.

The vs. 42-44 describe the visit of Nanda to Mathura for paying the taxes and his dialogue/discussion with Vasudeva. Vasudeva informing about the plans of Kaṁsa to kill the newly-born children.

The vs. 45-49 describe the Pūtanā incident.

The vs. 50 describes the anguish of Nanda due to experiencing the truth of the speech of Vasudeva about the plans of Kaṁsa to kill the children.

The vs. 51-54 describe the Tṛṇāvarta incident.

The vs. 55-56 describe the naming ceremony of the two sons by the family-priest (i.e. Garga Muni).

The vs. 57-65 describe the playful activities of Kṛṣṇa such as his smiling, crying or weeping, his rolling on the sides, crawling, walking with faltering steps, his taking support of some things to stand erect, his gluttony, in short, his giving pleasure to others by his playful and childish activities.

The last two verses (66-67) mention the name of the poet, his parents, name of the *kāvya* and the number of the *sarga*.

Canto - III :

The entire canto describes the activities of Kṛṣṇa as a child as well as a grown-up Kṛṣṇa.

The verses 1-12 describe the different childish activities of Kṛṣṇa, like breaking of the pitchers, stealing of butter, milk etc., releasing the cows from the bondage etc.

The vs. 13-16 describe the eating of mud by Kṛṣṇa and on being reprimanded by his mother, showing the worlds in his mouth to his mother, her seeing herself in his mouth and getting wonder-struck.

Vs. 17-22 describe his going to his mother for a suck, breaking the pitchers, churning rods etc.

Vs. 23-29 - his mother binding him to the mortar as a punishment.

Vs. 30-38. His approaching the two Arjuna-trees and breaking or uprooting them and releasing the sons of Kubera from the curse, pronounced on them by Nārada.

Vs. 39-52. Going to the New Settlement of Vrindavan and therein playing games, grazing the cattle, mock-court activities, bedecking their bodies with feathers of birds, garlands of flowers, imitating the sounds of different birds etc.

Vs. 53-55 - Dhenukāsura incident.

Vs. 56-58 - Bakāsura incident.

Vs. 59-68 - Aghāsura incident.

Vs. 69-73 - Going to the banks of the river Yamuna and partaking of food with his friends, telling them fascinating stories, satisfying the cattle by feeding it etc.

Vs. 74-92. Carrying away of the cows by Brahmadeva. Their disappearance causing anguish or distress to Kṛṣṇa, his assuming the forms of the cattle and his friends, for one full year, poetic description of the colourful dresses of the cow-herd boys, Brahmadeva astonished at this supernatural feat of Kṛṣṇa and his bowing down at the feet of Kṛṣṇa and begging his pardon and going back to his place at the behest of Kṛṣṇa.

Vs. 93 describes the return of Kṛṣṇa along with his friends to

Vraja at the end of the day (as usual), the narration of this incident by the *gopas* to Yaśodā and giving joy to everyone present there.

Vs. 94-95 - as usual supply the name of the poet, his parents, the name of the *kāvya* and the number of the *sarga*.

Canto - IV :

The brave exploits of Kṛṣṇa are continued in this *sarga* too.

Vs. 1-12 describe Kṛṣṇa taking the cattle for grazing. The poet says that wherever Kṛṣṇa went for this purpose, those places were the stepping-stones for his future training in duel fights and other acts of bravery i.e. these wanderings enabled him to know the geography of the different regions and the many games they played prepared them mentally and physically for displaying their prowess in future. That is, these were the training camps, as it were, for them for achieving their goals.

Vs. 13-18 - Going to the Tālavana, the forest infested with demons. They start felling the trees.

Vs. 19-24 - Dhenukāsura incident.

Vs. 25 describes the *gopas* enjoying the Tāla-fruits and praising Rāma and Kṛṣṇa for their prowess.

Vs. 26-50 - Kāliyāhi incident.

Vs. 51- The *gopas* return to their abodes in the evening along with Rāma and Kṛṣṇa.

Vs. 52-68 - The description of Nature, esp. the Summer-season (Grīṣma).

Vs. 69-75 - Pralaṁbāsura incident.

Vs. 76 - Rāma and Kṛṣṇa following the foot-prints of the cows, reach a forest place.

Vs. 77-82 - Description of the forest-fire.

Vs. 83-84 - The last two verses as usual give the name of the poet, his parents, name of the *kāvya* and the number of the *sarga*.

Canto - V :

The earlier portion of this canto is devoted to the description of Nature.

Vs. 1-14 - Description of the Rainy-season (Prāvṛṭ).

Vs. 15-29 - Description of autumn (Śarad).

Vs. 30-37 - Description of winter (Hemanta).

Vs. 38-57 - The famous incident of the carrying away of the clothes of the *gopīs* by Kṛṣṇa while they were observing the Kātyāyanīvrata. The dialogue between Kṛṣṇa and the *gopīs*.

Vs. 58-75 - Rāma and Kṛṣṇa having lunch with the *gopas* while wandering into the forests.

Vs. 76-110 - The well-known Indrayāga incident. Kṛṣṇa persuades his men to go in for the worship of the Govardhana mountain and the cattle instead of Lord Indra, the torrential rains unleashed by the enraged Indra, as a sort of punishment to Kṛṣṇa and his cow-herd friends for disrespecting/denying the share of Indra in the sacrifice. The defeat of Indra by Kṛṣṇa by removing his false pride in his supreme powers.

Vs. 111-124 - Nanda goes for a nocturnal bath to Yamunā, was carried away to Pātāla by the men of Varuṇa, Kṛṣṇa's personally going to Varuṇa for releasing his father, Varuṇa begs the pardon of Kṛṣṇa for his own sin of/in arresting and not releasing Nanda - the father of Kṛṣṇa - with a view to having a *darśana* of Lord Kṛṣṇa who would, he rightly thought, come to rescue his father, Varuṇa's satisfaction at the sight of Kṛṣṇa, 'his giving valuable gifts to Kṛṣṇa and finally the return of Kṛṣṇa along with Nanda to Vraja.

Vs. 125-126 - The last two verses as usual give the names of the poet, his parents, the name of the *kāvya* and the number of the *sarga*.

Canto - VI :

The sixth *sarga* is an illustration of the pedantic poetic genius of our poet/author. The first forty verses are couched in the style of a *Citrakāvya* - with *Yamaka* in the last quarter of every verse and abounding in *Anuprāsa* and clumsy/cumbrous constructions.

Vs. 1-32 - These are full of the beautiful description of Nature, esp. the Sun, Sun-rise, Sun-set etc. with a variety of novel and striking ideas, excellent *Utprekṣās* - showing the height of poetic fancy-quality of the author.

Vs. 33-72 - The description of Kṛṣṇa, playing on the Flute, the *gopīs* getting enchanted by its sweet notes/tunes, their natural haste and anxiety, eagerness to go near Kṛṣṇa - giving rise to funny situations. The dialogue between Kṛṣṇa and the *gopīs*, their keen interest in playing with Kṛṣṇa, Kṛṣṇa's promise to fulfill their desire for sports, their amorous sports described with minute details (which enabled Vātsyāyana to include these amorous activities in his work on Erotics (*Kāmasūtra*) with necessary divisions). Every *gopī* thought herself to be superior to any other one, because - she thought - she got full advantage of the vicinity of Kṛṣṇa and his love, thus, every *gopī* was proud of her fortune.

Vs. 73-74 - The last two verses as usual.

Canto - VII :

The entire *sarga* is the continuation of the previous topic of the amorous sports of Kṛṣṇa and the *gopīs*, Kṛṣṇa removing their pride etc. The whole *sarga* is full of the delicacy of words/style (*Mārdava*).

Vs. 1-11 - Disappearance of Kṛṣṇa from the scene, hectic efforts of the *gopīs* to trace him, their eager inquiries about his whereabouts addressing the trees, flowers etc. Here a number of *Utprekṣās* and delightful sayings hearten the readers.

Vs. 12-20 - The sight of the foot-prints of Kṛṣṇa along with that of another person, the search of *gopīs* for Kṛṣṇa and their lamentations giving vent to their feelings, emotions, affection for him etc.

Vs. 21-39 - The reappearance of Kṛṣṇa before the *gopīs* with the marks of satisfaction due to enjoyment with them.

Vs. 30-35 - Their amorous sports described. The search of the *gopīs* for the real cause of Kṛṣṇa's harsh attitude towards them.

Vs. 36-40 - Kṛṣṇa's explanation for his temporary disappearance and his re-appearance.

Vs. 41-55 - Kṛṣṇa's *Rāsakrīḍā* with the *gopīs.*

Vs. 56-58 - Kṛṣṇa's efforts to remove the fatigue of the *gopīs.*

Vs. 59-61 - With their amorous sports with Kṛṣṇa over, the *gopīs* go to their abodes in the morning and this *Rāsakrīḍā* is repeated every night.

Vs. 62-63 - The last two verses as usual.

Canto - VIII :

The canto opens with the visit of Nārada to Kaṁsa in order to make/let him know the reality, viz. immediately after the birth of the eighth child, the father (i.e. Vasudeva) removed it to the place of Nanda in Gokula and replaced it with the new-born daughter of Nanda and returned to the prison. That same child has killed the Dānavas like Tṛṇāvarta and other powerful enemies who had assumed different forms. The step-brother of that child (i.e. Balarāma) is also very powerful like him and out of your extreme pride in your prowess, you should not neglect them or connive at them (Vs. 1-12).

Kaṁsa invites and instructs Ariṣṭa and Keśī to kill Vāsudeva (Vs. 13) and orders Akrūra (14-15) to bring Balarāma and Kṛṣṇa for the *Dhanuryāga* in Mathura.

Vs. 16-24 - Ariṣṭāsura incident.

Vs. 25-111 - At the instance of Kaṁsa, Akrūra starts on his sojourn to Vraja (Gokula), description of Gokula, his reception by Nanda, deliverance of the message of Kaṁsa to bring R. & K. to Mathurā to see the *Dhanuryāga,* his decision to start for Mathurā the next morning, Kṛṣṇa's inquiry to Akrūra about his parents and their message to him, how Kaṁsa behaves with them, Akrūra's describing the facts to him (48).

Vs. 49-60 - Describe the lamentation of the gopīs at the burning news of Kṛṣṇa's going to Mathurā, their legitimate fears that he may not remember them (*gopīs*) after he reaches Mathura.

Vs. 61-69 - Beautiful descriptions of moonset, night, sunrise etc.

Vs. 70-111 - The return journey of Akrūra from Gokula to Mathura starts. The touching scene of the parting of R & K (73-77), Kṛṣṇa consoles *gopīs* (78-79).

Vs. 80-81 - The actual journey starts and within no time, the three (R.K. and Akrūra) reach the river Kālindī.

Vs. 82-87 - The *ṣaṭka* describes the river Kālindī.

Vs. 88-92 - Akrūra takes a bath in Kālindī and is surprised to see the chariot - which he had stationed at the bank of the river - in the water of the river and also sees the Ananta Śeṣa being praised by the gods.

Vs. 93-100 - This *Navaka* describes the person sitting on the lap of Śeṣa.

Vs. 101-109 - Akrūra praises that *Puruṣa*.

Vs. 110-111 - Kṛṣṇa asks Akrūra as to why he was delayed/late. On that Akrūra just asks him in wonder 'What is not known to/by you' and drives the chariot towards and reaches Mathurā.

Vs. 112-113 - The last two verses as usual.

Canto - IX :

This canto containing 98 verses is packed with incidents. The treatment of the incidents is very brief, almost sketchy. It is only the enumeration of events with very little details, covering a vast convass of incidents from the entry of R & K in Mathurā till the mention of the marriage of Balarāma with Rohiṇī. The life story of K. is hurriedly gone through.

Vs. 1-9 - Description of Mathurā.

Vs. 10-13 - People thronging to the windows to have a look at Kṛṣṇa.

Vs. 14-15 - The washerman/launderer (*Rajaka*) incident.

Vs. 16 - The weaver (*Vāyaka*) incident.

Vs. 17 - The hunch-backed lady (*Kubjā*). incident.

Vs. 18 - The garland-vendor (*Mālika*) incident.

Vs. 19 - The place of *Dhanuryāga*.

Vs. 20 - The breaking of the bow (*Dhanurbhaṅga*).

Vs. 21 - The killing of the guards (*Rakṣivadha*).

Vs. 22 - Returning home in the evening.

Vs. 23-28 - Kaṁsa remembers the speech of Nārada and sees ill- omens.

Vs. 29-34 - Kaṁsa summons and orders the wrestlers to kill Kṛṣṇa.

Vs. 35-38 - Killing of the elephant Kuvalayāpīḍa by Kṛṣṇa.

Vs. 39 - With the tusks in their hands, R & K enter the arena and Kaṁsa is frightened.

Vs. 40-51 - The Cāṇūra incident.

Vs. 52 - The killing of Muṣṭika.

Vs. 53 - Kaṁsa wonders as to how his powerful wrestlers were so easily killed.

Vs. 54 - R & K. start fighting with their equal-aged wrestlers.

Vs. 55 - Kaṁsa orders that R.&K. should be driven away from Mathurā, Nanda should be divested of his riches and Vasudeva and Devakī be killed.

Vs. 56-57 - Fight between Kṛṣṇa and Kaṁsa.

Vs. 58 - Death of Kaṁsa.

Vs. 59 - Death of the brothers of Kaṁsa.

Vs. 60-61 - Joy of the gods at the death of Kaṁsa.

Vs. 62 - Lamentations of the wives of Kaṁsa.

Vs. 63-65 - Kṛṣṇa bowing down to his parents and speaking with them.

Vs. 66 - Ugrasena installed on the throne of Mathurā.

Vs. 67 - Nanda returns to Vraja.

Vs. 68-74 - The Sāndipanī incident - that is R.&K. going to Sāndipanī, getting trained by finishing the education.

Vs. 75-77 - Jarāsandha attacks Mathurā.

Vs. 78-90 - These verses hurriedly mention the incidents of the death of Kālayavana, the creation of Dvārikā, Kṛṣṇa giving *darśana* to Mucukunda.

Vs. 91 - R. & K. return to Dvārakā, after killing the army of the enemies.

Vs. 92-93 - Jarāsandha confronts them on the way. They fled away to a mountain. Jarāsandha follows them and sets the mountain - wherein R & K. had hidden-on fire.

Vs. 94 - R. &K. leapt out of the burning mountain. Jarāsandha returns home thinking that R.& K. are dead.

Vs. 95 - R. & K. delight their relatives by returning to Dvārikā.

Vs. 96 - The marriage of Balarāma and Rohiṇī.

Vs. 97-98 - The last two verses as usual.

Canto - X :

The major or in fact the only event/incident in this *sarga* is the marriage of Kṛṣṇa and Rukmiṇī and its antecedents.

Vs. 1-8 - Description of Bhīṣmaka and his capital city Kuṇḍinapura.

Vs. 9 - Mention of his four sons and one daughter.

Vs. 10-11 - The description of Rukmiṇī.

Vs. 12 - Mutual longing of Kṛṣṇa and Rukmiṇī.

Vs. 13-15 - Rukmī's opposition to the marriage of Rukmiṇī with Kṛṣṇa.

Vs. 16-24 - Rukmiṇī sends a Brahmin messenger to Kṛṣṇa with her letter.

Vs. 25-31 - Kṛṣṇa along with the Brahmin messenger rushes to the city of Bhīṣma and the description of the city where the marriage is to be celebrated.

Vs. 32-41 - Arrival of Śiśupāla with his allies at Bhīṣmapurī, i.e. Kuṇḍinapura/rī.

Vs. 42 - The Brahmin Messenger delights Rukmiṇī with the welcome news of the arrival of the Kṛṣṇa in the city.

Vs. 43-51 - Rukmiṇī goes to the temple of Girijā for worship.

Vs. 52-60 - A beautiful *Navaka* describes the bride Rukmiṇī.

Vs. 61-66 - A graphic description of the mental attitude of the love-lorn kings assembled there.

Vs. 67-72 - Rukmiṇī worships Girijā, asks for a boon and sees Kṛṣṇa in the vicinity, as suggested by her.

Vs. 73-110 - Kṛṣṇa carries Rukmiṇī away by placing her in his chariot, the fight between Kṛṣṇa and Jarāsandha, Śiśupāla, Rukmī etc., his defeating them and successfully entering Dvārikā, along with Rukmiṇī.

Vs. 111-113 - The marriage of K & Rukmiṇī.

Vs. 114 - Other marriages of Kṛṣṇa.

Vs. 115-121 - The poet Nīlakaṇṭha describes his parentage, teachers, preceptors etc.

Vs. 122-123 - The last two verses as usual give the name of the parents of the poet, his name, the name of his poetic composition as well as the number of the *sarga*.

Here ends the *mahākāvya* containing ten cantos, dedicated at the feet of that Lord who had assumed ten incarnations.

CHAPTER - 6

ORIGIN AND DEVELOPMENT OF THE LIFE-STORY OF KṚṢṆA

After the summary of the poem, we turn to the actual sources of this composition.

As stated earlier, a mass of legends, myths, stories describing different aspects and characteristics and having local colouring/variations etc. has been woven around the personality of Kṛṣṇa - thus making him a complex amalgamation of the traits of differing personalities, bearing the common name Kṛṣṇa. The fact that there are many and differing accounts bearing on the same subject and details suggests that these texts were composed by different authors at different times and in different parts of India, obviously basing their compositions on the local or oral traditions existing or prevailing in those places and also suggests that Vyāsa alone was not the only composer of these differing accounts. This naturally leads us to the legitimate conclusion that the various details of the story of Kṛṣṇa yield to a variety of interpretations, at times, just opposite to each other and depending mainly on the comprehension of the individual scholar of a particular aspect of the life of Kṛṣṇa. Moreover, this has led to another situation - of getting only a partial picture of the personality of Kṛṣṇa, depending mainly on the attitude of the particular author/scholar towards the character of Kṛṣṇa. This accounts for the absence or non-availability of reference to certain incidents in the life of Kṛṣṇa. As a result, we do not get a complete and cohesive account of the entire life-span of Kṛṣṇa, in chronologically earlier compositions, such as the *Mahābhārata*, *Harivaṁśa* etc. But, it is the *Bhāgavata-purāṇa* which blends all these tit-bits from the various accounts of Kṛṣṇa, as obtained from these sources and supplies to us a skeleton of the story of Kṛṣṇa which later on was elaborated by other poets in their compositions, with some more stress on certain aspects and relegating the other non-important aspects to subordinate position or altogether dropping them. This is the reason why no single account could be considered to be the original one - the genuine and complete life-story of Kṛṣṇa in its entirety. Some sources like *Agnipurāṇa* mention certain incidents only, the order of some of them not being in consonance with the general tradition, while, some other sources like the *Liṅga-purāṇa, Vāyu-purāṇa* and *Devī-bhāgavata*, refer to the Kṛṣṇa story only incidentally, while the *Mahābhārata* describes the life of Kṛṣṇa as connected with the Pāṇḍavas and at places glorifies Kṛṣṇa to such an extent as to extol him to the skies and raise him to the divinity of Nārayaṇa, the Highest God. This is the reason why the present researcher does not desire to get entangled into the controversy of the genuine and the spurious accounts of the Kṛṣṇa-story and is obliged to rest content with just giving a comparative account of the different incidents in the life of Kṛṣṇa, as found in the various source-materials. It will show the changes in the story of Kṛṣṇa. One important thing to be noted is: The story of Kṛṣṇa as found in the *Bhāgavata-purāṇa* has generally been the main source of later writers for their compositions and the basic structure of the story was elaborated by the poets according to their tastes. Such tendency of the poets was the root-cause of the degenerating of the *Rāsalīlā* incident to such an extent that it has been a bane on the character of Kṛṣṇa and scholars and devout devotees of Kṛṣṇa have been ransacking their brains to keep Kṛṣṇa above such non-sensical allegations. Such incidents have not been examined in details in the present work, as being beyond the scope of the Thesis of this nature.

With this brief observation, we turn to the account of the "Origin and Development of the Life-story of Kṛṣṇa". It may be pointed out at the beginning itself that exhaustive and exhausting assessment of the theories about Kṛṣṇa-propounded by all the scholars till this day-is a Herculean task-which is very difficult to achieve. Only the salient points will be discussed and that too as briefly as possible, as volumes after volumes are written on Kṛṣṇa and his different aspects/characteristics etc. It will be much less pertinent to refer to all that in this work. I, still, however, try my hand at it in passing.

ORIGIN AND DEVELOPMENT OF THE LIFE-STORY OF KṚṢṆA

The most fascinating figure in the history of this land is that of Kṛṣṇa, the son of Vasudeva and Devakī. The etymology of the word Kṛṣṇa is *karṣati iti Kṛṣṇaḥ* - a person who attracts or forcibly drags (the attention/minds of others). This magnet-like power of Kṛṣṇa is quite manifest from the amount of stories, myths and a mass of literature centering round his personality. Owing to his appealing character, Kṛṣṇa attracted the attention of almost every individual from times immemorial. This has led to a vast mass of writing on different aspects of his life. It is a queer thing indeed that the same set of evidence should offer conflicting views of different scholars. This is the reason for the controversy surrounding Kṛṣṇa and his historicity, the problem about his identity etc. Thus, he has become a bone of contention, a controversial figure due to his various qualities which have been studied separately by different scholars. It has given rise to contradictory views about his total personality. Here is an humble attempt to deal with some aspects of the features, facts, connected with Kṛṣṇa, especially, his identity, his sports - *līlās*. At the outset, let me be frank enough about certain limitations regarding the approach to certain features, facts, the physical and intellectual impossibility of any individual scholar to embrace all the aspects/angles of the life and mission of Kṛṣṇa. Since Kṛṣṇa has literally pervaded the hearts of almost all individuals - not only indigenous but foreign scholars also - giving rise to multifarious theories and counter-theories, depending on the aspect chosen by a particular scholar, it is really a Herculean task to cover all the aspects of his personality in a Thesis of such a nature. It is equally beyond the intellectual reach of the present scholar to give justice to the Kṛṣṇa as he is represented in certain plastic arts, painting etc. In fact, covering all the aspects of Kṛṣṇa's life will require a set of volumes, relating to each art form, including the poetic one. It is needless to dilate upon poetic compositions describing Kṛṣṇa and his life. So, I limit/confine the scope of this note to only a few glaring characteristics of his many - faceted life. My main thrust will be on his identity and the examination of some of his actions like the *Rāsalīlā*, and consequently, his being dubbed as a licentious individual, not fit to be considered as the Highest God.

While considering his identity, historicity etc., our main stress will be on literary evidence, for obvious reasons. In literary evidence also, we will limit ourselves to only Brahmanical evidence, couched in the Sanskrit language, for reasons of brevity. In Brahmanical literature too, we will abide by the chronological aspect of the references to Kṛṣṇa as a seer, poet, person, warrior, statesman, friend of the Pāṇḍavas, Kṛṣṇa and his childhood and Kṛṣṇa, the preacher of the *Bhagavadgītā* etc. Here one thing must be borne in mind viz. the contradictory qualities to be found in the character of Kṛṣṇa, viz. his Godhood, his amours with the cow-herdesses, especially against the background of his teachings in the *Bhagavadgītā*, the treacherous or foul means he adopted while helping the Pāṇḍavas in their battle against the Kauravas etc. These contradictory qualities/characteristics seem to have been amalgamated in the totality of the personality of Kṛṣṇa, as gleaned from various sources, such as different oral traditions with local variations, literary reference to Kṛṣṇa mainly based on the similarity of names etc. I am fully aware of the many pitfalls in this kind of a scholastic effort, requiring utmost care in sifting the available material, with least concern for its genuine or spurious nature.

A resume of the occurrences of the word Kṛṣṇa in the Vedic literature will not be out of place here. Once the identity or otherwise of those Kṛṣṇas is fixed, it will be possible for us to turn to the different theories regarding Kṛṣṇa and his identity or otherwise. A look at those references in keeping with the chronological order will help us in deciding the identity.

(1) The first or earliest reference to Kṛṣṇa is found in RV. VIII. 3- 4. This Kṛṣṇa is termed as Āṅgirasa Kṛṣṇa in the *Anukramaṇī*. One Kṛṣṇa Āngirasa is also referred to in the *Kauṣītakī Brāhmaṇa* at XXX. 9.

(2) The second and last reference to Kṛṣṇa in the RV. is at VII. 96. 13-15. This Kṛṣṇa is said to have been a non-Āryan warrior, who was waiting with his 10,000 soldiers on the bank of the river Aṁśumatī (i.e. Yamunā) and was defeated by Indra.

(3) The third reference to Kṛṣṇa is to be found in the *Aitareya Āraṇyaka*, at III, 2.6, where this Kṛṣṇa Hārīta is mentioned as a teacher.

(4) The first reference to Devakīputra Kṛṣṇa (as he is traditionally known to be throughout the later post-Vedic literature) is to be found in the *Chāndogya Upaniṣad* at III. 17.6. He is said to be a Vedic seer having some conversation with Ghora Āṅgirasa. This association of Kṛṣṇa with Ghora Āṅgirasa led Śaṅkarācārya to think that he was the student of Ghora Āṅgirasa. This interpretation has no basis in the *Ch. Upaniṣad,* as there is no such clear statement in this passage suggesting that Kṛṣṇa is the disciple of Ghora Āṅgirasa. It is a dialogue, but, not between a teacher and a student, as here Ghora Āṅgirasa describes the life of a man in the form of a Soma sacrifice; the natural functions like eating, drinking, procreating etc. are interpreted as elements of the sacrifice and the cardinal virtues are described as the reward of the sacrifice.

These are the only references to Kṛṣṇa to be found in the Vedic literature. Now, we turn to the post-vedic or classical Sanskrit texts referring to Kṛṣṇa.

The texts in classical literature like the *Mahābhārata, Harivaṁśa* and different Purāṇas speak of Devakīputra and Vāsudeva Kṛṣṇa, i.e. Kṛṣṇa, the son of Devakī and Vasudeva - variously representing him as a human hero, a cow-herd, friend and counsellor of the Pāṇḍavas, a religious teacher, gradually raising him to divinity, as a semi-divine being, a partial and later on a full incarnation of Viṣṇu. The ultimate deification of this Kṛṣṇa as an incarnation of Viṣṇu culminating into his identification with the Highest Brahman is the final stage in the development of the character of this Kṛṣṇa. The Purāṇas describe Kṛṣṇa as a Yādava, who spent his early life in Gokula and later on in Dvārikā. At a much later stage, he was deified as an incarnation of Viṣṇu Nārāyaṇa.

One important detail to be noted is that except the *Ṛgveda*, and the Brāhmaṇa-works, all other literary authorities mention Kṛṣṇa as the son of Devakī as also Vāsudeva, i.e. son of Vasudeva. After having deified him as Vāsudeva, worship was also offered to him, which is borne out by Pāṇini in *sūtra*, *Vāsudevārjunābhyām vuñ*-IV. 3.98. It means that at least at the time of Pāṇini in the fifth century B.C. Vāsudeva along with Arjuna was an object of devotion-*bhakti*.

This in brief is the chronology of the occurrences of the word Kṛṣṇa in Vedic Sanskrit literature.

As stated earlier, we are not considering the other sources like Buddhist, Jaina, epigraphical, sculptural etc. being beyond the scope of the present study.

On the basis of this summarization of literary evidences, we shall try to discuss the problem of the historicity of Kṛṣṇa in respect of the following points :

(i) Whether Kṛṣṇa was a human being or a god in the beginning.

(ii) Whether there was one Kṛṣṇa or many Kṛṣṇas and

(iii) Various theories about Kṛṣṇa.

(i) The Vedic literature furnishes evidence about the human as well as the divine nature of Kṛṣṇa. In respect of the classical (i.e. post-vedic) literature, one point may be noted that there have been additions to the nucleus of the *Mahābhārata* (as well as to the Purāṇas). The earlier portions of the *Mahābhārata* do refer to the human character of Kṛṣṇa, while the later portions represent him as a semi-divine being and those portions that come still later, regard Kṛṣṇa as the Supreme God. There did exist a stage when the ordinary contemporaries of Kṛṣṇa like Śiśupāla, Duryodhana etc. regarded Kṛṣṇa as an ordinary cow-herd, while, some senior contemporaries like Vyāsa, Bhīṣma, Nārada etc. - endowed as they were with divine wisdom-regarded Kṛṣṇa as an *avatāra* of the Supreme Being, without forgetting his human elements. The Purāṇas composed by different authors at different times and regions present various stages in the process of the deification of the human hero Kṛṣṇa.

In sum, it may be stated that *Ṛgveda, Kauṣītakī Brāhmaṇa and Chāndogya Upaniṣad* etc. refer to Kṛṣṇa as a Vedic Seer, evidently, a human personality. Kṛṣṇa in the *Ṛgveda* VIII is a non-āryan king also points to his being just a human being and not a god at that period of time. Later on, gradually, he was raised to the status of a God (Viṣṇu), His full incarnation etc. - evidently because of the later legends coloured with mythology and looking at his stories from a different viewpoint.

(ii) Whether there was one Kṛṣṇa or many Kṛṣṇas has been a bone of contention, because we get so many self-contradictory traits in the present personality of Kṛṣṇa - which must have been an amalgamation of different qualities of Kṛṣṇa. Let us see it.

Before actually attempting to answer this tricky question, it is absolutely necessary to make a clear distinction between the Vedic Kṛṣṇa and the Puranic or post-vedic Kṛṣṇa, i.e. Kṛṣṇa mentioned in post vedic literature like the *Mahābhārata, Harivaṁśa,* Purāṇas etc., because, in this latter literature, Kṛṣṇa is the son of Vasudeva and Devakī - which is the prevailing tradition too.

(a) The Vedic Kṛṣṇa is a seer of hymns and connected with Āṅgirasa. The Puranic Kṛṣṇa is neither said to be a seer nor is he at all connected with Āṅgirasa - in any capacity whatsoever.

(b) The other Vedic Kṛṣṇa is the non-āryan army chief with 10,000 warriors standing on the bank of the Aṁśumatī River. The Puranic Kṛṣṇa is never mentioned to be a non-āryan or an *asura,* defeated by Indra. In the Purāṇas, it is Indra who is at the receiving end and Kṛṣṇa is victorious.

(c) Devakīputra Kṛṣṇa mentioned together with Ghora Āṅgirasa in the *Chāndogya Upaniṣad* has no connection with the Puranic Kṛṣṇa, except the similarity in the metronym. Moreover, the similarity of teachings of Ghora Āṅgirasa in the *Chāndogya Upaniṣad* and the *Bhāgavadgītā* cannot be taken to be a valid and sound reason of the influence of Ghora A. on Kṛṣṇa for two reasons: (1) The Upaniṣads and *Bhagavadgītā* have parallels in philosophical principles is well-known-as *Bhāgavadgītā* has culled passages from the Upaniṣads. The *Bhagavadgītā*, however, never mentions Ghora Āṅgirasa as the source of any teachings. Had Kṛṣṇa been the disciple of Ghora Āṅgirasa - as is supposed by many scholars - he would definitely have referred to his revered preceptor. In fact, the Purāṇas mention Garga and Sandīpanī as the family-priest and preceptor of Kṛṣṇa, respectively, and not Ghora Āṅgirasa, as is supposed to be stated in the *Chāndogya Upaniṣad*. Hence, the attempt to identify these two Kṛṣṇas does not seem to stand to reason.

In a nutshell, it may be said that the Kṛṣṇa mentioned in the Vedic texts is definitely different from the Puranic Kṛṣṇa.

(iii) Now we turn to the last important topic about some of the important theories about Kṛṣṇa.

As we have seen earlier, there were many Kṛṣṇas and the picture of Kṛṣṇa which we generally get is a sort of amalgamation of the traits of some of the accounts about the life of Kṛṣṇa, as gleaned from different sources, oral traditions with local variations. This has enabled the scholars to put forward their views, theories etc. from that material consisting of controversial matter. It is a sort of an irony that the same set of evidence should help scholars in advancing different theories about the original nature of Kṛṣṇa.

Herein we will just take a resume of certain theories only and not of all the theories - which is in fact beyond the purview of this Thesis. We will be dealing with that Kṛṣṇa which is found in the *Mahābhārata, Harivaṁśa* and the Purāṇas, that is, the non-vedic or *Paurāṇika* Kṛṣṇa.

The *Mahābhārata* is primarily concerned with the Kṛṣṇa which is connected with Pāṇḍavas and their heroic exploits, i.e. the history of the Bharatas. The *Harivaṁśa* deals with that life and history of Kṛṣṇa which is not covered in the *Mahābhārata,* i.e. the early and later life of Kṛṣṇa. Thus, these two sources together furnish a complete life story of Kṛṣṇa - which was later on nicely put together in the *Bhāgavatapurāṇa,* so much so that the *Bhāgavatapurāṇa* gives a connected and cohesive life story of Kṛṣṇa in its entirety. So, these three main sources and later on the other Purāṇas supply us the life of Kṛṣṇa from different angles and aiming at different aspects of his life. In fact, every writer has a different purpose to deal with or describe the Kṛṣṇa-story- with his flight of imagination and his perception of Kṛṣṇa and the events and incidents in his life. This has given rise to the later-day amours of Kṛṣṇa with the cow-herdesses etc. Such topics, in fact, need not detain us too much, but, they will be dealt with at their proper places, though their treatment in details falls beyond the scope of this work.

The different myths/stories etc. about the various incidents from the life of Kṛṣṇa were current in society for some centuries and hardly anybody doubted and tried to put them to critical study as it was considered tantamount to sacrilege. But, it must be noted that this tendency of mere belief or blind belief made the topic a very elusive one in the domain of Indian history and literature too. Owing to the individual perception and the fancy of the authors/poets of the compositions like Purāṇas etc., the character of Kṛṣṇa became an amalgamation of different conflicting - sometimes self-contradictory-characteristics and Kṛṣṇa almost represented a syncretism of more than one individual. The self-contradictory features in his character created scepticism in the minds of those scholars who were critical in their attitude and approach and they doubted the historicity of Kṛṣṇa and maintained that the life story of Kṛṣṇa is a mixture of various elements - some contradictory and some superhuman-suggesting thereby that the present picture of Kṛṣṇa is a mixture of the characteristics of more than one person. This fact goaded the scholars to delve deep into this aspect and propose their views.

It is not at all possible and advisable - in fact, it is redundant - to make even a passing reference to all such theories, as it wouldn't be pertinent to deal with this topic in a work of such nature. I, however, still would like to refer to only two scholars and the views put forward by them. The first is one of the earliest views and the second one is one of the recent ones. I have resisted myself from dealing with other views of other scholars for obvious reasons. The two views will also be dealt with in brief only.

(i) Sir R.G. Bhandarkar in his *'Vaiṣṇavism, Śaivism* and *Minor Religious Systems'* puts forward the view that Kṛṣṇa and Vāsudeva were two different persons and in course of time, they were merged into one single person. He argues that the cow-heard Kṛṣṇa of the Purāṇas is different from the Vṛṣṇi Prince Vāsudeva of the *Mahābhārata*. He further holds that Vāsudeva was not originally a patronymic, but, the name of a person of the Sātvata or Vṛṣṇi race - who was worshipped as a Supreme Being and the tradition of Kṛṣṇa as a sage is seen in the *Ṛgveda* and the *Chāndogya Upaniṣad*. Bhandarkar further proposes that the conception of Vāsudeva as a father (of Kṛṣṇa) arose at a later date and Vāsudeva was identified with Vedic sage Kṛṣṇa and a genealogy was given to him in the Vṛṣṇi race through Śūra and Vasudeva.

It may be pointed out here that these views, though subscribed to by Garbe, Grierson, Jacobi, Winternitz and other scholars, are not supposed to stand to reason and hence, rejected by Hopkins, Keith, Chaudhuri, Raychaudhuri etc. Firstly, the name Vāsudeva occurs in the Vedic literature at *Taittirīya Āraṇyaka* (x.1.6) as a name of Viṣṇu. (Cf. *Nārāyaṇāya vidmahe/Vāsudevāya dhīmahi/Tanno Viṣṇuh pracodayāt/*). Further, the *Bhagavadgītā, Mahābhāraṭa* etc. clearly state that Vāsudeva was a scion of the Vṛṣṇi-family. The *Mahābhārata* clearly states that the true Vāsudeva was the Kṛṣṇa of the Yādava, Vṛṣṇi or Sātvata family of Mathurā. The entire Puranic tradition records that Kṛṣṇa was the son of Vasudeva and Devakī and that Kṛṣṇa and Vāsudeva were the names of one and the same individual. Moreover, the mention of Vāsudeva Kṛṣṇa and Śūrasenas or Sātvatas together in one context definitely indicates the early and inseparable connection between these two. It seems probable that Vāsudeva and Kṛṣṇa were one and the same person and the deification of Vāsudeva Kṛṣṇa and his identification as an incarnation of Viṣṇu were complete before the date of Patañjali (150 B.C.) who accepts this fact (i.e. identity) when he says in his famous *Mahābhāṣya 'Asādhurmātule kṛṣṇaḥ/Jaghāna kaṁsam kila vāsudevaḥ/*.

(ii) Dr. Iravati Karve in her book *'Yugānta - the End of an Epoch'* puts forward the view, which is summarised under :

Kṛṣṇa the human hero of the Vṛṣṇi race was a very great and ambitious individual of his times. He had very many ambitions, the main amongst them were : some connected with his family, some with the Kṣatriya class and some were personal. These objectives or goals were achieved by him in his life span.

The Kṛṣṇa of the *Mahābhārata* was the real one and the one painted in the *Harivaṁśa* or the *Bhāgavatapurāṇa* is totally different from this Kṛṣṇa. The goals of Kṛṣṇa were for the overall benefit of the society. The killing of his maternal uncle was a goal personal as well as in the interest of his family at large. Killing of Jarāsandha etc. was necessary for the consolidation of the Kṣatriyas of his times. His only personal ambition was to become a Vāsudeva - which he achieved by killing the Vāsudeva Pauṇḍraka. The last argument of Dr. Karve is : The Ābhīras - a nomadic tribe - carried away the women-wolk of the Yādavas after the Civil war, even though they were being escorted by Arjuna. When these Ābhīras saw that Kṛṣṇa was not perturbed either by the civil war or by the kidnapping of the women, they were wonderstruck at the equillibrium of his mind. This particular Yogic attitude of his appealed them most and hence they deified him and tried to paint his childhood and other acts of valour and wonderment - which are not to be found in the *Mahābhārata*.

A few words about these won't be out of place.

Dr. Karve says that the main ambition of Kṛṣṇa was to become a Vāsudeva. She admits that this concept is not clear in Hindu literature, but, in the Jaina literature. The fact that she gets no authentic proof of the idea of *Vāsudevatva* in Hinduism and is obliged to refer to the Jaina literature for support is itself a proof of the untenable nature of her hypothesis. Secondly, her contention that the nomadic Ābhīras impressed by the attitude of Kṛṣṇa-deified him, also seems to be quite far-fetched. If that tribe is almost nomadic and barbaric in nature-will it be possible that the members of that tribe would have a culture and civilized attitude or bent of mind to understand the true nature of Kṛṣṇa and then to deify him in such glorious colours, that too by inventing stories which were not found in the *Mahābhārata*? Is it not tantamount to taxing the credulity ?

Other such theories also are advanced by many scholars. In fact, every person has a right to look at Kṛṣṇa from his angle and this has created a plethora of views - which fall beyond the purview of this Thesis. As stated earlier, it is physically impossible to embrace all the theories propounded about Kṛṣṇa and give due attention to them and to assess their merits or demerits in a work of such nature as this Thesis.

COMPARISON OF SOURCE-MATERIALS ON THE KṚṢṆACARITRA

As stated earlier, the life-story of Kṛṣṇa has been given in many works, such as the *Mahābhārata, Harivaṁśa* and the Purāṇas. Herein, our effort will be to give a comparison of the different sources with references to certain incidents in the life of Kṛṣṇa. The method followed is : Name of the incident; the place where it is found in the different Purāṇas and the *Mahābhārata*. We have refrained from giving the general description of the incidents in view of the fact that these are well-known. Our main aim in giving this information is to collect at one place all the accounts of the life story of Kṛṣṇa by dividing them into incident-units for our convenience.

Before we attempt this, we must give the details about the locations where the Kṛṣṇa-story occurs in different Purāṇas, *Mahābhārata* and the present *kāvya*.

(1) *Brahma Purāṇa* (BP) - *Adhyāyas* - 179-212; Ānandāśrama edition.

(2) *Viṣṇu Purāṇa* (VP) - *Aṁśa 5, adhyāyas* - 1-38; Vṛttadīpa Press.

(3) *Padma Purāṇa* (PP) - *Uttarakhaṇḍa, adhyāyas* - 272-379; Ānandāśrama. 1894.

(4) *Harivaṁśa* (HV) - *Adhyāyas* - 51-190; Calcutta edition.

(5) *Brahma Vaivarta Purāṇa* (BVP) - *Śrī-Kṛṣṇajanmakhaṇḍa.*

(6) *Bhāgavata Purāṇa* (BhP) - *Skandhas* - X, XI; Kumbhakonam edition.

(7) *Vāyu Purāṇa* (Vyp) - *Adhyāya*-96; Ānandāśrama edition.

(8) *Devī Bhāgavata Purāṇa* (DBh) - *Skandha* IV, *adhyāyas* - 18-25; Lele's edition.

(9) *Agni Purāṇa* (AP) - *Adhyāya* - 12; Ānandāśrama edition.

(10) *Liṅga Purāṇa* (LP) - *Adhyāya*-16; Calcutta edition by J. Vidyasagara.

(11) *Mahābhārata* - The Kṛṣṇa story is mixed with that of the Pāṇḍavas all over the epic; Kumbhakonam edition and

(12) *Yādavendramahodayakāvya - the present critical edition being brought to light for the first time.*

The numbering system is as follows : The first number denotes the *adhyāya* or *sarga* in the *Yādavendramahodaya* and the second number denotes the stanzas describing the incident. The Roman figures before the *adhyāyas* show the *parvans* in the *Mahābhārata* and the *skandhas* in the *Bhāgavata-purāṇa.*

With this explanatory note, we turn to the description of some of the incidents in the life of Kṛṣṇa.

I. THE EARTH'S APPROACH TO THE GODS :

The Earth afflicted by the sins of the demons approaches Brahmā, who along with other Gods, seeks the help of God Nārāyaṇa.

BP. 181. 5-20; VP. 1. 12-33; PP. 272. 12-18; HV. 52; BVP. 4. 2- 56; BhP. 1. 17-19; Vyp. no reference;

DBh. 18. 2-25; AP. no reference and LP. no reference; MBH. I. 65. 37-53; YM. I. 3-6.

II. GOD'S PROMISE:

The Gods along with Brahmā offer prayers to God Viṣṇu and the God Viṣṇu - having learnt their trouble, promises the Earth that her burden will be lessened by his taking birth as Kṛṣṇa, the son of Vasudeva. He also asked the other gods to assume various forms/characters for helping him in his cause.

BP. 181. 29-32; VP. 1. 33-65; PP. 272. 18-25; HV. 52-56; BVP. 4. 56-6.278; BhP. 1. 20-26; VyP. no mention; DBH. 18. 25-19.47; AP., LP. no reference; MBH. I. 65. 54-66.1 and VI. 66.2; YM. I. 7-10;

III. KṚṢṆA'S BIRTH:

Vasudeva married Devakī and while Kaṁsa was riding their chariot, a divine speech informs him that the eighth son of Devakī would kill him. The infuriated Kaṁsa was pacified by Vasudeva promising that he would hand over the children to Kaṁsa as soon as they are born. He kills six children, the seventh while in the womb was transferred from the womb of Devakī to that of Rohiṇī. Hence, Kaṁsa is more watchful at the time of the next son, which was born in the prison.

BP. 181. 32-182.11; VP. 1. 65-3, 7; PP. 272. 25-38; HV. 57-60; BVP. 7.1-74; BhP. 1. 27-3. 8; VyP. 96. 192-202; DBH. 20. 53-23- 21; AP. 12. 4-6; LP. 69. 46-48; MBH. I. 64. 141-145; YM. I. 16-58 (including other matters also).

IV. KṚṢṆA'S REMOVAL TO GOKULA:

Noticing the God in His divine form, Vasudeva requests him to assume a human form. He obliges and advises Vasudeva to take Him to Gokula and exchange with the daughter of Yaśodā and place it by the side of Devakī. When Kaṁsa tried to kill that daughter, she flew off from his hands and tells Kaṁsa that his killer is safe elsewhere.

BP. 182. 12-32; VP. 3. 8-29; PP. 272. 39-58; HV. 60; BVP. 7. 75- 132; BhP. 3. 9-4. 13; VyP 96. 203-210; DBh. 23. 22-48; AP. 12. 7-13; LP. 69. 49-61; MBH. no direct reference to these incidents, but, only indirect mention of Kṛṣṇa's deeds is made. YM. II. 1- 34.

V. KAṀSA'S SUBSEQUENT MOVE :

These incidents are from the life of Kṛṣṇa till he arrives in Mathurā. Though some of the incidents are ordinary, the Purāṇas capitalise on them to befit the life of the great hero These are divided as follows :

(a) PŪTANĀ:

BP. 184. 7-21; VP. 5. 7-23; PP. 272. 74-82; HV. 63; BVP. 10; BhP 6; YM. II. 45-50.

(b) ŚAKAṬA:

BP. 184. 22-28; VP. 6. 1-7; PP. 272. 82-85; HV. 62; BVP. 12. 1- 13; BhP. 7. 1-17; No mention in YM.

(c) KṚṢṆA AND THE MORTAR :

BP. 184. 31-42; VP. 6. 10-20; PP. 272. 89-97; HV. 64; BVP. 14; BhP. 9. 10; YM. III. 23-38.

(d) THE NEW SETTLEMENT:

Frightened by these incidents, Nanda decides to leave that area and go to Vṛndāvana, on the bank of the river Yamunā. The sports of the children there etc.

BP. 184. 42-60; VP. 6. 21-51; PP. 272. 97-99; HV. 65, 66; BVP. 16. 147-179; BhP. 11. 21-40; YM. III. 39-52.

(e) ḲĀLIYA, THE SERPENT:

BP. 185.1-56; VP. 7. 1-82; PP. 272. 128-134; HV. 68, 69; BVP. 19. 1-169; Bh. P. 15. 47-17.19; Ym. IV. 26-50.

(f) DHENUKA, THE ASS.

BP. 186. 1-13; Vp. 8. 1-13; PP. 272. 135-139; HV. 70; BVP. 22; Bh. P. 15. The Dhenuka incident it described twice in the Ym. at III. 53-54 & IV 19-24.

(g) PRALAMBĀSURA:

BP. 187. 1-30; VP. 9. 1-30; PP. 272. 140-143; HV. 71; BVP. 16. 14-19; BhP. 18. 17-32; YM. IV. 69-75.

(h) INDRA FESTIVAL:

This Indra Festival is variously termed as Śakramaha by BP, VP and HV., while, BhP. called it Indrayāga. This incident brings to light the greatness of Kṛṣṇa and in the end Lord Indra accepts the superiority of Kṛṣṇa.

BP. 187. 31-188.49; VP. 10. 1-12, 56; PP. 272. 181-217; HV. 72- 76; BVP. 21; BhP 24-27; YM. V. 76-110. This is one of the very few incidents from the life of Kṛṣṇa which has been dealt with in details by the author of YM, otherwise, generally his treatment is very brief, cornering on sketchy only.

(i) RĀSAKRĪḌĀ: (THE DANCE WITH THE GOPĪS):

Like the earlier one, this incident is also dealt with in much details, so much so that herein the poetic qualities of the author come to the fore and he seems to be in his colours, especially in the description of the amours.

BP. 189. 1-45; VP. 13; PP. 272. 158-180; HV. 77; BVP. 28-53. BhP. 10. 29-33; YM. VI. 33-72 and VII. 1-61.

A word about this incident may not be out of place. This incident has evoked greatest interest in the minds of the authors/poets etc. and everybody has tried his best to paint it in his own style. Here it may be said that in the beginning this was just a very ordinary dance amongst the males and females after the rainy season, but, later on it was transformed into amorous sports. In the VP, it seems to be holy without any tinge of *śṛṅgāra,* while, in VP it got some taste of the *śṛṅgāra,* the BhP. turned it into a very extra-ordinary *śṛṅgāra* with some minor details while, most unfortunately, it was full of *uttāna śṛṅgāra,* almost cornering or leaning on pornography in BVP. This over-indulgence later on became a fashion and almost every poet relished it and tried his best to delineate it, so as to surpass his predecessors, to such an extent that in course of time it degenerated to the lowest limits. This was the incident which goaded every poet to highest flights of fancy and it became customery to describe this in full details possible, without in any way giving any serious thought to its effects or repercussions on the masses.

(j) ARIṢṬA, THE BULL:

BP. 189. 46-58; VP. 14; PP. 272. 144-149ab; HV. 78; BVP. 16. 14- 19; BhP. 36. 1-15. This incident is not described in YM.

(k) KAṀSA ON THE ALERT:

This incident mainly deals with the going of Akrūra to Gokula to bring Balarāma and Kṛṣṇa to Mathurā to participate in the *dhanuryāga,* at the instance of Kaṁsa.

The Akrūra-mission is dealt with in details in the YM, the main aspects being Akrūra's arrival in Gokula, his reception by Nanda etc., his giving the message of Kaṁsa to Nanda and his task of taking Balarāma and Kṛṣṇa to Mathurā for the same purpose, the heart-rending lamentations of the gopīs, the wonderful sight of Kṛṣṇa in the river as well as in the chariot etc.

BP. 190. 1-21; VP. 15. 1-24; PP. 272. 217cd-230; HV. 79, 80; BVP. 63-65; BhP. 36. 16-34; DBh. 24. 109; YM. VIII. 25-111. This incident is continued in the following chapters of almost all the sources.

BP. 191. 192; VP. 17. 1-19, 9; PP. 272. 231-330; HV. 82. 34; BVP. 70. 1-72.14; BhP. 31. 1-41, 6. The YM. treats it at one place only.

IX. KṚṢṆA, THE DEATH OF KAṀSA:

Kṛṣṇa arrives in Mathurā and in due course kills Kaṁsa. But, before that, there are many incidents, which are dealt with in very brief in YM. It is almost a list of the events, without giving much details or information, possibly, the author thought that these are very common incidents.

BP. 192, 194. 17; VP. 19. 10-21.17; PP. 272. HV. 84-89; BVP. 12. 15-115; BhP. 41. 7-45.23; YM. IX. 1-58.

X. SĀNDĪPANI, THE TUTOR:

BP. 194. 18-22; VP. 81. 18-31; PP. 273. 1-5; HV. 90; BVP. 99-102; BhP. 45. 26-50. YM. IX. 68-74.

XI. JARASĀNDHA, THE LORD OF MAGADHA:

Jarāsandha is described twice. Once when he repeatedly attacks Mathurā after the death of Kaṁsa, his son-in-law and when he is with Śiśupāla, Rukmī etc. fighting against Kṛṣṇa and Balarāma after Kṛṣṇa carries Rukmiṇī away before their wide open eyes.

BP. 195-196. 1-197.7; VP. 22 and 23. 1-24.7; PP. 273. 6-33 and 33-70; HV. 91-99 and 100-109, 110-116; BVP. mere reference. 103. 13. BhP. 50. 1-43 and 52. 6-14, as well as 50. 44-52. 5; YM. IX 75-89.

XII. KṚṢṆA'S MARRIAGE WITH RUKMIṆĪ:

The author of YM devotes one full *sarga*, viz. the last one to the description of this major incident in the life of Kṛṣṇa. Herein, his celibre as a poet can be easily seen and relished.

BP. 199. 1-11; VP. 26. 1-11; PP. 274. 13-275.19; HV. 104-109; 117, 118; BVP. 105-109; BhP. 52. 16-54-60; YM. X. 1-113. The other sources also mention this incident with a few details.

CHAPTER - 7

CRITICAL APPRECIATION OF THE YĀDAVENDRAMAHODAYA

This last chapter will contain our observations about the following points :

(i) Traditional definition of a *Mahākāvya* and its applicability to YM.

(ii) Modern concept of a *Mahākāvya* and its applicability to YM. and

(iii) The scholarship of the author/commentator, grammatical, orthographical and linguistic peculiarities, figures of speech, metres used etc. It will be a very brief treatment and only references of the relevant verses will be given, because, the entire poem critically edited forms the second part of this Thesis. This is done to avoid duplication.

(I) The works like the *Agnipurāṇa* (33.24-32), *Kāvyādarśa* (1. 14-19) of Daṇḍin and *Sāhityadarpaṇa* (6. 315-325) of Viśvanātha give a general description of the main characteristics of a *Mahākāvya*. We shall consider in the light of the *Sāhityadarpaṇa*, how far, the present *Mahākāvya* conforms to these characteristics/norms and how much it deviates from these generally accepted principles. The characteristics are enumerated serially, as they are found in SD.

(1) A *Mahākāvya* is divided into *sargas*. YM. is in ten *sargas*.

(2) The hero is either a God or a Kṣatriya, born in a good family. Here Śrīkṛṣṇa is the hero born in a good family and considered to be a God.

(3) A *Mahākāvya* should have either *Śṛṅgāra, Vīra* or *Śānta* as a prominent *rasa* or sentiment and other sentiments are subsidiary to them. Herein *Śṛṅgāra* and *Vīra* are the dominant *rasas,* interspersed with *Adbhuta, Vātsalya* and *Karuṇa.*

(4) The story is taken from history or related to a noble person. The story of the YM. is taken mainly from the *Bhāgavatapurāṇa.*

(5) A *Mahākāvya* deals with the four goals of life and one of those is achieved.

In YM. all the four are dealt with and the first three are achieved.

(6) A *Mahākāvya* should begin with a salutation, benediction or the subject-matter.

The YM. starts with a salutation to Lord Kṛṣṇa.

(7) In a *Mahākāvya,* bad people are censured and good are praised. In YM. Kaṁsa and his allies/associates are censured and Kṛṣṇa is praised.

(8) The cantos in a *Mahākāvya* are neither small nor long and a *Mahākāvya* should possess more than eight *sargas.*

-The YM. has ten *sargas* which are neither too long nor too short.

(9) A canto should contain one metre which changes at the end of a *sarga* and a canto has a mixture of metres.

Both these norms are followed in the YM. (a look at the metres, arranged as per their occurrence in all the *sargas* will prove this).

(10) At the end of the canto, the subject-matter of the next canto is to be introduced.

This requisite is not followed in the YM.

(11) There is a description of twilight, sun, moon, night, darkness, day, morning, afternoon, hunting, mountains, seasons, forest, ocean, union of love and

separation, sages, heaven, cities, sacrifice, battle, journey, marriage, birth of a son etc.

Almost all these are found in the YM. which are given while giving the canto-wise summary of the poem.

(12) The title of the poem is after the poet or the hero of the work or the subject-matter.

The YM. is named after the subject matter and the hero of the work.

(13) The name of the canto is after the subject-matter of the canto. The author of the YM. does not give names of any of the *sargas* but, just gives the number of the canto in the last verse.

(II) The modern concept of a *Mahākāvya*:

When we try to test the YM. on the modern principles/concept of a *Mahākāvya*, we have to judge it from the following four major points:

(i) Continuity of the main-story, i.e. the sequence of events.

It will be clear from a glance at the contents of the cantos of the YM that the events described therein follow the regular course of the life of the hero, viz. the conditions prevailing before his birth, his birth and childhood, his extra-ordinary feats and achievements as a grown-up. In fact, his life as a whole is described till his marriage with Rukumṇī.

(ii) Selection of events that appeal to emotion.

When we look into this point, we are naturally struck by the easy flow of the events in the life of Kṛṣṇa, such as, his infancy, childhood, his changing his sides, crawling on his knees, his faltering steps, his trying to walk by holding the fingers of his mother, childish acts like butter-stealing, breaking the churning rod, his other playful activities etc. These descriptions appeal to everybody's mind or emotion, as almost every child in the house has similar traits like these which is directly experienced by almost all and it does appeal to everyone. In this way, the poet tries his best to mentally prepare us for looking forward to the heroic deeds of Kṛṣṇa - the hero of this poem.

(iii) Propriety of Time and Place :

This is a very important point and it is a touch-stone of the genius of a poet. Generally, an ordinary poet is not much keen on maintaining a balance of his time and the time of the hero of the poem and commits the mistake of describing the things like the food items etc. of his times and regions as having tasted by his hero, in his time and life-which is a wrong thing.

This sense of propriety of time and place is admirably maintained in the YM. by our poet. He never describes things which are not to be found in Gokula, Vraja or Mathurā or even Dvārikā. Moreover, there is no geographical discrepancy also in his descriptions of different places. Thus, it can easily be said that he is quite successful in maintaining a balance and does not get carried away too far by any emotion and does not lose sight of his topic and its relevance.

(iv) Adoption of a Style suitable to various episodes:

This is one of the most important factors and our author has proved his calibre and mettle as a poet of a high order. A lesser poet will not mind mixing many sentiments at one place or he may not be quite diligent in choosing appropriate words to suit the episode or the nature of the incident. Even during *Karuṇarasa*, he may induct some *śṛṅgāra*, which might mar the beauty of the situation. But, our poet never succumbs to this type of temptation.

When he describes the childhood of Kṛṣṇa, his style and diction is full of delicate words, befitting the occasion, while our poet is equally at ease while describing *śṛṅgāra* or *vīra* or *karuṇa rasas*, whenever they are depicted, by using the appropriate style having pleasing words, thundering sounds or soothing words respectively. The *śṛṅgāra* is seen in the *rāsakrīḍā* and other amorous sports of Kṛṣṇa and the *gopīs*; *karuṇa* is visible in the lamentations of the *gopīs* and *vīra* is found in the battles, heated discussions, involving Kṛṣṇa and his rivals, especially in the last canto. These incidents create an indelible mark on our minds about the calibre of our poet in describing different sentiments, in keeping with the nature of the incidents. His harsh words during heated discussions, harsh sounds in the battles, delicate words used during the treatment of *śṛṅgāra,* the description of the *gopīs* who are in a pitiable condition due to separation from Kṛṣṇa etc. testify to the ability and genius of our author as a poet of no mean order.

Thus, it can easily be said that our poet rises to the occasion and always proves his mettle by adopting suitable styles in keeping with the situation, mood and nature of the episode.

(III) Scholarship of the Author/Commentator

We next turn to this important point which will give a glimpse of the erudition of our poet as well as his commentator.

At the outset, it must be mentioned that our author is a very good poet, having sound grounding in grammar, prosody, mythology, lexicography etc. Some of his uses of unusual words or common words used in uncommon sense astonish us. His grammatical idiom is also seen in some of the forms which he has used. One more important aspect of his style is his very much use of the Aorist. It makes us feel that he is very much fond of this tense, possibly because, he is describing the events that have taken place in hoary past. Here is a list of a very few instances that are striking.

First, we take up his scholarship in grammar and lexicography.

(1) He is expert in using typical grammatical idioms, e.g.

Purā : I. 27; II. 44;

Adojagatī : VI. 18;

Idaṁpitarau: VI. 37;

Idaṁvadhūḥ : VII. 15;

Idamadriḥ : IX. 84;

Idamakṣīṇi : X. 87.

(2) He is very much fond of using obscure or uncommon or unusual words or those ordinary words that have an uncommon tinge to their meanings e.g.

Śiṣṭiḥ : II. 11;

Prahiḥ : III. 5;

Śakṛtkarī : III. 53;

Prasṛtiḥ : III. 83;

Netra : IV. 51;

Andhas : IV. 55;

Netiḥ : IV. 64, 67, 77;

Sauhitya : V. 70;

Rīḍhā : V. 75;

Dita-Yāpya : VI. 4;

Pitṛprasūḥ : VI. 12;

Sat : VI. 20;

Varṣman : VI. 22;

Ṛṇa : VI. 24;

Tānti : VI. 31;

Deva : VII. 26;

Bharma : VII. 27;

Vinna : VII. 51;

Prapadīna : VIII. 94;

Yathārthapañcatā : IX. 53;

Jagadaṇḍam : IX. 61;

Māṁsakartaḥ : X. 79;

Nikurumba : X. 93;

At all these places, the commentator also proves his

scholarship by explaining these words by the supporting evidence from lexicons, mainly *Amarakośa* and *Haima,* i.e. *Anekārthasaṅgaha* of Hemacandra.

(3) *Saṁbuddhi* and no *sandhi* :

Vibho iti - II. 60;

(4) *Pragṛhya* and no *sandhi* :

Padme adhya ..... IV. 5;

The *sūtra* of Pāṇini *'Oditaśca'* followed:

'Aho amuṣyām : IX. 6;

'Pyatho ahiṁsīt : IX. 38;

(5) *Tṛjanta*-forms:

Jagatpatiḥ : III. 12 and 80; V. 70;

Jagatsutam : III. 15;

Jagadbhayacchidaḥ : III. 38;

Vṛṣṭaḥ/Varṣitaḥ : III. 68;

(6) A typical use of the words

Prabhūṣṇu : IV. 7;

(7) Vedic root *lambh* used in VII. 18 and 26;

(8) *Nāmadhātu* : *Adadraḍhayat* : II. 50;

(9) *Śeṣe* or *saṁbandhe ṣaṣṭhī* : *Divaukasām asmarat* : III. 72;

(10) Word economy : *Nivaha* : IX.4; and

(11) Etymology of

Bhūripāda (Viṣṇu) : IV. 34 and

Dvārikā : IX. 81.

(12) He is very much fond of using the forms of Aorist which are scatterd throughout the poem, so are not specially mentioned here.

(d) Reference to different *śāstras* :

Vyākaraṇa : VI.49;

Nāṭyaśāstra : VII. 49;

Vātsyāyana (*Kāmaśāstra*) : VI.68;

Kāvyaśāstra : *Rūḍhyartha* (*Yoga*) : VIII.4;

Nyāyaśāstra : (esp. *Aṅghridṛś*) : II.39; IV. 66.V.20 (The word *tāntrika* used in the sense of a *Naiyāyika*).

After this, we turn our attention to the different *alaṅkāras* of *śabda* and *artha* that are used in this poem. As the entire text of the poem is given in the second part of the Thesis, I have refrained from repeating the illustrations here and only the number of the *sarga* and the *śloka* is given which can be verified by looking to the text at the end.

(e) *Alaṅkāras* :

While dealing with this interesting aspect of the poem, the following method is followed for reasons of brevity.

The actual quotations are not given here, only their locations in the poem are pointed to, since the *entire poem is brought to light for the first time at the end of this Thesis.* It may be remarked here that our poet has mainly used the major *alaṅkāras* only which are more popular and striking.

(1) *Upamā* : (78)

I. 2,7,11,16,22,25,34,55. (8)

II. 5,29,34,48. (4)

III. 28,37,42,49,53,55,56 (*Utprekṣā* too), 59 (mythological) 62,75,79,93. (12)

IV. 14,17,32 (philosophical), 33 (*Śleṣa* too), 49 (*Ārthītena tulyam kriyā cedvatiḥ*), 60. (6).

V. 2,7,8 (Śleṣa too), 9,31,32,46,84 (Mythological), 92,94 (10).

VI. 11,25,34,35 (4).

VII. 2,5 (*Pūrṇā*), 22,33,34 (5).

VIII. 10,13,17,20,21 (Philosophical), 22,46,49,50,51,80,96,99. (13).

IX. 12,17,34,89 (4).

X. 4 (*Śleṣa* too), 7, 14,29,37,41,46,53,71 (*Pūrṇā*), 72,90,96, 117 (13).

(2) *Utprekṣā* : (72)

I. 12,14,30,43 (4).

II. 16,44,61 (*Hetu*), (3).

III. 18 (*Hetu*), 22 (*Śleṣamūlaka*), 32,43 (*Hetu*), 56 (*Upamā* too), 57 (*Hetu*) 79 (7).

IV. 3 (*Hetu*), 11 (*Hetu*), 18, 29 (*Hetu*), 30,35,36,52,53 (*Śleṣa* too), 57,59,65,67 (*Śleṣamūlaka*), 80 (14).

V. 1 (*Śleṣamūlaka*), 3 (*Rūpaka* too), 11,14,17,18,27 (*Śleṣa* too), 33,59,94 (10).

VI. 6,14 (*Hetu*), 18,31 (*Rūpaka* too), 49,62,66. (7).

VII. 10,23,27,28,50,51,52,53,54 (9).

VIII. 57,67,68,81,82,83,84,85,86,87 (10).

IX. 1,15,92 (3).

X. 8 (*Śleṣa* too), 35,52,87,88 (5).

(3) *Śleṣa* : (80)

Here it may be noted that our author is very fond of this figure of speech and never leaves any occasion to resort to it.

I. 2,13,14,15 (4)

II. 13,38,40,41,64 (*Śleṣamūlaka virodha*). (5).

III. 6 (*Śleṣamūlaka virodha*), 16,17,22 (*Śleṣamūlaka utprekṣā*), 30 (*Sabhaṅga*), 32,44,68,80. (9).

IV. 1,8,12,24,26,31,32,33 (*Upamā* too), 38,51,53 (*Utprekṣā* too), 54,55,58,61,67 (*Śleṣamūlaka Utprekṣā*), 68,74,75,77. (20).

V. 1 (*Śleṣamūlaka utprekṣā*), 5,6,8 (*Upamā* too), 10,15,19,20,22,23,24,25 (*Yamaka* too), 27 (*Utprekṣā* too), 29,30,34 (*Sabhaṅga*), 51,53,56,80,100 (21).

VI. 3,5,10,17,20,24,32 (7)

VII. 11,24,26,46 (4).

VIII. 5,7 (*Sabhaṅga*), 34,61 (*Rūpaka* based on *śleṣa*), 62 (5).

IX. 96 (1).

X. 3,4 (*Upamā* too), 5,8 (*Utprekṣā* too) (4).

(4) *Rūpaka* : (21)

I. 29,51 (*Sāṅga*), 54 (3).
II. 10. (1).
III. 67 (1).
IV. 3 (*Utprekṣā* too), 26,75 (3).
V. 30,31 (*Utprekṣā* too) (2).
VI. 3,47,59,61 (*Rūpaka* based on *śleṣa*), 64,65,78,95 (8).
VII. 24,59 (2).
VIII. 2 (Ullekha too) (1).

(5) *Arthāntaranyāsa* : (12)

I. 5,26,41,44 (4).
II. 54. (1).
III. 29. (1).
IV. 40,50 (2).
V. 7,44 (2).
VI. 69 (1)
VII 50 (1).

Now a word about the excellent flights of the fancy of the poet would not be out of place. Only the numbers of the *sargas* and the stanzas are given for obvious reasons. This list is not exhaustive, just illustrative.

II. 16,29,60; III. 28,32,64; IV. 3,35,36,59; V. 49,93; VI. 7,11,15,19 (prevalent social belief); VII. 19,20,43,50,52,53,54; VIII. 5,17,62,64,65; IX. 24; X. 34,37,45,46,52,53,63,70,71,72,95.

After this, we turn our attention to some of the striking compositional peculiarities of this poetic piece. They lend poetic charm and are striking too. They also speak of the variety of poetic forms the author has successfully tried. This piece could be said to be forming one of the parts of *citrakāvya*. Only the more striking things are given here, as a kind of specimen.

They are arranged as per their first occurrence in the poem.

(1) *Saptaka* : I. 42-48;

(2) *Yugmam* : IV. 71-72; V. 30-31; 44-45; 61-62; 66-67; VIII. 19-20; 26-27; 37-38; 102-103; IX. 63-64; X. 38-39; 81-82.

(3) *Pañcakam*: VIII. 2-6;

(4) *Catuṣkam* : VIII. 31-34; IX. 83-86;

(5) *Ṣaṭkam*: VIII. 82-87;

(6) *Navakam*: VIII. 93-101. X. 52-60.

(7) Excellent construction : V. 21 and 22, an instance of *citrakāvya*.

(8) Independent excellent flight of the fancy of the poet: III. 20-22. No. 20 suggests his philosophical bent of mind and the three taken together provide mythological reference.

(9) Repetition of the words in either ab or bc or ac or bd quarters of the poem, recurrence of the same word in many verses, similar beginnings of certain verses, the whole verse in abcd is same, *Yamaka* in a continuous flow etc.

The word *Drāk* occurs at : IV. 59,60,62.

The word *Atha* occurs at : IX. 1,4,14,16,17,18,29,30,31.

The words *Tadālokana* and *Samunnatasthāna* used in X. 50-ac and bd.

The ab quarters same or common : IV. 78, 79. *Gaganagata* ....

The ac quarters same or common : VI. 22,23, 44; X. 5.

The bd quarters same or common : V. 22,23,24,25,34.

All the four quarters same : V. 21. *Vidyotamāna*.....

Same beginning of verses : Grīṣme IV. 65,66;

Udaya - VI. 22,23;
Ālūna - X. 92,93;

Yamaka in all the fourth quarters of the verses 1-40 in the sixth *sarga*, which is an excellent instance of *citrakāvya*.

Now we turn to the treatment of the various metres used by our poet in this Mahākāvya. As in the case of the figures of speech, here also, only the numbers of the *sargas* and the verses are given where a particular metre is used or employed. Moreover, the references are given according to their first occurrence in this poem. The metres are arranged *sarga*-wise and not according to their names in alphabetical order.

Sarga I :

Upajātī	: 1,3-57, 59;
Upendravajrā	: 2;
Mālinī	: 58 and
Anuṣṭubh	: 60.

It may be noted here only that the last verses in all the *sargas* are couched in the *Anuṣṭubh* metre invariably.

Sarga : II

Viyoginī	: 1-62;
Upajātī	: 63, 65, 66;
Vaṁśastha	: 64; and
Anuṣṭubh	: 67.

Sarga : III

Vaṁśastha	: 1-89;
Mālinī	: 90;
Praharṣiṇī	: 91,92;
Śikhariṇī	: 93;
Upajātī	: 94; and
Anuṣṭubh	: 95.

Sarga : IV

Śālinī	: 1-76;
Puṣpitāgrā	: 77,78,79,82;
Upajātī	: 80,83;
Praharṣiṇī	: 81 and
Anuṣṭubh	: 84.

Sarga : V

Anuṣṭubh	: 1-122,126;
Mālinī	: 123;
Śikhariṇī	: 124 and
Upajātī	: 125.

Sarga : VI

This is the *sarga* which contains a variety of metres as per the rules laid down and discussed earlier while examining this *kāvya* from the point of view of traditional definition.

Drutavilaṁbita	: 1-40;
Upajātī	: 41-44, 58,72,73;
Rathoddhatā	: 45;
Puṣpitāgrā	: 46;
Mālabhāriṇī	: 47,59;
Anuṣṭubh	: 48,64,69,74;
Vasantatilakā	: 49,54,55,63,65,67,68,70;
Svāgatā	: 51;
Śālinī	: 5;
Mālinī	: 53;
Indravajrā	: 56;
Upendravajrā	: 57;
Vaṁśastha	: 60;
Hāriṇī	: 61;
Gīti	: 62;
Śikhariṇī	: 66 and
Viyoginī	: 71.

Sarga VII :

Rathoddhatā	: 1-13, 15-58;
Gīti	: 14;
Mālinī	: 59;
Mandākrāntā	: 60;
Mālabhārinī	: 61;

Upajāti	: 62;
Anuṣṭubh	: 63.

Sarga VIII :

Anuṣṭubh	: 1-103, 113;
Vasantatilakā	: 104-107, 110;
Indravaṁśa	: 108;
Vaṁśastha	: 109;
Mālabhāriṇī	: 111;
Upajāti	: 112.

Sarga IX:

Mālabhāriṇī	: 1-95;
Śālinī	: 96;
Upajāti	: 97 and
Anuṣṭubh	: 98.

Sarga X:

Upājatī	: 1-7,9-83, 102,117,122;
Indravajrā	: 8;
Vasantatilakā	: 84-96,106-109,119;
Praharṣiṇī	: 97,98;
Mālinī	: 99,111, 120;
Mandākrāntā	: 100,110,121;
Mālabhāriṇī	: 101,112;
Upendravajrā	: 103;
Śikhariṇī	: 104;
Vaṁśastha	: 105;
Anuṣṭubh	: 118,123;
Gīti	: 113,116;
Sragdharā	: 114 and
Upagīti	: 115.

From this brief treatment, a reader would get a fairly good idea of the calibre of our author as a poet, well-versed in prosody, rhetorics as well as of his sound grounding in grammar. It must be said to the credit of our author that he never commits a grammatical mistake nor a prosodial. Thus, though he is a first- rate scholar, his work does not suffer from the fault of pedantry or verbosity. His language is full of *prasāda, mādhurya* and at times *ojas* too - in keeping with the situation -, but, his scholarship does not blunt his poetic taste or ability and he gives the glimpses of his poetic fancy which is a sheer joy, pure and simple/unmixed. His erudition does not mar the beauty of his composition, but, is complementary to it and enhances its value and makes it really worth relishing. No praise will be high as far as the poetic quality of the composition is concerned. The real joy will accrue from its reading only, which is never unpleasant.

A few words about the scholarship of the commentator will not be out of place here.

Our commentaror comes from a very learned family. He is also well-versed in different branches of learning. It can be inferred from his commentary wherein he has cited references from Vedic, classical literature, purāṇas, lexicons, grammatical works etc. His explanations of the verses are very good and to the point and speak of his scholarship and ability, especially when he explains some figures of speech. Of course, it must be admitted that since this is a *ṭippaṇa* and not a regular commentary, at times, his treatment is quite sketchy or insufficient as well as ambiguous. It should, still,however, be said to his credit that he has kept the works in currency by writing down his *ṭippaṇas* or notes on them and prevented them from being thrown into oblivion. This is his greatest contribution towards the furtherance of knowledge and the preservation of the works. In fact, without this *ṭippaṇa*, it will be very difficult to understand the sixth *sarga* which is full of *yamaka* and *śleṣa* - a very difficult nut to crack. It is almost a tribute to the scholarship of the poet Nīlakaṇṭha to have composed this *sarga* which will test the acumen of scholars. Herein, our commentator is very much helpful to us in getting a feel of the poetic composition.

A few words about the scribal peculiarities will be sufficient to give a fairly good idea of the calligraphy of the mss - which is definitely influenced by Marāṭhī typography. It is just possible that the scribe might be a Maharashtrian or a domicile of Maharashtra - because his style suggests his leanings towards Marāṭhī way of writing and spelling. Though the scribe is very meticulous, at times, he does prove the dictum : it is human to err. Here I point out only a few instances.

(1) Dropping of *Visarga/Anusvāra* and joining the two words :

II. 64; III. 18,21,54,56 (*anusvāra* dropped), 62,65,73 (*anusvāra* dropped), 87; IV. 4,33,35,69,80; V. 75,81 (*Anusvāra* dropped), 94; VI. 12, 47; VII. 20 (anu. dr.), 42; VIII. 28,29,37,86 (Anu. dr.), 87,106 (anu.dr.), 109; IX. 42; (anu. dr.); X. 14 (anu.dr.) 36,66,67,90 (anu.dr.) 96.

(2) Repetition of previous word : *Payas* - III.19;

(3) Illegible (not clear) writing due to overwriting: II.34; V. 122; IX. 65; X. 30,31,50,55,59,113.

(4) *Ti/Ni* written as *Gni* :

I. 16; II. 45,63; III. 14.42,55 (gvi); IV. 77,80,81; IX. 42 (*gdi*); IX. 56,91.

(5) ऊ written as उ॔ or अू or

I. 21; III. 39 (हु); IV 13 (मु), 71 (अू), 75 (उ॔); VI. 28 (अै in com.); 53 (अै in com.); VII. 10 (बु); IX. 35 (अै in com.); 71 (उ॔), 86.

(6) *Varṇavyatyāsa* or *varṇaviparyaya-Metathesis:*

I. 52; III. 1; IV. 24; VI. 67; VIII. 1, 94; IX. 21,38; X. 101;

(7) *Vīpsā* : I. 59 and X. 122 (in com.);

(8) -ह for ह्न : IV. 26; VI. 5,47; VIII. 83; X. 9,19 (न्हय), 46 (-हुः); 110 (-ही);

(9) Wrongly writing down without understanding:

II. 22, 50, 58; III. 59; IV. 40, 41; IX. 31,47;

(10) Marāṭhī words used :

Ḍerā-III. 22 (marginal gloss); *Tārāṅgaṇa*- VIII.34; *Mitrāḥ*-

X.2 (com.); *Saubhāgyavatī*- X. 55; *Dṛḍha*-X. 63.

(11) Persian word used : *Taravāri* (i.e. a sword) - V. 6 (com.);

(12) Wrong spellings - orthographical lapses :

II.23; III. 80,88,89; IV. 1,2,27; V. 25,36, VI. 15, 24,27,35,40,43,44,56,57,70; VIII. 3,80,84,93,105; IX. 23,47,68,93; X. 23,55,58,78,99,105,113;

(13) ज्झि used for ज्झि : III. 86; V. 30; VI.4, 19; VII. 5; X. 40;

(14) व for ब : VI. 67; X. 17, 48;

(15) ष्ट for ष्ठ : VI. 72; VIII. 32; X. 94;

(16) ध्या for द्ध्या : IV. 20;

(17) ध्द्द for द्ध : V. 5;

We conclude this treatment with giving instances where gloss, quotation or correction occurs in the margin.

(1) Marginal gloss :

I. 27; II. 52; III. 22; IV. 122 (additional information *kiṅkaraiḥ iti śesaḥ*); VI. 5 (add. inf. - *loka iti śeṣaḥ*); 7,11,30; VIII. 18,33,43,50,68; X. 94.

(2) Marginal quotations :

I. 11,12,15; II. 10; III. 53,83; V. 60,80; VI. 3,4,24,27; IX. 2,78; X. 54,70,84,93,94,95.

(3) Marginal corrections :

IV. 41,56,67; VII. 20,23,39; X. 64,86.

BIBLIOGRAPHY

PRIMARY SOURCES :

(1) *Agni-Purāṇa* - Anandashrama, Pune.

(2) *Bhāgavata-Purāṇa* - Kambhakonam.

(3) *Brahma-Purāṇa* - Anandashrama, Pune.

(4) *Brahmavaivarta-Purāṇa* - Anandashrama, Pune.

(5) *Devībhāgavata* - Lele, Pune.

(6) *Harivaṁśa* - Calcutta.

(7) *Liṅga-Purāṇa* - Jivananda Vidyasagar, Calcutta.

(8) *Padma-Purāṇa* - Anandashrama, Pune.

(9) *Vāyu-Purāṇa* - Anandashrama, Pune.

(10) *Viṣṇu-Purāṇa* - Vṛttadīpa Press, Pune.

SECONDARY SOURCES :

(1) Athavale, Pandurangashastri, *Shrikrishnajivanadarshana* (Guj.), Sadvichara Darshan Trust, Bombay, 1981.

(2) Bhandarkar, R.G., *Vaiṣṇavism, Śaiviṣm and Minor Religious Systems*, Bhandarkar Oriental Research Institute, Pune, 1928.

(3) Dange, Dr. Sindhu, S., The *Bhāgavatapurāṇa—Mytho-social Study*, Ajanta Publications, Delhi, 1984.

(4) Desai, Sushila S., *Bhāgavatapurāṇa - A Critical Study*, Parshva Prakashan, Ahmedabad, 1990.

(5) Karve, Dr. Iravati, *Yugānta - The End of an Epoch.*

(6) Kubba, Dr. Rajkumari, *Kṛṣṇakāvya in Sanskrit Literature*, Eastern Book Linkers, Delhi, 1982.

(7) Majumdar, Bimanbehari. *Kṛṣṇa in History and Legend*,

University of Calcutta, 1969.

(8) Pande, Smt. Vinapani, *Harivaṁśapurāṇakā Sānskritik Adhyayana* (Hindi), Publication Division, Information Centre, Uttar Pradesh, Lucknow, 1960.

(9) Pusalkar, A.D., *Studies in Epics and Purāṇas*, Bharatiya Vidya Bhavan, Bombay, 1955.

(10) Rai, Ramkumar, *Vedic Index*, Chowkhamba Vidyabhavan, Varanasi, 1962.

(11) Rukminī, R., *A Critical Study of the Bhāgavatapurāṇa*, Chowkhamba Sanskrit Series, Vol. LXXVII, Varanasi, 1970.

(12) Sandesara, U.J. *Shrikrishna-Purushottama ane Antaryāmī, Pūrvārdha ane Uttarārdha*, (Guj.), Gurjar Grantharatna Karyalaya, Ahmedabad, 1973, 1978.

(13) Sheth, Noel, S.J., *The Divinity of Krishna*, Munshiram Manoharlal, Delhi, 1984.

LEXICONS : ENCYCLOPAEDIAS :

(1) *Amaraliṅgānuśāsana* or *Amarakośa* of Amarasiṁha, with the *Rāmāśramī* (*Vyākhyāsudhā*), Commentary of Bhanuji Diksita (*Rāmāśrama*), edited with easy *Maṇiprabhā* (*Prakāśa*) Hindi Commentary and Notes etc. edited by : Pt. Haragovindashashtri, Chowkhambha Sanskrit Series, Varanasi, 1970.

(2) *Anekārthasaṅgraho nāma Koṣaḥ* of Hemachandracharya, ed. by : Pt. Jagannath Shastri Hoshing, Pt. Ghanananda Pandeya and Pt. Janardan Jyotirvit, Chowkhambha Sanskrit Samsthan, Varanasi, 2nd ed., 1969.

(3) Citrao, Siddheshvar Sastri, *Prāchīna Bhāratīya Charitrakosha* (Marathi), Pune, 1969.

(4) Joshi, Lakshmanshastri, *Marāṭhī Vishvakosha*, Vol. 4, Wai, 1976.

(5) Joshi, Mahadevashastri, *Bhāratīya Sanskritikosha*, Vol. 2, Pune, 1964.

(6) Ketkar, Dr. S.V., *Jñānakosha*, Vol. 11, 1925.

ARTICLES IN JOURNALS :

(1) Antarkar, Dr. W.R., "Śrīśaṅkarābhyudayakāvyam of Nīlakaṇṭha", *Journal of the University of Bombay*, September, 1964, Vol. XXXIII (New Series), Part-2, Arts Number, 39, pp. 128-167, Bombay.

(2) Tadpatrikar, S.N., "The Kṛṣṇa Problem", *Annals of the Bhandarkar Oriental Research Institute*, Vol. X., pp. 269-344, 1930.

PART - II

SANSKRIT TEXT

नीलकण्ठकविविरचितं यादवेन्द्रमहोदयकाव्यम् सटिप्पणम्

प्रथमः सर्गः

[१]गोवर्धनोद्धारणशान्तगर्वे पुरःस्थिते साञ्जलिबन्धमिन्द्रे ।
विवर्तितास्यं पशुपालमन्यमाभाषयन्तं प्रभुमाश्रयामः ॥१ ॥

श्रीगणेशाय नमः । श्रीसरस्वत्यै नमः । **यादवेन्द्रमहोदयकाव्यस्य टिप्पनमारभ्यते** गोवर्धन इति । साञ्जलिबन्धमिन्द्रे पुरःस्थिते सति पशुपालेन सह भाषणं कुर्वाणं प्रभुमाश्रयामः ॥१ ॥

गजा इवोद्भिन्नमदाः परं ये न दानवन्तः कुटिला नरेन्द्राः ।
कलेः पुरोगा इव किङ्करास्ते युगेऽभवन् द्वापरनामधेये ॥२ ॥

गजा इति । गजा इव मदोन्मत्ता एव, न दानयुक्ताः । दानं मदोदकं वितरणं च । कलेः पुरोगाः किङ्करा इव ॥२ ॥

अप्यन्यसाधारणदेहवद्भिरंहःशतापूर्णतयातिभारैः ।
क्षमापदं रूढमिवोद्वहन्ती तैर्मेदिनी कंसमुखैरखिन्त ॥३ ॥

अपीति । अखिन्त खेदं प्राप ॥३ ॥

साऽऽवेदयामास हिरण्यगर्भं व्यथामसद्राजमयीमनल्याम् ।
तया समं यज्ञविभङ्गदूनैः सुरैरपि प्राप पयोऽम्बुधिं सः ॥४ ॥

सेति । असद्राजेभ्यः (भ्य) आगता असद्राजमयी, ताम् ॥४ ॥

स देवकार्यार्थमभोजनः सन्नुपास्त भोगीन्द्रशयं दयालुम् ।
सतामुपेत्यापि शरीरखेदं निर्वर्तनीयो हि परोपकारः ॥५ ॥

---

१. P. begins with श्रीगणेशाय नमः । B. begins with श्री गणेशाय नमः । श्रीकृष्णाय नमः ॥

हरिर्गिरं[२] देवमतानुकूलामुवाच मन्द्रं द्रुहिणो[३]ऽश्रुणोत्ताम् ।
नान्ये सुराः सश्रवणाः सदेशा अप्यत्र विष्णोर्महिमैव बीजम् ॥६ ॥

हरेर्गिरोऽर्थं द्रुहिणोऽधिगम्य तेनापरान् संमदयाञ्चकार ।
अम्भः पयोधेरधिगम्य तेन देशानिवावग्रहिणोऽम्बुवाहः ॥७ ॥

सतां विपद्भिः सह[४] दुर्जनानां सुखानि लोप्तुं विहगेन्द्रकेतोः ।
उदेष्यतः[५] कौ वसुदेवगेहे श्रीमाननन्तो भविताऽग्रजन्मा ॥८ ॥

सतामिति । अनन्तः शेषः ॥८ ॥९ ॥१० ॥

मायाऽस्य नन्दस्य गृहे भवित्री तत्प्रीतये यादवतां भजध्वम् ।
सुरस्त्रियोऽपिस्त्रि[६] प्रभवन्तु[७] भूमौ तत्रापि सेवा परितोषबीजम् ॥९ ॥

एवं समादिश्य सुरान् विषण्णां भुवं समाश्वास्य स पद्मयोनिः ।
भेजे निजं स्थानमथो धरित्री[८] देवाश्च हृष्टा निलयानवापुः ॥१० ॥

यः शूरसेनात्मपदेन रूढ्या[९] योगेन साकं प्रतिपद्यमानः ।
द्विजैरमात्यैरिव साधुमन्त्रैः[१०] संवर्धितश्रीर्विषयोऽस्ति सोऽयम् ॥११ ॥

य इति । शूरा सेना यस्मिन्निति योगः । रूढिः समुदायशक्तिः । मन्त्रः(न्त्रो) वेदभेदः(दो) विचारश्च । 'वेदभेदे गुप्तवादे मन्त्रः' इति हैमः[११] (अमरः) ।(३.३.१६७) श्रीः सम्पत् शोभा च । विषयो देशः ॥११ ॥

पर्यन्तसञ्चारियमानुजायाः श्यामायमानो[१२]पवनावलीनाम् ।
कैदारिकाणां[१३] च रुचा य एष भातीव गारुत्मतरत्नमूर्तिः ॥१२ ॥

---

२. °गिरिं'।
३. °णाश्रुणोताम्;
४. स हि;
५. उदष्यतः;
६. °स्त्रयो° ;
७. °वन्ति ;
८. धरत्री;
९. रूप्या;
१०. P. Marginal quotation 'वेदभेदे गुप्तवादे मन्त्रः' इति हैमः ।
११. This quotation is from अमर & not from हैम. The actual reading of हैम is 'मन्त्रो देवादिसाधने ॥ वेदांशे गुप्तवादे च' । 2.448,449.
१२. °मानाप°;
१३. P. marg qu.. 'कैदारिकं स्यात्कैदार्यं क्षेत्रं केदारकगणे' इति अमरः ।

'पर्यन्त इति । कैदारिकाणाम् । कैदारि(र)कं स्यात्कैदार्यं क्षेत्रं केदारकं (कैदारिकं) गणे' इति **अमरः** (२.९.११) ॥१२ ॥

अनन्तमश्रान्तमुपाश्रयन्तो यानेत्य निर्यान्त्यफला द्विजेन्द्राः ।
न ताध्शा यत्र गृहाः पुरेषु वनेषु वृक्षाः सुमनोविहीनाः ॥१३ ॥

अनन्तमिति । अनन्तं गगनं विष्णुं **च** । अफलाः फलमप्राप्ताः । द्विजेन्द्राः पक्षिश्रेष्ठाः, ब्राह्मणश्रेष्ठाश्च । सुमनसः पुष्पाणि, पण्डिताश्च ॥१३ ॥

[14]तत्रास्ति काचिन्मथुराभिधाना शूराभिगुप्तेति परानवाप्या ।
पुरी भुवं[15] वीक्षितुमागतेव विभाति या भोगवती सभोगैः ॥१४ ॥

तत्रेति । शूरेणाभिगुप्ता संरक्षिता, अत एव परैः शत्रुभिराप्तुमशक्या । सभोगैः विलासिभिः, **पक्षे**-सर्पैः ॥१४ ॥

यां शूरसेनोऽधिवसन् पुरीं स्म संत्रायते तं विषयं पुरोक्तम् ।
प्रवर्त्य लोकानपि धर्ममार्गे निवर्तयन्नेव स धर्ममार्गात्[16] ॥१५ ॥

यामिति । धर्ममार्गे पुण्यमार्गे । धर्ममार्गात् यममार्गात् । **विरोधः** शब्दयोरेकार्थत्वात् । 'धर्माः पुण्ययमन्यस्वभावाचारसोमपाः' इति **अमरः** । (३.३.१३९) ॥१५ ॥१६ ॥१७ ॥१८ ॥१९ ॥

तस्यां पुरा देवकनामधेयो निजां ददौ शूरसुताय कन्याम् ।
तां प्राप्य तेनातितरां[17] ननन्दे नवाम्बुधारामिव चातकेन ॥१६ ॥

सा देवकी शूरसुतं समेत्य ननन्द कामं नयनाभिरामम् ।
वसन्तसङ्गे न कथं विकासमासादयेन्नाम रसालवल्ली ॥१७ ॥

सोऽग्रेसरस्यन्दनदन्तिवाजि[18]पादातमारुह्य रथं सदारः ।
गृहान् प्रवेष्टुं निरगात्तदानीं कंसोऽस्य सारथ्यमुरीचकार ॥१८ ॥

तदा तमामन्त्र्य बभाण वाणी तिरोहिताङ्गी भगिनीं हितां त्वम् ।
यां वेत्सि तस्यास्तनयोऽष्टमस्त्वां हनिष्यति भ्रान्तिमिमां त्यजेति[19] ॥१९ ॥

---

१४. कश्चिन्म°
१५. भवं;
१६. P. mg. qu. धर्माः पुण्ययमन्यायस्वभावाचारसोमपाः 'इति अमरः ।
१७. °ग्नि°. It is the peculiarity of the scribe of B. that he writes ग्नि instead of ति or नि.
१८. °वाजी°;
१९ त्यजन्ति·

श्रुत्वा चिकीर्षद्भगिनीवधं स तन्न प्रमाणं यदि किं वधेन।
नो चेदियं शक्यवधा नहीति तं नास्पृशन्मन्दमतिं विचारः ॥२० ॥

श्रुत्वेति। तत् आकाशात् श्रुतं (तदाकाशाच्छ्रुतं) वाक्यं प्रमाणं न चेत्, वधेन किं, किमपि प्रयोजनं न। प्रमाणं यदि, अस्या वध अशक्य इति विचारं नाकरोदित्यर्थः ॥२० ॥

जिघांसुमेनं वसुदेव ऊचे[२०] *स्त्रीघातिनस्तेऽद्य यशो विनश्येत्।*
दूरे भविष्यत्समये वपुस्तदहन्तुरत्रोचितमाचरेति ॥२१ ॥

जिघांसुरिति। अद्य हनिष्यसि चेत् यशः (चेद्यशो) विनश्येत् यशोनाशो भविष्यतीत्यर्थः। अद्य न हनिष्यसि चेत्कालान्तरेण वपुर्नश्येदित्यर्थः। 'सम्भावितस्या(स्य) चाकीर्तिर्मरणादतिचि(रि)च्यते।' **इत्युक्तेः**। (**भ. गीता**. २.३४) अद्य यशोहान्या मरणाधिकदुःखोत्पादनापेक्षया 'अद्य वाऽब्दशतान्ते वा मृत्युर्वै प्राणिनां ध्रुवः' इति **वाक्यात्** (**भाग.** १०.१.३८) मरणस्यावश्यंभावेन कालान्तरे वपुर्नाशाङ्गीकार उचित **इत्यभिप्रायः**। अत्र यदुचितं तत्कुर्वित्यर्थः ॥२१ ॥

तं[२१] **तद्वचो नैव निरोध्दुमैष्ट मृणालिकातन्तुरिव द्विपेन्द्रम्।**
स्वपुत्रदानो[२२]**श्रवणेन सोऽयं ररक्ष भार्यामथ कालधर्मात् ॥२२ ॥**

तमिति। स्वपुत्रदानाश्रवणेन स्वपुत्रदानप्रतिज्ञया। 'प्रतिज्ञा(नियमा)श्रवसंश्रवाः' इति **अमरः**। (१.५.५) कालधर्मात् मृत्योः ॥२२ ॥

कालेन गर्भं वसुदेवभार्या शोकेन साकं बिभराम्बभूव।
जातं सुतं शौरिरदान्महात्मा कंसाय हिंसापरमानसाय ॥२३ ॥

कालेनेति। गर्भं शोकेन साकं बिभराम्बभूव। स्वपत्युः पुत्रदानप्रतिज्ञया गर्भधारणादारभ्य शोकं चकारेत्यर्थः ॥२३ ॥२४ ॥

नायं वधार्हो न यदष्टमस्तं नयेति कंसो[२३] *यदुवाच हिंस्रः*[२४]*।*
आसादयत्तद्वचनं[२५] *रसालफलस्य निम्बप्रभवस्य साम्यम् ॥२४ ॥*

---

२०. B. writes as ऊ–a clear instance of Marathi influence.
२१. तन्तुद्वचो;
२२. दाप्राश्र;
२३. कंसा;
२४. हिंस्तः;
२५. °दयं तद्व°;

शौरेस्तदाकर्णयतस्तनूजानतीत्य षट् कंसवधस्य शङ्का।
आद्यात्सुतादष्टम एव सूनावह्नाय[२६] भेकीव समुत्पपात ॥२५ ॥

शौरेरिति। शौरेर्वसुदेवस्य कंसकर्तृकवधस्य शङ्का षट् पुत्रानतीत्य अष्टमसुते(त) एव समुत्पपात। यथा भेकी एकात्स्थानादुत्पु(त्प्लु)त्य मध्येऽन्तरं त्यक्त्वा स्थानान्तरं समुत्पतति तथा ॥२५ ॥२६ ॥

शौरेः षडासंस्तनया अथागात् स्वायम्भुवो देवऋषिर्महात्मा।
कंसान्तिकं तेन स[२७] पूजितोऽभूत् सतां प्रभावो यदसज्जनार्चा ॥२६ ॥

त्वां कालनेमिं जनने परस्मिन् 'पुराऽसुरं[२८] दैत्यरिपुर्निहन्ति'।
गृहीतजन्मा वसुदेवपत्न्या नागान्तको नागमिवातिवीर्यम्[२९] ॥२७ ॥

त्वामिति। परस्मिन् जन्मनि पूर्वजन्मनि। कालनेमिसंज्ञकमसुरं त्वां पुरा निहन्ति हतवान् अग्रे च हनिष्यति। 'यात्व(व)त्पुरानिपातयोर्भविष्यदर्थे लट्' (**पाणिनि**-३.३.४) 'पुरि लुङ् चास्म' (**पाणिनि**-३.२.१२२) इति भूते। नागान्तको गरुडः। नागं सर्पम् ॥२७ ॥२८ ॥

पिता तवायं वसुदेवमुख्या ये यादवा याश्च तदीयभार्याः।
नन्दादयो गोकुलवासिनश्च विरोधिनस्ते हि सुरांशजाताः ॥१८ ॥

इत्युक्तिदण्डेन निहत्य सुप्तं रोषोरगं कंसमनोबिलान्तः।
स[३०] बोधयामास ददंश सोऽथ हन्तृभ्रमेणानकदुन्दुभीयान् ॥२९ ॥

इतीति। सः (स) नारदः (दो) बोधयामास। एते (त) एव मम हन्तार इति धिया वसुदेवपुत्रान् ददंश मारितवानित्यर्थः ॥२९ ॥३० ॥

तौ देवकीं शूरसुतं च कंसः सबन्धनीकृत्य[३१] पदोर्न्यधत्त।
कारागृहे मानसराजहंसौ क्षाराम्बुवेशन्त इवातिपङ्के ॥३० ॥

---

२६. सूना बलाय;
२७. सुपूजितो;
२८. P. mg. gl. पुरा हतवान् अग्रे हनिष्यति च।
२९. °वीर्य;
३०. सम्बोधयामास;
३१. स बन्धनीकृत्य

प्रच्याव्य[३२] तातं स तदोग्रसेनं राज्याधिपत्यात् स्वयमीश्वरोऽभूत्।
सन्ताप्यमाना यदवोऽमुनाऽन्यदेशं गताः केऽप्यनुस[३३]स्त्रुरेनम् ॥३१ ॥

प्रच्याव्येति। एनं कंसम् ॥३१ ॥३२ ॥

स रोहिणीगर्भमपीष्यमाणो नेतुं रमाया रमणेन पूर्वम्।
अनायि देवक्युदरं फणीन्द्रो यियासयैवाष्टमपुत्रतायाः ॥३२ ॥

अथ स्वमायां हरिरादिदेश[३४] त्वं देवकीगर्भगतं विकृष्य।
निधेहि तस्या वसुदेवपत्न्या गर्भे पतिर्नन्दगृहे न्यधाद्याम् ॥३३ ॥

अथेति। देवकीगर्भगतं विकृष्य पतिः वसुदेवः (पतिर्वसुदेवो) यां नन्दगृहे न्यधात्, तस्या वसुदेवपत्न्याः (त्न्या) गर्भे निधेहि ॥३३ ॥

नन्दस्य धर्मैकरतस्य साधोरपत्यभावं भज गोकुले त्वम्।
परस्पराध्यासमवाप्स्यतो नौ माये[३५] स्वरूपे इव मातरौ च ॥३४ ॥

नन्दस्येति। नौ स्वरूपे इव नौ मातरौ परस्पराध्यासम् अन्योऽन्यस्मिन् अ(न्न) न्योऽन्यारोपम् अवाप्स्यतः (तो) गमिष्यतः। मन्माता त्वन्मातृत्वं त्वन्माता मन्मातृत्वं च। पुरुषः प्रकृतिधर्मं प्रकृतिः पुरुषधर्ममिवारोपेण गच्छत इत्यर्थः ॥३४ ॥

स्वमाययाऽऽज्ञप्तमकारि सर्वं मयेति विज्ञापित आदिदेवः।
इयेष देवक्युदरं प्रवेष्टुं कंसं हनिष्यन्[३६] जगतामघं[३७] च ॥३५ ॥

स्वमाययेति। अघं दुःखम्। 'अंहो दुःखव्यसनेष्वघम्' इति **अमरः**। (३.३.२७) ॥३५ ॥३६ ॥

गर्भत्वमासाद्य जगन्निवासो यथा यथा वृध्दिमवाप कुक्षौ।
तथा तथाऽवर्धत देवकीयो[३८] मनोरथो दोहदनामधेयः ॥३६ ॥

---

३२. प्रच्याव;
३३. °सस्तु°;
३४. B. lacuna for देश
३५. मायस्वरूपे;
३६. हनिष्यं (अनुस्वार for न्– Marathi influence);
३७. P. m.g. 'अंहो दुःखव्यसनेष्वघम्' इति **अमरः**।
३८. °कीया;

फणीन्द्रतल्पे शयितुं खगेन्द्रमारोढुमालापयितुं च लक्ष्मीम् ।
सुरार्थनां सार्थयितुं सुरारिवधं च कर्तुं चकमे धिया सा ॥३७ ॥

फणीन्द्रेति । सा देवकी धिया चकमे । इच्छामकरोदित्यर्थः ॥३७ ॥३८ ॥३९ ॥

शरीरसादो मुखपाण्डुता च विमुच्यमानाभरणत्वमस्याः ।
प्रागेव कारासदने बभूव गर्भात्परं चूचुकनैल्यमेव ॥३८ ॥

स्वभावमान्द्यं[३९] गमनस्य तस्या धृतान्दुकत्वादथ गर्भभारात् ।
गर्भस्य विश्वम्भरभावतश्च भेजे तदानीं परमाधिकत्वम् ॥३९ ॥

कृशं किलासीदुदरं पुराऽस्या महत्तमेभ्योऽपि महामहिष्ठे ।
तत्र प्रविष्टेऽपि हरावयासीदथोदरं तत्क्रशिमानमेव[४०] ॥४० ॥

कृशमिति । हरौ तत्र प्रविष्टे सत्यपि, उदरं क्रशिमानमेव अ(वा)यासीत् इति **विरोधः** । **पक्षे**-अथो दरम् इति **छेदः** । दरं भयम् । 'दरोऽस्त्रियां भये' इति **अमरः** । (३.३.१८४) ॥४० ॥

सत्यप्रतिज्ञानमपीश्वरं तमार्ताः[४१] पुनः प्रार्थयितुं सुरेन्द्राः ।
पुरस्कृतब्रह्मशिवास्तदाऽऽयन् दुःखायितारो न विलम्बसाहाः ॥४१ ॥

सत्येति । तदा आयन् आगताः ॥४१ ॥

नमो नमद्दुःखतमोविमर्दचन्द्रायितोद्यन्नखमण्डलाभ्याम् ।
रमाशयव्याजसरोजलब्धसेवासुखाभ्यां[४२] भगवन् पदाभ्याम् ॥४२ ॥

नम इति । नमतां दुःखरूपं तमः, तस्य विमर्दे नाशे चन्द्रायितम् । उद्यन्नखमण्डलं ययोस्ताभ्यां, शयः (यो) हस्तः ॥४२ ॥

ये[४३] योगिभिः पुण्यसमूहमूल्यसङ्क्रीयमाणे इव तन्मनःसु ।
अनारतं[४४] निश्चलवासमेतस्ताभ्यां नमस्ते चरणाम्बुजाभ्याम् ॥४३ ॥

---

३९. °माद्यं
४०. तत्कुशि°;
४१. तमाताः;
४२. °लब्धं सेवा;
४३. य;
४४. °रतन्नि°–तं + नि = तन्नि— Marathi influence.

ये इति । ये योगिभिः पुण्यसमूहरूपमूल्येन सङ्क्रि(ङ्क्री) यमाणे इव तेषां मनःसु निरन्तरं वासमेतः ॥४३ ॥

नीरन्ध्रमाकाशमतिग्मपादैः पूर्येत [४५] यावद्धरिदश्वबिम्बैः ।
यत्कान्ति तावत्तुलनानुवादेऽप्यनुन्मुखत्वं हि महाकवीनाम् ॥४४ ॥

नीरन्ध्रमिति । अतिग्मपादैः अतीक्ष्णकिरणैः ॥४५-४८ ॥(४४-४७) ॥

नानाकिरीटोज्ज्वलमस्तकाग्रधृतामितश्वेतमहातपत्रम् ।
समुच्चलत्काञ्चनचारुदण्डैः संवीज्यमानं सितचामरौघैः ॥४५ ॥

प्रसन्ननानावदनारविन्दं [४६] नानानिशातायुधबाहुदण्डम् ।
आपादलम्बैर्नवमल्लिकानां हारैर्मणीनां च विराजितोरः ॥४६ ॥

हिरण्यगर्भाण्डकुलाधिवासनानामनोज्ञोदरराजमानम् ।
अनेकपादाम्बुजमम्बरोध्दं [४७] पीतं दधानं शशिपाण्डुरं च ॥४७ ॥

सुगन्धलिप्तं सकलाङ्गकेषु योग्यैर्महार्घाभरणैरुपेतम् ।
गुणप्रसूनैर्निगमार्चितं यत्तत्ते स्वरूपं भगवन्नमामः ॥४८ ॥

सुगन्धेति । गुणा एव प्रसूनानि, तैः **करणैः** निगमैरर्चितम् । निगमवर्णितगुणमित्यर्थः ॥४९ (४८) ॥

यं वीतरागा अपि कामयन्ते निरन्तरं वीक्षितुमम्बुजाक्ष ।
सौन्दर्यसाराञ्चितसर्वगात्रं तं त्वां प्रपश्येम सदेति कामः ॥४९ ॥

यमिति । तं त्वां सदा पश्येम इति कामः(मो) मनोरथः । अस्तीति शेषः ॥५०(४९) ॥

सतां मनःस्वन्यमनःसु देव मोदं च खेदं बहुमादधानम् ।
भास्वन्तमब्जेषु विकासमग्निं शिलास्विवेच्छेम विलोकितुं त्वाम् ॥५० ॥

सतामिति । अन्ये दुष्टाः । अब्जेषु विकासं शिलासु अग्निमादधानं भास्वन्तमिव सूर्यमिव ॥५१(५०) ॥

---

४५. यो बद्धरि°;
४६. °विन्दनाना°;
४७. P. °रोद्यं

विलूनसत्पद्मतया विपुण्यगन्धां जनानन्दमरन्दशून्याम् ।
दैवादनष्टां कुमहीन्द्रनागैर्भूपद्मिनीं वर्धय तद्वधेन ॥५१ ॥

विलूनेति । विलूनानि सन्त एव प[द्]मानि यस्यास्तत्तया । विगतः पुण्यमेव गन्धः (न्धो) यस्याः । जनानन्द एव मरन्दः, तद्रहिताम् । दैवादनष्टाम् अनुत्पाटिताम् । महीन्द्रा एव नागाः (गा) गजाः । भूरेव प[द्]मिनी, ताम् ॥५२-५३(५१-५२) ॥

षडग्रजांस्ते निजघान योऽयं बध्नाति मातापितरौ तवेमौ[४८] ।
तव द्विषन्पापजनाग्रगण्यः कंसो जहीमं त्वरितं महेश ॥५२ ॥

स्थित्वाम्बरे देवगणा इतीशं प्रणम्य नुत्वेहितमर्थयित्वा ।
आश्वास्य शौरिं सहधर्मदारं प्रणम्य भूयो निलयानवापुः ॥५३ ॥

स्थित्वेति । ईहितम् इष्टमर्थयित्वा ॥५४(५३) ॥

कंसस्य यः स्वान्तशिलां बिभेद मूर्ता वरीयोभयवज्रपातैः ।
ववर्ष साधुप्रमदाम्बु सोऽथ हरेर्नभा[४९] वैजननो बभूव ॥५४ ॥

कंसस्येति । स्वान्तमन्तःकरणम् । तद्रूपां शिलाम् । श्रेष्ठभयान्येव वज्राणि, तेषां पाताः, तैः । साधूनां प्रमदरूपमम्बु ववर्ष । नभाः श्रावणः । वैजननः । 'सूतिमासो वैजननः' इति **अमरः** ।(२.६.३९) ॥५५-५६ (५४-५५) ॥

तदैव बन्धालयरक्षकाणां कंसोऽप्रमादां स्थितिमादिदेश ।
ते किङ्करास्तत्सदनं ररक्षुर्निधिं भुजङ्गा इव वीतनिद्राः ॥५५ ॥

नभो वलक्षेतरपक्षमध्यतिथौ[५०] तुरीयेऽप्यथ वारतारे ।
जातो हि देवक्युदरान्निशीथे[५१] चन्द्रांशुधौते भगवान्मुरारिः[५२] ॥५६ ॥

नभ इति । नभसः श्रावणस्य कृष्णपक्षमध्यतिथौ अ(थाव) ष्टम्यां तुरीये चतुर्थे । तुरीयो वारः सौम्यवारः । तुरीया तारा रोहिणी ॥५७(५६) ॥

तद्दीपशून्यं सदनं स्वकान्त्या बालं वितन्वानमनन्धकारम् ।
असूतिदुःखा गतगर्भभारा साऽबोधि दृष्ट्वाऽहमसोषि हीति ॥५७ ॥

---

४८. तमेवौ Metathesis;
४९. हरेर्नभार्वै°;
५०. तिथो;
५१. °शीथचन्द्रा°;
५२. °रि;

तदिति । असूतिदु:खा सूतिदु:खरहिता । गतः(तो) गर्भभारो यस्याः । अहम् असोषि प्रसूतवतीति । अबोधि ज्ञातवती ॥५८-५९(५७-५८) ॥

कृतजयजयशब्दैस्त्यक्तनव्यप्रसूनैः ।
विधृतकनककोणैस्ताडितानां सुरेन्द्रैः ।
जगदिदमभिपूर्णं दुन्दुभीनां निनादैः
नटनमकृत रम्भामुख्यवाराङ्गनौघः ॥५८ ॥

यध्द्वीर्जगज्जातमिवासुरारेस्तनूरखेदाऽभृत शास्त्रजातम् ।
त्रिविक्रमाभिख्यतदात्मजन्मा यः पार्वतीनन्दनतामयासीत् ॥५९ ॥

यध्धी(ध्दी)रिति । असुरारेस्तनूर्यथा जगज्जातं तथा । यध्धीः(ध्दीः) शास्त्रजातम् । अखेदा सती अभृत धारितवती । **त्रिविक्रमाभिख्यश्चासौ** स च **त्रिविक्रमाभिख्यः,** सः **त्रिविक्रमाभिख्य[:]** तस्य आत्मजन्मा, **त्रिविक्रमाभिख्यतदात्मजन्मा** ॥६०(५९) ॥

इति नीलकण्ठकविकृत-यादवेन्द्रमहोदयाख्यकाव्यस्य रानडे-इत्युपनामक श्यामरायाङ्गजविष्णु(ष्णु) कृतटिप (प्प)न्यां प्रथमः सर्गः ॥२ ॥

नीलकण्ठेन तेनास्मिन् यादवेन्द्रमहोदये ।
कृते काव्ये प्राथमिकः सर्गः सम्पूर्णतां गतः[५३] ॥६० ॥[५४]

५३. गताः;
५४. B. adds इति प्रथमसर्ग [:] समाप्तः ॥

द्वितीय :सर्गः

[१]अथ शौरिरवेतनन्दनप्रभवः सम्मदवारिणा प्लुतः ।
हरिचिन्तनमातनोत्पदे स तदात्वप्रविधेयकर्मणाम् ।।१ ।।

अथ द्वितीयः सर्गः । अथेति । अवेतः (तो) ज्ञातः (तो) नन्दनप्रभवः सुतोत्पत्तिर्येन सः । हर्षजलेन प्लुतः । तदात्वप्रविधेयकर्मणां जन्मकाले कर्तुं योग्यानां दानादिकर्मणां पदे स्थाने कारास्थितित्वात् दानादिकर्मण्यपटुः सन् हरिचिन्तनमेवाकरोदित्यर्थः ।।१ ।।

जगतांपतिरात्मनस्ततो घटिकाजातमजातरोदनम् ।
अतनोदतिसुन्दरं महाभरणं षोडशहायनं वपुः ।।२ ।।

जगतामिति । घटिकाजातं घटिका जातस्य (जाता) यस्य तत् ।
घटिकात्मककालपरिच्छिन्नमित्यर्थः ।।२ ।।३ ।।

अतिविस्मयमानमानसौ जनयित्रीजनकौ कृतस्तवौ ।
सदरस्मितमम्बुजे[२]क्षणो वचनैर्मोदयितुं प्रचक्रमे ।।३ ।।

वसुदेव पुरा भवानभूत् सुतपा नाम तवेयमङ्गना ।
अपि पृश्न्यभिधा तदा युवां व्यधिषाथां परमोत्तमं[३] तपः ।।४ ।।

वसुदेव इ(वे)ति । व्यधिषाथां कृतवन्तौ ।।४ ।।

तदिदं सुतकामनावशादपि दातुं पटु मोक्षसम्पदम् ।
लघुतां तु बभाज मूषकग्रहणार्थं खननं गिरेरिव ।।५ ।।

तदिदमिति । तत् इदं (तदिदं) तपः(पो) मोक्षसम्पदं दातुं पट्वपि सुतकामनावशात् लघुतां बभाज ।।५ ।।

प्रचकास्य वपुः कृपावशाद्वृणुतं मां वरमित्यवादिषम् ।
अवनिष्टमुभौ सुतं तदा मदभिप्रायवशेन मां[४] सुतम् ।।६ ।।

---

१. P. & B. begin with श्रीकृष्णाय नमः ।।
२. °ज°;
३. परमान्तमं;
४. मा;

प्रचकास्येति । मामप्रधानं **कर्म** । मां मद्रूपं वरमिति **च** प्रतीयते । अवनिष्टम् अयाचतम् ॥६ ॥

जनने तदनन्तरे युवां समभूतं त्वदितिश्च कश्यपः ।
अनु देवकशूरनन्दनौ त्रिजनुष्यात्मजतां गतोऽस्मि वाम् ॥७ ॥

जनने(न) इति । समभूतं जातौ । वां युवयोः ॥७ ॥

अनुरागवतां शरीरिणां मयि नैवार्थिकमात्रकं ददत् ।
विरमत्यभिलाषपूरणान्मम तुष्यत्यभिपूर्य वा मनः ॥८ ॥

अनुरागेति । मम मनः अ(नोऽ)र्थितमात्रकं ददत् अ(द)भिलाषपूरणात् न(न्न) विरमति । अभिपूर्य वा न तुष्यति । अतः(त) एकजन्मनि पुत्रत्वेन प्रार्थितोऽपि जन्मत्रये पुत्रतां प्राप्तोऽस्मीत्यर्थः ॥८ ॥

असुखं च यदौग्रसेनिना भवतोर्दत्तमिदं च वेद्म्यहम् ।
मदनुग्रहतो जगद्दृशः किमुताहं सकलाश्च योगिनः ॥९ ॥

असुखमिति । औग्रसेनिः कंसः । मदनुग्रहतः (तो) मदनुग्रहात् सकलाश्च योगिनः (नो) जगद्दृशः, अहं किमुत । सर्वज्ञत्वादहं जानामीत्यर्थः ॥९ ॥

तमसाधुदिवान्धसेवितं विनिहत्योन्मदयिष्य एवं वाम् ।
अचिरेण [५]सुरोत्तमः परं प्रशमय्येव तमोविलोचने ॥१० ॥

तमिति । असाधव एव दिवान्धाः, तैः सेवितं कंसं तमश्च । सुरोत्तमः सूर्यः । 'सुरोत्तमो धामनिधिः' इति **अमरः** । (१.३.३०[४१]) ॥१० ॥

अयि नन्दसुतां तदालये निदधन्मामधुना समुद्भवाम् ।
समुपाहर गोकुलादितो मम शिष्टिः सकलान्तरायनुत् ॥११ ॥

अयीति । अयि वसुदेव, मां तदालये नन्दालये निदधन् सन् अ(न्न)धुना समुद्भवामिदानीमेवोत्पन्नां नन्दसुतां गोकुलादुपाहर आनय । ननु निगडादिप्रतिबन्धकसद्भावात् मद्गमनं गोकुले कथं भविष्यतीति चेत्तत्राह ममेति । मदाज्ञा सर्वविघ्नध्वंसकारिण्यस्तीत्यर्थः ॥११ ॥

प्रथमं हरिरित्यवोचत प्रथमं वा शिशुतामशिश्रियत् ।
अपि भावयतोस्तयोरभूत् पटिमा नान्यतरार्थनिश्चये ॥१२ ॥

---

५. P. marginal quotation 'सुरोत्तमो धामनिधिः' इति **अमरः** ।

प्रथममिति। हरिरिति प्रथममवोचत वा प्रथमं शिशुतामशिश्रियद्वा द्वयोर्मध्येऽन्यतरस्य विनिश्चये पटिमा नाभूत् ॥१२॥

हरिशासनमाचरन् यदाशयविन्यस्तमहेश्वरोऽभवत्।
वसुदेव उवाह तत्क्षणे गतिविद्वेषणबन्धशून्यताम् ॥१३॥

हरिरिति। शयः हस्तः आशयश्च। गतिर्गमनं परलोकगतिश्च ॥१३॥

विवृता अभवन् कपाटिकाः स्वयमेनं रुरुधुर्न रक्षिणः।
इतरेतरजाड्यचेतनाव्यतिहत्येव महेशनिर्गमे ॥१४॥

विवृता इति। व्यतिहत्या विनिमयेन ॥१४॥

अनुगस्य फणैर्महामणिद्युतिभिः कुण्डलिनामधीशितुः।
निबिडाम्बुदवृन्दसम्भवं तिमिरं वारि च वारितं तदा ॥१५॥

अनुगेति। फणैर्वारि वारितं, महामणिद्युतिभिस्तिमिरं वारितम् ॥१५॥

परिबृंहितमम्बु यामुनं हरिवाहे वसुदेव आगते।
अनुगच्छदहीन्द्रफूत्कृ[६]तिज्वलनैः पीतमिवाल्पतां ययौ ॥१६॥

परीति। यामुनं यमुनाया इदम् ॥१६॥१७॥

शिशुरोदनसूचिताध्वना स यशोदा[७]सदनावधि व्रजन्।
अवबोधयुतं ददर्श तद्गृहदीपं न परं तु कञ्चन ॥१७॥

तनयेन तदात्मजामयं विनिमित्य द्रुतमागतो गृहान्।
निगडादि यथा पुराऽभवच्छिशुरेषा च रुरोद तत्परम् ॥१८॥

तनयेनेति। विनिमित्य विनिमयं कृत्वा। तत्परं तदनन्तरम् ॥१८॥

गृहपालमुखाद्यदुद्गतं प्रसवोऽभूदिति तस्य भोजराट्।
अशृणोत्प्रथमं स्वमन्दिरे चरमं बन्धनमन्दिरे[८]ऽक्षरम् ॥१९॥

गृहं इ(हे)ति। प्रथमाक्षरं मन्दिरे श्रुतवान्। चरमाक्षरं बन्धनमन्दिरेऽश्रुणोदिति। त्वरिततरं तत्रागतवानित्यर्थः ॥१९॥

---

६. °पूत्कृ°;
७. यशोदां सद°;
८. मन्दिरक्षरम्;

जहिहीदमपत्यमन्तिमं स्त्रियमित्यस्य भगिन्यवोचत।
अथ हन्तुमुपाददे शिशुं स तदालम्भविधिभ्रमादिव ॥२०॥

जहिहीति। जहिहि त्यज। तदालम्भविधिभ्रमात्-तस्या आलम्भः, स विधिः हिंसाविधिः, तस्य भ्रमात्। नाशयेत्यर्थक जहीति (जहि इति) **पदच्छेदात्** स **भ्रमः** ॥२०॥२१॥

अथ सोत्पतिताम्बराङ्गणे शिशुभूतं वपुरात्मनः क्षणात्।
अतिभीषणमष्टबाहुकं निशितास्त्राञ्चितमूर्जितं व्यधात् ॥२१॥

किमरे दयनीयताश्रयान्निजदिष्टान्तनिवारणेच्छया।
विनिहत्य शिशून् महानले परितापे[९] क्षतये स्वपन्नभूः ॥२२॥

किमरे इति। दिष्टान्तं मरणम् ॥२२॥

इयतापि यतो वधस्तवाकथि घातो न बभूव तस्य हि।
न शशाम रुजापि भक्षिते लशुने न्यायपदं भवानभूत् ॥२३॥

इयतेति। तव वधोऽकथि कथितः। तस्य च घातो न बभूव। यथा लशुनभक्षणेन व्याधावशान्ते सति तत्भ(द्भ)क्षणजन्यं पापमेव भक्षणफलं न व्याधिशान्तिस्तथेत्यर्थः ॥२३-२७॥

पुरुषं वददष्टमं मृषावचनं देवकनन्दनात्मजम्।
इति माऽस्तु मतिः पुमानसावुदितः क्वाऽपि विराजते भुवि ॥२४॥

इति सोक्तवती जगत्प्रसूरचलं विन्ध्यमुपाश्रयद्गता[१०]।
नमनोद्यतदेवदानवावलिसम्बाधमहाम्बराध्वना ॥२५॥

इति तज्जगदम्बिकावचः श्रुतवान् भोजपतिर्व्यचारयत्।
न मृषाऽष्टमगर्भपुंस्त्ववागिति वाचेयमपीरिताऽनृता ॥२६॥

गिलितो[११] बहिरेति मानवः कृतयत्नोऽजगरोदरादपि।
बहुभिः परिरक्षिताद्भटैर्न पुनर्मामकबन्धनालयात् ॥२७॥

---

९. तापा°; The B. scribe could not understand the sign of deletion in प like this (/), hence writes पा;
१०. श्रयद्दृताः
११. बहुरेति;

अनुतप्य वृथा विहिंसिताः पृथुका इत्यपनीतबन्धनौ ।
भगिनीभगिनीपती तदा मदयामास ससान्त्वनोक्तिभिः ॥२८ ॥

अन्विति । पृथुका बालाः । मदयामास आनन्दयामास ॥२८ ॥

उदयावनिभृ[१२]त्किरीटतामुपयाते सति भानुमण्डले ।
स ययौ दनुजावृतां सभां मृगराडुग्रमृगाटवीमिव ॥२९ ॥

उदय इ(ये)ति । भानुमण्डले उदयं प्राप्ते सति ॥२९ ॥३० ॥

अवदच्च निशाकथां वदन् किमु मिथ्याऽष्टभुजोक्तवागुत ।
मम बन्धगृहाद्बहिर्गतोऽष्टम एतत्सुविमृश्यतामिति ॥३० ॥

अथ [१३]ते निशमय्य भोजराट्कथितां[१४] वाचमिदं बभाषिरे ।
अपि मन्दधियो निशाचरा विबुधंमन्यतया प्रणोदिताः ॥३१ ॥

अथेति । निशाचराः(रा) मन्दधियोऽपि विबुधंमन्यतया प्रणोदिताः सन्तः(न्तो) बभाषिरे ॥३१ ॥

स्वसुरष्टम आत्मजः पुमान् ध्रुवमन्यत्र गतश्च तद्गृहात् ।
उपपद्यत एव तद्गतिर्भयदं रूपमदः शिशोरिव ॥३१(३२) ॥

स्वसुरिति । अदः शिशोः अ(र)मुष्याः शिशोः भयदं(शिशोर्भयदं) रूपम् अष्टभुजरूपमिव तस्याष्टमपुत्रस्य गतिः उ(रु)पपद्यत एव ॥३२ ॥

तदमुष्य वधो यदीष्यते शिशुहीनां कुरु मेदिनीमिमाम् ।
अभिनन्दिततद्वचाः खलः शिशुघाताय शशास पूतनाम् ॥३२(३३) ॥

तदिति । शशास आज्ञातवान् ॥३२ ॥३३ ॥(३३ ॥३४) ॥

रुधिरा[१५]मिषनित्यकामुका वचनेनास्य निरस्तयन्त्रणा ।
विचचार शिशून् विनिघ्नती भुवि सा व्याघ्रवधूर्मृगानिव ॥३३(३४) ॥

अथ नन्दवधूर्विनिर्गते वसुदेवेऽजनि जातजागरा ।
पुमपत्यमभून्ममेत्यहो हरिमायाऽपगमेऽपि साऽभ्रमीत् ॥३४(३५) ॥

---

१२. भक्ति;
१३. तैः;
१४. कथितं वच॰;
१५. रमिष;

अथेति। हरिप्रेषितमायाया:(या) अपगमेऽपि सा भ्रमं प्रापितवती। **विरोधः स्पष्टः** ॥३४(३५)॥

तनयोदयवार्तया मुदं प्रतिपन्नोऽजनि यां व्रजेश्वरः।
श्रुतिबोधितकाष्ठया मुदा तनयस्यास्य न साऽत्यशीयत ॥३५(३६)॥

तनयेति। अस्य तनयस्य श्रुतिर्वेदः, तद्बोधितोत्कर्षया मुदा सा मुत् ना(न्ना)-तिक्रान्ता। वेदान्तप्रतिपाद्यब्रह्मसाक्षात्कारापेक्षयाऽपि तनयोदयेनात्यन्तं मुमोदेत्यर्थः ॥३६॥

समयोजयदात्मनः सुतं [१६]द्विजवर्यैरथ जातकर्मणा।
द्विजसादकरोद्[१७]व्रजेश्वरो द्रविणं भूरि मुदा तदुत्सवे ॥३६(३७)॥

सममिति। द्रविणं द्रव्यम्। द्विजेभ्य:(भ्यो) ददावित्यर्थः ॥३७॥

जगति प्रतिपन्नवाञ्छिता न हि याचन्त्यमुना तु धीमता।
अपि लम्भितसर्वकामिता अभवन्नर्थिन एव मार्गणाः ॥३७(३८)॥

जगतीति। प्रतिपन्नवाञ्छिताः सम्पन्नमनोरथाः। अर्थिन:(नो) याचका:(का) **धनिनश्च** ॥३८॥

प्रसरन् परितो मृषागिरः कृतवान् मङ्गलतूर्यनिस्वनः।
वदतो गगनैकदेशगो ध्वनिरित्यङ्घ्रिह[१८]शोऽनुयायिनः ॥३८(३९)॥

प्रसरन्निति। शब्दगुणकमाकाशमिति वादिनो नैयायिकान् मृषागिरः कृतवान्, शब्दस्य सर्वत्र प्रसृतत्वात् ॥३९॥

दिवि च व्रजराजमन्दिरे समुदा गोपतिना नियोजिता।
अनटन् वरवारयोषितो जगुरुच्चैर्मधुरं च गायनाः ॥३९(४०)॥

दिवि चेति। गोपतिना इन्द्रेण नन्देन **च** ॥४०॥

विधृतोत्तमभूषणाम्बरप्रमदापूरुषरत्नभूषितः।
अपि नन्दयुतो महाव्रजः स तदानन्दयुतो व्यराजत ॥४०(४१)॥

१६. सुतद्विज°;
१७. °द्वृ°;
१८. B. lacuna for दृशो;

विधृतः इ(ते)ति । नन्देन युतः(तो) युक्तोऽपि अनन्दयुक्त इति **विरोधः** । **पक्षे**-आनन्दयुतः ॥४१ ॥

दिवसेषु गतेषु केषुचिद्विदधानोऽवनिभृत्करार्पणम् ।
मथुरां गतवान् व्रजाधिपः सुहृदा सङ्गतवांश्च शौरिणा ॥४१(४२) ॥

दिवसे(ष्वि)ति । अवनिभृत् राजा, तस्य करो बलिः षष्ठांशः, तस्यार्पणं कर्तुमिच्छुः ॥४२ ॥४३ ॥

वसुदेवनिवेदितार्भकव्रजघातोद्यमनो महीपतेः ।
कृतकार्य उपागमद्द्रुतं[१९] व्रजमात्मीयमयं सुतप्रियः ॥४२(४३) ॥

शिशुमारणकर्मकर्तृतापदमेधी[२०]त्युभयार्थशासनात् ।
अधिगम्य तदीयकर्तृतामथ सम्प्राप्तुमिवास्य कर्मताम् ॥४३(४४) ॥

शिशुरिति । शिशुमारणरूपं यत्कर्म तस्य कर्तृतायाः पदं स्थानम् । एधि भव इत्येको**ऽर्थः** । शिशोर्मारणं शिशुमारणं, कर्तरि षष्ठ्यन्तेन समासः । शिशूनां मारणं शिशुमारणं, कर्मणि षष्ठ्यन्तेन समासः । The portion after this is in the upper margin & the letters are very faint and difficult to read or decipher from the xerox-copy and no access was possible to the original manuscript. तदीयकर्तृतां शिशुकर्मकमारणकर्तृताम् । अस्य शिशुकर्तृकमारणस्य कर्मतां प्राप्तुमिव व्रजमापेति **उत्तरेणान्वयः** ॥४४ ॥

समितां सजिघांसयानिशं[२१] स्वधिया स्वां विषपूरितां तनुम् ।
प्रियदर्शनतां नयन्त्यसौ बत नन्दव्रजमाप पूतना ॥४४(४५) ॥

समितामिति । विषपूरितामत एव अ(वा)निशं जिघांसयासहितया स्वधिया समितां समीकृताम् ॥४५ ॥

अतिलङ्घ्य जनान् बतासुरी हरिमापानुपशान्तमानसा ।
अधिरोप्य तमङ्कमेषका गरलापूर्णमपाययत् स्तनम् ॥४५(४६) ॥

अतिलङ्घ्येति । जनान् लोकान् अ(न)तीत्य । अज्ञाता ए(तै)षा एषका अज्ञातकुलगोत्रादिका पूतना ॥४६ ॥

१९. मद्धुतं;
२०. °यु°;
२१. यग्निशं;(ग्नि for नि–scribal peculiarity).

स्तनचूषणमाचरन्नयं तदसूनप्ययतिष्ट चूषितुम् ।
अलमित्यसमापिताक्षरं ब्रुवती साऽमृत पूर्वरूपभाक् ।।४६(४७) ।।

स्तनेति । अयतिष्ट यत्नमकरोत् । अमृत मृतवती ।।४७ ।।

अवतार्य शनैस्तमुन्नताद्गिरिशृङ्गादिव पूतनास्तनात् ।
भयविह्वलचेतसेऽर्भकं शिशुमात्रे धृतिमन्त आर्पयन् ।।४८ ।।[२२]

अवतार्येति । शिशुमात्रे बालमातायै ।।४८ ।।४९ ।।५० ।।

विनिकृत्ततदङ्गकोच्चये परिशुष्केन्धनमध्यंवर्तिनि[२४] **।**
पवमानसखस्य तर्पणं विदधाने व्रजमाप गोपतिः ।।४८(४९) ।।

वसुदेववचःप्रमाणता व्यथयामास मुहुर्व्रजेश्वरम् ।
व्रजवृत्तममूमदद्रढत्[२५] **सुखयामासतमां तथापि तम् ।।५० ।।**

वसुदेव इति । अमूं वसुदेववचः प्रमाणताम् अ(म)दद्रढत् दृढीचकार । तथापि व्यथाजनकवसुदेववचःप्रमाणतादृढीकारकत्वेऽपि ।।५१(५०) ।।

अथ भोजपतिर्निशाचरीं शिशुना दण्डधरातिथीकृताम् ।
प्रजिघाय निशम्य दानवं स तृणावर्तममुष्य शान्तये ।।५३(५१) ।।

अथेति । दण्डधरो यमः । 'कालो दण्डधरः श्राध्ददेवः' इति **अमरः** ।(१.१.५९) अमुष्य बालस्य शान्तये नाशाय ।।५४-५६(५२-५३) ।।

स च चक्रसमीरणो भवन् व्रजमासाद्य विकीर्णधूलिकः ।
प्रतिगृह्य [तमर्भकं नभो गमयामास ततो निपा[२६]**तयन्**[२७]**] ।।५४(५२) ।।**

---

२२. P. has the following additional verse in the upper margin, mentioning just the line no. 5 without actually indicating the place where it is to be inserted.
विषपास्तु परोऽमृतापरेत्यद आसीन्नहि विस्मयापदम् ।
फलमर्पयितारमेव यत्परमेशार्पि[२३]तमापयेदतः ।।४८ ।।A

२३. Marginal gloss —वस्तु;

२४. वर्तिनी;

२५. °मभूमदिद्र° The B. scribe could not understand the sign of deletion like this (दि) which is shown in the P.

२६. निपातन्;

२७. [..][27] P. marginal gloss निपातयन् सन् नभो गमयामास ।

शिशुरस्य निपीडयन्नभूद्ग[२८]लमात्मीयभुजाभिवेष्टितम् ।
स गतो गमनोन्मुखासुतां निजरूपेण पपात दानवः ॥५५(५३) ॥

निपिपातयिषुं दिवः[२९] स्वमप्यमुमारोहयदीश्वरो दिवम् ।
अपकुर्वति सन्नुपक्रियां कुरुते किं पुनरेष सत्तमः ॥५६(५४) ॥

निपिपातमिति । दिवः अन्तरिक्षात्, दिवं स्वर्गम् । सन् साधुः । अयं तु सत्तमः ॥५७(५४) ॥

यदुवंशपुरोहितो मुनिर्व्रजमेत्य व्रजराजसन्निधौ ।
विजनेऽकृत नामनी शुभे स यशोदासुतरौहिणेययोः ॥५७(५५) ॥

यदुरिति । शुभे नामनी अकृत कृतवान् ॥५८-५९ (५५-५६) ॥

प्रथमस्य तु वासुदेव इत्यभिधां व्यकृत कृष्ण इत्यपि ।
अथ राम इतीतरस्य तां मुनिवर्यो बलभद्र इत्यपि ॥५८(५६) ॥

भुवि दुर्लभमिष्यतेऽखिलं विदतो बालिशताऽतिदुर्लभा ।
अत एव समस्तवेदिनां प्रथमो बालिशतामलष्यत ॥(५७) ॥

भुवीति । अखिलं विदतः पण्डितस्य बालिशता मौर्ख्यं बाल्यं **च** । बालिशतां बालकर्म मौर्ख्यं **च** ॥६०(५७) ॥

द्रविणं बहु वीक्ष्य चापि मे न हि मां श्रीनिलयं विदुर्जडाः ।
अहसत्स[३०] इतीव हा भवे परिखिद्यन्त इतीव चारुदत् ॥[५८] ॥

[द्रविणमिति ।] द्रविणं धनं बलं **च** । 'द्रविणं तरः सहोबलशौर्याणि स्थाम शुष्मं **च** ।' इति **अमरः** । (२.८.१०२) श्रीनिलयं लक्ष्मीसम्पन्नं विष्णुं **च** । प्राणिनः संसोर(संसारेऽ) खिद्यन्त, हा इति अरुदत् ॥६१(५८) ॥

परिवृत्तिमहोऽभवद्धरे[३१]स्तदनन्धः सुखगाम्यभूज्जनः ।
तदहीन्द्रशयस्य वा शिशोः परिवृत्तिर्न हरेर्व्यशिष्यत ॥६१(५९) ॥

---

२८. B. omits ल;

२९. दिवस्वम° generally the scribe does not write the विसर्ग & joins the two words at many places.

३०. अहत्स B. scribe did not understand the स added after ह & before त्स in the lefthand margin in P., hence copied the reading without adding the marginal स.

३१. °वद्धरस्त°;

परिवृत्तिमिति। परिवृत्तिमहः परिवर्तनोत्सवः अ(वोऽ)भवत्। 'मह उध्ध(द्ध)व उत्सवः' इति **अमरः**। (१.७.३८). तत् तस्माद्धेतोः। अनन्धः (न्धो) जनः सुखगामी अभूत्। अनन्धः सुखगामी अन्नसुखमप्राप्त इति **च** प्रतीयते। 'भिःसा स्त्री भक्तमन्धोऽन्न' इति **अमरः**। (२.९.४८). फणीन्द्रशयस्य हरेः' परिवृत्तिः, शिशोर्हरेः परिवृत्तिश्च। परिवृत्तिः भा (र्भा) द्रपदशुक्लैकादशी परिवृत्तिवाच्या ॥६२-६३(५९-६०)॥

उरसा परिसर्पतो हरेर्गमनं तस्य रुरोध देहली।
जडतां हर मामिकां विभो इति सम्प्रार्थ्य नतेव दण्डवत् ॥६२(६०) ॥

दिविजानुचरत्वगामिनो मम नेदं समुपार्जयाम्यतः।
भुविजानुचरत्वमाददे न्विति बालेन सुरारिविद्विषा ॥६३(६१) ॥

दिविजेति। दिवि जानुचरत्वं गच्छतीति, तस्य। **पक्षे**-दिविजा देवा अनुचरा यस्य, तस्य भावस्तत्त्वं गच्छतीति, तस्य मम भुवि जानुचरत्वं नास्तीति हेतोः पृथिव्यां जानुचरत्वम् आ(मा)ददे नु ॥ ६४-६५(६१-६२)॥

उदतिष्ठदुपाश्रितः किमप्यथ सञ्चारमपि स्खलत्पदम्।
व्यदधादुपचारयत्प[३२]दान्यसमग्रं बत सर्वशक्तिमान् ॥६४(६२) ॥

पूर्णः परात्मैव न चान्य एवं श्रुतिर्वदन्ती वितथीकृतेति[३३]।
रुषेव पूर्णं शिशुभावगामी परेश्वरो रेचयति स्म पूर्णः ॥६५(६३) ॥

पूर्ण इति। पूर्णं दधिदुग्धादिना पूरितं भाण्डादि ॥६८(६३)॥

असङ्करायैव स लब्धसम्भवः पदार्थजातस्य चकार सङ्करम्।
अपङ्कता यस्य सदातनी श्रुता स पङ्कसङ्गी मुदमन्वविन्दत ॥६४॥

असङ्करेति। असङ्कराय वर्णाश्रमधर्मपरिपालनाय। सङ्करं चतुर्वर्णमिश्रणम्। **पक्षे**-पदार्थानामेकीकरणम्। अपङ्कता निष्पापता। पङ्कः पापः कर्दमश्च ॥६४॥

सर्वेऽपि यद्वीक्षितबालभावा वृद्धाः स एवं समवाप्तबाल्यः।
लीलाभिरानन्दितवानशेषान् परात्मजः[३४] सन् जगतां प्रसूतिः ॥६७(६५) ॥

---

३२. °यत्प्रदा°;
३३. °ग्नि–scribal peculiarity of writing ग्नि for ति or नि.
३४. °त्मज सन्;

सर्वेऽपीति। येन वीक्षितः(तो) बालभावो बाल्यं मौर्ख्यं **च** येषां ते। वृद्धाः पण्डिता जरठाश्च। 'बुध वृद्धौ पण्डितेऽपि'। 'मूर्खेऽर्भकेऽपि बालः स्यात्' इति च **अमरः**।(३.३.१०० and ३.३.२०५)। जगतां प्रसूतिः सन् परात्मजः ॥६५॥

इति नीलकण्ठकविकृतयादवेन्द्रमहोदयकाव्यस्य टिप्पण्यां द्वितीयः सर्गः ॥२॥

यद्धीर्जगज्जातमिवासुरारेस्तनूरखेदाऽभृत शास्त्रजातम्।
त्रिविक्रमाभिख्यतदात्मजन्मा यः पार्वतीनन्दनतामयासीत्। ।६८(६६) ॥

नीलकण्ठेन तेनास्मिन् यादवेन्द्रमहोदये।
कृते काव्ये द्वितीयोऽपि सर्गः सम्पूर्णतां गतः। ।२॥[३५](६७) ॥

---

३५. B. adds इति द्वितीयसर्ग[ः] समाप्तः॥

तृतीयः सर्गः

[1]हरिश्चतुःपञ्चशरद्वयास्ततः[2] समं वयस्यैः पशुपालदारकैः ।
चकार खेलां[3] दुरितौघनाशिनीं विलोकमानेक्षणसाफलीमपि ॥१ ॥

अथ तृतीयसर्गटिप्पणम् । हरिरिति । खेलां क्रीडाम् ॥१ ॥

स बालभावोचितभूषणाञ्चितो विलोक्यमानः स्पृहया व्रजालयैः ।
समं वयस्यैर्मृदुपादपल्लवश्रमानवेक्षी विचचार वीथिषु ॥२ ॥

स इति । व्रजालयैः व्र(व्रै)जस्थैः ॥२ ॥

क्षणं सखीकृत्य यमेष खेलितः क्षणेन तं रो[4]दयति स्म ताडयन् ।
कदाचन क्रीडनके परैर्हृते रुदन् स्वमात्रे तदुपागतोऽब्रवीत् ॥३ ॥

क्षणमिति । खेलितः क्रीडितः । क्रीडनके क्रीडासाधने ॥३ ॥४ ॥

[5]बहिर्विहारोत्सुकमानसे हरावनागते भोजनकालमप्यति ।
यया बहिर्देहलिकाऽपि नेक्षिता[6] तया स मात्रा मृगितोऽखिले व्रजे ॥४ ॥

बबन्ध सद्मानि चखान च प्रहीन् प्ररोहयामास महीरुहाङ्कुरान् ।
क्षणे[7] न कस्मिंश्चिदपि[8] क्षणं ययौ ध्रुवं सिसृक्षाद्यतिवासनावशात् ॥५ ॥

बबन्धेति । चखान अखनत् । कस्मिंश्चिदपि क्षणे काले क्षणं निर्व्यापारस्थितिं न ययौ । 'निर्व्यापारस्थितौ कालविशेषोत्सवयोः क्षणः ।' इति **अमरः** ।(३.३.४७) ॥५ ॥

हरन् दृशं तत्परिरक्षिणां हरिः प्रगृह्य पीयूषमथानुवर्तिनः ।
अपाययत्पूर्वमपौरुषेण तत्कृतं करोम्यद्य सपौरुषो न्विति ॥६ ॥

हरन्निति । पीयूषम् अ(म)भिनवं पयः । अनुवर्तिनः(नो) गोपबालान् । 'पीयूषोऽभिनवं पयः' इति **अमरः** । (२.९.५४) **पक्षे**-पीयूषम् अ(म)मृतम् ।

---

१. P. begins with श्रीकृष्णाय नमः । B. begins with श्रीगणेशाय नमः ।
२. °द्वयास्तः;
३. लेखां –metathesis.
४. राद°;
५. विहि°;
६. भेक्षिता;
७. क्षणेन;
८. °दविक्षणं;

अनुवर्तिनः(नो) देवान्। पूर्वमपौरुषेण पुरुषरूपभिन्नेन स्त्रीरूपेणेत्यर्थः। अद्य सपौरुषः सन् अ(त्र)हं तत्कृतं करोमीति बुद्ध्या नु गोपानपाययदित्यर्थः ॥६ ॥

सदध्नि भाण्डे स विधाय मूत्रणां कृतक्रुधं काञ्चिदुवाच मथ्नतीम्।
हितानभिज्ञे परिपूर्णमस्तु ते कथं न्वमूत्रे दधिभाजनं मयि ॥७ ॥

सदिति। अमूत्रे मूत्रशून्ये मयि सति। **पक्षे**-'ईश्वरस्य मूत्रं वृष्टिः' इति **श्रुतिसिद्धेः**। अवृष्टौ सत्यां तव भाण्डं कथं नु पूर्णं भविष्यतीति हेतोः म(र्म)या मूत्रणं कृतमित्यर्थः ॥७ ॥

अनुद्रुतां स्वं नवनीतहारिणं पलायमानं विदितात्मलम्भनः।
पलायतैकां क्षमणागिरो वदन् पतन् पदोस्तौ[९] विनिकृष्य पातयन् ॥८ ॥

अनुद्रुतामिति। नवनीतहारिणं पलायमानं स्वम् अ(म)नुद्रुताम् ए(मे)काम्। विदितम् आ(मा)त्मलम्भनम् आ(मा)त्मप्राप्तिर्येन, तादृशः सन् क्षमणागिरः सान्त्वनवाक्यानि वदन् सन् पदोः पतन् तौ पादौ विनिकृष्य तां पातयन् सन् पलायत ॥८ ॥

कयाचन स्तन्यपिबे निजे शिशौ पयःपिबं वारयितुं[१०] बिडालकम्[११]।
नियोजितः प्रस्तरखण्डमीरयन् न तं जिहिंसापि तु तं पयोघटम् ॥९ ॥

कयाचनेति। पिबतीति पिबः, तस्मिन्। तं बिडालकं न जिहिंस न ताडितवान् अपि तु पयोघटं जिहिंस ताडितवान् ॥९ ॥

गृहेषु कासाञ्चन चौर्यतः पयो निपीय तच्छेषमवाहयत् क्षितौ।
अशेषभोगाधिगमोऽस्य जायतां जनस्य वाञ्छामकरोद्यदित्यसौ ॥१० ॥

गृहेष्विति। अस्य जनस्य अ(स्या)शेषभोगाः सर्वभोगाः, तेषामधिगमः प्राप्तिर्जायताम्। **पक्षे**-शेषस्य अ(स्या)वशिष्टस्य भोगः, तस्य अ(स्या)धिगमः प्राप्तिः, तदभावः अ(वो)शेषभोगाधिगमः। जायतामितीच्छया पीतशेषं भूमौ अ(माव)-वाहयत् ॥१० ॥

गृहे न कुत्राप्यभवत्स वत्सको न यस्य दामापहृतं मुरारिणा।
हतानि दामानि शिलासु योजितान्यपातयद्भूरि जले महाप्रहौ ॥११ ॥

---

९. पदास्तै;
१०. °यितु;
११. बिडालम्;

गृहे(ह) इति। महाप्रहौ महाकूपे। 'पुंस्येवान्धुः प्रहिः कूपः' इति **अमरः** ।(१.१०.२६) ॥११ ॥

[१२]उपद्रुतास्तेन तथा व्रजालयाः स्त्रियोऽखिला एत्य हरेर्विचेष्टितम् ।
अवेदयन्नन्दवधूं तथापि नो जगत्पतिं गोपवधूरदण्डयत् ॥१२ ॥

उपद्रुतेति। गोपवधूः यशोदा। 'स्थायुकोऽधिकृतो ग्रामे गोपो ग्रामेषु भूरिषु।' इति **अमरात्** । (२.८.७) कतिपयग्रामाधिपपत्नीत्वात् जगत्पतिं नो अदण्डयत् । दण्डनाभावे गोपवधूत्वं हेतुः ॥१२ ॥१३ ॥१४ ॥

अथैकदा रामपुरोगमार्भका गता यशोदान्तिकमेवमब्रुवन् ।
मृदं यशोदे तनयश्चखाद ते निवार्यमाणः[१३] शपते स्म नः क्रुधा ॥१३ ॥

अथ स्वमाहूय सुतं जगाद सा कुतो मृदं भक्षितवान् भवानिति[१४] ।
स नेत्यथ व्यात्तमुखो [१५]भवेति सा तथा कृते तत्र जगन्ति सैक्षत ॥१४ ॥

सुताननालोकितलोक आत्मजं स्वमप्यवैक्षिष्ट तदानने पुनः ।
जगत्सुतं स्वं च परम्परामिमामनन्तगां वीक्ष्य महाद्भुतं गता ॥१५ ॥

सुतेति। पुत्रमुखावलोकिते लोके(क) आत्मजं स्वं च। तत्र स्थितस्यापि मुखे जगत्सुतं स्वं च। एवम् अ(म)नन्तां परम्परां दृष्ट्वा आ(ष्ट्वाऽऽ)श्चर्यं प्राप ॥१५ ॥

ययानुभावं निजमैक्षत[१६] प्रसूर्जहार तां लोकपतिर्दृशं[१७] पुनः ।
प्रतीक्ष्य तद्दण्डविलोकनोत्सुकाश्चिरं[१८] निराशा न्यवृतंस्ततोऽर्भकाः ॥१६ ॥

ययेति। लोकपतिर्जगत्पतिः। लोकपतिः द(र्द)र्शनपतिरिति **च** प्रतीयते। न्यवृतन् निवृत्ताः ॥१६ ॥

कदाचनाथोदधिमन्थमातनोत्प्रयोजनीकृत्य महामृतोद्भवम् ।
प्रिया हि नेत्रं कृषती व्रजेशितुर्मन्थाचलेनैव सुरासुरावलिः ॥१७ ॥

---

१२. अप°;
१३. °माण (omits the विसर्ग);
१४. भवग्निति;
१५. सवेति;
१६. मैक्ष तत्र°;
१७. °र्दशं;
१८. श्चिरन्नि (म् + न = न्न- Marathi influence)

कदाचनेति। महामृतस्य घृतस्योद्भवो यस्मात्तत्, नवनीतमित्यर्थः। **पक्षे**-पीयूषम्। नेत्रं रज्जुम्। 'मन्थारं मन्दरं कृत्वा नेत्रं कृत्वा च वासुकिम्।' इति **भागवते (विष्णुपुराणे)** [१.९.८४]. दधिमन्थम् उदधिमन्थं **च** ॥१७॥

तदा हरिः[१९] स्तन्यमयाचतोंगतो[२०] विलम्बिते मन्थनदण्डमग्रहीत्।
तिरोहितां स्वामिव दण्डधारतां स्फुटीचिकीर्षन् जगतामधीश्वरः ॥१८॥

तदेति। दण्डधारतां निग्रहप्रापकत्वम्। दण्डः खलनिग्रहः ॥१८॥

विसृज्य मन्थोद्यमनं तमात्मजं न्यपीप्यत स्तन्यपयः ततः[२१] प्रसूः।
अशेषभुङ्[२२]नापिबदेव देवकीस्तनं परोच्छिष्टतयेव यः प्रभुः ॥१९॥

विसृज्येति। अशेषभुक् शेषमवशिष्टं भुनक्तीति, न तथा। ***पक्षे***-समस्तपालकः ॥१९॥

स्रुतं पयः कृष्णमुखे विमुञ्चति स्तने हरेर्मातुरमुष्य यः समः।
अमुञ्चतोत्सेकमिषात्पयः स्रुतं हरेर्मुखेऽग्नौ सपयोधरो[२३] घटः ॥२०॥

स्रुतमिति। हरेर्मुखेऽग्नौ अ(ग्नाव)मुञ्चत। 'अग्निमुखा वै देवाः।' इति **श्रुतिः**। ॥२०॥

य एष साक्षादमृतं विमुच्य तं पयः[२४]स्पृहा हन्त जगाम गोपिका।
यतो जगत्यां पशुपालजातिजा जडोपमानत्वमवाप्नुवंस्ततः ॥२१॥

य इति। अमृतं पयः। **पक्षे**-मोक्षस्वरूपम्। पयसः स्पृहा यस्याः सा गोपिका जगाम। उत्सिक्तं घटं प्रति चलिता ॥२१॥

कृशानुभावं गत एव स व्यधाद्घटाधिरोपाभिभवप्रतिक्रियाम्।
महानुभावोऽभिभवं क्षमे कथं न्वितीव रुष्टः स बभञ्ज मन्थनीम्[२५] ॥२२॥

कृशेति। कृशानुभावम् अ(म)ल्पसामर्थ्यं गतोऽपि। **पक्षे**—कृशानुभावमग्नित्वम्। स्वस्मिन् यो घटाधिरोपरूपः पराभवः त(स्त)स्य प्रतिक्रियां

१९. हरिस्तन (विसर्ग dropped & jointly written);
२०. °चप्ता;
२१. पयप्रसूः (repetition of previous word)
२२. °भूं;
२३. B. lacuna for धरो;
२४. Omits the विसर्ग;
२५. P. marginal quotation 'मन्थनी गर्गरी समे' इति **अमरः**।

दुग्धोत्सेकरूपां व्यधात्। 'महानुभाव: अ(वोऽ)हं, मां त्यक्त्वा पयोघटं प्रति गमनरूपं पराभवं कथं क्षमे नु' इति धिया मन्थनीं गर्गरीं बभञ्जेति। 'मन्थनी[२६] गर्गरी समे' इति अमरः। (२.९.७४) ॥

अथागता वीक्ष्य सुतस्य दुर्नयं व्रजेश्वरी बन्धनताड[२७]नेच्छया।
उपासृपत्तं स गृहीततन्मनाः पलायतैषापि[२८] तमन्वधावत ॥२३॥

अथेति। उपासृपत् समीपं गता ॥२३ ॥२४ ॥२५ ॥

श्रमानभिज्ञामनुधावनश्रमं गतां महान्तं स विलोक्य मातरम्।
दयालुरागाद्वशमेनमम्बिका निबन्धुकामा पशुरज्जुमाददे ॥२४॥

[२९]यदैकदामाऽपटु तस्य वेष्टने बभूव दामान्तरयोजितं तदा।
तथाभवत्तच्च तथा कृतं पुनर्गतान्तमेवं गृहदामसंहतिः ॥२५॥

प्रसूरिदं वीक्ष्य परं विसिष्मिये न बन्धयत्नाद्विरराम मायिनः।
स्वभक्तशापान्तचिकीर्षया परं ततो जनन्या कृतबन्धनोऽभवत् ॥२६॥

प्रसूरिति। विसिष्मिषे(ये) विस्मयं प्राप ॥२६ ॥

यया स रज्ज्वा परयोगदीर्घया सुवेष्टिताङ्[३०]गो भगवांस्तदन्तयोः।
उलूखलं दारुविकारमन्तरा विधाय सा ग्रन्थिमदादृढं प्रसूः ॥२७॥

ययेति। परयोगदीर्घया अन्यरज्जुसम्बन्धेन महत्या। तदन्तयो:(यो) रज्जोः प्रान्तयोः ग्र(ग्रं)न्थिमदात् दारुविकारमुलूखलमन्तरा स्थापयित्वा ॥२७ ॥२८ ॥

निबध्यमानो भगवानुलूखले भृशं [३१]व्यराजद्बहुवेष्टनाञ्चितः।
सगण्डशैलान्तिकवल्लिकान्तरप्रवेशनिष्यन्द इवेभशावकः ॥२८॥

ततो रुडन्तर्धिमवाप नाप्नुयात् प्रभोर्विरोधे सति कस्तिरोहितम्।
तथापि नामुञ्चत सा सुतं यतो न युज्यते शीघ्रमनुग्रहः[३२]क्रुधि ॥२९॥

---

२६. P1 marginal gloss. The Marathi word डेरा given as an equivalent to मन्थनी & गर्गरी.

२७. °न°;

२८. °तेषाःपि;

२९. वदेक°

३०. °ष्टितां भोगगवां;

३१. °व्यथा राज°;

३२. कधि (Marathi influence, cf. कधी (हि));

तत इति। रुट् क्रोधः शान्तः। प्रभोर्विरोधे जाते सति कः ति(स्ति)रोहितम् अ(म)न्तर्धिं नाशं च नाप्नुयादपि तु सर्वोऽपि। ननु क्रोधशान्तौ सत्यां कृष्णं किमर्थं न मुमोचेत्यत आह न युज्यते (त इ) ति ॥२९॥

स दारुणाश्लिाष्टरथः सुरोत्तमो दिवं वितन्वन् वसुजातसङ्गताम्।
तमोऽ[३३]भिभूताशुचिपक्षमन्तयन् हरिर्ययावर्जुनपादसन्निधिम् ॥३०॥

स दारुणेति। दारुणा उलूखलरूपेणाश्लिष्टरथः(थ) आश्लिष्टशरीरः। 'रथस्तु स्यन्दने पादे शरीरे वेतसद्रुमे।' इति **हैमः**। (**अनेकार्थसङ्ग्रहः**-२.२२४) **पक्षे**-अरुणेनाश्लिष्टस्यन्दनः। 'सुरोत्तमः' उभयत्र समानम्। दिवं स्वर्गम् अन्तरिक्षं **च**। वसुः कुबेरः, तज्जातौ पुत्रौ, ताभ्यां *सङ्गताम्*। **पक्षे**-वसुजातं किरणसमूहः। तमोऽभिभूताः त(स्त)मोगुणेनावृताः, ये अ(येऽ)शुचयः, तेषां पक्षं सहायम् अ(म)न्तयन् सन् अ(न्र)र्जुनवृक्षमूलसन्निधिम्। **पक्षे**-तमोऽन्धकारः। अशुचिपक्षः कृष्णपक्षः। अर्जुनपादः शुभ्रपादः चन्द्रः (न्द्र) इति यावत् ॥३०॥

[३४]विवेश देवोऽर्जुनपादपान्तरं ततो महास्थूलमुलूखलं तु न।
तदाकृष[३५]त्तत्स महाबलो हरिर्बभञ्ज तेनार्जुनपादपद्वयम् ॥३१॥

विवेशेति। उलूखलं तु न विवेश। तस्मादाकृषत् ॥३१॥

त्रिलोकपूज्यस्य तवाङ्घ्रिसङ्गमो बभूव[३६] नौ क्षाम्यतु तं भवानिति।
विभङ्गशब्दस्य कृतार्थनमिषात्तरुद्वयं तच्छिरसाऽस्पृशद्भुवम् ॥३२॥

त्रिलोकेति। तव नौ आवयोः अ(र)ङ्घ्रिसङ्गमः पादसङ्गमः। **पक्षे**-मूलसङ्गमः ॥३२॥३३॥

ततः पुमांसौ विरजोत्तमाम्बरौ महार्घभूषाञ्चितसुन्दराङ्गकौ।
विनिर्गतौ तत्तरुकोटरान्तरात्परं पुमांसं शिरसा प्रणेमतुः ॥३३॥

कृतानुयोगौ हरिणा तमूचतुर्महेश्वरावां तनयौ धनेशितुः।
वधूसुरासङ्गमवेक्ष्य नारदः शशाप नौ शापमहन् भवा[३७]निति ॥३४॥

कृतेति। कृतानुयोगौ कृतप्रश्नौ। 'प्रश्नोऽनुयोगः पृच्छा च' इति **अमरः**।

---

३३. तमौभि°;
३४. विशेष;
३५. °कृषन् तत्स;
३६. बभौ वनौ;
३७. भवम्निति;

(१.६.१०) हे महेश्वरेति सम्बोधनम्। वधूनां सुरायाश्च यो(य) आसङ्गः (ङ्ग) आसक्तिः। तम् अ(म)वेक्ष्य अ(क्ष्या)वलोक्य ॥३४॥३५॥

अथानुमान्य प्रणतौ महेश्वरं गतौ पदं वैश्रवणात्मजौ[३८] निजम्।
ततः श्रुतात्यन्तभयङ्करध्वनिस्तमेत्य नन्दस्तरुभङ्गमैक्षत ॥३५॥

कृतं सुतेनेदमिति व्रजार्भकैरुदीर्यमाणं वचनं गवेश्वरः।
मृषेति मत्वा समुपागतं कमप्यमन्यतोत्पातमवेक्ष्य तान् पुरा ॥३६॥

कृतमिति। पुरा पूर्वं तान् उ(नु)त्पातान् अ(न)वेक्ष्य अ(क्ष्या)न्यतः समुपागतम् उ(मु)त्पातममन्यत ॥३६॥

उदायतोलूखलनध्दमात्मजं गवेषिताध्वानममुं शिफान्तरे।
सपाण्डुराम्भोधरखण्डसङ्गतं शरत्तुषारांशुमिव व्यलोकत ॥३७॥

उदिति। उदायतम् उत् आयतं विस्तीर्णं यदुलूखलं शिफान्तरे शाखान्तरे। शरत्तुषारांशुः शरच्चन्द्रः, तमिव ॥३७॥

भयङ्गतस्येव जगद्भयच्छिदो विमुच्य बन्धं जनबन्धहारिणः।
निनाय धामैष पिता जगत्पितुर्हरिं[३९] जगद्धाम महाकलेवरम् ॥३८॥

भयङ्गतस्येति। सर्वत्रापि **शब्दतः(तो) विरोधाभासः**। भयच्छिदः(दो) भयङ्गतस्य **च**। जनबन्धहारिणः (णो) बन्धं विमुच्य। धाम गृहं, जगद्धाम जगन्निवासम् ॥३८॥

बृहद्वने वीक्ष्य बहू[४०]नुपद्रवान् स मन्त्रयित्वा स्थविरैर्विसृज्य तत्।
इयेष[४१] वृन्दावननामकं वनं पशव्यमावस्तुमदुष्टसत्त्ववत् ।३९॥

बृहदिति। पशव्यं पशुसमूहः। आवस्तुं वृन्दावननामकं वनम् इ(मि)-येष ॥३९॥

यदन्तिकोत्स[४२]र्पिकलिन्दकन्यका गिरिश्च गोवर्धननाम भाजनम्।
निसर्गरम्यं नयतो द्युतिं परां फलप्रसूनावनतोन्नतद्रुमम् ॥४०॥

---

३८. °जै;
३९. °त्पितु ह°,(Omits the विसर्ग (i.e.) रेफ);
४०. P. writes हू as हु (Marathi influence on spelling);
४१. इयेष्ट;
४२. कात्स;

यदिति। निसर्गरम्यं तद्वनं कालिन्दी गोवर्धनश्च द्वावपि परां द्युतिं नयतः प्रापयतः। 'तत्र उभावपि वर्तेते' इत्यर्थः ॥४० ॥

निवर्तितैः शृङ्गरवेण गोधनैर्वधूजरद्बालपरिच्छदान्वितैः।
सहानसां च प्रकरैस्तदासदद्वनं स नन्दः सकलैश्च बल्लवैः ॥४१ ॥

आसदत् प्राप्तवान् सकलैश्च बल्लवैः ॥४१ ॥

वनं तदाभात्पशुपैरधिष्ठितं व्रजाङ्गनाभिर्भृशपाण्डुगोधनैः।
विनीलसालैश्च सतारकं नभः सपाण्डुराभ्रं सतमो[४३] निशास्विव ॥४२ ॥

वनमिति। निशासु सतमः सतारकं सपाण्डुराभ्रं नभ इव तद्वनम् आ(मा)भात् ॥४२ ॥४३ ॥

महेश्वरः सन्नतलोकपालको जगाम कालेन सवत्सपालताम्।
महत्पदं प्राप्तवतोऽवरं पदं प्रयापयेत् काल इतीव बोधयन् ॥४३ ॥

समित्रवृन्दौ बलभद्रकेशवावदूरगौ चारयतः स्म वात्सकम्।
अनन्तरागैर्हरिपाददुर्गमे चिखेलतु[४४]श्चांशुमदात्मजातटे ॥४४ ॥

समि[त्रे]ति। वात्सकं वत्ससमूहः। अनन्तराः (रा) निबिडा ये अगाः(गा) वृक्षाः, तैः। हरिः सूर्यः, पादः चरणः किरणा(ण)श्च। तैर्गन्तुमशक्ये यमुनातटे चिखेलतुः चि(श्चि)क्रीडतुः ॥४४ ॥

नृपायितं प्राप्य कदाचन प्रभुः समं गतैः कैश्चन राजसेविताम्।
स निग्रहानुग्रहयोरनुक्रियां चकार तद्योग्यपदावलम्बिषु ॥४५ ॥

नृपायितमिति। राजसेवितां गतैः कैश्चन समम्। तद्योग्यं निग्रहानुग्रहयोग्यं यत्पदं तस्यावलम्बिषु विषये निग्रहानुग्रहयोः अ(र)नुक्रियां चकार। निग्रहयोग्यस्य निग्रहम् अ(म)नुग्रहयोग्यस्य अ(स्या)नुग्रहं चकारेत्यर्थः ॥४५ ॥

गतैरिवैकाग्रमतिं निजानने दृशं ददद्भिर्धृतपर्णपुस्तकैः।
हरिर्वयस्यैः परिवारितो वने कदाचिदासीज्जगतांगुरुर्गुरुः ॥४६ ॥

गतैरिति। जगतांगुरुः ह(र्ह)रिः कदाचित्(द्) गुरुरासीत् ॥४६ ॥

परस्परौपम्यजुषां द्वियूथिकां विधाय यूथं स्वयमेकमाददत्।
प्रदाय रामाय परं च यूथगौर्जि[४५] तस्य जैत्रोद्वहने पणीकृते ॥४७ ॥

४३. सतगोग्निशा°;
४४. °त°;
४५. °गौर्जित्तस्यस्य;

परस्परेति । परस्परसाम्यजुषां द्वयोर्यूथयो: समाहार: द्वियूथी । सैव द्वियूथिका, ताम् । जितस्य जैत्रोद्वहने, जेतु: उ(रु)द्वहने पणीकृते सति । जितेन जेतु: उ(रु)द्वहनं कार्यमिति पणीकृत्वा (त्य) यूथमाददिदित्यन्वयः । ।४७ ॥

जितत्वजेतृत्वविपर्ययोऽनयोर्न यावता स्यात्समयेन तावता ।
कदाचिदीशो विजहार कन्दुकैः स जातु लाक्षामयगोलकैरपि ।।४८ ॥

जितत्वेति । यावद्विपर्यय:(यो) नाभूत्तावत्पर्यन्तम् ।।४८ ॥

निमील्य चोन्मील्य तदीक्षणे हरिर्जयं फलन्तं स्वपराङ्गयोगतः ।
तिरोहिताङ्गेषु वयस्यमेकदा परेषु नाराचमिव व्यमुञ्चत ।।४९ ॥

निमील्येति । तस्य वयस्यस्य ई(स्ये)क्षणे पूर्वं निमील्य पश्चादुन्मील्य स्वस्य पराङ्गसङ्गात् ज(ज्ज)यं फलन्तं जयं सम्पादयन्तं वयस्यं तिरोहिताङ्गेषु अ(ष्व)न्येषु वयस्येषु विषये नाराचमिव व्यमुञ्चत । **बाणपक्षेऽपि विशेषणानि योज्यानि** ।।४९ ॥

सभासदः केचन केचनाभवन्नटाः कदाचिन्नटतामुपेयुषाम् ।
विलोक्य नाट्यं बहुपारितोषिकं प्रसूनमाल्यादि [४६]फलाद्यदुः परे ।।५० ॥

सभासद इति । परे केचन पारितोषिकमदु: दत्तवन्त: ।।५० ।।५१ ॥

प्रमादसंत्यक्तविषाणकादीन् परे परेषामपहृत्य तान् पुनः ।
भृशाकुलान् वीक्ष्य चिरेण तान् ददुर्मृगद्विजादीननुकृत्य चारमन् ।।५१ ॥

सुरूषिता गैरिकधातुरेणुना प्रवालपिञ्छाकुसुमाद्यलङ्कृताः ।
धृतोरुगुञ्जामणिमालिका अमी वने चरन्तो विदधुर्मुदं दृशाम् ।।५२ ॥

सुरूषितेति । रूषिता वेष्टिता:, गैरिकेण कृताङ्गरागा इत्यर्थ: ।।५२ ॥

कदाचिदीशे सति चारयत्यमूं शकृ[४७]त्करीभूय तृणादनक्रियाम् ।
विवेश वत्सावलिमेत्य दानवः सुरावलिं राहुरिवाश्नतीं सुधाम् ।।५३ ॥

कदाचिदिति । तृणादनक्रियां तृणादनकर्त्रीम् अ(म)मूं वत्सावलिम् । शकृत्करीभूय वत्सो भूत्वा । 'शकृत्करिस्तु वत्सः स्यात्' इति **अमरः** । (२.९.६२) ।।५३ ॥

---

४६. पला°;
४७. P. mg. qu. 'शकृत्करिस्तु वत्सः स्यात्' इति **अमरः** ।

**रुरोज[४८] कांश्चिच्छिरसाल्पशृङ्गको[४९] जघान कांश्चिच्च स पश्चिमाङ्घ्रिणा ।
न पीडितस्तेन न कोऽपि वत्सको हरिः[५०] स्वपक्षाभिभवात्तदाऽक्रुधत् ।।५४ ।।**

रुरोजेति । रुरोज पीडामकरोत् । तेन कोऽपि वत्सकः (को) न पीडित इति न, अपि तु सर्वोऽपि पीडित इत्यर्थः । स्वपक्षाणां योऽभिभवस्तस्मात् ।।५४ ।।

**[५१]प्रगृह्य तं पश्चिमपादयोर्नयन्[५२] भ्रमं महान्तं स कपित्थपादपान् ।
अभि त्यजंस्तत्फलपातनेच्छया वि[५३]मुक्तचक्रो दनुजेष्विवाबभौ ।।५५ ।।**

प्रगृह्येति । तत्फलपातनेच्छया । कपित्थपादपान् अ(न)भि कपित्थपादपोन्मुखं तं त्यजन् सन् विमुक्तचक्रः(क्रो) विमोक्तुमारब्धचक्र इव बभौ । **एकस्यैवोपमेयोपमानत्वम्** । ।५५ ।।

**हरौ कदाचित् ससखौ कलिन्दजां गते समं वत्सगणैर्बकाभिधः ।
हरिं[५४] विदित्वेव झषाकृतिं खलो[५५] निहन्तुमागाद्बकरूपमाश्रितः ।।५६ ।।**

हराविति । ससखौ मित्रसहिते हरौ यमुनां प्राप्ते ।।५६ ।।

**जगन्निवासोदरता यशस्विनं निधाय कुक्षौ परमं यशो लभै ।
इतीव कीर्तिप्रियतां गतो महातनुः स चञ्च्वा प्रजहार तं ह्यदन् ।।५७ ।।**

जगदिति । जगन्निवासोदरता यशस्विनमेनं स्वकुक्षौ निधाय परमं यशः(शो) लभै प्राप्नुयामिति हेतोः ।।५७ ।।

**वधेच्छया तं परमात्मनो बकं तदोपसृप्तं हतवान् मुरान्तकः ।
न नोपसर्पन् हरिमाप वाञ्छितं यतो हतेऽस्मिन् मुदिताः कुमारकाः ।।५८ ।।**

वधेच्छयेति । मुरान्तकः परमात्मनः(नो) वधेच्छया उ(यो)पसृप्तं तम् आ(मा)त्मनः परं स्वस्यैव वधेच्छया उ(यो)पसृप्तमिति च प्रतीयते, बकं हतवान् । यतः(तो) हेतोः ह(र्ह)रिमुपसर्पन् वाञ्छितं नापेति न, **अत इति पूर्वेणान्वयः** । कुमाराः(रा) मुदिताः ।।५८ ।।

---

४८. सुरोज;
४९. °ङ्गका;
५०. हरिस्व° (विसर्ग dropped & jointly writtten);
५१. मगृ°;
५२. °र्नयंन् (अनुस्वार + न्—Marathi influence);
५३. ग्विमु° (Scribal peculiarity of writing additional ग् before वि)
५४. हरिवि° (अनुस्वार dropped & jointly written);
५५. खले;

अथाघनामा बकपूतनानुजो निगारकामो बकपूतनाद्रुहः ।
अशेत घो[५६]राजगराकृतिं भजन् हरेः पथीन्दोरिव सिंहिकासुतः ॥५९ ॥

अथेति । पूतनाद्रुहः कृष्णस्य कृष्णं प्रतीत्यर्थः । निगारकामः(मो) गिलितुकामः । हरेः पथि अशेत्(त) ॥५९ ॥

अनेकदा दृष्टमपीश्वरानुगाः प्रयापितं नूतनतां दुरात्मना ।
शिलोच्चयाकारशरीरगामिना वनं न्यविक्षन्त गृहीतवत्सकाः ॥६० ॥

अनेकेति । ईश्वरानुगाः ते(स्ते)न दुरात्मना नूतनतां प्रयापितं वनं न्यविक्षन्त प्राविशन् ॥६० ॥

निरन्तरानोकहतान्धकारितं वनान्तघण्टापथमाकलय्य ते ।
अवेशयन् व्यात्तमहाशनाननं स्ववात्सकं स्वेऽप्यविशन्ननन्तरम् ॥६१ ॥

निरन्तरेति । स्ववात्सकं स्ववत्स[स]मूहं व्यात्तं यन्महाशनस्य राक्षसस्य आ(स्या)ननं प्रति अ(त्य)वेशयन् ॥६१ ॥

निवृत्तिकामा अपि पूर्वगामिनः परप्रवृत्तैः पुरतः[५७] प्रणोदिताः ।
महाशनोद्यज्जठरानलान्तरेऽविशन् प्रवाहा इव वाडवेऽम्बुधेः ॥६२ ॥

निवृत्तीति । वाडवे वडवाग्नौ, अम्बुधेः प्रवाहा इवाविशन् ॥६२ ॥

महाशनप्राणगमागमैरमी गतोदराः क्लिष्टगमागमासुकाः ।
प्रतापिताश्चोदरजातवेदसा मृताः प्रयाता अपि सम्मुखोरगाः ॥६३ ॥

महाशनेति । क्लिष्टौ गमागमौ येषां ते क्लिष्टगमागमाः । तादृशा असवो येषां ते ॥६३ ॥

गतेऽखिलेऽप्याननशुक्तिरागमस्पृहा हरिस्वात्यमृतस्य यातुनः ।
सुमुक्ततायै रदनच्छदाभिधे न योजयामास दले उभे अपि ॥६४ ॥

गतेति । अखिले गोपसमूहे गते सति अ(त्य)न्तः प्रविष्टे सति यातुनः राक्षसस्य आ(स्या)ननरूपा शुक्तिः, सुमुक्ततायै सुमुक्ताप्राप्त्यर्थं हरिरूपस्वात्यमृतस्य आ(स्या)गमे स्पृहा यस्या[ः] सा, तादृशी सती रदनच्छदाभिधे ओष्ठनामके उभे दले न योजयामास, न संयोजितवती ॥६४ ॥

---

५६. घोरां जं°; The B. scribe could not understand the अनुस्वार deleted by the sign & hence retains it.

५७. °तप्र° (विसर्ग dropped & jointly written);

प्रविश्य तस्याननकन्दरान्तरं हरिः[५८] स्वदन्तच्छदयोजनोद्यमम् ।
वितन्वतोऽमुष्य गले निजां तनूमवर्धयद्यद्बलिनिग्रहोद्यतः ॥६५ ॥

प्रविश्येति । यत् यस्मात्कारणात् बलवतां निग्रहे दण्डे विषये (य) उद्यतः, तस्मात्, तनूमवर्धयत् ॥६५ ॥६६ ॥

स तिर्यगूर्ध्वं च विवृद्ध ईश्वरे निरुध्यमानासुगतिः स्थिराशयः ।
विमुक्तभोगो गलिताघसङ्गमो विवेश तेजोमय ईशमीदृशम् ॥६६ ॥

मृतान् सवत्सानथ वत्सपालकान् स जीवयित्वा करुणामृतोक्षणैः ।
हरिः समं तैर्निरगात्तदाननात्तिरोहिताघान्तविधायिविग्रहः ॥६७ ॥

मृतानिति । करुणैवामृतं, तस्य उक्षणैः प्रोक्षणैः ॥६७ ॥

अथाघविध्वंसकृतीश्वरेश्वरे हरौ महामोदयुतो रसान्वितः ।
सगायनालिः सुमनोगणो महान् बभूव वृष्टोऽपि च वर्षितोऽपि[५९] च ॥६८ ॥

अथेति । अघासुरनाशके(क) ईश्वरेश्वरे हरौ । आमोदो गन्धः हर्षश्च । रसः मकरन्दः प्रीतिश्च । सगायना अलयो यस्मिन्, गायनालिः गन्धर्वपङ्क्तिः, तत्सहितश्च । सुमनोगणः पुष्पसमूहः, वृष्टः(ष्टो) बभूव । **पक्षे**-सुमनोगणः(णो) वर्षिता बभूव । **एकस्यैव सुमनोगणस्य कर्मकर्तृविरोधस्तु शब्दतः, परिहारस्तु अर्थतः** ॥६८ ॥

पिपासितैरप्यशनायितैर्भृशं सवत्सकैर्मित्रगणैः समं हरिः ।
निरन्तरच्छायमिनात्मजातटं ययौ हिमं सञ्चरदम्बुमारुतैः ॥६९ ॥

पिपासितैरिति । तृषितैः क्षु(क्षु)धितैश्च । इनः सूर्यस्तस्यात्मजा यमुना, तस्यास्तटम् ॥६९ ॥

निपाय्य[६०] तृण्यास्ववसज्जय वत्सकानघोदरोदन्तमवस्थितं पुरः ।
अवेक्षमाणान्[६१] वलयायितावलीन् सखीन् विधाय स्वयमन्तरे स्थितः ॥७० ॥

निपाय्येति । निपाय्य पाययित्वा तृण्यासु तृणसमूहेषु । 'तृण्या तृणसमूहे स्यात्' इति **हैमः** । अवसज्ज्य योजयित्वा । सखीन् मित्राणि । वलयायितावलीन् वलयाकारेण स्थितान् विधाय स्वयं मध्ये स्थितः ॥७० ॥

---

५८. हरिस्व° (विसर्ग dropped & jointly written);
५९. वर्षितो°;
६०. निपाप्य;
६१. [-] अवेक्षमाणावलयीकृतावलीन् विधाय स्वरम°;

प्रचक्रमे तैः सह भोजनक्रियां कथाभिरस्वाद्वपि[६२] रस्यतां नयन् ।
अनाभिमुख्यं स हि श्रुण्वतां कथां निजां न कस्यापि ययौ महेश्वरः ।।७१ ।।

प्रचक्रमे (म इ)ति । अस्वाद्वपि वस्तु कथाभिः गो(गो)ष्ठीभिः (भी) रस्यतां स्वादुत्वं नयन् निजां कथां श्रुण्वतां मध्ये कस्यापि अ(प्य)नाभिमुख्यम् अ(म)साम्मुख्यं न ययौ । मध्येस्थितत्वात् सर्वस्यापि साम्मुख्यं ययावित्यर्थः ।।७१ ।।

निरीक्ष्य तत्प्रत्यवसानमुत्तरं महाशनोदर्यधनञ्जयौषणात् ।
विषानलप्लोषणतः[६३] परं सुधां दिवौकसामस्मरदीश्वरोऽश्नताम् ।।७२ ।।

निरीक्ष्येति । महाशनस्य उदर्यो यो धनञ्जयः, तत्कर्तृक ओषणात् प्लोषणात् उ(दु)त्तरम् उ(मु)त्तरकालभावि प्रत्यवसानं भोजनं निरीक्ष्य । ईश्वर:(रो) दिवौकसां देवान् अ(न)स्मरदित्यर्थः ।।७२ ।।

ततर्प तद्वत्सपवृन्दमन्धसो[६४] वचोऽमृतानां[६५] न तु दानवद्विषः ।
हरेर्मुखेन्दुस्मितचन्द्रिकालिहः परं बभूवुः सखिदृक्चकोरकाः ।।७३ ।।

ततर्पेति । तत् व(द्व) त्सपवृन्दम् अ(म)न्धसः (स) अन्नेनेत्यर्थः । ततर्प । दानवद्विषः कृष्णस्य वचोऽमृतानां वागमृतैः न(र्न) ततर्प, अलं बुद्धिं न प्रापेत्यर्थः । मुखेन्दुस्मितचन्द्रिकालिहः परं बभूवुः, अन्यत्र दृष्टवन्त इत्यर्थः ।।७३ ।।

जरद्गवीनां च ममाप्रसूतिता मनश्च पीयूषरुचेर्वशंवदम् ।
लभेय कालेन फलं हरन्नमूनितीव[६६] वत्सानहरत्तदा विधिः ।।७४ ।।

जरदिति । मम जरद्गवीनां वृद्धानां गवां श्रुतीनामिति च प्रतीयते । अप्रसूतितां गर्भमोचनराहित्यम्, उत्पत्तिराहित्यम् अ(म)पौरुषेयत्वात् ।।७४ ।।

कथाविरामे सति तन्मुखाम्बुजाद्दृशं विभक्तामथ वत्सपालकाः ।
स्ववत्ससञ्चारधरामयापयन् धियं समाधेर्जगतीमिवोत्थिताः ।।७५ ।।

कथेति । समाधेरुत्थिताः पुरुषाः (षा) धियं जगतीमिव ।।७५ ।।७६ ।।

---

६२. °स्वाद्दपि;
६३. °णल°;
६४. °मन्धसा;
६५. °नान (अनुस्वार dropped & jointly written);
६६. °न्नमूनी°;

अवी[६७]क्ष्य वत्सान् भृशतप्तचेतसो गवेषणोद्योगजुषः क्लमान्वितान्।
दया[६८]निसर्गो भगवान्निवार्य तान् स्वयं विचेतुं गहनं व्यगाहत ॥७६ ॥

इतो विधाताऽहृत वत्सपालकान् श्रुतानुभावस्तमवेक्षितुं हरेः ।
निवृत्य तानप्यविलोक्य सर्ववित् सखीन् ययौ वत्सपवत्सतामपि ॥७७ ॥

इत इति । इतः प्रदेशे हरेः श्रुतानुभावः श्रुतसामर्थ्यः(र्थ्यो) विधाता ब्रह्मा तमनुभावमवेक्षितुं वत्सपालकान् अ(न)हृत हृतवान् । वत्सावलोकनार्थं गतो हरिः त(स्त)त्र वत्सानदृष्ट्वा निवृत्य परावृत्य अ(त्या)त्रापि तान् सखीनविलोक्य वत्सपत्वं वत्सतां च स्वयवाप ॥७७ ॥

अशोकतास्या अभिवाञ्छिता यतो न्यपीयत स्तन्यपयश्च विष्णुना ।
व्रजाङ्गनानां च गवां च संहतिस्ततोऽत्यशेतानकदुन्दुभिप्रियाम् ॥७८ ॥

अशोकतेति । यतः(तो) विष्णुना अ(नाऽ)स्याः (स्या) व्रजाङ्गनानां संहतेः अ(र)शोकता शोकराहित्यमभिवाञ्छिता अ(ताऽ)स्या गवां संहतेश्च पयः(यो) न्यपीयत । ततः त(स्त)स्मात् व्र(द्व्र)जाङ्गनासंहतिः ग(र्ग)वां संहतिश्च आ(श्चा)नकदुन्दुभिप्रियाम् अ(म)त्यशेत अतिक्रमितवती । देवक्याः(क्या) जन्मारभ्य स्वाऽदर्शनेन शोकजननात्, दुग्धाऽपानाच्च ॥७८ ॥

स पेयखाद्यान्यनुभूय तृप्ततां नयन्न[६९]मून् पद्मभवात्मसात्कृतान् ।
पुरार्पिततद्रचितक्रियाफलोऽकरोदिव प्रत्युपकारमच्युतः ॥७९ ॥

सेति (स इति) । पुरा अर्पितानि एतैर्वत्सवत्सपालैः(लै) रचितानां क्रियाणां फलानि यस्मै सः (स) कृष्णः प्रत्युपकारमकरोदिव ॥७९ ॥

अखेलदेवं शरदं जगत्पतिश्चतुर्मुखर्तुः शरदन्त आगतः ।
महीतलं शान्तरुचीभवद्धरिः समानशे मोहतुषारविभ्रमैः ॥८० ॥

अखेलदिति । शरदन्ते शरत्कालान्ते संवत्सरान्ते च महीतलमागतः । चतुर्मुखः (ख) एव ऋतुः अर्थात् हेमन्तऋतुः । शान्ता रुचिः कान्तिर्यस्य, तादृशी(शो) भवन् हरिः सूर्यो यस्मिन् । शान्ता रुचिः प्रीतिर्यस्य तादृशी(शो) भवन् हरिः कृष्णु यस्मिन् (कृष्णो/विष्णुर्यस्मिन्) सः । मोह एव तुषारविभ्रमास्तैः समानशे व्याप्तः ॥८० ॥८१ ॥८२ ॥

---

६७. B. अवेक्ष्य;
६८. दयो नि°;
६९. °न्नभून्;

परे हृतेभ्यः क इमे हृताः पुनः समाहृताः किं नु न तेऽधुनेक्षिताः ।
निधानभूमौ वितथा अमी मम भ्रमो हृतेर्वेत्यभजन्मतीर्विधिः ॥८१ ॥

अपारसन्देहजुषा स्वयम्भुवा तदा व्यदृश्यन्त सवत्सवत्सपाः ।
प्रसन्नपूर्णेन्दुमनोरमाननाः प्रलम्बपीताम्बरनीलविग्रहाः ॥८२ ॥

विलोचनाख्यप्रसृ[७०]तिप्रसारितैर्दयारसैः शान्तनताघपावकाः ।
ससान्ध्यकान्तीन्दुमयूखसुन्दरारुणाधरोद्योतयुतस्मितांशवः ॥८३ ॥

विलोचनेति । विलोचनाख्या या प्रसृतिः नि(र्नि)कुब्जपाणिः । 'पाणिर्निकुब्जः प्रसृतिः' इति **अमरः** । (२.६.८४) तेन प्रसारितैर्दयारसैः । शान्तः(न्तो) नतानामघमेव पावकः यैस्ते । सान्ध्यकान्तिसहिताः(ता) ये(य) इन्दुमयूखाः, तद्वत् सुन्दराः, अरुणाधरोद्योतयुताः स्मितांशवो येषाम् । अरुणाधरोद्योतस्य अ(स्या)रुणत्वात् सान्ध्यकान्तिसाम्यं, स्मितांशूनाम् इ(मि)न्दुमयूखसाम्यम् ॥८३ ॥८४ ॥

किरीटमूर्धान उदारकुण्डलप्रकाशनीराजितगण्डमण्डलाः ।
सहेमकेयूरभुजा चतुष्टया गदारथाङ्गाम्बुजकम्बुपाणयः ॥८४ ॥

करस्थनिर्वाणधना[७१]वनेच्छया सुवर्णसालै रचितैरिवोज्ज्वलैः ।
विराजमाना वलयैर्महाधनैः सहारदोरन्तरशोभिकौस्तुभाः ॥८५ ॥

करस्थेति । करस्थं निर्वाणरूपं यत् धनं, तस्य अ(स्या)वनेच्छया संरक्षणेच्छया रचितैः सुवर्णसालैः सुवर्णप्राकारैरिव वलयैः कटकैः वि(र्वि)राजमानाः । 'प्राकारो वरणः सालः' इति **अमरः** ।(२.२.३)' कटको वलयोऽस्त्रियाम्' (**अमरः** २.६.१०७) इत्यर्थः । सहारं हारसहितं यद्दोरन्तरं तत्र शोभिनः कौस्तुभा येषां ते ॥८५ ॥

महोन्नतस्थानजुषाऽपि नोज्झिते हरेर्विधेये चरणाम्बुजे इति ।
गतांसयाऽप्यङ्घ्रिसरोरुहस्पृशा निवीतिभाजा वनमालयाञ्चिताः[७२] ॥८६ ॥

मह इति । महोन्नतस्थानजुषाऽपि मया हरेर्विधेये पूज्ये चरणाम्बुजे मया नोज्झिते इति ज्ञापनायेव प्राप्तांसयाऽपि अ(प्य)ङ्घ्रिसरोरुहस्पृशा वनमालया अञ्चिताः । 'आपादलम्बिनी माला वनमालेति गीयते' इति ॥८६ ॥

---

७०. P. mg. qu. पाणिर्निकुब्जः प्रसृतिः' इति **अमरः** ।
७१. धनो व°;
७२. °लयान्विताः (Difficult reading is generally older and hence preferred).

महार्घशोणोपलमेखलाजुषो मनोज्ञमञ्जीरपदाम्बुजद्वयाः ।
युता महाराजपरिच्छदैः[७३] शुभैरुपास्यमाना दिविजैः पृथक् पृथक् ॥८७ ॥

महार्घेति । शोणोपलाः (ला) माणिक्यमणयः । मञ्जीरः पादभूषणम् । शुभैरुत्तमैः महाराजपरिच्छदैः महाराजयोग्यैर्वस्त्रैर्युताः ॥८७ ॥

विलोकमानस्य हरेरिमास्तनूर्बभूव खेदो[७४] हृदये महान् विधेः ।
तदाभिमुख्यं युगपच्चतुष्टयी निजाननानां न यतोऽन्वविन्दत ॥८८ ॥

विलोकेति । यतः(तो) निजाननानां चतुष्टयी युगपत् आ(दा)भिमुख्यं न अ(ना)न्वविन्दत, ततः(तो) महान्खेदोऽभूत् । युगपत्मु(न्मु)खचतुष्टयस्य तदभिमुखीकरणाभावेन अ(ना)ष्टनेत्रैर्भगवतः(तो) युगपत्द(द्द)र्शनं नानुभूतमिति खेदकारणम् ॥८८ ॥

पुरा यदीया सखिवत्ससंहतिर्हृता मयैषां कतमो न्वसाविति ।
विचिन्तवत्येव विधौ तिरोहिता अमी विचिन्वन् ददृशे परं हरिः ॥८९ ॥

पुरेति । यदीया सखिवत्ससंहतिः र्म(म)या हृता, असौ सः (स) एषां सर्वेषां तुल्यानां मध्ये को नु इति विधौ विचिन्तवत्येव अमी तिरोहिताः विचिन्वन् हरिः परं हरिरेव ददृशे दृष्टः ॥८९ ॥

अथ चरणसरोजोपान्तमासाद्य विष्णोरपहृतचरमस्मै वत्सतत्पालवृन्दम् ।
अनमदुपहरंस्तं क्षान्तमन्तूकरिष्यंश्चरणनखमयूखैश्चन्द्रमस्यत्किरीटः ॥९० ॥

अथेति । अपहृतचरं पूर्वमपहृतम् । चन्द्रमस्यत् चन्द्रमसमिवात्मानमाचरत् किरीटं यस्य सः ॥९० ॥

उत्तिष्ठेत्यभिहित ईश्वरेण वेधा उत्तस्थौ विरमि(चि[७५]तदण्डवत्प्रणामः ।
पाणिभ्यां सविनयमञ्जलीकृताभ्यां व्याहार्षीदिति भगवन् क्षमस्व मन्तून् ।९१ ॥

उत्तिष्ठेति । हे भगवन्, मन्तून् अपराधान् क्षमस्वेति व्याहार्षीत् व्याजहार ॥९१ ॥

---

७३. °च्छदैशु° (विसर्ग dropped and jointly written);
७४. खेदा;
७५. P. & B. °मि°;

अस्माकं प्रणमनतः परं विदध्याद्यश्चित्ते[७६] पदमयमस्ति नैव मन्तुः ।
स्वस्थानं व्रजतमितः[७७] परं न कुर्या इत्युक्त्वा व्यसृजदमुं हरिर्विरिञ्चम् ॥९२ ॥

अस्माकमिति । प्रणमनतः परं प्रणामोत्तरम्, अस्माकं चित्ते यः पदं विदध्यात् तादृशः (श) अपराध एव नास्तीत्यर्थः ॥९२ ॥

दिनान्ते[७८] गोविन्दो व्रजमभजदानन्दितजनः
स्ववत्सैस्तत्पालैः सह खमिव पूर्णेन्दुरुडुभिः ।
समान्ते ते बाला अजगरमहन्नद्य तनयो
यशोदाया एवं जगुरजनि हृष्टो व्रजजनः ॥९३ ॥

दिवा(ना)न्ते (न्त) इति । समान्ते वर्षान्ते ते बालाः "अद्य यशोदायाः तनयः अजगरम् अहन् हतवान्" एवं जगुः ॥९३ ॥

यद्धीर्जगज्जातमिवासुरारेस्तनूरखेदाऽभृत शास्त्रजातम् ।
त्रिविक्रमाभिख्यतदात्मजन्मा यः पार्वतीनन्दनतामयासीत् ॥९४ ॥

नीलकण्ठेन तेनास्मिन् यादवेन्द्रमहोदये ।

कृते काव्ये तृतीयोऽपि सर्गः सम्पूर्णतां गतः ॥६ ॥[९९]

इति रानडे इत्युपनामकश्यामरायतनूजविरचितायां यादवेन्द्रमहोदयटिप्पण्यां तृतीयः सर्गः समाप्तः ।।

---

७६. °द्यच्चित्ते;
७७. व्रजमितः (drops त);
७८ दीनान्ते;

चतुर्थः सर्गः

[1]कृष्णः श्रीमान् लोकपालार्चिताङ्घ्रिर्गोत्रारक्षादाक्ष्यमालोच्य पित्रा।
गोत्रागुप्तौ शिष्ट एनं स नावेद्भूमिं प्राप्तं येन गोत्रावनाय ॥१॥

अथ चतुर्थः सर्गः। कृष्ण इति। गोत्रा गोसमूहः तस्याः(स्या) रक्षायां दाक्ष्यं सामर्थ्यमवलोक्य गोत्रागुप्तौ गोसमूहपालने अशिष्ट (शिष्ट) आज्ञातवान्। सः नन्दः येन यस्मात् गोत्रावनाय पृथ्वी (पृथिवी)परिपालनाय भूमिं प्राप्तम् एवं नावैत् न ज्ञातवान्। **तस्मादिति पूर्वेण सम्बन्धः**। 'गोत्रा कुः पृथिवी पृथ्वी' इति **अमरः**। (२.१.३) 'गव्या गोत्रा गवाम्' इति **अमरः**। (२.९.६०) ॥१॥

प्रातः प्रातः पाण्डुभैर्गोसमूहैः सार्धं लोकान् नन्दयन्निर्जगाम।
मित्रोपेतो रौहिणेयानुजन्मा कृष्णीभावं[2] यन् विधुश्चित्रमेतत् ॥२॥

प्रातरिति। गोसमूहैः गवां समुदायैः किरणसमूहैश्च। पाण्डुभिः पाण्डुकान्तिभिः, पाण्डुभिर्नक्षत्रैश्च। मित्राणि सखायः, मित्रः सूर्यश्च। रौहिणेयो बुधः बलभद्रश्च। कृष्णीभावं वासुदेवत्वं नीलत्वं **च**। विधुर्विष्णुश्चन्द्रश्च। **चित्रपक्षे**-मित्रोपेतत्वे सति चन्द्रस्य लोकानन्दजननाभावात्, रौहिणेयो बुधः त(स्त)दनुजन्मत्वाभा[वा]त्च्च (च्च), नीलत्वाभावाच्च **चित्रत्वम्** ॥२॥

आसन्नानामीशितुश्चक्रपाणेर्गोगोपानां[3] गोष्ठनिर्याणकाले।
आसीन्नूनं[4] पादसम्पर्कपुण्यो द्यामारूढो रेणुपुञ्जो महीयान् ॥३॥

आसन्नानामिति। महीयान् रेणुपुञ्जः(ञ्जो) द्यामन्तरिक्षमारूढ आसीत्। द्यां स्वर्गमिति **च** प्रतीयते, तत्र भगवतः सान्निध्यभाजां पादसम्पर्कपुण्यं **हेतुत्वेनोत्प्रेक्षितम्**।।३॥

दण्डाघातं द्वारपैर्वार्यमाणाः[5] स्प्रष्टुं देवा नाशकन् ये शिरोभिः।
ताभ्यां देवः पादपङ्केरुहाभ्यां रक्षन् धेनूः कानने सञ्चचार ॥४॥

दण्डेति। द्वारपैः दण्डाघातं दण्डेन आहत्य इति दण्डाघातम्। अव्ययमिदम्। दण्डाघातेनेत्यर्थः। वार्यमाणाः देवाः ॥४॥

---

१. P. begins with श्रीकृष्णाय नमः। B. begins with श्री गणेशाय नमः।
२. °भावयन् (अनुस्वार dropped & jointly written);
३. आसंन्नां° (अनुस्वार retained + अनुनासिक -Marathi influence;)
४. न्रनं;
५. °माणास्प्र° (विसर्ग dropped & jointly written);

सुस्पर्शोऽवाद्वायुरुष्णांशुरासीन्मन्दोष्णांशुर्वारिदच्छायमिन्द्रः ।
चक्रे भीत्या कानने कृष्णगम्ये नागादग्निः श्वापदात्मा च मृत्युः ॥५ ॥

सुस्पर्शेति । वायुः सुस्पर्शः अवात् ववौ । उष्णांशुः सूर्यः मन्दोष्णांशुः अशि(शी)-तोष्णांशुः आसीत् । इन्द्रः(न्द्रो) भीत्या भयेन कृष्णगम्ये कानने वारिदच्छायं चक्रे । छायाबाहुल्ये नपुंसकमिति । (**पाणिनि** २.४.२२) अग्निः नागात्, श्वापदरूपः(पो) मृत्युश्च नागात्, व्याघ्रादयो हिंस्राः त(स्त)त्र नागमन्नित्यर्थः ॥५ ॥

निष्पाद्यं नः किं फलं वा प्रसूनं काले कस्मिन्नेष वाञ्छेन्महेशः ।
नाभूदाज्ञा चैककालप्रवृत्तौ सर्वर्तूनामित्यभूदाकुलत्वम् ॥६ ॥

निष्पाद्यमिति । नः अस्माभिरित्यर्थः । निष्पादितुं योग्यं फलं प्रसूनं वा कस्मिन् काले कदा वाञ्छेत् । एककालप्रवृत्तौ तु आ(त्वा)ज्ञा नासीत् । तस्मात् किं क्रियतामिति चिन्ताकुलत्वमभूत् ॥६ ॥७ ॥

यद्यद्देशे चारयामास धेनूर्मित्रैः क्रीडन्नेष वृन्दावनस्य ।
आसीत्सा साऽभ्यासशाला प्रभूष्णोर्विष्णोर्[६]मल्ल द्वन्द्वयुद्धादिकानाम् ॥७ ॥

[७]यद्द्रोश्छायामाश्रयल्लोकनाथस्तस्यैवासीत् साधुगोत्रोदितत्वम् ।
जन्मस्थानस्यैकभावेऽपि चासन् वृक्षा अन्ये हा कुजन्मान एव ॥८ ॥

यदिति । लोकनाथः(थो) यद्द्रोः यस्य वृक्षस्य छायामाश्रयत् त(त्त)स्यैव वृक्षस्य साधुगोत्रोदितत्वम् उत्तमकुलोत्पन्नत्वम् । **पक्षे**-गोत्रोदितत्वं पृथ्वीसम्भूतत्वं, साधु सम्यक् । जन्मस्थानस्यैकभावेऽपि जन्मस्थानस्यैकत्वेऽपि, अन्ये वृक्षा [:] कुजन्मान एव कुत्सितजन्मवन्त एव । **पक्षे**-कुः पृथ्वी, तदुत्पन्ना एव अनेन भगवदाश्रितस्यैव जन्मसाफल्यं, तदितरेषां जन्मनैरर्थक्यं च सूचितम् ॥८ ॥

विष्णोः पादाज्जाह्नवीं निस्स[८]रन्तीं दृष्ट्वाऽन्तःस्थां तत्तनोर्भावयन्त्याः ।
कालिन्द्याश्चातादृशो[९](शी) या व्यथाऽभूत् सा निर्वाणं विष्णुपीताम्भसोऽगात् ॥९ ॥

विष्णोरिति । अतादृशः(शो-शी) विष्णुशरीरान्तरस्थितिरहितायाः कालिन्द्याः गङ्गेव मम विष्णुशरीरान्तःस्थितिर्नास्तीत्याकारका या व्यथा आ(थाऽऽ)सीत् सा

६. ष्णो म° (omits the रेफ);
७. यद्रोछाया (द् & विसर्ग (=श्) dropped) ;
८. निसरन्ती (विसर्ग & अनुस्वार dropped);
९. P.& B. °शो

विष्णुकर्तृकस्वजलपानेन निर्वाणम् अ(म)गात्। पानेन स्वस्यापि तदन्तस्थिति-सम्पादनात् सा व्यथाऽऽगतेत्यर्थः ॥९ ॥

भ्रान्त्वा छायामाश्रितं श्रान्तमेनं गोपालांस्तान् पादसंवाहनाद्यैः ।
दृष्ट्वा रामः सेवमानान् स्वसेवां स्मृत्वा लुप्तां विव्यथेऽन्तर्नितान्तम्[१०] ॥१० ॥

भ्रान्त्वेति । रामः तान् सेवकान् दृष्ट्वा ज्येष्ठत्वेन लुप्तां स्वकर्तृकसेवां स्मृत्वा अन्तः अभ्यन्तरे नितान्तं विव्यथे व्यथां प्रापेत्यर्थः ॥१० ॥

सान्द्रच्छायाऽध्यासिता जग्धपीता रोमन्थायोद्गीर्णफेनाश्च गावः ।
अह्नो[११] मध्ये लोचनैर्मीलितार्धै[१२]र्ध्यायन्त्यो वा तस्थुरम्भोजनेत्रम् ॥११ ॥

सान्द्रेति । सान्द्रच्छायायाम् अध्यासिताः(ता) आसन्नाः, जग्धपीताः पूर्वं कृतभक्षणाः पश्चात् कृतपानाः । रोमन्थस्य करणं रोमन्थाया, तया उ(यो)द्गीर्णफेनाः (ना) गावः(वो) मीलितार्धैर्लोचनैः अ(र)म्भोजनेत्रं ध्यायन्त्य इव तस्थुरित्युत्प्रेक्षा ॥११ ॥

वेणुक्वाणानन्दपूर्णान्तरङ्गा गावो लेढुं यत्पदे प्राक्रमन्त ।
विष्णोरम्भोजातजातार्चिते तद्युक्तं यस्मात्सोऽमृतोद्गारिपादः ॥१२ ॥

वेणुरिति । गावः विष्णोः अ(र)म्भोजजाता कमलोद्भवा लक्ष्मीरिति यावत्, तया अर्चिते पादे लेढुं प्राक्रमन्त इति यत् तत् युक्तम् । कुतः सः (स) विष्णुः अमृतं जलं तज्जनकचरणः, विष्णुपादस्य जलोत्पत्तिस्थानत्वात् जलपानार्थमेव लेढुं प्राक्रमन्त । अमृतं मोक्षश्च ॥१२ ॥१३ ॥१४ ॥

श्रीदामाख्यः कृष्णमचे[१३] कदाचिद्गोपः[१४] कृष्णोपान्तदेशेऽस्त्यरण्यम् ।
तालैः पूर्णं दानवानां निवासस्तालीयानां नोऽस्ति वाञ्छा फलानाम् ॥१३ ॥

लोकस्वामी वाचमाकर्ण्य साकं भ्रात्रा चान्यैर्धेनुपालैः सगोत्रैः ।
अभ्यैत्तालान् देवसेनां विकर्षन् स्कन्दोपेतो दैत्यसै[१५]न्यानिवेन्द्रः ॥१४ ॥

अस्मिन् दैत्यैः सेव्यमाने प्रवेशो युष्माकं[१६] नो युज्यते हे कुमाराः ।
एवं शंसत्पर्णशब्दापदेशात् प्रापुर्गोपास्तद्वनं साम्बुजाक्षाः ॥१५ ॥

---

१०. °थन्तर्नि°;
११. अलो;
१२. °तार्धौर्ध्या°;
१३. P. writes मू as मु (Marathi influence on spelling);
१४. गोप्यः;
१५. °सेन्या°;
१६. युष्माकन्नो (म् + न् = न्न – Marathi influence);

अस्मिन्निति । पर्णशब्दापदेशात् पर्णशब्दमिषात् एवं श[ब्द]पूर्वोक्तं शंसत् वनं प्रापुः ॥१५ ॥

तालं कञ्चिद्रौहिणेयोऽध्यरोहन्मित्रप्रीत्यै पातयंस्तत्फलानि ।
आरूढोऽयं नीलमेघानुषक्तं तारानाथं स्मारयामास तत्र ॥१६ ॥

तालमिति । तालस्य नीलमेघसाम्यं, रौहिणेयस्य चन्द्रसाम्यम् ॥१६ ॥

अग्रादग्रे निष्पतत्तालपङ्क्तेस्तालद्रूणामुत्पतन् रौहिणेयः ।
शीर्षाच्छीर्षं[17] निःस्रवद्रक्तधारान्मातङ्गानां यन्निवाभा[18]न्मृगेन्द्रः ॥१७ ॥

अग्रेति । मातङ्गानां गजानां निःस्रवद्रक्तधारात् शीर्षात् शीर्षं यन् गच्छन् मृगेन्द्र इवाभात् ॥१७ ॥

तालीयानां तैः समूहैः फलानां भूमिः पूर्णा रामनिष्पातितानाम् ।
दैतेयानामप्रवेशस्य हेतोरास्तीर्णाङ्गारैव तत्राबभासे ॥१८ ॥

तालीयानामिति । तालफलानां रक्तवर्णत्वात् अङ्गारत्वनोत्प्रेक्षितानि । ।१८ ॥

अस्मद्भीत्या शङ्किनो नो शकुन्ता यस्मिन्नस्मिन् के नु शब्दायमानाः ।
ते स्युर्येषां स्यात्तनूर्दुर्भरे ति ध्यायन्ना[19]गाध्देनुको नाम दैत्यः ॥१९ ॥

अस्मदिति । येषां तनूः दुर्भरा दुःखेन भर्तुं पोषितुं धर्तुं वा अशक्या (शक्या) ते (त) एवात्र शब्दायमाना इति ध्यायन् । भृञ् धारणपोषणयोः ॥१९ ॥

अत्रायास्यन्नेष बुद्ध्या परं नो गात्रेणापि प्राप मायी खरत्वम् ।
रामं प्राप्तस्तालसालावरूढं पादेनाहन् पश्चिमेनाशु दैत्यः ॥२० ॥

अत्रेति । एषः (ष) धेनुकः (को) बुद्ध्या परं बुद्ध्यैव केवलं खरत्वं न प्राप । खरत्वं तीक्ष्णत्वं रासभत्वं च । 'तिग्मं तीक्ष्णं खरम्' इति **अमरः** । (१.३.३५) गात्रेणापि खरत्वं प्राप ॥२० ॥

रामस्याङ्गे कोमले या खुरस्य प्राभून्मुद्रा नीलतापन्नरक्ता ।
दैत्यस्यासौ निष्कलङ्कत्वमूलं चन्द्राद्रामस्योत्तमत्वं लुलोप ॥२१ ॥

रामस्येति । चन्द्रात् प्रसिद्धचन्द्रमसः रामस्य बलरामस्य निष्कलङ्कत्वमूलं

---

१७. °र्षन्नि° (अनुस्वार (म्) - अनुनासिक (न्) - Marathi influence);
१८. °वाभा मृ°;
१९. °यन् प्रागा°

यदुत्तमत्वं तत् **कर्म**, दैत्यस्य पादाघातजन्या मुद्रा लुलोप लोपं प्रापितवती, मुद्रायाः (या) नैल्यात् ॥२१ ॥

क्रुद्धस्तेनात्यन्तमेषोऽभवद्यो देवानीकैर्वन्द्यमानाङ्घ्रिपीठः ।
श्रेष्ठश्चैषां मन्युवश्योरगाणां पादाघातं मृष्यतां केन सोऽयम् ॥२२ ॥

क्रुद्ध इति । देवसमूहैर्वन्द्यमानचरणः(णो) मन्युवश्याः(श्या) ये(य) उरगास्तेषां मध्ये श्रेष्ठश्च-बलदेवस्य शेषांशत्वात् । केन हेतुना पादाघातं मृष्यताम् । न केनापि हेतुनेत्यर्थः ॥२२ ॥

आदायाङ्घ्री भ्रामितत्यक्तमेतद्गात्रं निष्क्रान्तासु सम्प्राप्य तालान् ।
अस्मत्स्वामी लोकमन्यं सहायैरेभिः साकं यात्वितीव व्यभाङ्क्षीत् ॥२३ ॥

आदायेति । अङ्घ्री चरणौ आ(णावा)दाय भ्रामितत्यक्तं भ्रामितं सत् त्यक्तं तद्गात्रं तालान् व्यभाङ्क्षीत् ॥२३ ॥

दृष्ट्वोत्क्रान्तप्राणमात्माधिनाथं दैत्या अन्ये ये शिवात्मत्वभाजः ।
रामं[२०] कृष्णं हन्तुमायन्नमूभ्यां[२१] ते जीयन्ते मृत्युना स्मेति चित्रम् ॥२४ ॥

दृष्ट्वेति । शिवात्मत्वभाजः क्रोष्टीस्वरूपभाजः, हन्तुमायन् आ(न्ना)गताः । अमूभ्यां रामकृष्णाभ्यां मृत्युना ते जीयन्ते स्म, रामकृष्णाभ्यां मृत्युं प्रापिता इत्यर्थः । **चित्रपक्षे**-शिवस्वरूपाः(पा) मृत्युना जिता **इत्याश्चर्यं,** शिवस्य मृत्युञ्जयत्वात् ॥२४ ॥

तृण्यां[२२] स्फीतां तत्र सत्त्वाप्रवेशाज्जक्षुर्[२३]गावो रामवीर्यार्जितानि ।
तालान्यादन् रौहिणेयाच्युताभ्यां साकं गोपा रामवीर्यं स्तुवन्तः ॥२५ ॥

तृण्यामिति । स्फीतां वृद्धां तृण्यां जक्षुः भ(र्भ)क्षितवत्यः । गोपाः(पा) रामवीर्यार्जितानि तालानि तालफलानि अ(आ)(न्या) दन् भक्षितवन्तः ॥[२४]

प्राप्तोदन्यं गोपगोवृन्दमागात्कालिन्दीयं तं ह्रदं[२५] कालियाहिः ।
तार्क्ष्याद्भीतो लीनवान् यत्र वार्धौ मैनाको वा रत्नवच्छीर्ष इन्द्रात् ॥२६ ॥

---

२०. सामं;
२१. °न्नभूम्यां (Metathesis);
२२. °ण्या (drops the अनुस्वार);
२३. °शाच्चक्षु°;
२४. Lower marginal note not clear in the xerox-copy
२५. P. writes as -हदं (Marathi influence) B. लदं;

प्राप्तेति। प्राप्तोदन्यं प्राप्ततृष्णम्। 'उदन्या [तु] पिपासा तृट्' इति **अमरः**। (२.९.५५) मैनाकोऽपि रत्नवच्छीर्षः रत्नवन्ति शीर्षाणि शिखराग्राणि यस्य। **पक्षे**-रत्नवत् रत्नयुक्तं शीर्षं मस्तकं यस्य, फणामणित्वात् ॥२६॥

तेनोद्गीर्णक्ष्वेलयोगान्नु येन प्राप्ता नीलत्वेन साकं विषाख्या।
प्लुष्टोपान्तद्रोर्जलं तद्हृदस्य प्राश्य प्राप्नोदद्[२३]दो हा मृतत्वम् ॥२७॥

तेनेति। येन जलेन तेन काली(लि)येन उद्गीर्णविषयोगान्नु विषयोगादिव नीलत्वेन साकं विषाख्या प्राप्ता। तज्जलं प्राश्य अदः(दो) गोपगोवृन्दं मृतत्वं प्राप। मृतमित्यर्थः। हा इति खेदे ॥२७॥

तानुज्जीव्याम्भोजनेत्रः सगोत्रान् गोपान्[२७] दण्डं प्रापयन् कालियाहिम्।
आरुह्यैकं[२८] वृक्षमास्फोट्य बाहुं तस्मादम्भस्युत्पपात ह्रदस्य ॥२८॥

तानिति। सगोत्रान् गोसमूहसहितान्। तस्मात्(द) वृक्षात् ह्रदस्याम्भसि उत्पपात ॥२८॥२९॥

मीनो भूत्वा यां पयोधावकार्षीत् क्रीडां तामत्रातनोदादिदेवः।
वेलातीतैर्वारिभिस्तैर्ह्रदो[२९]ऽयं पुस्फोरेव[३०] श्रीपतिप्राप्तिहर्षात् ॥२९॥

तल्पीकृत्योद्वेजयन्नस्मदीशं तद्विश्रान्त्यै नाभ्यनुज्ञो[३१]मदाद्यः।
ईशप्रीत्यै तं हनानीति नूनं क्रुद्धः कृष्णं कालियाहिर्ददंश ॥३०॥

तल्पीति। अस्मदीशं शेषाहिम्। ईशप्रीत्यै स्वामिप्रीत्यै। तं कृष्णं हनानि मारयामि इ(मी)ति हेतुना ददंशेत्युत्प्रेक्षा ॥३०॥

दष्ट्वा[३२] भोगेनास्य देहं विवेष्टे नागः कृष्णेऽप्येवमागश्चकार।
यस्तेनैव न्यस्तनागस्वभावः सोऽनागः स्यात्किं प्रति[३३]भ्रान्तिशून्यम् ॥३१॥

दष्ट्वेति। नागः कालियाहिः दष्ट्वा दंशं कृत्वा, कृष्णमिति शेषः। अस्य कृष्णस्य

२६. प्रामोद°;
२७. गोपां (न् written as म् (अनुस्वार) (Marathi influence);
२८. आरुह्येकं;
२९. °ह° (drops the रेफ);
३० पुंस्फो°
३१. °नुद्या°;
३२. दृष्ट्वा;
३३. छाति°;

देहं भोगेन स्वशरीरेण विवेष्टे वेष्टितवान्। कृष्णेऽपि ए(प्ये)वमागश्चकार। यः ते(स्ते)नैव कृष्णेनैव न्यस्तः(स्तो) नागस्वभावो यस्मिन् ए(न्ने)तादृशः सः (स) भ्रान्तिशून्यं प्रति अनागः सर्पभिन्नः स्यात् किम्। अनागः स्यात्किम् अनपराधी स्यात्किमिति **च** प्रतीयते ॥३१ ॥

सर्वज्ञोऽयं भोगिनः शीघ्रमन्योर्मन्दप्रज्ञस्यापराधावसाने।
सम्प्राप्तान्ते वादिनः पूर्वपक्षे सिद्धान्तीव प्रायतिष्टारिभङ्गे[३४] ॥३२ ॥

सर्वज्ञ इति। सर्वज्ञः अयं भोगिनः अ(नोऽ)पराधावसाने अ(नेऽ)रिभङ्गे प्रायतिष्ट। वादिनः पूर्वपक्षे सम्प्राप्तान्ते सति समाप्ते सति सिद्धान्तीव। विशेषणानि तु **सर्पपक्षे वादिपक्षे च** योज्यानि ॥३२ ॥

अङ्गस्फात्या सोऽथ निर्वेष्टनः[३५] सन् फूत्कुर्वाणस्यास्य कोपाद्दिदंक्षोः।
आरूढोऽभूदुच्छ्रितानेकमूर्ध्नो[३६] मूर्ध्न्येकस्मिन् क्ष्माधरस्येव मेघः ॥३३ ॥

अङ्गेति। सः (स) हरिः अ(र)ङ्गस्फात्या अङ्गवृद्ध्या निर्वेष्टनः सन्। कोपात् फूत्कुर्वाणस्य दिदंक्षोः द(दं)ष्टुमिच्छोः, उच्छ्रितानेकमूर्ध्नः तस्य सर्पस्य एकस्मिन् मूर्धनि क्ष्माधरस्य मूर्धनि मेघ इव आरुरोह। उच्छ्रितेति विशेषणं **पर्वतपक्षेऽपि** योजनीयम्। 'स्फातिर्वृद्धौ' इति **अमरः**। [३.२.९] ॥३३ ॥

मूर्ध्नो मूर्धन्युत्पपातास्य कृष्णः पर्यायेणैवाश्वसन्निग्रहीता।
दृष्टो नैकोऽप्यङ्घ्रिशून्यो हि मूर्धा विष्णोः सोऽस्मात्कीर्त्यते भूरिपादः ॥३४ ॥

मूर्ध्न इति। असन्निग्रहीता कृष्णः आशु पर्यायेणैव मूर्ध्नः(र्ध्नो) मूर्धनि उत्पपात उत्पतनमकरोत् ॥३४ ॥

दष्टुं[३७] कोपादुच्छ्रितैः पादघाताद् भीत्या पश्चान्नामितैर्दीप्तरत्नैः।
नागेनायं मस्तकैरङ्घ्रिमुक्तैः कृष्णः[३८] प्रीत्येवास्त नीराज्यमानः ॥३५ ॥

दष्टुमिति। कोपात् दष्टुमुच्छ्रितैः पादाघातात् भीत्या नामितैः अङ्घ्रिमुक्तैः दीप्तरत्नैर्मस्तकैर्नागेन प्रीत्या नीराज्यमान इव आस्त। नीराजनायामपि दीपानाम् ऊ(मू)र्ध्वाधोनयनं प्रसिद्धम् ॥३५ ॥

---

३४. P. भगे;
३५. °ष्टन सन् (विसर्ग dropped & jointly written-Marathi influence);
३६. मूध्नो & मूध्न्ये° (omits the रेफ);
३७. दंष्टं;

पादाघातैः पीड्यमानः स नागो वान्तैक्ष्वेलैः शोणितैश्चातिमात्रम्।
विष्णोः पादासङ्गपुण्यैरिवाभून्मुञ्चन् भावांस्तामसान् राजसांश्च ॥३६॥

पाद इति। क्ष्वेलैः विषैः, विषाणां नैल्यात् तामसभावत्वं, शोणितानां रक्तवर्णत्वात् राजसभावत्वं **चोत्प्रेक्षितम्** ॥३६॥

पश्चान्मोहं[३८] चाप्यवापेत्ययुक्तं वक्तुं यस्मान्मोहमाप्यैव स घ्नन्।
अभ्यैत्कृष्णं पन्नगारातिसेव्यं मृत्योर्मृत्युं विष्यतां तस्य जानन् ॥३७॥

पश्चादिति। पश्चातꣳ क्ष्वेलस्य वमनोत्तरं मोहं मूर्च्छां मोहं मतिभ्रमं प्रोयेति वक्तुमयुङ्क्त। यस्मातꣳ सः(स) मोहेमाप्यैव मोहं प्राप्यैव ध्ननꣳ हन्तुमिच्छनꣳ पन्नगारातिसेव्यं मृत्योर्मृत्युं कृष्णं तस्य कृणस्य विष्यतां विषेण वध्यतां जानन् सन् अभ्यैत्। विष्णो(ष्यो) विषेण यो वध्यः' इति **अमरः**।(३.१.४५) तादृशविशेषयुक्तस्य कृष्णस्य हन्तुमिच्छया यत्सम्मुखगमनं तदेव मोहकारणम्। तस्मात्पूर्वमेव मोह प्राप्तः(प्तो) न तु विषवमनोत्तरमिति ॥ ३७ ॥

तत्प्रेयस्यो भर्तुरेतामवस्थां बुद्ध्वा विष्णोः सम्प्रसादेऽयतन्त।
अप्येतस्मान्माधवं प्राप्ततापो वाञ्छावर्षं को नु नाराधयेन्तम् ॥ ३८ ॥

तत्प्रेयस्य इति। एतस्मान्माधवता् प्राप्ततोपोऽपि, वाञ्छां वर्षतीति वाञ्छावर्षः तं कामप्रदं माधवं विष्णुम्। **पक्षे**-वाञ्छ(ञ्छय) त इति वाञ्छा, वाञ्छावर्षं यस्मिन् तं माधवं वैशाखं कः ना अराधयेत् वैशाखभिन्नं ब्रूयात् नु। वैशाखे माधवो राधः इति **अमरः** (१.४.१६) ॥ ३८ ॥

उद्यान्तीनामम्भसस्तद्वधूनां पूर्वोद्यातैः कान्तरत्नैफैगाग्रैः[३९]।
एति त्रातुं नागराज स्वगृहयं पातालदित्यभ्रमन् वीक्षितारः ॥ ३९ ॥

उद्यान्तीनामिति। पूर्वोद्यातैः पूर्वमुपर्यागतैः कान्तरत्नैः फणाग्रैः। वीक्षितारः अभ्रमन् ॥ ३९ ॥

आगत्यैता योषितो दैन्यभाजः पादन्यस्तैर्मस्तकैर्लोकनाथम्।
शान्तक्रोधं प्रार्थयन्ते स्म तस्माद्दुर्विज्ञाना यन्महच्चित्तवृत्तिः ॥४०॥

आगत्येति। यत् यस्मात् महतां चित्तवृत्तिर्दुर्विज्ञाना ज्ञातुमशक्या, अतः शान्तक्रोधमपि प्रार्थयन्ते स्म ॥४०॥

---

३८. कृष्णप्री° (विसर्ग dropped & jointly written-Marathi influence);
३९. फणाग्नैः;

स्वामिन् दण्डं प्रापितोऽस्माकमीशः कस्मान्मन्तोश्चेदमन्तुस्तवाघम्[४०] ।
इत्याचष्टे शास्त्रमंहोऽप्यकार्यं यस्तूच्छास्त्रः स त्वया दण्डनीयः ॥४१ ॥

स्वामिन्निति । हे स्वामिन्, अस्माकमीशस्त्वया कस्मात् दण्डं प्रापितः । मन्तोः अपराधात् हेतोः दण्डं प्रापितश्चेत् तव अमन्तुः त्वज्ञानरहितस्य अघं पापम् इति शास्त्रम् आचष्टे कथयति । तव अमन्तुः अपराधाभाव एव अघमिति च प्रतीयते । शास्त्रम् अंहः पापम् अकार्यमित्यपि आचष्टे । तथा च प्रकृते अमन्तोरघत्वात् मन्तोरेव कर्तव्यतया न तस्य दण्डहेतुरिति भावः ॥४१ ॥

स्वाच्छन्द्यं चेद्दर्शयिष्यन्नकार्षीर्दण्डं जाता तावकीनेष्टसिद्धिः ।
अप्येतावत्कर्मणा जीवयैनं निर्यत्प्राणं भोः कृपादृष्टिपातैः ॥४२ ॥

स्वाच्छन्द्यमिति । स्वाच्छन्द्यं दर्शयिष्यन् सन् दण्डमकार्षीश्चेत् तावकीना दण्डप्रापणरूपा या इष्टसिद्धिः सा एतावत्कर्मणापि जाता । अधुना ए(नै)नं कृपादृष्टिपातैर्जीवय ॥४२ ॥

यस्मात्सेव्यो देव नागान्तकेन ध्वस्ते तस्मिन् यासि नागान्तकत्वम् ।
तस्मादेतज्जीवनं प्रार्थनीयं नन्वस्माकं यद्वदेवं तवापि ॥४३ ॥

यस्मादिति । हे देव यस्मात्कारणात् त्वं नागान्तकेन गरुडेन सेव्यः । अस्मिन्नागे त्वया ध्वस्ते सति नाशिते सति नागान्तकत्वं गरुडत्वं, **पक्षे**-सर्पनाशकत्वं यासि । सेव्यः सन् सेवकत्वं यासीत्यर्थः । तस्मात् हेतोः अ(र)स्माकं यद्वत् यथा एतज्जीवनं प्रार्थनीयं वर्तते तद्वत् तथा तवापि वर्तत इति ॥४३ ॥

इत्येताभिः प्रार्थ्यमानो मुरारिर्नागं चक्रे मुक्तपादप्रहारम् ।
मोहातीतः शान्तगर्वः स नागः प्राणंसीत्तं योगिसंस्मा(स्म) र्यपादम् ॥४४ ॥

इतीति । स नागः तं(स्तं) प्राणंसीत् प्रणाममकरोत् ॥४४ ॥

पर्यायेण श्रीनिवासाङ्घ्रिपद्मे अध्यारूढा तच्छिरःपङ्क्ति[४१]पङ्क्तिः ।
स्वाध्यारूढारोहणाख्यां तदानीमातन्वानेवाद्युतद्वैरशुद्धिम् ॥४५ ॥

पर्यायेणेति । श्रीनिवासपादपद्मे पर्यायेण अध्यारूढा तच्छिरसां याः पङ्क्तयः दशकानि तासां पङ्क्तिर्द(द)शकं, शतं शिरांसीति यावत् । स्वस्मिन् अ(न्र)ध्यारूढं यत् पादपद्मं तस्मिन् आ(न्रा)रोहणाख्याम् आरोहणाभिधां वैरशुद्धिम् आतन्वानेव अद्युतत् शुशुभे ॥४५ ॥

---

४०. °वाद्यम्; B scribe could not understand/make out the द्य corrected to घ in the margin in P.

४१. पङ्क्तिपङ्क्तिः;

क्षन्तव्यस्ते देव मन्तुर्ममैवं कर्तव्या नो प्रार्थना क्षान्तमन्तौ ।
त्वय्यस्माकं गेहमेत्यास्मदर्चां लब्ध्वा कार्यं जन्मनः सार्थकं ते ॥४६ ॥

क्षन्तव्येति । हे देव, त्वयि क्षान्तमन्तौ सति मम एवं मन्तुः अपराधः ते त्वया क्षन्तव्य इति प्रार्थना नो कर्तव्या, कर्तुमयोग्या, मयेति शेषः । ते त्वया अस्माकं गेहमागत्य पूजां च लब्ध्वा जन्मनः सार्थकं कार्यम् । मद्‌गृहागमनेन पूजाप्राप्त्या च मज्जन्मनः साफल्यं भविष्यतीति भावः ॥४६ ॥

एवं तेन प्रार्थितस्तन्निकाय्यं गत्वाऽऽसाद्याप्येतदर्चामवोचत् ।
न स्थेयं ते प्राणिसेव्योदकेऽस्मिन् पूर्वं स्थानं याहि दाराद्युपेतः ॥४७ ॥

एवमिति । तन्निकाय्यं गृहं गत्वा पूजां लब्ध्वापि अस्मिन् ह्रदे त्वया न स्थेयमित्याद्यवोचत् । 'निकाय्यनिलयालयाः' इति **अमरः** ।(२.२.५) ॥४७ ॥

शापात्ताक्ष्र्यो नैव[४२] तत्रापि [४३]भोगिन्नस्मत्पादाघातचिह्ना[४४]वलोकात् ।

बाधेत त्वां नेत्युदीर्य ह्रदात्तं प्रस्थाप्या[४५]स्मान्निर्ययौ दानवारिः ॥४८ ॥

शापादिति । गरुडः त(स्त)त्रापि मत्पादचिह्नावलोकनात् त्वां न बाधेत इत्युक्त्वा तं तस्मात् ज(ज्ज)लाशयात् प्रस्थाप्य अस्मात् ह्रदात् दा(द्दा)नवारिः कृष्णः(ष्णो) निर्ययौ ॥४८ ॥

नागाधीशप्रत्तसद्रत्नभूयोभूषातेजोमण्डलान्तर्विभान्तम् ।
उद्यातं तं वीक्ष्य गोपा अनन्दन्नुद्यच्चन्द्रारक्तबिम्बाङ्कतुल्यम् ॥४९ ॥

नागादि(धी)शेति । नागाधीशः कालियाहिः, तेन प्रत्तानां दत्तानां सद्रत्नानां भूयसीनां भूषाणां तेजोमण्डलान्तः विभान्तं चन्द्रस्य अ(स्या)ङ्केन कलङ्केन तुल्यम् ॥४९ ॥

उद्युञ्जानस्तद्ह्रदाम्भः सुपेयं कर्तुं कृष्णो निर्विषं तं विधाय ।
लोकैरासीत्[४६] स्तूयमानः प्रभूणां सर्वं कर्म स्तूयते तद्भयेन ॥५० ॥

उदिति । कृष्णः तद्ह्रदाम्भः सुपेयं कर्तुमुद्युञ्जानः सन् उद्युक्तः सन् तं ह्रदं निर्विषं निर्जलं, **पक्षे** विषरहितं विधाय । निर्जलं कृत्वाऽपि लोकै[:] स्तूयमानः (न) आसीत् ।

---

४२. त्रेव;
४३. भोगीन्न°;
४४. °चिलाव°;
४५. P. °प्यां°;
४६. Omits त्;

तस्मात्प्रभूणां सर्वं कर्म तद्भयेन प्रभोर्भीत्या स्तूयते। 'सर्वं कर्म' इत्यनेन अनुचितमपि कर्मेति व्यज्यते। 'निर्जलीकरणेनापि लोके [:] स्तुतः इति **चमत्कारः**। **पक्षे**-स्पष्टम् ॥५१(५०)॥

ताभ्यां साकं सायमागत्य गोष्ठं गोपा वर्णै रामकृष्णानुषक्तैः।
श्रद्धालेपान्निर्मलाश्चित्तभित्तीर्गोष्ठस्थानां प्राप्तचित्रा वितेनुः ॥५१॥

ताभ्यामिति। रामकृष्णसम्बद्धैः वर्णैः स्तुतिभिः। **पक्षे**-श्वेतनीलसम्बद्धैर्वर्णैः हरितादिवर्णैश्च। 'बले रामो नीलचारुसिते त्रिषु।' इति **अमरः**। (३.३.१४०) 'वर्णो द्विजादौ शुक्लादौ स्तुतौ वर्णं तु वाक्षरे।' इति **अमरः**। (३.३.४८) गोष्ट(ष्ठ)स्थानां चित्तभितीः (त्तीः) प्राप्तचित्राः प्राप्तालेख्याः प्राप्ताश्चर्याश्च वितेनुः ॥५२(५१)॥

क्रीडत्येवं वासुदेवे धरित्रीं[४७] भूयस्तापो ग्रीष्मनामर्तुरागात्।
तापापन्नैः सेव्यमानं मुरारिं तापोत्सादायेव सेविष्यमाणः ॥५२॥

क्रीडेति। भूयान् तापो यस्मिन् सः(स) ग्रीष्मनामऋतुरागात्। भूयान् तापो यस्येति च प्रतीयते। तापापन्नैः त्रिविधतापसन्तप्तैः। **पक्षे**-तापः(पो) दाहः तद्युक्तैः। तापोत्सादाय तापदूरीकरणाय सेविष्यमाण इव आगादिति **उत्प्रेक्षा** ॥५२॥

जातोऽत्यन्तं मे तपस्यानुषङ्गो नाहं श्यामां कामभोगं ददानाम्[४८]।
तत्सामीप्यप्राप्तरागोऽप्यविन्दं तापं भेजे भानुरेवं महान्तम् ॥५३॥

जात इति। मे मम तपस्या तपश्चर्या, तस्याः अनुषङ्गः। **पक्षे**-तपस्य ग्रीष्मस्यानुषङ्गः, अत्यन्तं जातस्तथापि कामभोगं मदनविलासम्। **पक्षे**-यथेच्छभोगं ददानां श्यामां रात्रिं षोडशवार्षिकीं स्त्रियं **च**। तस्याः रात्र्याः स्त्रियश्च सामीप्येन। **पक्षे**-सामीप्येन प्राप्तः रागो रक्तिमा अनुरागश्च। यस्य तादृशोऽपि नाविन्दं न प्राप्तवान् इति हेतोः म(र्म)हान्तं तापं दाहकत्वं सन्तापं **च** भेजे ॥५३॥

भासा [४९]दृश्यव्रातमुद्योतयन्तं वेदात्मानं हंसमप्राप्तदृष्टिः।
लोकः पूर्वं सद्विजाधीशपादस्पर्शात्तापं प्राप पश्चान्मुदं च ॥५४॥

भासेति। भासा कान्त्या स्वचैतन्यभासा **च**। दृश्यव्रातं पदार्थसमूहम् **उभयत्रापि समानम्**। उद्योतयन्तं प्रकाशयन्तं **समानमेव**। वेदात्मानं वेदस्वरूपं ज्ञानस्वरूपं **च**। हंसं सूर्यं परमात्मानं **च**। अप्राप्तदृष्टिः अप्राप्ता दृष्टिः नेत्रं यस्य। **पक्षे**-अप्राप्ता दृष्टिः बुद्धिः यस्य, एतादृशो लोकः। सद्वि(द्वि)जाधीशपादस्पर्शात् चन्द्रकिरणस्पर्शात्, पूर्वं प्राक् तापं प्राप, चन्द्रकिरणस्पर्शोत्तरं मुदं प्राप। **पक्षे**-सतां द्विजानां च योऽधीशः, तस्य पादस्पर्शात् पूर्वं प्राक् तापं पश्चात् मुदं चित्सुखजन्यहर्षम् ॥५४॥

---

४७. °र°

४८. ददानम्;

४९. दिश्य°;

सर्वत्रेनाद्युक्तदण्डान्महोग्रात्तापोद्रेकं प्राप्य संत्यक्तगेहाः ।
लोकास्त्यक्त्वान्धांसि पीत्वा विषाणि प्राप्ताः[५०] संस्थां वृक्षमूलेष्वभूवन् ॥५५ ॥

सर्वत्रेति । सर्वत्र सर्वप्रदेशे, **पक्षे**-साधुष्वसाधुषु **च**। युक्तदण्डात् प(पा)रिपार्श्वकयुक्तात् । 'माठरः पिङ्गलो दण्डश्चडांशोः पारिपार्श्व(र्श्वि)कः ।' इति **अमरः** । (२.३.३१) **पक्षे**-कृतदण्डात् इनात् सूर्यात्, **पक्षे**-प्रभोः । 'इनःसूर्ये प्रभावपि (प्रभौ राजा) ।' इति **अमरः** । (३.३.१११) तापोद्रेकं सन्तापाधिक्यं, **पक्षे**-त्रासाधिक्यम् । विषाणि जलानि हालाहलानि **च**। संस्थां स्थितिं मरणं **च** ॥५५ ॥

ग्रीष्मे लोकैः कारणं तस्य जज्ञे यत्कीनाशो जीवनान्तं करोति ।
[५१]यद्दृष्टोऽर्को जीवनान्तं वितन्वन् पुत्रैर्धर्मो[५२] धार्यमाणः पितुश्च ॥५६ ॥

ग्रीष्म इति । कीनाशो यमः । जीवनान्तं प्राणान्तम् उदकनाशमिति **च** प्रतीयते । जीवनान्तम् उदकान्तम् ॥५६ ॥

क्लृप्ताहारानन्तरिक्ष[५३]च्युतेन क्षीरेणैव प्रीणयित्वा द्विजान् द्राक् ।
अग्रे कीर्तिं भूतले भावयामी[५४]त्यादत्तेनस्तत्र[५४] गोक्षीरजातम् ॥५७ ॥

क्लृप्तेति । आ(अ)न्तरिक्षच्युतेन आकाशाद्गलितेन, **पक्षे**-अयाचितेनेत्यर्थः । क्षीरेण जलेन दुग्धेन **च**। क्लृप्ताहारान् द्विजान् पक्षिणः, चातकानिति यावत् । **पक्षे**-ब्राह्मणान् । द्राक् प्रीणयित्वा कीर्तिं पङ्कं यशश्च भावयानि इति हेतोः, इनः ।

सूर्यः तत्र ग्रीष्मौ गौक्षीरजातं महीतलवर्ति जलसमूहम् । पक्षे गवां क्षीरं दुग्धं, तस्य जातं समूहम्, आदत्तेत्युत्प्रेक्षा ॥ ५७ ॥

संज्ञां प्राप्ता इत्यदः क्षान्तमागश्छायां कान्तां कामयन्तेऽध मन्दाः ।
इत्यासाद्येवातिकोपं विवस्वान् चक्रे लोकान् जीवनक्लेशभाजः ॥ ५८ ॥

संज्ञे(ज्ञामि)मि । संज्ञाम् अभिधां, पक्षे-स्वस्य तन्नमिकां भार्यां प्राप्ताः इति । अदः एतत् अ(आ)गः अपराधः क्षान्तं सोढम् । छायाम् अनातपम्, एतन्नामिकां भार्यां चू ।

---

५०. प्राताः;
५१. P. marginal correction- त changed to य;
५२. °र्धमो (रेफ dropped);
५३. रीय·५४· P. marginal correction– नी changed to ceer, but, the commentator (P1) takes it as efve only thourgh the context is evidently in favour of मी as नाr misses the mark.
५४. र
५५. वपु;

छाया सूर्याप्रिया कान्तिःप्रितिबिम्बमनातपः ।' इति **अमरः** । (३.३.१५७) जीवनमुदकं जीवितं च ॥ ५८ ॥

नुन्नग्रावाधीतदेहाभिद्यातासतत्स्त्रीर्नेयान् द्रागिवाध्वन्यलेखान् ।
उद्बिभ्राणः शुष्कपाण्डुच्छदौघं निर्मर्यादास्ते ववक्षुण्डवाताः[५५] ॥ ५९ ॥

नन्नेति । नुन्नाः(न्ना) ये ग्रावाणाः पाषाणाः, नैरधीतः(तो) देहाभिघातो येभयस्ते । पाषाणपातवत्कठिणस्पर्शा इत्यर्थः । तत्स्त्रीः अध्वन्यस्त्री प्रति नेयान् अध्वन्यानां लेखानिव शुष्कपाण्डुपत्रौघम् उदाव्भ्राणाः(णा) वाताः ववुः ॥ ५९ ॥

द्रागापूर्णा रेचिता द्राक् च कुम्भा वार्याहारै[५६]श्चाध्वनीनैः प्रपासु ।
द्राक् पूर्णानि द्राक् च रिक्तानि राज्ञः कोशागाराणीव दातुर्विरेजुः ॥६० ॥

द्रागिति । वार्याहारैः वारि जलम् आहरन्ति आनयन्ती(न्ति) ते वार्याहारास्तैः ज(र्ज)लवाहकैः । आपूर्णाः भरिताः, अध्वनीनैः(नै) रेचिताः कुम्भाः कोशागाराणीव रेजुः ॥६० ॥

नित्यानन्तापन्नगूढामृतानां सस्थैर्याणामक्षमात्यागभाजाम् ।
प्राप्तोद्रेका नैव तापा असह्या जाता अन्यैः प्राणिभिर्दुःसहाये ॥६१ ॥

नित्येति । नित्यम् अनन्तायाः पृथ्व्याः आपन्नं प्राप्तं गूढं छन्नम् अमृतं जलं यैः, तेषाम् । **पक्षे**-अनन्तात् भगवतः प्राप्तम् अमृतं मोक्षः यैः । सस्थैर्याणां निश्चलानां **समानमेव** । अक्षमात्यागभाजाम् अत्यक्तावनितलानां, **पक्षे**-क्षमायुक्तानामित्यर्थः । एतादृशां वृक्षाणां जनानां **च** । प्राप्तोद्रेकाः अन्यैः प्राणिभिः दु(र्दु)ःसहाश्च ये तापाः ते असह्या न जाताः । **पक्षे**-तापाः त्रिविधतापाः ॥६१ ॥

लुम्पन्तीभिर्निष्क्रमाणां पिपासामभ्यायातो[५७] द्राङ्मृगीवाहिनीभिः ।
वृद्धिं प्राप्तो दीप्तवैरोचनोस्त्रैर्वेलामत्यैद् दृश्यमात्राम्बुरब्धिः ॥६२ ॥

लुम्पन्तीभिरिति । निष्क्रमाणां पिपासां लुम्पन्तीभिः लोपं प्रापयन्तीभिः । **मृगीपक्षे**-पिपासां लुम्पन्तीभिः सतीभिः स्वपिपासां लोप्तुमिच्छावतीभिः, मृग्य एव वाहिन्यः, ताभिः अभ्यायातः अभिमुखं प्राप्तः । दीप्ताः ये, विरोचनः सूर्यः, तस्य इमे वैरोचनाः, उस्राः किरणाः, तैः । **पक्षे**-दीप्ताः ये, विरोचनश्चन्द्रः, तस्य इमा (मे) वैरोचनाः किरणाः, तैः । वृद्धिं प्राप्तः **उभयत्र समानम्** । दृश्यमात्राम्बुः दर्शनमात्रफलः, पानानुपयुक्तजलत्वात् । **पक्षे**-मृगतृष्णिकारूपः अब्धिः समुद्रः वेलामत्यैत्, वेलामतिक्रान्तवान् ॥६२ ॥६३ ॥

मल्लीगन्धाघ्राणनिर्वाणभाजां सर्पौघाणां विस्मृताहारभावात् ।
पीनाङ्गत्वं किं न्वभून्मारुतानां सर्पाहारत्वेन ये दैवक्लृप्ताः ॥६३ ॥

---

५५. वपुः
५६. °होरैः

काष्ठानीकं हेतिभिश्चित्रभानोः प्लुष्टं दृष्ट्वाऽऽकाशमध्यस्थितस्य ।
स्मृत्वा दाहव्यापृतिं स क्षमास्थो[५८] भस्मीचक्रे सर्वतः काननानि ॥६४ ॥

काष्ठेति । काष्ठानीकं दिग्स(क्स)मूहः इन्धनसमुदायश्च । आकाशमध्यस्थितस्य चित्रभानोः सूर्यस्य अग्नेश्च हेतिभिः किरणैः ज्वा(र्ज्वा)लाभिश्च प्लुष्टं सम्बद्धं दग्धं **च** । दृष्ट्वा सः (स) क्षमास्थः पृथ्वीतलवर्ती चित्रभानुः वह्निः स्वस्य दाहव्यापारं स्मृत्वा सर्वतः काननानि भस्मीचक्रे ॥६४ ॥

ग्रीष्मेऽह्नां चेद्दैर्घ्यमल्पा निशा स्यादध्वन्यानां रात्रिदैर्घ्यं सुदृग्भिः ।
जज्ञे नास्माद्रात्रिरल्पा स दुःखं कालं दीर्घं वेत्ति लोकस्ततः सः ॥६५ ॥

ग्रीष्मे (ष्म इ)ति । अध्वन्यानां सुदृग्भिः रात्रिदैर्घ्यं जज्ञे, तस्मात् रात्रिरल्पेति वक्तुं न युक्तम् । सुदृग्भिरिति साभिप्रायं, पण्डितैरिति । ननु ग्रीष्मे प्रतीयमानं दिनानां दैर्घ्यम् असत्यमिति वक्तुं न युज्यते । तत्र का गतिरिति चेत् तत्राह-लोकः सः (स) दुःखं कालं दीर्घं वेत्ति । अत्र तापप्रयुक्तदुःखम् । ततः हेतोः स ग्रीष्मे अ(ष्मेऽ)ह्नां दैर्घ्यव्यवहारः (रो) लोकानां दुःखनिमित्त एव न वास्तव इत्यर्थः ॥६५ ॥

ग्रीष्मे लोकैः पाटलामोदसाक्षात्कारं प्राप्तैर्ये गुणानां गुणित्वम् ।
प्रत्याचख्युर्द्रव्यमात्राश्रितत्वान्न्यायज्ञास्तद्वागसत्येति मेने ॥६६ ॥

ग्रीष्मे (ष्म) इति । ग्रीष्मे पाटलामोदसाक्षात्कारं-पाटलानां य आमोदः, तस्य पाटलाकुसुमगन्धसाक्षात्कारम् । **पक्षे**- पाटलश्चासावामोदश्चेति । पाटलरूपविशिष्टः (ष्टो) य आमोदः, तस्य साक्षात्कारं, प्राप्तैः लो(र्लो)कैः, गुणानां द्रव्यमात्राश्रितत्वात्, गुणानां गुणित्वं ये न्यायज्ञाः प्रत्याचख्युः निराचक्रुः, तेषां मते गुणे गुणानङ्गीकारात् । तेषां वाक् असत्येति मेने ज्ञाता । अत्र पाटलरूपविशिष्टामोददर्शनात् गुणे गुणाङ्गीकारत्वमेवेति **चमत्कारः** । ।६६ ॥

योऽसौ चक्रे बन्धुजीवोपघातं स्वार्थं तीक्ष्णीभूतहेत्यावलीनः ।
ग्रीष्मेऽरण्ये किं न हन्यात्स पान्थानस्यान्तश्चेन्नो हरेः कर्मणा स्यात् ॥६७ ॥

य इति । यः तीक्ष्णीभूता हेत्यावलिः किरणपङ्क्तिः यस्य, तादृशः इनः सूर्यो यस्मिन् सः ग्रीष्मः, स्वार्थं स्वप्रयोजनं, बन्धुजीवोपघातं-बन्धुजीवः पुष्पभेदः, तन्नाशं चक्रे । **पक्षे**-यः अवलीनः प्रच्छन्नः सन्, स्वार्थं धनार्थं बन्धूनां जीवघातं चक्रे, सः ग्रीष्मः पुरुषविशेषश्च । अरण्ये पान्थान् न हन्यात् किम्, अपि तु निहन्यादेव । हरेः सूर्यस्य सिंहस्य **च** कर्मणा गमनागमनरूपेण, **पक्षे**-मारणरूपेण च । अस्य ग्रीष्मस्य पुरुषविशेषस्य **च**, अन्तो नाशः(शो) न स्याद्यदि न भवेद्यदि तदा निहन्यादेव । हननाभावे हरिकर्म हेतुत्वेन **कल्पितम्** ॥६७ ॥

---

५८. क्षमास्था;

लोकोद्वेगं भावयन् ग्रीष्मनामा[५९] वृन्दारण्ये स्वं वसन्तं वितन्वन्।
चक्रे प्रीतिं लोकनाथस्य सर्वः स्वामिप्रीतिं पाति यत्नाज्जगद्विट् ॥६८ ॥

लोक इति। वृन्दारण्ये स्वं वसन्तं वसन्तस्वरूपं स्थितिमन्तं **च** वितन्वन् लोकनाथस्य प्रीतिं चक्रे ॥६८ ॥

तस्मिन्काले रामकृष्णौ समित्रौ वाह्यो जैत्रो वाहकश्चेतरः[६०] स्यात्[६१]।
इत्थं निर्णीयातनिष्टां विहारान् दैत्यस्तत्रागात् प्रलम्बाभिधानः ॥६९ ॥

तस्मिन्निति। जैत्रः जेता वाह्यः, इतरः जितः वाहकश्चेति निर्णयं कृत्वा विहारान् अतनिष्टाम् ॥६९ ॥

मायाछन्नस्वाकृतिर्दानवोऽसावेकं यूथं यूथयोराविवेश।
रामस्तत्रागात् प्रतिद्वन्द्विभावं जिग्यै दैत्यो रामवोढा च जातः ॥७० ॥

मायेति। मायया छन्ना आच्छादिता स्वाकृतिः स्वस्वरूपं येन। दैत्यः जितः रामवोढा रामवाहकश्च जातः ॥७१(७०) ॥

ऊढ्वा[६२] गच्छंश्चिन्तयामास कंसो राजाऽस्माकं धेनुकं यं निशम्य।
उत्क्रान्तासुं[६३] दुःखमापादि तद्यत् स्वाङ्गच्छेदात्तन्निहन्तारमेनम् ॥७१ ॥

ऊढ्वेति **युग्मम्**। अस्माकं राजा कंसः उत्क्रान्तासुं यं धेनुकं निशम्य यत् स्वाङ्गच्छेदात् दुःखं भवति तत् तादृशं दुःखं प्राप। तन्निहन्तारं धेनुकनिहन्तारमेनं कृष्णं स्वामिप्रीत्यै अद्रिशृङ्गात् पातयामीति चिन्तयामासेति **पूर्वेणान्वयः**। अथ चिन्तानन्तरम् अवरोहप्रदेशम् अवतारणप्रदेशम् अत्याय्य अतिक्रम्य दूरं यातः सन् स्वस्वरूपं बभाज सेवितवान्। रामस्तदा तं दानवम् अवेत् ज्ञातवान् ॥७२ ॥७३ ॥(७१-७३) ॥

स्वामिप्रीत्यै[६४] पातयाम्यद्रिशृङ्गादित्यत्याय्याथावरोहप्रदेशम्।
यातो दूरं स्वस्य रूपं बभाज श्रीमान् रामो दानवं तं तदाऽवैत् ॥७२ ॥

---

५८. क्षमास्था;
५९. °नाम;
६०. °श्चै°;
६१. °तरस्या° (विसर्ग dropped & jointly written-Marathi influence);
६२. P. writes ऊ as अू (Marathi influence) & B. writes ऊ as ऊ (= ओ);
६३. °न्तासं;
६४. स्वामी°;

रामप्रोद्यन्मुष्टिनिर्घातभिन्नादेतन्मूर्ध्नो[६५] **निःसृतास्त्रस्त्रवन्त्याः (न्ती) ।**
युक्तावान्तासृङ्नदी पादमस्य प्राप्ता देहद्रुः पपातास्य पश्चात् ।।७३ ।।

कुर्वाणानां यो जगत्प्राणजग्धिं श्रेष्ठः सर्गात्[६६] **स क्षमाधारणां च ।**
मुञ्चन्[६७] **यातः शूरसन्तानजत्वं किं नो हन्याद्राम एनं जिघांसुम्**[६८] **।।७४ ।।**

कुर्वाणानामिति । यः सर्गात् स्वभावात् निसर्गत इति यावत् । जगत्प्राणः समीरणः । 'जगत्प्राणसमीरणः' इति **अमरः** । (१.१.६२) **पक्षे**-जगतां जगदन्तर्वर्तिनां प्राणाः जीवाः तेषां जग्धिं भक्षणं कुर्वाणानां सर्पाणां मनुष्याणां **च** । श्रेष्ठः स क्षमा पृथ्वी तितिक्षा **च** । शूरः यादवभेदः पराक्रमविशिष्टश्च ।।७४ ।।

यातूढं तं बलं निःशलाकं स्थानं निन्ये कामसम्मर्दहेतोः ।
विन्दन्तस्यास्वङ्गसम्मर्दसौख्यं प्रत्यावृत्तो वाच्यमर्थं स ऊचे[६९] **।।७५ ।।**

यात्विति । यातु राक्षसः, उदूढं स्कन्धारूढं तं बलं बलदेवं कामं यः सम्मर्दः युद्धं, तद्धेतोः निःशलाकं विजनं स्थानं निन्ये । **पक्षे**-या काचित्स्त्री उदूढम् उद्वाहितं बलं बलवन्तं तं कञ्चित्पुरुषं, कामसंमर्दः रतिः । 'विविक्तविजनच्छन्ननिःशलाकास्तथा रहः ।' इति **अमरः** । (२.८.२२) सः (स) बलः तस्य राक्ष[स]स्य असूनां प्राणानाम् अङ्गानाम् अवयवानां च संमर्दसौख्यं विन्दन् सन् प्रत्यावृत्तः सन् वाच्यं तन्मारणरूपमर्थम् ऊचे । **पक्षे**-सः (स) पुरुषः तस्याः शोभनानि यानि अङ्गानि स्वङ्गानि, तेषां संमर्दसौख्यं सङ्गसौख्यं विन्दन् वाच्यं रतिक्रीडादिकमर्थं कथितवान् ।।७५ ।।

क्रीडासक्ते गोपवृन्दे तदैव प्राप्तो मुञ्जारण्यमुस्त्रा[७०] **समूहः ।**
अन्विष्यन्तस्तत्खुरन्यासचिह्नैर्यातास्तत्ते रामकृष्णान्यगोपाः ।।७६ ।।

क्रीडेति । मुञ्जास्त्र(स्तृ)णविशेषाः । उस्त्राः गावः । 'उस्त्रा माता च शृङ्गिणी' इति **अमरः** । (२.९.६६) तत् वनम् ।।७६ ।।

गतधनपुनराप्तिजातहर्षे पशुपगणेऽथ ततो[७१] **निवर्तमाने ।**
सकलसरणिरोध्र्युपात्तहेतिः[७२] **स्ववदुपघातकरः स कोऽपि जातः ।।७७ ।।**

---

६५. °मुध्नो (omits the रेफ) ;
६६. P. marginal gloss सर्गात् = स्वभावात्;
६७. °च° (ञ् dropped) ;
६८. °सु (म् dropped) ;
६९. B. writes ऊ as उ
७०. °मुस्ता°;
७१. ततेग्निव° (ग्नि for नि–scribal peculiarity).
७२. °राध्यु°;

गतेति । धनं गोधनं द्रव्यं **च** । पशुपगणे पशुपालगणे जडजने **च** । ततः वनात् कस्मादपि स्थानात् । निवर्तमाने सति । उपात्तहेतिः गृहीतज्वालः स्ववतां स्वाश्रयाणाम् उपघातकरः नाशकः, अग्निरिति यावत् ।' आश्रयाशो बृहद्भानुः' इति **अमरः** । (१.१.५४) सकलसरणिरोधी सकलमार्गनिरोधकः, सः कः स वायुश्चापि जातः । 'को ब्रह्मणि समीरात्मयमदक्षेषु ।' इति **एकाक्षरात्** । **पक्षे**-उपात्तायुधः स्ववतां धनवतामुपघातकरः कोऽपि सकलसरणिरोधी जातः ॥७७ ॥७८ ॥७९ ॥

गगनगतममन्दधूमवृन्दं वनशिखिनः परितः समुत्थितस्य ।
वनमिव तदतिप्रवृद्धवह्न्युत्तपनभयोत्पतितं दिवि व्यराजत् ॥७८ ॥

गगनगतममन्दधूमवृन्दं वनशिखिनः परितः समुत्थितस्य ।
गगनचरतरङ्गिणी जलान्तर्वनमिव तत्प्रतिबिम्बितं बभासे ॥७९ ॥

अन्तः[७३]स्फुरद्भिर्बहुभिः स्फुलिङ्गैर्धनञ्जयस्य ज्वलतोऽस्य धूमः ।
खद्योतजालाकलितान्तरालो व्यद्योतितेवातिघ[७४]नान्धकारः ॥८० ॥

अन्तरिति । धूमः(मो) घनान्धकार इव व्यद्योतत । स्फुलिङ्गानां खद्योतसाम्यं, धूमस्य घनान्धकारसाम्यम् ॥८० ॥

आक्रन्दं स सुरभिधेनुपालकानां श्रुत्वेशो द्रुतहृदयो नि[७५]जानुभावात् ।
वह्नेस्तान् बहिरनयन्निरुद्धमार्गात् स्वोपान्तं तदविदितं क्षणादतापान् ॥८१ ॥

आक्रन्दमिति । तदविदितं तैरज्ञातं यथा स्यात्तथा, स्वोपान्तमनयत् ॥८१ ॥

दहनवलयनिर्गमक्रमाज्ञैः पशुविचयादि मृषेति मन्यमानैः ।
सह सखिभिरगाद्व्रजं दिनान्ते हरिरतिमोदयुतैर्गवां गणैश्च ॥८२ ॥

दहन इति । दहनवलयनिर्गमस्य क्रमाज्ञैः क्रमानभिज्ञैरत एव पशुविचयादिकं मृषेति मन्यमानैः ॥८२ ॥८२ ॥८४ ॥

इति रानडे [झा]त्युपनामकशामरायतनूजविरचितायां नीलकण्ठकविकृत-यादवेन्द्रमहोदयकाव्यस्य टिप्पण्यां चतुर्थः सर्गः ॥४ ॥

यद्धीर्जगज्जातमिवासुरारेस्तनूरखेदाऽभृत शास्त्रजातम् ।
त्रिविक्रमाभिख्यतदात्मजन्मा यः पार्वतीनन्दनतामयासीत् ॥८३ ॥

नीलकण्ठेन तेनास्मिन् यादवेन्द्रमहोदये ।
कृते काव्ये तुरीयश्च सर्गः सम्पूर्णतां गतः ॥८४ ॥

---

७३. अतस्फु° (न् dropped & विसर्ग dropped & jointly written-Marathi influence);
७४. °वग्नि (ग्नि for ति–scribal peculiarity);
७५. °ग्नि° (ग्नि for नि–scribal peculiarity).

पञ्चमः सर्गः

[१]ततः प्रावृडुपायाता गां प्रस्नुतपयोधरा।
द्रष्टुकामेव गोविन्दं चिरविश्लिष्टमात्मजम् ॥१ ॥

पञ्चमः सर्गः। तत इति। ताः पयोधराः मेघाः यस्याम्। **पक्षे**-प्रस्नुतौ पयोधरौ स्तनौ यस्याः सा। गां पृथ्विम्। आत्मजम् आत्मनि जातः, तम्। भगवतः (तो) वर्षाकालोत्पन्नत्वात्। **पक्षे**-पुत्रम् ॥१ ॥

शैलानामिव मेघानां व्रातेन स्रवदम्भसाम्।
अत्युन्नतानामापूर्णा भूरिव द्यौरराजत ॥२ ॥

शैला इति। स्रवदम्भसाम् अत्युन्नतानां चेति विशेषणं **पक्षद्वयेऽपि** योजनीयम् ॥२ ॥

यद्वासराः सान्धकारा मन्ये रविद[२]शेन्धनः।
शान्त आसन्नशान्तित्वात् प्रागतिज्वलितोऽपि च ॥३ ॥

यदिति। यत् यस्मात्। रविरेव दशेन्धनः (नो) दीपः शान्त इति मन्ये। स्वोक्तस्य दृढीकरणायाह- अपि चेति। आसन्नेति। वर्षाकालात् प्राक् ग्रीष्मकाले(ल) इति यावत्। अतिज्वलितः-दीपस्य निर्वाणात्पूर्वम् अ(म)तिज्वलनं लोके प्रसिद्धम्। तदनुचिन्त्य शान्त इत्येव सत्यमिति मन्ये। 'दशेन्धनो गृहमणिः स्नेहाशः' इति **कोशः** ॥३ ॥४ ॥

वर्षाम्बुमन्ति शीर्षाणि तरूणां परिकम्पयन्।
उत्पादयामास परां वृष्टिं वनसमीरणः ॥४ ॥

गजग्राहिमहापङ्करुद्धाध्वाध्वगयोषिताम्।
जीवनग्रहणादासीन्मेघवृन्दं सजीवनम् ॥५ ॥

गजेति। रुद्धाध्वानः ये अ(येऽ)ध्वगास्तेषां योषितां जीवनं प्राणः (णा) उदकमिति **च** प्रतीयते। सजीवनं सजलं सप्राणमिति **च** ॥५ ॥

वाहिनीभिरसङ्ख्याभिः प्रभूततरवारिभिः।
व्यद्योततेव कालोऽयं सेनानीः पुष्पधन्वनः ॥६ ॥

---

१. P. begins with श्रीकृष्णाय नमः। B. begins with श्रीगणेशाय नमः।
२. °रशे°;

वाहिनीभिरिति । वाहिन्यो नद्यः सेनाश्च । प्रभूततरं वारि यासु । **पक्षे**-तरवारि खड्गः । सेनानीरिव सेनानायक इव व्यद्योतत ॥६ ॥

कदम्बकुटजामोदवाही वर्षासमीरणः ।
चचार शब्दमातन्वन् गन्धविक्रयिको यथा ॥७ ॥

कदम्बेति । आमोदवाही गन्धवाही । **पक्षे**-सुगन्धिद्रव्यवाहकः । गन्धविक्रयिकः सुगन्धिद्रव्यविक्रेता ॥७ ॥

सदांसीव[३] सरांस्यासन् हंसानामिव धीमताम् ।
निवहैर्दूरमुक्तानि सृजतां मधुरां गिरम् ॥८ ॥

सदांसीति । मधुरां गिरं सृजतां धीमतां निवहैर्मुक्तानि सदांसीव गृहाणीव हंसानां निवहैर्मुक्तानि सरांस्यासन् । **हंसपक्षेऽपि**-मधुरां गिरं सृजतामिति विशेषणं योज्यम् । वर्षाकाले हंसानां मानससरोगमनात् नि(न्नि)[:]श्रीकाणि सरोवराण्यासन्नित्यर्थः ॥८ ॥

आश्रित्य कञ्चिदुद्देशं त्यक्तसञ्चरणक्रियाः ।
अभवन् विहगाः सर्वे सत्परिव्राजका इव ॥९ ॥

आश्रित्येति । कञ्चिदुद्देशमाश्रित्य त्यक्तसञ्चरणक्रियाः त्य(स्त्य)-क्तगमनव्यापाराः (रा) अभवन् ॥९ ॥

हरेः स्वार्थकृतो गोभिश्चर्व्या[४] दूर्वा विनाशयत्
हरेः परस्य गोवृन्दं घनै[५]रिन्द्रो न्यवारयत् ॥१० ॥

हरेरिति । स्वार्थकृतः स्वार्थसम्पाद[क] स्य हरेः वि(र्वि)ष्णोः गो(र्गो)भिः च (श्च)— र्वितुं योग्याः दूर्वाः विनाशयत् नाशकरं, परस्य अ (स्या) न्यस्य शत्रोरिति **च** प्रतीयते । हरेः सूर्यस्य विष्णोरिति **च** प्रतीयते । गोवृन्दं किरणसमूहः, गवां वृन्दं **च** । इन्द्रः (न्द्रो) घनैर्मेघैः मु(र्मु)द्गरैश्च । 'द्रुघणे मुद्गरघनौ' इति **अमरः** । (२.८.९१) ॥१० ॥

नीलजीमूतसन्दोहो[६] रेजे दानववैरिणा ।
निजैश्वर्यं दर्शयितुं कायव्यूह इवादृतः ॥११ ॥

---

३. °दा° (omits the अनुस्वार);
४. P. चर्व्याः (retains the विसर्ग to show plurality);
५. घने°;
६. °सन्देहो;

नील इति । कायव्यूहः कायसमूहः ॥११ ॥

वने सर्वपथीनेन व्याप्ते पङ्केन धेनवः ।
स्फीतदूर्वाङ्कुरग्रासपीनाङ्गा मन्दमभ्रमन् ॥१२ ॥

वने(न) इति । सर्वपथं व्याप्नोतीति सर्वपथीनः, तेन । मन्दभ्रमणे पङ्कः पीनाङ्गत्वं च कारणम् ॥१२ ॥

एवंकारं प्रवृत्तासु वर्षासु ससुहृद्गणः ।
प्रावृष्येण्यविहाराणां जज्ञे कर्ता जनार्दनः ॥१३ ॥

एवमिति । वर्षासु ए(स्वे)वंकारम् इ(मि)त्थं पूर्वोक्तप्रकारेणेत्यर्थः । प्रवृत्तासु सतीषु ॥१३ ॥

ततो निववृते प्रावृडम्बरान्तरसंस्थितम् ।
अन्विष्यन्तीव विभ्रष्टं विद्युच्चामीकरोत्करम् ॥१४ ॥

तत इति । अम्बरमाकाशं वस्त्रं च विभ्रष्टम् । विद्युदेव चामीकरं, तत् अ(द)-न्विष्यन्तीव निववृते (त) **इत्युत्प्रेक्षा** ॥१४ ॥

पद्मकोशस्तनोद्भेदरम्या सिञ्जानहंसका ।
उपतस्थे शरत्कान्ता कृष्णं तं निर्जरोत्तमम् ॥१५ ॥

पद्ममिति । पद्मकोशौ कमलकुड्मलावेव स्तनौ, तयोरुद्भेदेन प्रादुर्भवेन रम्या, सिञ्जानशब्दं कुर्वाणा, हंसा एव हंसकौ पादकटकौ यस्या [:] सा ।'हंसकः पादकटकः 'इति **अमरः** ।(२.६.११०) शरदेव कान्ता । निर्जरोत्तमं युवश्रेष्ठं देवश्रेष्ठं **च** ॥१५ ॥

सिंहाः सप्तच्छदामोदमाघ्राय पवनाहृतम् ।
तुल्यं गजमदामोदैः परितो वनमभ्रमन् ॥१६ ॥

सिंहा इति । गजमदामोदतुल्यत्वात्(द्) गजभ्रान्त्या अ(न्त्या)-भ्रमन् ॥१६ ॥१७ ॥

पाण्डुरैर्हंसनिवहैर्दूरोत्पतनपण्डितैः ।
दिवाऽपि व्यक्तनक्षत्रमिवाम्बरमरोचत ॥१७ ॥

नीलं चरत्सिताम्भोदमस्तनीलाम्बुदं नभः ।
मृगेन्द्राक्रान्तमुन्मुक्तं गजैर्वनमिवाबभौ ॥१८ ॥

नीलमिति । सिताम्बुदमृगेन्द्रयोः साम्यम् । नीलाम्बुदगजयोः साम्यम् ॥१८ ॥

तरङ्गिणीनितम्बिन्यः कामवेगवशंवदाः ।
अतिसङ्गरुजा पत्युर्नूनं कार्श्यमुपागताः ॥१९ ॥

तरङ्गिणीति । तरङ्गिण्य एव नितम्बिन्यः । कामं वेगः(गो) जवः कामवेगः(गो) मदनवेगः । पत्युः समुद्रस्य वल्लभस्य **च**। अतिसङ्गात् मैथुनातिप्रसङ्गात्, **पक्षे**-निरन्तरसंश्लेषात् ॥१९ ॥

नाकाशकुसुमोद्भेदः शरद्येव सदैव तम् ।
असन्तं वदतां जज्ञे तान्त्रिकाणां वचो मृषा ॥२० ॥

नाकाशेति । आकाशकुसुमोद्भ(द्भे)दः शरद्येव शरत्काल एव न । एवकारेण शरद्व्यतिरिक्तेषु कालेषु वर्तत इति ज्ञायते । तं(त)माकाशकुसुमोद्भेदं सदैव असन्तं वदतां तान्त्रिकाणां वचः(चो) मृषा जज्ञे जातम् । **पक्षे**-काशकुसुमोद्भ(द्भे)दं शरद्यैव ना (न) सदैव । शरत्कालातिरिक्तकाले तस्यानुदुद्गमात् ॥२० ॥

विद्योतमानहंसाब्जं निर्मलं पुष्करं बभौ ।
विद्योतमानहंसाब्जं निर्मलं पुष्करं बभौ ॥२१ ॥

विद्योतमान इति । विद्योतमानौ हंसाब्जौ सूर्याचन्द्रमसौ यस्मिन् । पुष्करमाकाशम् । विद्योतमानानि हंसाः अब्जानि च यस्मिन् । पुष्करं जलम् । 'पुष्करं खे जलेऽपि च' इति **कोशः** ॥२१ ॥

आघ्राय मुदितो लोकः सरोजवनमारुतम् ।
अलिवृन्दमगात् पद्मसरोजवनमारुतम् ॥२२ ॥

आघ्रायेति । लोकः सरोजवनमारुतं कमलष(=ख)ण्डसमीरणमाघ्राय मुदितः । आरुतं शब्दं कुर्वत्, जवनं वेगवत्, अलिवृन्दं पद्मसरः अगात् ॥२२ ॥

स्पृहयेन्न कलत्राय रणत्सारसनायकः ।
दृष्टो यदि वनोद्देशो रणत्सारसनायकः ॥२३ ॥

स्पृहेति । रणन्तः शब्दं कुर्वन्तः सारसनायकाः पक्षिविशेषश्रेष्ठाः यस्मिन् एतादृश उद्देशः प्रदेशः(शो) दृष्टो यदि कः पुरुषः, रणत् सारसनं मेखला यस्य, तस्मै कलत्राय भार्यायै न स्पृहयेत्, अपि तु सर्वोऽपि स्पृहयेदित्यर्थः । 'क्लीबे सारसनम्' इति **अमरः** ।(२.६.१०९) 'कलत्रं श्रोणिभार्ययोः' इति **अमरः** ।(३.३.१७८) ॥२३ ॥

बाष्पवर्षैरन्वकुर्वन् वियुक्तकमलेक्षणाः ।
अमूर्वर्षाजागरितवियुक्तकमलेक्षणाः ॥२४ ॥

बाष्पवर्षैरिति । जागरितेन जागरेण वियुक्तः रहितः कमलेक्षणो विष्णुर्यासु ताः, अमूः वर्षाः, बाष्पवर्षैः-बाष्पस्थानीयानि वर्षाणि, तैः, वियुक्ताः(क्ता) या[ः] कमलेक्षणाः स्त्रियस्ताः(स्ता) अनुकुर्वन् अ(न्न)नुकरणं कृतवत्यः ॥२४ ॥

दीप्तकामं[७] नभो वीक्ष्य शुकमालिकयाऽऽवृतम् ।
निन्ये रतिं काऽ[८]प्यानीतं शुकमालिकया वृतम् ॥२५ ॥

दीप्तमिति । काऽपि स्त्री शुकमालिकया कीरपङ्क्त्या आ(ङ्क्त्याऽऽ)वृतं व्याप्तं नभः (नभो) वीक्ष्य दीप्तकामम् आ(मा)लिकया सख्या आ(ख्याऽऽ)नीतं वृतं स्वेन अ(ना)भिलक्षितं शुकं रतिं निन्ये रतिं प्रापितवती । शुकस्य जितेन्द्रियत्वेऽपि तत्थै(द्धै)र्यच्युतीकरणपटुः स समय **इति भावः** ॥२५ ॥

परस्पराभिमुख्येन सम्पतद्भिः शिलीमुखैः ।
आचख्ये शम्बरारातिर्जगद्विजयसङ्गरः ॥२६ ॥

परस्परेति । शिलीमुखा भ्रमरा एव बाणाः, तैः । शम्बरारातिर्मदनः । 'शम्बरारिर्मनसिजः' इति **अमरः** ।(१.१.२६) ॥२६ ॥

जलपानावतीर्णानां पाण्डूनां निवहैर्गवाम् ।
रिक्ता पूर्णेव रुरुचे यमुना पाण्डु[९]सैकता ॥२७ ॥

जलमिति । रिक्ताऽपि यमुना पाण्डूनां गवां निवहैः पूर्णेव रुरुचे । गवां जलानामिति **च** प्रतीयते । गवां जलानां **च** पाण्डुत्वेन साधर्म्यात् । 'दिग्दृष्टिदीधितिस्वर्गवज्रवाग्बाणवारिषु । गोशब्दः ॥२७ ॥

रामणीयकमालोक्य शरदः परमात्मना ।
तत्सन्निधानकामेन मार्गशीर्षत्वमाददे ॥२८ ॥

रामणीयकमिति । मार्गशीर्षत्वं मार्गशीर्षमासत्वम् । 'मासानां मार्गशीर्षोऽहम्' इति **गीतायां भगवदुक्तेः** [१०.३५] ॥२८ ॥

अनासादितमार्गत्वाद्विचचार वनेषु या ।
सा शरन्मार्गमासाद्य क्षयमेवान्वविन्दत ॥२९ ॥

---

७. °कामन्नभो (म् = (अनुस्वार) + न = न्न -Marathi influence) ;
८. काऽप्य° ;
९. पाडु° (drops the अनुस्वार (अनुनासिक)) ;

अनेति। मार्गः सरणिः मार्गशीर्षमासश्च। वने विचरणं तु वृक्षाणां फलपर्णादिना शोभासम्पादकत्वम्। मार्गं सरणिं मासविशेषं च। क्षयं गेहं नाशं च। मार्गशीर्षान्ते शरन्नाशात्॥२९॥

चतुष्टये स्वबाणानां वसन्ताद्यपदेशिनि।
अपराद्धे सरोषेण शम्बरारातिनोज्झितः[१०]॥३०॥

चतुष्टये (य इ) ति। **युग्मम्**। वसन्ताद्यपदेशिनि वसन्तादिसंज्ञके। आदिपदेन ग्रीष्मवर्षाशरदः। अपराद्धे लक्षाच्च्युते सति। 'अपराद्धपृषत्कोऽसौ लक्ष्याद्यश्च्युतसायकः।' इति **अमरः**। (२.८.६८) अमोघः पञ्चमो बाण इव। आवृतशरीराणां कवचादिना आ(नाऽऽ)च्छादितगात्राणाम्, कञ्चुकादिभिराच्छादितगात्राणां **च**॥३१(३०)॥

अमोघः पञ्चमो बाण इव गात्राणि कम्पयन्।
अप्यावृतशरीराणां हेमन्तऋतुरागतः॥३१॥

क्षोणीतलं विसृमरैरनुष्णैर्मिहिरांशुभिः।
निषिक्तं सर्वतो रेजे शातकुम्भद्रवैरिव॥३२॥

क्षोणीति। शातकुम्भद्रवैः सुवर्णद्रावैः, निषिक्तमिव रेजे॥३२॥

विदिद्युते तुषाराणां संहतिः पटमन्दिरम्।
जेतुं प्रस्थास्यमानस्य[११] जगन्तीव मनोभुवः॥३३॥

विदिद्युत इति। तुषाराणां संहतिः ज(र्ज)गन्ति जेतुं प्रस्थास्यमानस्य मनोभुवः पटमन्दिरमिव विदिद्युते॥३३॥

अतुद[१२]त्कस्य न सरः शान्तता[१३]मरसं मनः।
योगिनामपि तत्याज शान्तताम रसं मनः॥३४॥

अतुददिति। शान्तानि आह्लादजनकानि तामरसानि पद्मानि यस्मिन् तत् सरः सरोवरं कस्य मनः(नो) न अ(ना)तुदत्। उद्दी[प]कत्वात् सर्वस्यापीति **भावः**। योगिनाम् अरसं रसशून्यमपि मनः शान्ततामिन्द्रियनिग्रहं तत्याज॥३४॥

---

१०. °ताः;
११. B. lacuna for स्य;
१२. °क्तस्य;
१३. °तामनरसं;

यूनां तुहिनभीरूणामभवत्कारणं[१४] द्विधा ।
सोष्मस्तनस्वरमणीगाढाश्लेषमहोत्सवे ॥३५ ॥

यूनामिति । द्विधा कारणमभवत् । गाढालिङ्गनविषये(य) एकं कामबाणरूपं, द्वितीयं शैत्यम् ।

कूपोदकं वटच्छाया ताम्बूलं तरुणीस्तनः ।
शीतकाले भवेदुष्णमुष्णकाले च शीतलम् ॥ इति ॥३५ ॥

दीपितानां हुतभुजां[१५] धूमैः शीतापनुत्तये ।
छन्नो हिमैश्च सविता स्वं ददर्श स्वयं[१६] न वा ॥३६ ॥

दीपितानामिति । धूमैः हि(र्हि)मैश्च छंन्नः[१७](=छन्नः) सूर्यः स्वं स्वयमेव स्वयमात्मानं ददर्श वा न वेति, तादृशः छ(श्छ)न्न इति **पूर्वेण सम्बन्धः** ॥३६ ॥

ससौरभोऽपि मन्दोऽपि वायुरत्यन्तशीतलः ।
सुरतामर्दखिन्नानां परमानन्दकोऽभवत् ॥३७ ॥

ससौरभ इति । सुरतामर्दखिन्नानां परं तेषामेव आ(वा)नन्दकः, नान्येषामित्यर्थः ॥३७ ॥

मार्गशीर्षे कुमारीणां नन्दव्रजजुषां ततिः ।
कृष्णं रमणमीप्सन्ती कात्यायन्यर्चनं व्यधात् ॥३८ ॥

मार्गेति । कात्यायनी गौरी ॥३८ ॥३९ ॥

मासनिर्वर्तनीयस्य गौरीपूजाव्रतस्य ताः ।
पूर्वाङ्गं स्नानमातन्वन्नुषःसु यमुनाम्भसि ॥३९ ॥

कृष्णो मासान्त्यदिवसे गौरीमात्मानमर्थितम् ।
निष्पन्नं बोधयन्नेताः प्रत्यूषे यमुनां ययौ ॥४० ॥

कृष्णे (ष्णं) इति । कृष्णः(ष्णो) गौरीमुदि(द्दि)श्य अ(श्या)र्थितं कृतार्थनमात्मानं निष्पन्नं सम्प्राप्तम् इ(मि)ति बोधयन् सन् यमुनां ययौ ॥४० ॥

---

१४. °कारुणं;
१५. °भूजां;
१६. स्वयन्न°;
१७. छंन्न (अनुस्वार changed to next अनुनासिक & अनुस्वार & अनुनासिक both used-Marathi influence);

कृष्णशृङ्गरवाज्जातजागराः सह गोधनैः ।
अन्वयुः सत्वरं गोपा विस्मृताहार्यसङ्ग्रहाः ॥४१ ॥

कृष्णे इति (कृष्णेति) । विस्मृतः(त) आहार्यसङ्ग्रहो भक्षणीयपदार्थसङ्ग्रहो यैस्ते ॥४१ ॥

अथ स्नानावतीर्णानां तासां दिग्वाससां हरिः ।
तीरन्यस्तानि वासांसि जहार तदवीक्षितः ॥४२ ॥

अथेति । दिग्वाससां नग्नानाम् । तदवीक्षितः ता(स्ता)भिरनवलोकितः ॥४२ ॥

सान्द्रानुरागा गोविन्दे तं सर्वत्रैव सर्वदा ।
पश्यन्त्यो[१८] नूनमायातं नापश्यंस्तं कुमारिकाः ॥४३ ॥

सान्द्रेति । गोविन्दे सान्द्रानुरागाः (गा) अत एव तं सर्वत्रैव सदा पश्यन्त्यः (न्त्य) अतः (त) आयातं तं नापश्यन् इ(न्नि)ति नूनं शङ्के ॥४३ ॥

अथारुह्य कदम्बाग्रं तस्थौ पश्यन्निमा हरिः ।
स्वानुरागेण महता सुसहीभाविते‌ऽम्भसि ॥४४ ॥

अथेति । **युग्मम्** । स्वानुरागेण स्वविषयकप्रीत्या । सुखेन सह्यत इति सुसहम् । असुसहं सुसहं भावितं सुसहीभावितं, तस्मिन् अ(न्न)त्यन्तशीतले अ(ले‌ऽ)म्भसि आ(स्या)कण्ठं मग्नाः । द्विर्भावः(वो) द्वैगुण्यम् ॥(४४) ॥४५ ॥

अत्यन्तशीतले मग्ना आकण्ठं वदनैः शुभैः ।
[१९]तत्कालोत्फुल्लराजीववनद्विर्भावकारिणीः ॥४५ ॥

[२०]अभात्कृष्णो‌ऽनेकवर्णशाखालम्बाम्बरैर्वृतः ।
नदीभिर्भिन्नवर्णोर्वीरेणुहृद्भिरिवार्णवः ॥४६ ॥

आ(अ)भादिति । नीलवर्णत्वात् कृष्णसमुद्रयोः साम्यम् । विचित्रवर्णवस्त्राणां भिन्नरेणुधारिणीनां नदीनां साम्यम् ॥४६ ॥

अथारोहणकामास्ता आरोहसरणौ दृशम् ।
विन्यस्य तत्र नापश्यन्नम्बराणि वराङ्गनाः ॥४७ ॥

---

१८. पश्यन्तो;
१९. °सत्का;
२०. अभकृष्णा°;

अथेति । आरोहः जलावतारः । तस्य सरणौ मार्गे ॥४७ ॥४८ ॥

समन्तात्प्रहितैर्नेत्रैः कदम्बशिखरस्थितम् ।
हृतवाससमैक्षन्त जगदीशं कुमारिकाः ॥४८ ॥

तदा हर्षो भयं क्रोधो ह्रीश्च तासां हृदङ्गणे ।
अयुध्यन्त मिथस्तेषु हर्ष ईषद्बलाधिकः ॥४९ ॥

तदेति । कृष्णप्राप्त्या हर्षाधिक्यम् ॥४९ ॥

ततो मन्दाक्षभारेण रुद्धवाणीकमाननम् ।
व्याहारोन्मुखतां निन्ये हिमं तासां निरङ्कुशम् ॥५० ॥

तत इति । निरङ्कुशमत्यन्तं हिमं व्याहारोन्मुखतां निन्ये । हिमेन पीडिताः सत्यः ऊचुरित्यर्थः ॥५० ॥

स्वामिन्नेत्रासङ्गमस्मद्गात्राणां रचितं त्वया ।
कामयामह एनं त्वं कुरु दासीर्दयस्व नः ॥५१ ॥

स्वामिन्निति । हे स्वामिन्, त्वया रचितम् अ(म)स्मद्गात्राणां नेत्रासङ्गं वस्त्रासङ्गं कामयामहे । 'त्वमस्माकं वस्त्राणि देहि ।' **इत्येकोऽर्थः** । त्वया रचितम् अ(म)स्मद्गात्राणां नेत्रस्य नयनस्य आ(स्या)सङ्गं कामयामहे । 'त्वया अ(याऽ)स्माकं शरीरमवलोकनीयमितीच्छामहे'। इति **द्वितीयोऽर्थः** । नेत्रानियामकेन पत्या त्वया रचितम् अ(म)स्मद्गात्राणाम् आ(मा)सङ्गं कामयामहे ।' त्वमस्माकं पतिर्भूत्वा अस्मच्छरीरसङ्गं कुरु ।' इति **तृतीयोऽर्थः** । ।५१ ॥

ऋजूनामपि भावानुसारि[२१] तासां वचो हरिः ।
निशम्य व्याजहारेदं सर्वार्थानुगुणं वचः ॥५२ ॥

ऋज्विति । भावानुसारि स्वाभिप्रायानुरोधि । सर्वार्थानुगुणं पूर्वो(र्व)-श्लोकोक्तार्थानुगुणम् ॥५२ ॥

वारिणो यदि निर्यान्ति भवत्यो मीनलोचनाः ।
भवद्वाञ्छितमाप्नोति तदा सिद्धिमसंशयम् ॥५३ ॥

वारीति । वारिणः जलात् यदि निर्यान्ति तदा नेत्रासङ्गं वस्त्रासङ्गरूपं

२१. °नुः सारि;

नयनासङ्गरूपं **च**, वारयतीति वारी, निवारकः गुरुबन्धुजनादिः, तस्मात् यदि निर्यान्ति तदा मत्पत्नीत्वेन मत्समागमरूपं **च** वाञ्छितं सिद्ध्येदित्यर्थः ॥५३ ॥

आकर्ण्य तन्निरगमं[२२]न्नम्भसस्ता नताननाः ।
वराङ्गस्तनमाच्छाद्य पाणिभ्यां वामलोचनाः ॥५४ ॥

आकर्ण्येति । वराङ्गं गुह्यम् ॥५४ ॥

ललाटलग्नाञ्जलिका सङ्घाद्बहिरुपागता ।
मद्वितीर्णाम्बरं वस्तामेकैकेत्युक्तवान् प्रभुः ॥५५ ॥

ललाटमिति । वस्ताम् आच्छादयतु धारयत्वित्यर्थः ॥५५ ॥

अङ्गीकृततदुक्तार्थाः सर्वाङ्गेषु वधूरिमाः ।
नेत्रेणाच्छादयामास द्विविधेन जनार्दनः ॥५६ ॥

अङ्गीकृत इति । द्विविधेन नेत्रेण वस्त्रेण नयनेन **च**। आच्छादयामास आच्छादनं चकार । नयनेन आच्छादयामास अवलोकयामासेत्यर्थः ॥५६ ॥५७ ॥ ५८ ॥५९ ॥

ललितापाङ्गवलनैः स्वमापृच्छ्य महेश्वरः ।
निर्यान्तीस्ता[२३] उवाचेदं मत्सङ्गं प्राप्स्यथाचिरम् ॥५७ ॥

ता विसृत्याथ गोपालैः सह चारितगोधनः ।
विजहार वनान्तेषु सरामो नन्दनन्दनः ॥५८ ॥

ततो गगनमध्यस्थां तृषिता इव धावनैः ।
तरङ्गिणीमुपायाता भानवीयास्तुरङ्गमाः ॥५९ ॥

तदा गोविन्दमवदन् गोपा दीप्ताशनायिताः ।
प्रभवन् विस्मृताहार्यानशनाया[२४] दुनोति नः ॥६० ॥

तदेति । दीप्तम् अशनायितं बुभुक्षा येषां ते । हे प्रभवन् प्रभो, विस्मृताहार्यान् नः अशनाया क्षुधा दुनोति ।'अशनाया बुभुक्षा क्षुत्' इति **अमरः** । (२.९.५४) ॥६० ॥

---

२२. °मंत्र° (अनुस्वार + अनुनासिक-Marathi Incluence);
२३. निर्यातीस्ता;
२४. P. marginal quotation 'अशनाया बुभुक्षा क्षुत्' इति **अमरः** ।

यज्वनामाश्रमोऽदूरे वदान्यानां विपश्चिताम् ।
अस्ति तान्[२५] याचतां वः स्यात्किमन्नमपि दुर्लभम् ।।६१ ।।

यज्वनामिति । **युग्मम्** । अवदान्यानामत एव भवतां किमन्नमपि कुत्सितान्नमपि दुर्लभं स्यात् । अतस्तान् मुक्त्वा ताः स्त्रीः याचतेति **भगवदभिप्रायः** । वदान्यानामत एव भवतामन्नमपि दुर्लभं स्यात् किं, तस्मात् स्त्रीः मुक्त्वा तान् याचतेति **गोपाभिप्रायः** । शाब्दभ्रमेण ते गत्वा तान् [अ] याचन्त ।।(६१) ।।६२ ।।

ततो याचत तान्मुक्त्वा तत्पत्नीरित्यवोचत ।
भगवानथ ते शाब्दभ्रमाद्गत्वाऽऽर्थयन्त[२६] तान् ।।६२ ।।

अलब्धवाञ्छिता एत्य हरये तन्न्यवेदयन्[२७] ।
पूर्वोक्तवाक्यं व्याख्याय सप्रमानकरोत्स तान् ।।६३ ।।

अलब्ध इति । पूर्वोक्तवाक्यं व्याख्याय स्वोक्ताभिप्रायमुक्त्वा तान् सप्रमान् यथार्थज्ञानयुक्तान् अकरोत्, स्वाभिप्रायज्ञानवन्तः कृतवानित्यर्थः ।।६३ ।।

तास्तेऽथ गत्वाऽयाचन्त सरामं कृष्णमागतम् ।
आकर्ण्य तास्तद्वचनक्रमाद्धर्षमुपागताः ।।६४ ।।

ता इति । ताः तद्वचनक्रमात् तेषां वचनपरिपाट्या सरामं कृष्णमागतमाकर्ण्य हर्षमुपगताः ।।६४ ।।६५ ।।

अन्नं रसवदादाय यत्र तौ रामकेशवौ ।
निर्जगामाभि तं देशं यायजूकाङ्गनाजनः ।।६५ ।।

प्रागसङ्ख्येषु जननेष्वदृष्टसमसुन्दरम्[२८] ।
सबलं ता अवैक्षन्त कृतपुण्या महेश्वरम् ।।६६ ।।

प्रागिति । **युग्मम्** । अदृष्टः समः सुन्दरो यस्य तम् । दन्तच्छेदवत् अवदातया धवलया रामकान्त्या मिलितया त्विषा संभिन्नगङ्गायमुनां दर्शयन्तम् । रामस्य धवलवर्णत्वात् गङ्गासाम्यम् । स्वस्य नैल्यात् यमुनासाम्यम् । तादृशम् अवैक्षन्त इति **पूर्वेणान्वयः** ।।[६६]६७ ।।

---

२५. तांन्या° (अनुस्वार + अनुनासिक-Marathi influence);
२६. °भ्रमान् ग°;
२७. तन्य°;
२८. B. repeats the line स जननेष्वदृष्टसमसुन्दरम् after 'b' in the text.

रामकान्त्या मिलितया दन्तच्छेदावदातया ।
संभिन्नगङ्गायमुनां दर्शयन्तं त्विषाऽटवीम् ॥६७ ॥

भगवद्दर्शनानन्दबाष्पजम्बालिता मही ।
तासां भगवदासत्तौ चक्रे किञ्चिद्विलम्बितम् ॥६८ ॥

भगवदिति । [जम्बालिता] पङ्किला मही तासां भगवदासत्तौ भगवत्सान्निध्ये विषये किञ्चिद्विलम्बितं चक्रे कृतवती ॥६८ ॥६९ ॥

मुमुदे ससखा देवो भुञ्जानोऽन्नं तदर्पितम् ।
यथा तत्प्रेमरसतस्तथा नैव[२९] रसान्तरात् ॥६९ ॥

सौहित्यकाष्ठामापन्ने मित्रवृन्दे जगत्पतिः ।
ता उवाच प्रतीक्षन्ते पतयो गम्यतामिति ॥७० ॥

सौहित्यमिति । सौहित्यं तृप्तिः, तस्याः काष्ठामुत्कर्षम् । अतिशयितां तृप्तिमित्यर्थः ॥७० ॥७१ ॥७२ ॥

निषिद्धागमना अस्मानुल्लङ्घ्याज्ञामिहागताः ।
कथं गृह्णन्ति पतयस्त्वं गतिर्नः प्रभो इति ॥७१ ॥

तासां वचनमाकर्ण्य भगवानेवमब्रवीत् ।
नाथा गृह्णन्ति वः शान्तचित्तमालिन्यजक्रुधः ॥७२ ॥

जग्धमन्नं जरयति पश्चात्तद्यस्य देहिनः ॥
स्वं तस्य चित्तमालिन्यं पूर्वं मज्जठरानलः ॥७३ ॥

जग्धमिति । मज्जठरानलः जग्धं भक्षितम् अन्नं यस्य देहिनः स्वं तस्य देहिनश्चित्तमालिन्यं पूर्वं जरयति पश्चादन्नं जरयति । मद्भक्षितान्न(न्नात्) स्वामिनश्चित्तमालिन्यं तत्क्षण एव नश्यतीत्यर्थः ॥७३ ॥

प्रभोरादेशमासाद्य प्रत्यावृत्ता व्यथामयुः ।
ताः प्रागतीव मुदिताः स्वर्गारूढच्युता इव ॥७४ ॥

प्रभोरिति । प्राक् भगवद्दर्शनेन मुदिताः पश्चाद्वियोगेन दुःखमाप्ता इत्यर्थः ॥७४ ॥

---

२९. चैव;

ता गृहीताः[३०] स्वपतिभिः कृष्णरीढो[३१]नुतापितैः ।
कालार्णवं तरन्ति स्म कृष्णचिन्तातरीश्रिताः ।।७५ ।।

ता इति । कृष्णस्य या रीढा अवज्ञा, तया अनुतापितैः पश्चात्तापं प्राप्तैः । रीढावमाननावज्ञा' इति **अमरः** ।[१.७.२३] कृष्णस्य चिन्ता स्मरणं, तदेव तरी नौका, तामाश्रिताः ।।७५ ।।७६ ।।७७ ।।

कदाचिदूचे भगवानिन्द्रयागार्थमुद्यतान् ।
नन्दादीनयमुद्योगः किमुद्दिशति वः फलम् ।।७६ ।।

तदा नन्द उवाचेदं कृष्णं वत्स यजामहे ।
भगवन्तं ब(व)लारातिं काम्या वृष्टिर्हि तद्वशे ।।७७ ।।

[३२]तदोवाच हरिः प्रीतो यदि यागेन वो वृषा ।
वर्षत्यनीप्सितां वृष्टिमूषरे[३३] किं करोति वः ।।७८ ।।

तदेति । वः अनीप्सितां वृष्टिम् ऊषरे किमर्थं करोति । तस्मात् वृष्टिकरणं तस्य स्वभाव एव न, यागहेतुका प्रीतिरिति **भावः** ।।७८ ।।

किं चेन्द्रस्य वशे वृष्टिरित्यपि व्याहृतं मृषा ।
तथा चेत् स्वमनःकान्ते नन्दने किं न वर्षति ।।७९ ।।

किं चेति । नन्दने तत्संज्ञकस्वारामे । वृष्टेः स्वाधीनत्वं चेत् नन्दने कुतो न वर्षति ।।७९ ।।

दृष्ट्वैव[३४] वः फलानाप्तिः कदाचिद्यजतामपि ।
अतो न वृष्टिकाम्यानां याज्यो जीमूत[३५]दारकः ।।८० ।।

दृष्टै(ष्ट्वै)ति । जीमूतान् मेघान् दारयतीति दारकः नाशकः इति **चमत्कारः** । **पक्षे**-जीमूतान् पर्वतान् दारयतीति पर्वतनाशकः इन्द्रः । 'जीमूतौ मेघपर्वतौ' इति **अमरः** । [३.३.५८] ।।८० ।।८१ ।।८२ ।।

---

३०. ता (omits the विसर्ग);
३१. °रूढा°;
३२. तदे°;
३३. °रेतिं;
३४. °वं;
३५. P. marginal quotation जीमूतौ मेघपर्वतौ' इति **अमरः**

युष्माभिर्भृतसम्भारैर्याज्यो गोवर्धनाचलः ।
त्राता गवामयं[३६] यन्नः स्थिरभूर्यम्बुपादपः ।।८१ ।।

युक्तिमद्वचनं विष्णोर्नन्दाद्यैरनुमोदितम् ।
गोब्राह्मणाग्नीन् संतर्प्य गिरये बलिमार्पयन् ।।८१ ।।

बल्यन्नराशिं भगवान् गोवर्धनमिवोन्नतम् ।
रूपान्तरमधिष्ठाय किञ्चिच्छेषमभक्षयत् ।।८३ ।।

बल्यन्नमिति । गोवर्धनमिवोन्नतम् इति अन्नराशेः रूपान्तरस्य अपि **विशेषणम्** । किञ्चिच्छेषं यस्य सः, तम् ।।८३ ।।८४ ।।

तं रामकृष्णप्रमुखाः सर्वे चक्रुः प्रदक्षिणम् ।
महनीयं सुवर्णाद्रिं चन्द्रसूर्यादिका इव ।।८४ ।।

ते सेष्टप्रार्थनं नत्वा दण्डवद्यावदुत्थिताः ।
तावदन्तर्धिमगमत्तद्रूपं परमात्मनः ।।८५ ।।

त इति । सेष्टप्रार्थनम् इष्टप्रार्थनया सहितं यथा [स्यात्] तथा ।।८५ ।।८६ ।।८७ ।।

बहुकृत्वः कृतेज्योऽपि नेन्द्रो दृग्गोचरोऽभवत् ।
कृष्णोक्तकारिणां नोऽद्य गिरिः प्रत्यक्षतां गतः ।।८६ ।।

इति ब्रुवन्तः सानन्दा नन्दगोपपुरोगमाः ।
ततो निजनिजावासान् प्रयाता धेनुपालकाः ।।८७ ।।

ततः स्वयागभङ्गेन क्रुद्ध इन्द्रो बलाहकान् ।
नन्दव्रजविनाशाय शशासोद्वेलवृष्टिभिः ।।८८ ।।

तत इति । उद्वेलाः निर्मर्यादाः याः वृष्टयस्ताभिः ।।८८ ।।८९ ।।

अथाम्बुदानां निवहैरापूरि गगनाङ्गणम् ।
विच्छिन्नशृङ्खलोद्भ्रान्तदिव्यदन्तावलायितैः ।।८९ ।।

घनान्धकारसंरुद्धचाक्षुषे समये तदा ।
नीलाम्बुवाहसन्दोहो गर्जितेनान्वमीयत ।।९० ।।

---

३६. °मययन्नः(अनुस्वार dropped & jointly written) .

घन इति । चाक्षुषं चक्षुर्जन्यविषय (यं) प्रत्यक्षम् ॥९० ॥

व्रजभाजामजायन्त शार्करैश्चण्डमारुतैः[३७] ।
भञ्जद्भिः पादपव्रातं दुर्लभोन्मीलना दृशः ॥९१ ॥

व्रज इति । शार्करैः । शर्करा सिकता, तद्युक्तैः ॥९१ ॥

गोवर्धनो गुहास्येन गर्जितप्रतिनादिना ।
दशां दधौ गुरुमनु छात्रेस्य[३८] पठितश्रुतेः ॥९२ ॥

गोवर्धन इति । गुहैवास्यम् । गुरुमनु पठितश्रुतेः छात्रस्य दशां दधौ ॥९२ ॥

अम्भोधिशायिनो वासादम्भोधि[३९]भ्रान्तिगा इव ।
नन्दव्रजे पयोवाहा अवर्षन्नं[४०]म्बुधाविव ॥९३ ॥

अम्भोधिरिति । अम्भोधिशायिनः हरेः वासात् अम्भोधिरिति भ्रान्तिगाः सन्तः अम्बुधौ यथा वर्षन्ति तद्वत् अ(द)वर्षन् ॥९३ ॥

धाराः[४१] स्थूला अजायन्त व्रजनाशार्थमीरितैः ।
प्रसारिता इव करा ऐरावतकुलैर्गजैः ॥९४ ॥

धारा इति । ऐरावतस्य कुलमिव कुलं येषां तैः । एरावतकुलोत्पन्नैर्वा ॥९४ ॥

तावदम्बु ववर्षात्र व्रजे वारिमुचां गणः ।
बभूवाम्भोनिधिः शून्यो यावति प्रोद्धृतेऽम्भसा ॥९५ ॥

तावदिति । यावति अम्बुनि प्रोद्धृते सति, अम्भोनिधिः अम्भसा शून्यो बभूव तावदम्बु ववर्षेति ॥९५ ॥९६ ॥९७ ॥९८ ॥ (wrong) ॥

अतिवर्षातिवाताभ्यां पीड्यमाना व्रजौकसः ।
गोभिः सह जगन्नाथं शरणं प्रतिपेदिरे ॥९६ ॥

स गोवर्धनमुत्पाट्य कनिष्ठाग्रेन धारयन् ।
सर्वे विशत गर्तेऽस्मिन्निर्भया इत्यवोचत ॥९७ ॥

---

३७. °रेश्च°;
३८. °त्रे°;
३९. °दि.....का;
४०. अवर्षंन्न (अनुस्वार + अनुनासिक-Marathi Influence);
४१. °रा (विसर्ग dropped)

तद्वचःप्रत्ययात् सर्वांस्तं प्रविष्टान् सगोधनान् ।
नाऽबाधेतां वर्षवातौ[४२] सप्ताहान्येवमत्यगुः ॥९८ ॥

तद्वच इति । तद्वचःप्रत्ययात् तद्वाक्यविश्वासात् । तं (=गर्तं) प्रविष्टान् सर्वान् वर्षवातौ न अबाधेताम् । एवं सप्ताहम् अत्यगुः ॥[९८] ॥९९ ॥१०० ॥

आस्वादितमुरारातिसुन्दरास्यस्मितामृतान् ।
सर्वान् व्रजौकसस्तत्र न काऽपि विपदस्पृशत् ॥९९ ॥

जीमूतोद्यमवैफल्यं जीमूतोद्यमतो हरेः ।
अवेक्ष्य वारयामास जलदान् पाकशासनः ॥१०० ॥

जीमूत इति । हरेः कृष्णस्य जीमूतोद्यमतः पर्वतोद्यमात् जीमूतोद्यमवैफल्यं मेघोद्योगविफलत्वमवलोक्य । 'जीमूतौ मेघपर्वतौ' इति **अमरः** । [३.३.५९] ॥[१००] ॥१०१ ॥१०२ ॥(wrong) ॥

कृष्णो विद्योतमानार्कं गलिताम्बुदमम्बरम् ।
वीक्ष्य निर्याप्य तान् गर्तात् स्वस्थाने निदधे गिरिम् ॥१०१ ॥

अथ कृष्णं महेशानं जानानः पाकशासनः ।
एत्य मन्तूनपमृजंस्तत्पादौ शिरसाऽस्पृशत् ॥१०२ ॥

अथेति । मन्तूनपराधान् अपमृजन् सन् तत्पादौ शिरसाऽस्पृशत् ॥[१०२] ॥ १०३ ॥१०४ ॥

लोकातिशायिसौन्दर्यमुत्थायावेक्ष्य तं प्रभुम् ।
इन्द्रः सफलतां मेने सहस्रस्यात्मनो दृशाम् ॥१०३ ॥

उवाच च प्रभो नैव जाने तत्त्वमहं तव ।
ततो विहतयागत्वादकार्षं मन्तुमीदृशम् ॥१०४ ॥

आ[४३]गोऽप्युपाकुरुत मे भवद्गोचरमीदृशम् ।
त्वां[४४](त्वाऽऽ) वेदयत्प्रणामस्ते नोपकुर्यात्कथं न्वयम् ॥१०५ ॥

आगोऽपीति । भवान् गोचरो यस्मिन् तत् आगोऽपि अपराधोऽपि त्वाम्

---

४२. °वातो;
४३. अनोऽ°;
४४. P & B. both read त्वां वेद°;

आवेदयत् सत् उपाकुरुत, प्रणामः(मो) नोपकुर्यादिति कथम्, उपकुर्यादेव ॥[१०५] ॥१०६ ॥(wrong) ॥

शिक्ष्य[४५] एव यदीष्टोऽहं पातयेर्मां निजात्पदात् ।
तथाऽप्यस्ति व्यथा नैव त्वत्पदालम्बिनो मम ॥१०६ ॥

शिक्ष्य एवेति। त्वत्पदालम्बिनः त्वच्चरणाश्रयिणः। त्वत्पदं वैकुण्ठश्च। तस्याश्रयिणः। स्वर्गाऽपेक्षयाऽपि वैकुण्ठस्याधिक्यात् ॥[१०६] ॥१०७ ॥ १०८ ॥(wrong) ॥

इति प्रगल्भया वाचा पौरन्दर्या प्रतोषितः ।
विहस्योवाच भगवान् प्रीतोऽस्मि व्रियतां वरः ॥१०७ ॥

न तं पश्यामि भगवन् यस्त्वामवरयन् वरः ।
गोचरं मनसो नित्यं ततस्त्वां तादृशं वृणे ॥१०८ ॥

न तमिति। हे भगवन्, तं वरं न पश्यामि यः वरः नित्यं मनसः गोचरं त्वाम् अवरयन् अपकृष्टं कुर्वन् तादृशं न पश्यामीत्यर्थः। ततः(तो) हेतोः तादृशं मनसः नित्यं गोचरं त्वां वृणे। 'नित्यं मन्मनसः गोचरो भव' इत्येव कामये, नान्यदित्यर्थः ॥[१०८] ॥१०९ ॥११० ॥(wrong) ॥

इत्यर्थितेऽभ्यनुज्ञाते हरिणेन्द्रः प्रणम्य तम् ।
अनुज्ञाप्य दिवं भेजे प्राप्तानन्देन चेतसा ॥१०९ ॥

स्वस्य स्वर्गादपेतस्य पुरे[४६]वाधिगमे दिवः ।
हेतुं कृष्णप्रणा[४७]माख्यान् मेने चेन्द्रः शतं[४८] क्रतून् ॥११० ॥

स्वस्येति। स्वर्गादपेतस्य स्वर्गाद्वियुक्तस्य। पुरेव पूर्वमिव ॥[110] ॥१११ ॥ ११२ ॥११३ ॥(wrong) ॥

एकादशीमुपवसन्नन्दः प्रत्यूषविभ्रमात् ।
कदाचिद्यमुनावारि निशीथे स्नातुमाविशत् ॥१११ ॥

तमकाले प्रविष्टाम्बुं पाशै रचितबन्धनः ।
निनाय[४९] स्वप्रभूपान्तं सलिलाधीशकिङ्करः ॥११२ ॥

---

४५. शीक्ष्य;
४६. °पुरोवाग्धि°;
४७. कृष्णं प्र.....न्मुने;
४८. शतक्रतून्;
४९. विनाय;

जलान्नँन्दमनुन्मग्नं[५०] समयेनापि भूयसा।
यादसा गिलितं मत्वा विलेपुर्व्रजवासिनः ॥११३ ॥

जलादिति। यादसा जलजन्तुना। 'यादांसि जलजन्तवः' इति **अमरः**। [१.१०.२०] ॥[११३] ॥११४ ॥११५ ॥

तदा विदितसर्वार्थो भगवानाविशञ्ज[५१]लम्।
ययौ[५२] प्रत्याहरन्नन्दं वरुणं[५३]स्वामिकां पुरीम् ॥११४ ॥

आगतं कृष्णमालोक्य प्रांशोः[५४] सिंहासनादयम्।
अवरुह्याभिगम्याशु तत्पादौ शिरसाऽस्पृशत् ॥११५ ॥

आगतमिति। प्रांशोः उन्नतात् ॥[११५] ॥११६ ॥११७ ॥११८ (wrong) ॥

विधिवत्पूजितस्तेन सूपविष्टो[५५] वरासने।
बद्धाञ्जलिमुवाचेदं[५६] तिष्ठन्तं[५७] वरुणं हरिः ॥११६ ॥

अज्ञानाध्रियतां[५८] नाम किङ्करेण पिता मम।
ज्ञातैश्वर्येण भवता किं[५९]न प्रत्यर्पितोऽभवत् ॥११७ ॥

तमूचे वरुणः स्वामिन् मदान्नानर्पणं पितुः।
किन्तु त्वद्दर्शनेच्छतस्तथाऽप्याग इदं ध्रुवम् ॥११८ ॥

तमिति। अनर्पणं मदात् न, किन्तु त्वद्दर्शनेच्छयेति। तथापि त्वद्दर्शनार्थप्रयत्ने सत्यपि इदं मदाचरितम् आग एव ध्रुवम् ॥[११८] ॥११९ ॥१२० ॥(wrong) ॥

---

५०. °न्नद°;
५१. °विशं (= शन्) (अनुस्वार for अनुनासिक- Marathi influence);
५२. ययो;
५३. °णः स्वा;
५४. प्राञ्चोः;
५५. सूपं°;
५६. °ञ्जुलिमवा°;
५७. तिष्ठतं;
५८. तांन्नाम; (अनुस्वार + अनुनासिक- Marathi influence);
५९. किन्न;

आगो[६०] हि किङ्करत्वस्य व्यापकं भवति प्रभो ।
तदभावादकैङ्कर्यं स्यादितीदं मया कृतम् ॥११९ ॥

आगस्कृद्दण्ड्य[६१] इत्येतद्द्वितीयादिकगोचरम्' ।
आकर्ण्येदं प्रसादं स्वं स्मितेन व्याञ्जयद्धरिः ॥१२० ॥

आग इति । 'आगस्कृत् दण्ड्यः' इत्येतद्वाक्यं द्वितीयादिकगोचरं द्वितीयतृतीय-अपराधः गोचरः यस्मिन् तत् । तद्वाक्यं प्रथमा(म)कृतापराधिनः दण्ड्यरं[६२] न किन्तु द्वितीयादि अपराधपरेण योजनीयम् । स्मितेन प्रसादं व्याञ्जयत् व्यक्तीकृतवान् ॥[१२०] ॥१२१ ॥(wrong) ॥

ऐश्वर्यकाष्ठां विश्रान्तां वरुणे जानतामयम् ।
शान्तो बभूव सभ्यानां श्रुतोभयगिरां भ्रमः ॥१२१ ॥

ऐश्वर्यमिति । ऐश्वर्यकाष्ठां वरुणे विश्रान्ताम् इति जानतां, श्रुता उभयोः गीः यैः तेषां सभ्यानां श्रमः शान्तो बभूव । 'कृष्णदर्शनात्पूर्वं वरुणः एव सर्वश्रेष्ठः इति तेषां भ्रमः, सः तदानीं शान्तः' इत्यर्थः ॥[१२१] ॥१२२ ॥ (wrong) ॥

आनीतो यादसां पत्युर्दृशा संसूचितानयैः[६३] ।
वीक्ष्य तत्रापि सोत्कर्षं कृष्णं नन्दोऽत्यमोदत[६४] ॥१२२ ॥

आनीत [इति.॥ यादसां पत्युः दृशा संसूचितः आनयो(यः) आनयनं येषां तैः । किङ्करैरिति शेषः । आनीतः नन्दः ॥[१२२] ॥१२३ ॥ (wrong) ॥

तदुपहृतममूल्यं वस्तुजातं परेषाम्
असुलभमनुगृह्णन्[६५] दर्शनेनाप्तकामः ।

अनुगतम[६६]तिदूरं संनिवर्[६७]त्याम्बुनाथं
व्रजमभजद[६८]थेशो नन्दमादाय तूर्णम् ॥१२३ ॥

---

६०. अगो;

६१. °दण्ड;

६२. दण्ड्यरं (= दण्डयं) (= दण्डार्हं) दण्डाय अलं दण्ड्यलं (रलयोरभेदः) -Marathi influence);

६३. P. marginal gloss किङ्करैरिति इति शेषः।

६४. ह्यत्यमोदित first letter not clear due to over-writing.

६५. °गृह्णद्द°;

६६. °मिति दूरं;

६७. °निवृत्या°;

६८. °दशेशो;

तदिति। आप्तकाम अत एव दर्शनेनैव अनुगृह्णन् ॥[१२३] ॥१२४ ॥ (wrong) ॥

सकृष्णं तं दृष्ट्वा व्रजपतिमथैतेन गदितं
स्ववृत्तान्तं सर्वं वरुणविभवं चानुपमितम्।
नतिं कृष्णे तस्याप्यनुपहतवीर्ये[६९] श्रुतवतां
तदीयानां हर्षः परिमितिमगान्नो गुणतया ॥१२४॥

सकृष्णमिति। तदीयानां हर्षः गुणतया परिमितिं परिमाणं न अगात्। अपरिमितः (तो) हर्षः(र्षो) बभूवेत्यर्थः। हर्षस्यापि गुणत्वात्। परिमितिरूपं गुणं नागादिति **च**। गुणे गुणानङ्गीकारात् ॥१२५ ॥१२६ ॥१२७(१२४ ॥१२५ ॥१२६) ॥

[इति रानडे इत्युपनामक श्यामरायसूनुविष्णुविरचितायां नीलकण्ठकविकृत- यादवेन्द्रमहोदयकाव्यस्य टिप्पन्यां पञ्चमः सर्गः] ॥५ ॥

यद्धीर्जगज्जातमिवासुरारेस्तनूरखेदाऽभृत[७०] शास्त्रजातम्।
त्रिविक्रमाभिख्यतदात्मजन्मा यः पार्वती नन्दनतामयासीत् ॥१२५॥

नीलकण्ठेन तेनास्मिन् यादवेन्द्रमहोदये।
कृते काव्ये पञ्चमश्च सर्गः सम्पूर्णतां गतः ॥१२७(१२६) ॥५॥

---

६९. वीर्ये;
७०. °भृशं (श due to the following श)

षष्ठः सर्गः

[1]अथ कदाचिदयं जगतांपतिः क्वचन रम्यविहारभुवि स्थितः ।
रमयितुं रमणीश्चरितव्रता अतनुतातनुतापजुषो मतिम्[2] ॥१ ॥

अथेति । अतनुतापजुषः मदनतापभाजः तरुणीः रमयितुं मतिम् अतनुत कृतवान् ॥१ ॥

अ[3]परवारिनिधौ शतपर्विकाभ्रमवतामसिते रथवाजिनाम् ।
विचकृषे निवहेन तदाऽनु तं रविरथोऽविरथों[4]न्नततां जहौ ॥२ ॥

अपरि(रे)ति । तदा कृष्णेप्सितरमणीक्रीडनकाले असिते अपरवारिनिधौ पश्चिमसमुद्रे, तस्य अ(स्या)सितत्वात् । शतपर्विका दूर्वेति भ्रमवतां रथवाजिनां निवहेन रविरथः तमनु समुद्रमनु समुद्राभिमुखं विचकृषे कृष्टः । अविः सूर्यः, उन्नततां जहौ अस्ताद्रिं जगामेत्यर्थः । 'दूर्वा तु शतपर्विका' 'अवयः शैलमेषार्काः', इति च **अमरः** ।(२.४.१५८ and ३.३.२०७) ॥२ ॥

क्षितिभृता वसुमान् यदि मन्यते हृतवसुर्भवतीति विजानता ।
उपयता रविणा[5]स्तमहीभृतं वसुगणोऽसुगणोऽपिदधे द्रुतम् ॥३ ॥

क्षितिरिति । क्षितिभृता राज्ञा पर्वतेन **च** । वसुमान् द्रव्यमान् किरणवांश्च । मन्यते यदि ज्ञायते यदि । तदा हृतवसुः हृतद्रव्यः हृतकिरणश्च । भवतीति विजानता रविणा अस्तमहीभृतम् अस्ताचलम् । अस्तः निन्द्यः (न्द्यो) दुष्ट इति यावत् यः (यो) महीभृत् राजा, तं च उपयता गच्छता सता, असुगणः असङ्ख्यः वसुगणः द्रव्यगणः किरणगणश्च । द्रुतं शीघ्रम् अपिदधे आच्छादितः । 'सूर्योऽस्तं गत' **इत्यर्थः** । 'वसुर्हृदेऽग्नौ रश्मौ च वसु तोये धने मणौ ।' इति **हैमः** । 'नुत्तनुन्नास्तनिष्ठ्यूत(ता)-विद्धक्षिप्तेरिताः समाः ।' इति **अमरः** ।(३.१.८७) ॥३ ॥

रविरम[6]न्यत सन्निहितान्ततां यदत उज्झितवान् परितापनाम् ।
भवति सन्निहितान्ततया स्वया विदितया दितया[7]प्यगुणो जनः ॥४ ॥

---

१. P. begins with श्रीकृष्णाय नमः । B. begins with श्री गणेशाय नमः ।
२. मतिः;
३. अपरि° (रि due to the following रि);
४. °थोंन्न (अनुस्वार + अनुनासिक- Marathi influence)
५. P. marginal quotation नुत्तनुन्नास्तनिष्ठ्यूतविद्धक्षिप्तै(प्ते)रिताः समाः । इति **अमरः** ।
६. °मंन्यत (additional अनुस्वार-scribal peculiarity-Marathi influence);
७. P. marginal quotations 'छिन्नं छातं लूनं कृत्तं दातं दितं छितं वृक्णम् ।' इति **अमरः** । & 'निकृष्टप्रतिकृष्टार्वरेफयाप्यवमाधमाः ।' इति **अमरः** ।

रविरिति। यत् यतः रविः सन्निहितान्ततां समीपनाशताम् अमन्यत, अतः परितापनां तापजनकत्वम् उज्झितवान्। स्वया स्वकीयया सन्निहितान्ततया विदितया सत्या जनः दितयाप्यगुणः दिताः खण्डिताः याप्याः निकृष्टाः गुणाः, दोषा इत्यर्थः यस्य तादृशः(शो) भवति। 'छिन्नं छातं लूनं कृत्तं दातं दितं छितं वृक्णम्।' इति **अमरः**। (३.१.१०३) 'निकृष्टप्रतिकृष्टार्वरेफयाप्यवमाधमाः।' इति **अमरः**। (३.१.५४) ॥४॥

महस एष विरोचनजन्मनो विधृतवान् [८]ह्रसिमानमुपानयन्।
हरिरवामनभावमनातपो व्यथयतोऽथ यतो भयमत्यगात्[९] ॥५॥

महस इति। व्यथयतः यतः विरोचनजन्मनो महसः सकाशात् भयं **कर्म**, अति अतिशयेन अगात्, लोक इति शेषः। तस्य विरोचनजन्मनो महसः सूर्योत्पन्नतेजसः बलिपराक्रमस्य **च** अनातप एव हरिर्विष्णुः, अवामनभावं दैर्घ्यं त्रिविक्रमत्वं **च** धृतवान् ॥५॥

चलतरोरपराह्णसमीरणैरयमकम्पत नूनमनातपः।
गत उदेत्य तमो ग्रसते न इत्यसुतरां सुतरां भयपूर्णताम् ॥६॥

चलतरोरिति। चलश्चासौ तरुश्च, तस्य अनातपः अपराह्णसमीरणैः अ(र)कम्पत। तमः उदेत्य नः ग्रसते इति सुतराम् अत्यन्तम् असुतरां दुस्तरां भयपूर्णतां गतः सन् अ(न्र)कम्पतेति नूनं शङ्के, **इत्युत्प्रेक्षा**।।६॥

प्रथमदिग्दयितामहिमांशुना स्वमभि संदिशता द्रुतमागमम्।
निहितदौत्य इवायमनातपो गततया[१०] ततया ददृशेऽभि[११] तम् ॥७॥

प्रथममिति। प्रथमदिगेव दयिता, तां, स्वं स्वकीयं द्रुतं शीघ्रम् आगमं संदिशता अहिमांशुना सूर्येण निहितदौत्य इव अयमनातपः ददृशे, लोकैरिति शेषः। तामभि पूर्वदिशाभिमुखं ततया विस्तृतया, गततया गत्या उपलक्षितः इति अनातपविशेषणम् ॥७॥

सविधमम्बुजिनीविरहं विदन् ज्वलितशोक हुताशनतापितः।
अरुणिमानमविन्दत भानुमांश्चरमगोऽरमगोचरतां भजन् ॥८॥

---

८. Both P. & B. write -हसि° a clear case/instance of the influence of the Marathi way of writing/spelling in Devanāgarī.

९. P. Marginal gloss लोक इति शेषः।

१०. P. marginal gloss गत्या उपलक्षितः।

११. °शोऽभि;

सविधमिति । चरमगः पश्चिमाद्रिगः भानुमान् अरम् अत्यन्तम् अगोचरतां भजन् सन् अरुणिमानमविन्दत । शोकहुताशनतापितत्वम् अरुणिम्नि हेतुः ॥८ ॥

रविहयैर्विकलाङ्गनियन्तृकैर्विषमदेशमपूर्वमहीभृतः ।
गमित एकरथाङ्गरथोऽपतत्सहहयोऽहह योऽम्बुधिमाप सः ॥९ ॥

रविरिति । विकलाङ्गः न्यूनावयवः नियन्ता येषां तैः रविहयैः यः एकं रथाङ्गं चक्रं यस्य एतादृशो रथः पूर्वमहीभृतः विषमदेश (शं) गमितः सन् अपतत् । सः रथः सहहयः हयैः सहितः अम्बुधिमाप । अहह इति खेदे ॥९ ॥

चरमदिश्यरुणोऽन्य उदित्वरो[१२] विघटितप्रियचक्रवधूगणः ।
वितनुते स्म तमःसखतां गतः कमलिनीमलिनीप्रियवर्जिताम् ॥१० ॥

चरमेति । चरमदिशि उदित्वरः अन्यः अरुणः अरुणिमा अरुणश्च । प्रसिद्धारुणपेक्षया अस्य वैपरीत्यं कथयति । प्रसिद्धारुणः घटितप्रियचक्रवधूगणः, नाऽयं तथा । स तमोनाशम् अलिनीसहितां कमलिनीं च करोति । अयं तमःसख्यं गतः सन् अलिनीप्रियवर्जितां कमलिनीं वितनुते ॥१० ॥

प्रकृतसान्ध्यि[१३]करैररुणं जगद्विनशन[१४]क्षमया समतां ययौ ।
दलितकौरवसैन्यतनूसृतक्षतजयात्तजयार्जुनसायकैः ॥११ ॥

प्रसृत इति । प्रसृता[:] सन्ध्यायां भवाः सान्ध्या ये कराः, तैः अरुणं जगत्, आत्तजया[:] प्राप्तजया ये अर्जुनसायकाः तैः, दलितं कौरवसैन्यं, तस्य तनूसृतं क्षतजं रक्तं यस्यां सा । तया विनशनक्षमया कुरुक्षेत्रभूम्या समतां ययौ । कराणामरुणत्वात् क्षतजयुक्तभूम्याः साम्यम् ॥११ ॥

रविरुचिक्षयकारिपितृप्रसूसमयरागविलोप्युदितं तमः ।
तमस आहतसत्त्वरजः[१५]क्षयं विदधतोऽदधतोपमितिं पराम् ॥१२ ॥

रविरिति । रविरुचिक्षयकारी यो (यः) पितृप्रसूसमयरागः सायंसन्ध्याऽरुणिमा, तस्य विलोपि उदितं तमः, आहतं सत्त्वं सत्त्वगुणो येन तादृशं यद्रजः रजोगुणः, तस्य क्षतं विदधतः तमसः तमोगुणस्य पराम् उपमितिम् उपमानम् अदधत । रविरुचेः सत्त्वसाम्यं, रागस्य रजः साम्यं, तमसः तमोगुणसाम्यम् ॥१२ ॥

---

१२. °त्वरे;
१३. °साध्य° (अनुस्वार dropped) ;
१४. P. marginal gloss- कुरुक्षेत्रं;
१५. रजक्षयं (विसर्ग dropped & jointly written);

तदुपकण्ठरथाङ्गवियोगिनीध्वनितदैन्यरवश्रवणाज्जनाः ।
विलपतीत्यविदुर्गतभर्तृका कमलिनी मलिनीकृतमानसा ॥१३ ॥

तदिति । तस्याः कमलिन्याः उपकण्ठे समीपे रथाङ्गवियोगिनीनां ध्वनितं दैन्यं यस्मिन् तादृशो यो रवः, तस्य श्रवणात् जनाः, गतभर्तृका अत एव मलिनीकृतमानसा कमलिनी विलपतीति अविदुः ज्ञातवन्तः ॥१३ ॥

गलितचाक्षुषताऽसुभृतां तदा न तिमिरान्निबिडत्वमुपेयुषः ।
भुवनचक्षुष एव विलोपतस्त[१६]नुभृतो नु भृतोरुतरभ्रमाः ॥१४ ॥

गलितेति । तदा सायङ्काले असुभृतां प्राणिनां गलितचाक्षुषता निबिडत्वमुपेयुषः तिमिरात् अ(द)न्धकारात् चक्षुर्जन्यप्रत्यक्षराहित्यम् । न जाता किन्तु भुवनचक्षुषः सूर्यस्य भुवनानां नेत्रस्य **च**। **जात्यभिप्रायेणैकवचनम्**। विलोपत एव। तनुभृतः प्राणिनः, भृतः उरुतरः भ्रमः तिमिरेणैव गलितचाक्षुषत्वमित्याकारकः यैः तादृशः(शा) भवन्ति । भुवनचक्षुषः(षो) विलोपादेव आन्ध्यं न तु तिमिरादिति **कवेः कल्पना**। **नु वाक्यालङ्कारे**। 'कर्मसाक्षी जगच्चक्षुः इति **अमरः** ।(१.३.३१) [३९] ॥१४ ॥

जगति वस्तु न कृष्णविवर्जितं निगमतत्त्वविदां यदितीरि[१७]तम् ।
तदृतमातनुताम्बुदमेचकं बत तमस्ततमस्तमिताधिकम् ॥१५ ॥

जगतीति । कृष्णः विष्णुः नैल्यमिति **च** प्रतीयते । तद्विवर्जितं वस्तु जगति नास्तीति निगमरहस्यज्ञातृणां यत् ईरितं तत् **कर्म**, अम्बुदमेचकं मेघवन्नीलं, ततं विस्तृतम्, अस्तमितम् अधिकं यस्मात्, सर्वोत्कृष्टमिति यावत्, तमः **कर्तृ**, ऋतं सत्यम् अतनुत । सर्वत्रान्धकारस्य सद्भावात् ॥१५ ॥

अपगतान्यविलोकनमीक्षिताम्बुदविनीलवपुः सु[१८]दृशां गणैः ।
उदरवर्तितसर्वजगत्तमो रुचितमाचितमाधवतौ[१९]ल्यकम् ॥१६ ॥

अपगत इति । सुदृशां दृष्टिमतां स्त्रीणां **च** गणैः, अपगतान्यविलोकनं यथा स्यात्तथेति **माधवपक्षे** क्रियाविशेषणम् । ईक्षितम् अम्बुदवन्नीलं वपुर्यस्य । **पक्षे**-अपगतम् अन्यविलोकनं यस्मिन् तत्, तमसोऽपि ईक्षितं दृष्टम् अम्बुदवन्नीलं वपुर्यस्य तत् । उदरवर्तितसर्वजगत् सर्वत्र तमोव्यापनात्, **पक्षे**-ब्रह्माण्डोदरत्वात् । आचितं माधवस्य विष्णोस्तौल्यकं साम्यं येन तत् तमः रुचितम् अरोचतेत्यर्थः ॥१६ ॥

---

१६. °स्तुनु° (उ on the strength of the following उ);
१७. तं् (wrongly spelt for तं/तम्- orthographical lapse);
१८. स°;
१९. °तो°;

गुरुकुलायगतं द्विजमण्डलं विगलिताध्ययनध्वनि सर्वतः ।
निबिडसंतमसे[२०] समये तदा स्वपनमाप न मानमिदं पुनः ॥१७॥

गुरुरिति । गुरुर्महान् यो(यः) कुलायो नीडं, तस्मिन् गतम् । **पक्षे**-गुरुकुलाय गुरुगृहं प्रति गतं प्राप्तम् । 'गत्यर्थकर्मणि द्वितीयाचतुर्थ्यौ चेष्टायामनध्वनि ।' इति **सूत्रात्** । (**पाणिनि**-२.३.१२) द्विजमण्डलं पक्षिसमूहः, **पक्षे**-बटुसमूहः । सर्वत्र । विगलितः, अधि उपरि, अयनं गतिः, तेन ध्वनिर्यस्य तत् । **पक्षे**- स्पष्टम् । स्वपनं स्वापमाप । इदं स्वपनं पुनः मा(र्मा)नं परिमाणं न आप-अतिशयितां निद्रां प्रापेत्यर्थः ॥१७॥

प्रतिनिशान्तसमिन्धितदीपिकामषिकयोद्गतया तिमिरच्छलात् ।
इदमदोजगदन्तरमायतं निजगलेऽजगलेन ससाम्यया ॥१८॥

प्रतीति । अजगलेन हरकण्ठेन ससाम्यया साम्यवत्या उद्गतया प्रतिनिशान्तं प्रतिगृहं समिन्धिता या दीपिकाः, तासां मषि(षी)कया तिमिरच्छलात् अ(द)-न्धकारकपटात्, इदं दृश्यमानम् आयतं दीर्घम्, अदोजगदन्तरम्-इदं च अदश्च अमू, अमू च ते जगती च अदोजगती-एतल्लोकपरलोकावित्यर्थः । द्वयोरन्तरं मध्यं निजगले गिलितं-भूम्यन्तरं च तमोग्रस्तमभूदित्यर्थः । 'अजा विष्णुहरछा(च्छा)-गाः ।' इति **अमरः** । (३.३.३०) ॥१८॥

नयनसञ्जितसन्तमसां जनैः परमदृश्यत नाधिगतो निधिः ।
स्वसदनेऽथ जनैर्भृशतारकोत्करमयो रमयोज्झितसन्निधौ ॥१९॥

नयनमिति । रमया लक्ष्म्या स्वसदने स्वगृहे कमले **च** उज्झितसन्निधौ त्यक्तसान्निध्ये सति, नयनयोः सञ्जितं योजितं सन्तमसमेव अञ्जनं यैस्ते, तैः ज(र्ज)-नैः भृ(र्भृ)शं यस्तारकाणामुत्करः समूहस्तन्मयः तद्रूपः निधिः अदृश्यत, परं केवलं दृष्टः न अधिगतः न आसादितः न प्राप्त इत्यर्थः । निधिदर्शनार्थं नेत्रे अञ्जनं क्रियते' **इति सर्वप्रसिद्धम्** ॥१९॥

स्वमवदातगुणं स्म यतः स्वयं प्रकटयन्ति तमःसमयोदिताः ।
अपि खला इव ता लघवोऽ[२१]भवन् बत सदात्तसदाख्यकतारकाः ॥२०॥

स्वमिति । सद्भ्यः साधुभ्यः आत्ता प्राप्ता सदिति आख्या याभिस्ताः सदाख्या[:] ता एव सदाख्यकाश्च तास्तारकाश्च । **यद्वा**- सदेति भिन्नं पदम् । सत् उत्तमः, सत् इति नक्षत्रपर्यायश्च । यतः हेतोः तमःसमये उदिताः सत्यः, स्वं स्वकीयम् अवदातगुणं

---

२०. °सन्तमसत्स°;
२१. °वा भ°;

नैर्मल्यगुणम् । अवदातः निर्दोषः य गुणः शौर्यादिस्तं च । स्वयं प्रकटयन्ति स्म । अतः खला इव दुष्टा इव लघवः स्वल्पपरिमाणाः नीचाश्च अभवन् । तमःसमयोदिता इति विशेषणं **खलपक्षेऽपि** योजनीयम् । 'इन्द्रोऽपि लघुतां याति स्वयं प्रख्यापितैर्गुणैः ' **इत्युक्तेः** । समयाः शपथाचारकालसिद्धान्तसंविदः ।' इति **अमरः** । (३.३.१४९) ॥२१ ॥(२०) ॥

समयजारसमागमतः सुधाकिरणगर्भमुपेत्य दिगङ्गना[२२] ।
दशशताक्षवधूर्मुखपाण्डुतामधिगताधिगता च वियोगिनी ॥२१ ॥

समय इति । दशशताक्षः इन्द्रः, तस्य वधूः दिगङ्गना दिगेवाङ्गना, पूर्वदिगित्यर्थः । समयः सायङ्काल एव जारः, तत्समागमात् । सुधाकिरणश्चन्द्र एव गर्भः, तम् उपेत्य मुखपाण्डुताम् अधिगता तां दृष्ट्वा वियोगिनी वियुक्ता, **जात्येकवचनम्** । आधिगता आधिं मनोव्यथां गता प्राप्ता । दशशताक्षेतिपदेन इन्द्रस्य नेत्रबाहुल्येऽपि वध्वा जारसमागमः कृत **इति आश्चर्यम्** ॥२१ ॥

उदयशैलतिरोहितवर्ष्मणो हिमरुचेः[२३] प्रसृता किरणावलिः ।
उदयजौषधिकान्तिरिति भ्रमं व्यधित साधितसान्द्रतमश्छिदा ॥२२ ॥

उदय इति । साधिता सान्द्रतमसः छिदा छेदो यया सा किरणपङ्क्तिः उदयपर्वतसम्बन्धिनीनामोषधीनां कान्तिरियमिति भ्रमं व्यधित कृतवती, जनानामिति शेषः ॥२२ ॥

उदयगैरिकभूमिचरानिलाऽऽहितरजोऽमृतमूर्तितयाऽरुणः ।
उदयसानुगतः समबोधयद्धिमकरो मकरोत्तमकेतनम् ॥२३ ॥

उदय इति । उदयपर्वतसम्बन्धिनी या गैरिकभूमिः, तस्यां सञ्चरणशीलो योऽनिलः वायुस्तेन आहितं रजो यस्यां सा । अमृतं जलं पीयूषं [च], तत्स्वरूपा मूर्तिर्यस्य, तस्य भावस्तत्ता, तया अरुणः । चन्द्रः(न्द्रो) मकरोत्तमकेतनं मदनं समबोधयत्, मदनोद्दीपनं चकारेत्यर्थः ॥२३ ॥

अनृ[२४]णतां नयता भुवनं तदा करकशाभिहतं वसुमालिना ।
तिमिरकश्मलमाप विधुः करामृतमदस्तमदै[२५]स्तदिहाकरोत् ॥२४ ॥

---

२२. दिदङ्गना (द due to the preceding दि);
२३. °रुचः;
२४. P. marginal quotation-'ऋणं देये जले दुर्गे च' इति हैमः ।
२५. °स्तमदः स्तदिहाकरत् । (विसर्ग + स् both used-scribal peculiarity-an instance of local (Marathi) influence.

अनृणतामिति । अनृणतां ऋणराहित्यं जलराहित्यं **च** । नयता प्रापयता वसून् किरणान्, वसूनि धनानि **च** । मलते धारया(य)तीति, तेन सूर्यणे (सूर्येण) धनिकेन **च** । करा एव कशाः ताडनरज्जवः, **पक्षे**-कराभ्यां कशया **च** । **यद्वा**-करधृता या कशा तया **च,** अभिहतं ताडितं, भुवनं जगत् लोकश्च । तिमिरमेव कश्मलं मोहम् आप । तमदः-तमु ग्लानौ, तमः ग्लानिः अन्धकारश्च । तं द्यति खण्डयतीति तमदः विधुः चन्द्रः । तत् तस्मात् मूर्च्छितत्वाद्धेतोः, अदः एतत् करामृतं किरणरूपममृतं करस्थितजलं **च,** इह जगति आकिरत् । 'ऋणशब्दो दुर्गभूमौ जले च' इति **कौमुद्यम्** । 'ऋणं देये जले दुर्गे' इति **हैमः** । (२.१३५). भुवनं तोयलोकयोः' इति **अमरः** । अश्वादेस्ताडनी कशा' इति **अमरः** [२.१०.३१] । वसुर्हृदेऽग्नौ रश्मौ च वसु तोये शने मणौ ।' इति **अमरः** ।मल मल्ल धारणे । मूर्च्छा तु कश्मलं मोहः' इति **अमरः** ।(१.८.१०९) ॥२४ ॥

विरलभूमिरुहा वनराजयः श्रितसितासितगोमहिषा इव ।
विधृतसंतमसाः क्वचिदन्यतो रुरुचिरे रुचिरेन्दुकरान्विताः ॥२५ ॥

विरला इति । विरला भूमिरुहा वृक्षा यासु ताः वनराजयः, क्वचित् विधृतसंतमसत्वेन सितगोसाम्यं, क्वचित् रुचिरेन्दुकरान्वितत्वेन असित-महिषसाम्यम् । रुरुचि [रे] शोभिता इत्यर्थः ॥२५ ॥

हरिरनन्तसखः श्रयतेऽधुना सितममुं कलशाब्धिमसाविति ।
अकुरुतेन्दुकरैरतिपाण्डुरा वसुमती सुमतीनपि सभ्रमान् ॥२६ ॥

हरिरिति । इन्दुकरैरतिपाण्डुरा वसुमती सुमतीनपि असौ अनन्तः शेषावतारत्वात् बलभद्रः, तत्सखः हरिः अधुना सितममुं कलशाब्धिं श्रयते इति भ्रमसहितान् अकुरुत । इन्दुकरकृतधावल्यस्य कलशाब्धिना क्षीरसमुद्रेण साम्यात् । क्षीरसमुद्रे भगवद्वास्तव्यात् सशेषः हरिरेवात्र वसतीति भ्रमं कृतवतीत्यर्थः ॥२६ ॥

हततमोवसनां करमर्दितक्षितिधरोरुपयोधरमण्डलाम् ।
निहिततेजसमातनुतावनीप्रियतमां यतमाननिशापतिः ॥२७ ॥[२६]

हतमिति । यतमानः उद्यन् यत्नं कुर्वन् स चासौ निशापतिश्चन्द्रः जारश्च । हतं तमोरूपं वसनं यस्या[:] सा । करैः किरणैः कराभ्यां **च** । मर्दितं स्पृष्टं धृतं **च** । क्षितिधराः पर्वतास्त एव उरु उत्कृष्टं पयोधरमण्डलं यस्याः सा । अवनी एव प्रियतमा, ताम् । निहितं तेजो(जः) प्रकाशः शुक्रं **च** यस्यां सा, तादृशीमतनुत कृतवान् । 'शुक्रं तेजोरेतसी च' इति **अमरः** ।(२.६.६२) ॥२७ ॥

---

२६. P. marg. qu. शुक्रं तेजोरेतसी च' इति **अमरः** ।

द्रवमयान् हृदयानि कृतक्रुधां मृगदृशां सह चान्द्रमसोपलैः ।
विकसितं च तदीशमुखैस्तदा सकुमुदैः कुमुदैन्दवरश्मिभिः ॥२८ ॥

द्रवमयानिति । कोः पृथिव्याः मुदः लोकसुखकरा इति यावत्, ये औ(ऐ)न्दवरश्मयः तैर्हेतुभिः चान्द्रमसोपलैः चन्द्रकान्तमणिभिः सह कृतक्रुधां मानिनीनां सुदृशां स्त्रीणां हृदयानि द्रवम् अयान् प्राप्तानि । तदा तस्मिन् काले सकुमुदैः नीलोत्पलैः सह, तदीशमुखैः तासां स्त्रीणां ये ईशाः भर्तारस्तैर्विकसितम् ॥२८ ॥

दलितनीलसरोजनवासवग्रसनमत्तमधुव्रतगुञ्जितैः ।
मधुलिहां कमलोदरभाग्ययौ समुदयो मुदयोगमनु व्यथाम् ॥२९ ॥

दलितमिति । दलितानि विकसितानि यानि नवसरोजानि नूतनकमलानि, तेषां यो नवासवः नूतनमकरन्दः तस्य ग्रसनेन भक्षणेन मत्ता ये मधुव्रताः भ्रमराः, तेषां गुञ्जितैः **हेतुभिः**, कमलोदरभाक् कमलोदरबद्धः यः मधुलिहां भ्रमराणां समुदयः, मुदः अयोगं हर्षाभावमनु व्यथां ययौ । प्रथमं कमलोदरबद्धत्वेन हर्षाभावं पश्चात् सजातीयमत्तमधुकरगुञ्जितश्रवणेन व्यथां प्रापेत्यर्थः ॥२९ ॥

तुहि[२७]नदीधितिकान्तितिरोहिता [धवलमाल्यधरा धवलाम्बरा][२८] ।
प्रियमभिप्रययौ मदनेरिता सुरमणी रमणीयगुणं तदा ॥३० ॥

तुहिनदीधितिरिति । तुहिनदीधितेश्चन्द्रस्य कान्त्या तिरोहिता कृतावगुण्ठना, धवलमाल्यधरा, धवलमम्बरं वस्त्रं यस्या[:] सा । **पक्षे**-धवलम् आकाशं यया सा, मदनेन ईरिता सुरमणी अर्थात् उक्तविशेषणैः ज्योत्स्नाभिसारिका रमणीयगुणं प्रियं चन्द्रमभि चन्द्रं प्रति ययौ ॥३० ॥

मिलितनीलसरोरुहकैरवद्युतिमिषेण विशालसरोऽङ्गणे ।
तिमिरशीतमयूखरुची तदा व्यतनुतां तनुतान्तिकरं रणम् ॥३१ ॥

मिलितेति । तिमिरकान्तिः शीतमयूखकान्तिश्च । द्वे अपि, विशालसर एव अङ्गणं युद्धाङ्गणं, तस्मिन् मिलिता मेलनं प्राप्ता, नीलसरोरुहाणां कैरवाणां श्वेतकमलानां या द्युतिः त(स्त)न्मिषेण तत्कपटेन तनोस्तान्तिकरं ग्लानिसम्पादकं रणं व्यतनुताम् । नीलसरोरुहकान्तितिमिरकान्त्योश्च साम्यम् । कैरवद्युतिचन्द्रद्युतेश्च साम्यम् ॥३१ ॥

---

२७. °नु° (on the analogy of previous उ in तु);
२८. [ ] P. marg. gloss- अर्थात् ज्योत्स्नाभिसारिका ।

महितपादमजाड्यवतां परं प्रशमयन्तममन्दतरं तमः ।
हरिमवेक्ष्य न यः सुरताश्रयी क्लमयुजामयुजां च युजां न सः ॥३२ ॥

महितमिति । अजाड्यवतां सन्तापशालिनां, **पक्षे**-पण्डितानां, महिताः पादाः किरणाः, **पक्षे**-महितौ पूजितौ पादौ यस्य तम् । अमन्दतरं बहलं तमः तमिस्त्रम् अज्ञानं **च** । प्रशमयन्तं हरिं चन्द्रम् अवेक्ष्य, क्लमयुजां दुःखितानां, अयुजां युज्यन्त इति युजः, न युजः अयुजः, तेषां वियुक्तानां मध्ये यः सुरताश्रयी देवत्वाश्रयी न जातः ता(स्ता)दृशः (शो) नासीत् । चन्द्रस्योद्दीपनविभावत्वात् वि(द्वि)युक्ता, मृता इत्यर्थः । युजां स्त्रीयुक्तानां मध्ये यः सुरताश्रयी सुरतस्य निधुवनस्याश्रयी न जातः सः (स) नासीत् । स्त्रीयुजः सर्वेऽपि मैथुनासक्ता जाता इत्यर्थः । **पक्षे**-हरिं विष्णुम् अवेक्ष्य क्लमयुजां श्रमभाजां, युजां योगिनां, अयुजाम् अयोगिनां च मध्ये यः सुरता ऐश्वर्यं, तदाश्रयी न जातस्तादृशः(शो) नासीत् । हरिदर्शनात् योगिनः अ(नोऽ)योगिनोऽपि ऐश्वर्यं प्राप्नुवन्तीत्यर्थः । सुरेश्वर्ये (सुर ऐश्वर्ये) इति धातोः ॥३२ ॥

प्रसरदिन्दुकरैरतिपाण्डुरं[२९] वनमवेक्ष्य तदा जगतांपतिः ।
अरणयन्मुरलीमथ तद्रवं निशमयन् शमयन् न हि कोऽप्यभूत् ॥३३ ॥

प्रसरदिति । जगतांपतिः मुरलीम् अरणयत् । अथ तद्रवं मुरलीनिनादं निशमयन् श्रवणं कुर्वन् कोऽपि जनः शं सुखम् अयन् अप्राप्नुवन् नाभूत्, सर्वोऽपि जनः सुखं प्रापेत्यर्थः ॥३३ ॥

श्रुतिसुखं जनयन्मुरलीरवो वच इवाजनि दूतिकयेरितम् ।
प्रहितया हरिणाऽस्पृहयन् श्रियः पतिमभीतिमभीकमतोऽङ्गनाः ॥३४ ॥

श्रुतिरिति । श्रुतिसुखं कर्णसौख्यं जनयन् मुरलि(ली)रवः हरिणा प्रेरितया दूतिकया ईरितमुक्तं वच इवाजनि । अङ्गनाः(ना) अभीतिं भीतिरहितं श्रियः पतिम् अभीकं कामुकम् अस्पृहयन् अपेक्षितवत्य इत्यर्थः । 'अभीकः कामुके क्रूरे' इति **अमरः (मेदिनी)** ॥(३.१.२४) ॥(४.४१) ॥३४ ॥

व्रजभुवां सुदृशां सकलक्रिया विरमयन्नभवन्मुरलीरवः[३१] ।
भगवतोऽर्थपरं वचनं यथा सुमनसामनसारमकामिनाम् ॥३५ ॥

व्रजभुवामिति । मुरलीरवः सुदृशां स्त्रीणां सकलव्यापारान् विरमयन् अ(न्न)-भवत् । यथा भगवतः अनसारं सारवत् । 'द्वौ नयौ(ञौ) प्रकृतमर्थं सातिशयं गमयतः ।' अर्थपरं गीतारूपं वचनम् अकामिनां सुमनसां विदुषां सकलव्यापारवि-

---

२९. पाडुरं (omits the अनुस्वार- अनुनासिक);

३१. भवंन्मु (अनुस्वार & अनुनासिक bothused-Marathiinfluence

रामकारि भवति तद्वदित्यर्थः ॥३५ ॥

पतिमपास्य रतिस्पृहयालुकं सपदि काऽप्यपरा स्तनपं शिशुम् ।
पचनमप्यपरा परिदोहनं द्रुतमगात्तमगों[३२]धगुणं वधूः ॥३६ ॥

पतिमिति । रतिं स्पृहयते, तच्छीलस्तं पतिम् ॥३६ ॥

जगत एव पतिर्हरिरेव मे पतिरिदंपितरौ श्वशुरौ मम ।
इति परा श्वशुरादिनिषेवणाद्विरतिगा रतिगा भगवत्यगात् ॥३७ ॥

जगत इति । हरिर्जगत एव पतिर्जगदन्तःपातित्वात् । हरिरेव मे पतिः, इदंपितरौ अस्य कृष्णस्य पितरौ इदंपितरौ मम श्वशुरौ इति बुद्ध्या परा काचित्स्त्री श्वशुरादीनां निषेवणात् विरतिगा विरामं प्राप्ता भगवति रतिगा प्रीतिगा सती अगात् ॥३७ ॥

विनिहितं वदने कवलं परा गिलितवत्ययनार्धगताऽश्नती ।
अपरिपूर्णविभूषणयाऽन्यया द्रुतमितं तमितं मृदुलं वपुः ॥३८ ॥

विनिहितमिति । अश्नती परा काचित् वदने निहितं कवलम् अयनार्धे मार्गमध्ये गता सती गिलितवती । अपरिपूर्णविभूषणया अन्यया कयाचित् द्रुतं शीघ्रम् इतं प्राप्तं, शीघ्रमागतेत्यर्थः । शीघ्रागमनेन मृदुलं वपुः तमितं ग्लानिं प्रापितम् । ।३८ ।

विसृजती रचितैकदृगञ्जनाऽञ्जनविधिं गमनाय परोद्यता ।
इदमनक्तमिति ब्रुवती सखीं [३३]भ्रममयाममया इति साऽब्रवीत् ॥३९ ॥

विसृजतीति । परा काचित् रचितम् एकदृशि अञ्जनं यया सा, गमनाय उद्यता अत एव अञ्जनविधिं विसृजती सती इदमनक्तम्-इदं नेत्रमनक्तम् अनञ्जितम् । अनक्तं रात्रिभिन्नमिति च प्रतीयते । इति वदतीं सखीं त्वम् अयामं दुर्निवारं भ्रमम् अयाः इति अ(त्य)ब्रवीत् । नक्तं सदपि त्वम् अनक्तमिति वदसि तस्मात्त्वं भ्रमं प्राप्ताऽसीत्यब्रवीदित्यर्थः ॥३९ ॥

हरिमभि प्रसरद्व्रजसुन्दरीसमुदयेन वचांसि निषेधताम् ।
अनुसृतान्यपनीतनञर्थकं विदधिरे दधिरे न तु वैफलीम् ॥४० ॥

हरिमिति । हरिमभि हरिं प्रति । प्रसरद्व्रजसुन्दरीसमुदायेन निषेधतां- 'मा व्रजं गच्छत' इति निषेधं कुर्वतां श्वशुरादीनां वचांसि नञर्थं विना-निषेधको यो नञः (ञ), तद्विना-अनुसृतानि विदधिरे न तु वैफलीं विफलतां विदधिरे । नञर्थं विना वचोऽङ्गीकारात् साफल्यम् ॥४० ॥

---

३२. हा
३३. भ्रमया (drops म);

व्रजाङ्गनानां सरणिं निरुध्य व्यामेन तासां पतयोऽस्थुरेते ।
अतीत्य यातास्वपि तास्वजानन्नवस्थिता एव हरेः प्रभावात् ॥४१ ॥

व्रजेति । अस्थुः स्थितवन्तः । हरेः प्रभावात् तासु अतीत्य यातासु सतीषु ताः अजानन् अवस्थिता[ः] स्थिताः ॥४१ ॥

गता अपश्यन्नरविन्दनेत्रं निशाकरोद्योतनिवारिताऽन्यत् ।
तमो हरं तं तरुमूलभाजं निजांशुभिर्वासवनीलजैत्रैः ॥४२ ॥

गता इति । निशाकरस्य उद्योतेन निवारितात् अन्यत् तरुमूलभाजं तमः, वासवनीलाः इन्द्रनीलाः, तज्जैत्रैर्निजांशुभिः हरं तं हरिं गताः सत्यः अ(त्योऽ)-पश्यन् ॥४२ ॥

यं सुन्दरं वर्णयितुं प्रवृत्तास्त [द्] ध्यानधारापहृतान्यधीत्वात् ।
अर्थानुरूपं पदमस्मरन्तो मौनं[३४] महान्तः कवयो भजन्ते ॥४३ ॥

यमिति । तत्ध्या(द्ध्या)नेन अपहृता अन्यधीः पदार्थान्तरस्मरणं येषां (ते), तेषां भावस्तस्मात् । अर्थानुगुणं पदम् अस्मरन्तः सन्तः(न्तो) महान्तः कवयो मौनं भजन्ते ॥४३ ॥

स्वध्यानभाजां सुदृशां समूहं यः शान्तकामं विदधन्महात्मा ।
स्वध्यानभाजां सुदृशां समूहं प्रदीप्तकामं वितनोति देवः ॥४४ ॥

स्वध्यानमिति । यः सुदृशां पण्डितानां शान्तं कामं वीतरागं विदधत् । सुदृशां स्त्रीणां समूहं दीप्तः कामः पञ्चेषुःर्यस्मिन् (पञ्चेषुर्यस्मिन्) [सः] , तम् । **विरोधः स्पष्टः** ॥४४ ॥

मन्दमन्दमरविन्दलोचनोपान्तमेत्य सरतित्रपा इमाः ।
तस्थुरानमितसुन्दराननं ता उवाच जगतां महेश्वरः ॥४५ ॥

मन्दमन्दमिति । रतिश्च त्रपा च, ताभ्यां सहिताः । आगमने रतिर्हेतुः । मुखाधःकरणे त्रपा हेतुः ॥४५ ॥

अधिरजनि भयङ्करैः कुसत्त्वैर्वनमबलाः परिवार्यमाणमेतत् ।
सहजमपि भयं विधूय कस्मादभजत पूर्णशशाङ्कसुन्दरास्याः ॥४६ ॥

---

३४. मोनं;

अधीति। अधिरजनि रजन्यां हे शशाङ्कसुन्दरास्याः वनं कस्माद-भजत ॥४६ ॥

इति वादिनि सर्वलोकनाथेऽप्यवलम्ब्यासत मौनमेव कान्ताः ।[३५]
[३६]ह्रियमीषदपास्य[३७] भूरियत्नान्नयनान्तैश्चरणौ[३८] हरेः[३९] स्पृशन्त्यः ॥४७ ॥

इतीति। मौनमेवालम्ब्य आसत स्थिताः ॥४७ ॥

ततः सर्वविदां श्रेष्ठो विचार्यैव क्षणं हरिः ।
व्याजहार[४०] प्रियतमाः समन्दहसितं वचः ॥४८ ॥

तत इति। सर्वविदपि साधारण इव विचार्यैव विचारं कृत्वैव ॥४८ ॥

नूनं भवत्य इह मत्परिरम्भकामा
आयन् यतः परवधूरवलोक्य सा माम् ।
रक्षेदमन्मथवशा स्वपतिव्रतात्वं
वन्ध्योदरं श्रितवती जननाय या स्यात् ॥४९ ॥

नूनमिति। यतः या जननाय जननार्थं वन्ध्योदरं श्रितवती स्यात् सा परवधूः मामवलोक्य अमन्मथपरवशा सती स्वपतिव्रतात्वं रक्षेत्, अतः(तो) मत्परिरम्भकामाः भवत्यः इह आगता **इति शङ्के** ॥४९ ॥

एकोऽहमेकसमयेन मनोरथं वः कुर्यां कथं नु परिपूर्णमतोऽखिलानाम् ।
युष्माकमेत्यनुमतेन ममोपकण्ठं या या स्ववाञ्छितमसौ भजतां क्रमेण ॥५० ॥

एक इति। या युष्माकं मतेन ममान्तिकम् एति सा सा क्रमेण क्रमेण वाञ्छितं भजतां सेवताम् ॥५० ॥

सङ्गमः प्रियतमेन परस्याः प्राङ्मया कथमिवास्त्वनुमान्यः ।
अन्यया मम च याऽहमिवोत्केत्यव्यथन्त वनिता हरिवाक्यात् ॥५१ ॥

---

३५. प्यवलं व्यासतमेवेनमेव;
३६. P.&B. write ह्रि as ह्रि- a clear influence of Marathi orthography;
३७. मि;
३८. drops श्च;
३९. हरेस्पृ॰ (विसर्ग dropped and jointly written (Marathi influence);
४०. हाष्य;

सङ्गम इति । मया प्राक् मत्सङ्गमात्पूर्वं परस्याः परकीयायाः प्रियतमेन कृष्णेन सह सङ्गमः कथम् अनुमान्यः । या मत्सदृशा उत्का उत्कण्ठिता, अन्यया तया मम च प्रियतमेन सह सङ्गमः कथं वाऽनुमान्यः । द्वयमपि असुघटमिति हेतोः हरिवाक्यात् वनिताः अव्यथन्त व्यथां प्राप्ता इत्यर्थः ॥५१ ॥

तत्सन्तापं वीक्ष्य जातानुकम्पो यावत्यस्तास्तावदासीन्महेशः ।
एकैकेन स्वात्मनैकैककानां भुक्तां कुर्वन्न[४१]प्रतीतान्यमूर्तिः ॥५२ ॥

तदिति । अप्रतीता अन्याभिर्मूर्ति[ः] यस्य सः । एकैकेन स्वात्मना एकैकां भुक्तां कुर्वन् तावत् तावत्सङ्ख्याकः(क) आसीत् ॥५२ ॥

तदनु[४२] युवतयस्ताःस्वं स्वमातन्वता द्राक्
स्मरसमरसुखाय स्वानुकूल्ये प्रयत्नम् ।
अनुरहसमवाप्तोपान्तमैक्षन्त तेन
त्रिभुवनपतिना न स्वेतरा गोपकान्ताः ॥५३ ॥

तदन्विति । ताः युवतयः स्वं स्वं द्राक् स्मरसमरसुखाय स्वानुकूल्ये प्रयत्नम् आतन्वता तेन त्रिभुवनपतिना अनुरहसं रहसि अवाप्तोपान्तम् ऐक्षन्त, स्वेतरा[ः] स्वभिन्नाः गोपकान्ताः न औ(ऐ)क्षन्त ॥५३ ॥५४ ॥

आनम्रमाननसरोरुहमुन्नमय्य
सिञ्जानकङ्कणकरेण निवारयन्त्याः ।
पाणी निजौ स भगवानधरं प्रियाया
बिम्बातिशोणममृतान्मधुरं चुचुम्ब ॥५४ ॥

आतन्वती बहिरसौ प्रतिकूलभावं विष्णोर्ननन्द हृदये सुतरां मृगाक्षी ।
प्राग्जन्मभिर्बहुभिरातनवं तपांसि यान्यद्य तानि युगपत्फलितानि हीति ॥५५ ॥

आतन्वतीति । काचित् बहिः प्रतिकूलभावमातन्वती सती यानि बहुभिर्जन्मभिः तपांसि आतनवं तानि अद्य कृष्णप्राप्त्या युगपत् फलितानि हि निश्चयेन इति हेतोः हृदये ननन्द ॥५५ ॥

यावत्करं कञ्चुकमोचनाय व्यापारयामास हरिर्नतभ्रूः ।
निरोधनायास्त्रसदस्य तावद्ग्रन्थिः प्रमोदस्फुरिताङ्गकायाः ॥५६ ॥

---

४१. कुर्वंन्न (अनुस्वार + अनुनासिक both used-Marathi influence)
४२. P. तयः स्ताः (विसर्ग & स् both used-scribal peculiarity) .

यावदिति। यां(या)वत् हरिः कञ्चुकमोचनाय करं व्यापारयामास यावत् नतभ्रूः निरोधनाय करं व्यापारयामास तावत् अस्य कञ्चुकस्य ग्रन्थिः अस्रसत् स्रसनं प्राप ॥५६ ॥

विमोचितापाण्डुरकञ्चुकं [४३]तत्कुचद्वयं तेन तदा बभासे।
गङ्गाम्बुमग्नोत्थितचक्रवाकयुगं यथाऽन्योन्यमिलच्छरीरम् ॥३५ ॥

विरिति (विमोचितेति)। तेन हरिणा निष्कासितकञ्चुकं तत्कुचद्वयं तदा चक्रवाकयुगमिव बभासे ॥५७ ॥

व्रजेश्वरस्यात्मज इत्यकामां मामन्यभार्यामुपभोक्तुमिच्छेः।
निवेदितागास्तव दण्डकृत्स्यात् स भोजराजो न जहासि चेन्माम् ॥५८ ॥

व्रज इति। अकामाम् अन्यभार्यां माम् उपभोक्तुमिच्छेः इच्छसि। भोजराजः कंसः ॥५८ ॥५९ ॥

इति तां ब्रुवतीं विमृद्यमानस्तनकुम्भां विरचय्य सस्मितं सः।
कथमप्यपसृत्य गन्तुकामामथ रुन्धन्निव सान्द्रमालिलिङ्ग ॥५९ ॥

ममागतायाः समयोऽत्यगान्महान्न बुध्यते यावदतीवकोपनः।
पतिर्ममाहं यदि तावदाप्नुयां स्ववेश्म जीवामि न चेन्न मुञ्च माम् ॥६० ॥

मम इ(मे)ति। यावदतीवकोपनः(नो) मम पतिर्न बुध्येत तावत् स्ववेश्म आप्नुयां जीवामि च एवं न चेत् न जीवामि। तस्मात् मां मुञ्च ॥६० ॥६१ ॥

इति मृदुगिरा प्रार्थं प्रार्थं प्रयासनिरर्थताम्
उपगतवतीं कान्तां रत्यां प्रवृद्धमनोरथः।
अशिथिलभुजाश्लेषं चुम्बन्मुहुर्वदनाम्बुजं
शयनमनयद्रम्यं दूर्वामयं मृदुलं हरिः ॥६१ ॥

विस्रंसितनीवीकं कथमप्यस्या निरस्य मानपटौ।
मरुता हृतत्वचाविव रम्भास्तम्भावराजतामूरू[४४] ॥६२ ॥

विस्रंसितमिति। पटत्वचोः साम्यम्। ऊरुकदल्योः साम्यं च ॥६२ ॥

---

४३. तत् त्कु (additional त् used-scribal peculiarity);
४४. भुरू;

दन्तक्षताधरमेपतदयं विदीर्णवक्षोजकुम्भमतितीक्ष्णतरैर्नखाग्रैः ।
आनन्दमेव विदधन्मिलतोर्द्वयोश्च तद[द] द्वन्द्वयुद्धमजनि[४५] स्मरदत्तसाक्ष्यम् ॥६३ ॥

दन्त इति । स्मराय दत्तं साक्ष्यं साक्षिकर्म यस्मिन् तत् ॥६३ ॥६४ ॥

धारावाहिमहानन्दज्ञानतां प्राप्तयोर्द्वयोः ।
विधून्वती जगद्भानं दशा[४६] काचित्तयोरभूत्[४७] ॥६४ ॥

चक्लाम तत्सुरतनिर्दयमर्दनेन कान्तं मृणालमृदुलं वपुरङ्गनायाः ।
स्वेदाम्बुसान्द्रमुरुनिःश्वसिताहतार्द्रदन्तक्षतं जनितसीत्कृति मीलिताक्षम् ॥६५ ॥

चक्लामेति । चक्लाम क्लमं प्राप ॥६५ ॥

त्रुटद्धारोन्मुक्तैरिव वसुमतीमौक्तिकगणैः
अभूषि स्वेदाम्भःकणसमुदयैर्गात्रलतिका ।
क्षतैर्दन्तानां चाधर इव नखानां कुचयुगं
तदास्या ध्यायन्त्या इव रतिसुखं मीलितदृशः ॥६६ ॥

त्रुटदिति । मौक्तिकगणस्वेदाम्भःकणयोः साम्यं, वसुमतीगात्रलतिकयोश्च साम्यम् । 'रतिसुखं ध्यायन्त्यः इव मीलितदृशः अस्याः ॥६६ ॥

अन्या प्रगल्भयुवतिः पुरुषायमाणा संसक्तकृष्णकरशोणरुचानुलिप्तौ ।
बालातपच्छुरितकोकरुचिं दधानौ वक्षोरुहावतितरामनयत्प्रकम्पम्[४८] ॥६७ ॥

अन्येति । पुरुषायितत्वेन कुचौ प्रकम्पम् अनयत् ॥६७ ॥६८ ॥

एवं परा अपि वधू रमयाम्बभूव
बन्धैः स तैरभिमतैः सुरतानुकूलैः ।
वात्स्यायनो मुनिरवेत्य स यान् स्वशास्त्रे
बन्धानलक्षयदिमान् व्यभजच्च सम्यक् ॥६८ ॥

क्लान्ता आनन्दयामास यामुनो मन्दमारुतः ।
प्रीतये मरुतां पत्युरिव तस्य प्रियाङ्गनाः ॥६९ ॥

---

४५. जविस्म;
४६. दृशा;
४७. त्र;
४८. प्रपङ्कम् metathesis;

क्लान्ता इति । मरुतां वायु(यू)नां देवानां च पत्युः कृष्णस्य प्रीतये ॥६९ ॥

प्राग्यस्तुषारकिरणो जगदीशसङ्गात् ताः कृष्णसक्तमनसो व्यथयाञ्चकार ।
पश्चात्स एव नितरां मदयाञ्चकार लोका यदीश्वरकृतादरमाद्रियन्ते ॥७० ॥

प्रागिति। कृष्णसङ्गात् प्राक् विरहकाले व्यथयांश्च(याञ्च)कार। पश्चात् कृष्णसमागमोत्तरम्। यत् यस्मात् ईश्वरः प्रभुः, तेन कृतादरं पुरुषं लोकाः आद्रियन्ते ॥७० ॥

युगपत्सफलत्वमाप्नुवन् व्रजकान्तागुणरूपयौवनम् ।
यमुनातटरम्यभूमयो रजनी चापि सपूर्णचन्द्रमाः ॥७१ ॥

युगपदिति। व्रजकान्तानां गुणाः रूपं यौवनं च समाहारद्वन्द्वः। यमुनातटरम्यभूमयः सपूर्णचन्द्रमाः रजनी च युगपत् सफलत्वं प्राप्नुवन् ॥७१ ॥ ७२ ॥७३ ॥७४ ॥

इति रानडे इत्युपनामकशामरायाङ्गजेन विष्णुविरचितायां नीलकण्ठकविकृत- यादवेन्द्रमहोदयकाव्यस्य टिप्पन्यां षष्ठः सर्गः । ।६ ॥

एवं महेशात्समवाप्तकामा अता[४९]दृशीरन्यवधूर्विदित्वा ।
वरिष्ठमात्मानमवेत्य ताभ्यो महान्तमानन्दमिमा अविन्दन् ॥७२ ॥

यद्धीर्जगज्जातमिवासुरोरस्तनूरखेदाऽभृत शास्त्रजातम् ।
त्रिविक्रमाभिख्यतदात्मजन्मा यः पार्वतीनन्दनतामयासीत् ॥७३ ॥

नीलकण्ठेन तेनास्मिन् यादवेन्द्रमहोदये ।
कृते काव्ये षष्ठ एष सर्गः सम्पूर्णतां गतः ॥७४ ॥६ ॥

---

४९. अना;

सप्तमः सर्गः

[1]गर्वितं तदनु गोपसुन्दरीवृन्दमस्तमदतां निनीषुणा।
सर्वशक्तिनिलयेन योगिनामीश्वरेण निमिषात्तिरोदधे ॥१ ॥

श्रीगणेशाय नमः। **सप्तमसर्गप्रारम्भः**। गर्वितमिति। अस्तः मदो यस्य तत् अस्तमदं, तस्य भावः, तत्ता, तां निर्मदत्ता(ता)म् ॥१ ॥

विद्युतामिव हरेस्तिरोहितैर्लोचनानि हृदयान्यनन्तरम्।
प्राक्तनातिशयितं प्रपेदिरे दुःखमन्धतमसं मृगीदृशाम् ॥२ ॥

विद्युतामिति। हरेस्तिरोहितैः तिरोधानादनन्तरं मृगीदृशां हृदयानि, प्राक् संयोगात् पूर्वं भवं प्राक्तनं, तस्मात् अ(द)तिशयितं दुःखं प्रपेदिरे। विद्युतां तिरोहितैरनन्तरं प्राक्तनातिशयितम् अ(म)न्धतमसं लोचनानीव लोचनानि यथा प्राप्नुवन्ति तथैवेति **सम्बन्धः** ॥२ ॥३ ॥

किं निमित्तमपहाय मां ययौ यो मयि प्रणयसारवानभूत्।
चिन्तयन्त्य इति न प्रपेदिरे कारणाधिगममम्बुजेक्षणाः ॥३ ॥

अप्रयत्य न विषादतः फलं यं विना सकलमेव निष्फलम्।
तं वनेषु विचिनोमि वल्लभं निश्चिकाय मनसेति यौवतम् ॥४ ॥

अप्रयत्येति। अप्रयत्य प्रयत्नमकृत्वा विषादतः खेदात् फलं न भवति। यं विना यं वल्लभं विना सकलमेव निष्फलं तं विचिनोमीति निश्चिकाय निश्चयं कृतवत् [तत् यौवतम्] ॥४ ॥

ता विचेरुरटवीषु वल्लभेनोज्झिता सुरमणीयमूर्तिना।
दत्तसङ्गमसुखेन तारकाः कृष्णपक्षगतयामिनीष्विव ॥५ ॥

ता इति। सुरमणीयमूर्तिना चन्द्रेण कृष्णेन **च** ॥५ ॥

ता मिथोऽथ समगंसताध्वनि स्वोपमानदशतां च तद्गिरा।
अप्यमंसत ततो जगत्पतिं काननेषु मिलिता व्यचिन्वत ॥६ ॥

ता इति। अथ ताः मिथः परस्परं समगंसत सङ्गताः। तद्गिरा तस्याः (स्या)

---

१. P. begins with नमःश्रीकृष्णाय भगवते। B. begins with श्रीगणेशाय नमः।

अन्यस्याः (स्या) गिरा वाण्या स्वोपमानदशतां तस्या अपि स्वसादृश्यावस्थतामपि अ(प्य)मंसत ॥६ ॥

नावलोक्य हरिवेदिनो जनानन्वयुञ्जत वनोद्भवांस्तरून् ।
पञ्चबाणविकलीकृतात्मनां दुर्लभैव सविवेकिता यतः ॥७ ॥

नावलोक्येति । हरिवेदिनः जनान् नावलोक्य वनोद्भवान् तरूनन्वयुञ्जत ॥७ ॥

पीनतुङ्गकुचकुङ्कुमं दधत् श्लिष्यदम्बुजदृशो निजोरसा ।
नेत्रचुम्बनकृताञ्जनाधरश्चम्पके ह किमुपागतो हरिः ॥८ ॥

पीन इ(ने)ति । श्लिष्यदम्बुजदृशः पीनतुङ्गकुचकुङ्कुमं निजोरसा दधत् । नेत्रचुम्बनेन कृतम् अञ्जनं यस्मिन् तादृशः(श) अधरो यस्य ॥८ ॥९ ॥

आम्रपादप निजेन पाणिना गौरवर्णवति पक्वतां गते ।
स्वप्रियास्तनसमे स्पृशन् फले त्वां व्रजन् किमवलोकितो हरिः ॥९ ॥

बिम्बिके हरिरिहागतो ध्रुवं स्वप्रियाधर[२]धिया फलं तव ।
यच्चुचुम्ब यदि नास्य शीर्णताकारणं किमथ स क्व वा गतः ॥१० ॥

बिम्बिक इति । हे बिम्बिके तुण्डिकेरि, यत् यस्मात् स्वप्रियाधरबुद्ध्या तव फलं चुचुम्ब तस्मात् ह(ध्द)रिः इ(रि)ह आ(हा)गतः(तो) ध्रुवं निश्चितम् । चुम्बनचिह्नमाह-चुम्बनं यदि न कृतं चेत् अ(द)स्य फलस्य शीर्णताकारणं किम् । शीर्णत्वादेव चुम्बनं ज्ञायते । पक्वं फलं शीर्णं भवति तदुपरि **कवेरुत्प्रेक्षा** ॥१० ॥

ब्रूहि[३] कुत्र कुमुदिन्यगाद्धरिर्नागतोऽत्र यदि किं मृषा बुधैः ।
नान्तरेण हरिपादसङ्गमं कैरवं विकसतीत्युदीरितम् ॥११ ॥

ब्रूहीति । हरिश्चन्द्रः (हरिः चन्द्रः), तस्य पादाः किरणाः, तेषां सङ्गमम् । **पक्षे**-हरिपादः विष्णुपादः, तत्सङ्गमं विना कैरवं न विकसतीति बुधैरीरितं मृषा स्यात्किम् । तस्मात्तव विकासदर्शनेन हरिरिहागत **इति मन्ये** ॥११ ॥

इत्यरण्यभुवि सञ्चरिष्णवो योषितो दयितलाभकाम्यया ।
वन्दितां ददृशुरीश्वरेश्वरैर्मुद्रिकां हरिपदाम्बुजन्मनः ॥१२ ॥

---

२. B. lacuna for र;

३. P. writes ब्रू as बु (Marathi influence on orthography);

इतीति । ईश्वरेश्वरैर्वन्दितां हरिपदाम्बुजन्मनः(नो) मुद्रिकां ददृशुः ॥१२ ॥

तामवेक्ष्य कुलिशाङ्कुशध्वजैर्मण्डितां भगवदेकलक्षणैः ।
यामयुर्मुदममूर्व्रजाङ्गनास्तां न कृष्णपरिरम्भणादपि ॥१३ ॥

तामिति । तामवेक्ष्य यां मुदम् अयुः ता कृष्णपरिरम्भणादपि न अयुः न प्रापुः ॥१३ ॥१४ ॥

ऐक्षत प्रियतमाङ्घ्रिमुद्रिकासन्निधावपरपादमुद्रिकाम् ।
श्लिष्टयोरनु ममे[४](मै) तयोर्गतिं यौवतं भृशमतप्यताप्यथ ॥१४ ॥

आदृताऽन्यवनिता विमुञ्चता या वधूर्भगवताऽथ गर्विता ।
साऽपि तद्विरहिता वने चरन्त्याप सङ्गतिमिदंवधूजनैः ॥१५ ॥

आदृतेति । अन्यवनिताः(ता) विमुञ्चता भगवता या वधूः आदृता सा गर्विता जाता, अत एव साऽपि तद्विरहिता वने चरन्ती सती इदंवधूजनैः इमाश्च ताः वध्वश्च इदंवध्वः, तासां जनैः सङ्गतिं समागमम् आप ॥१५ ॥

मार्गयन् हरिममुष्य दौर्लभीं स्त्रीजनो निरचिनोत्तथा यथा ।
सर्व एव चरणव्यधाद्वने कण्टकाः सफलजन्मतां ययुः ॥१६ ॥

मार्गयन्निति । यथा सर्वे एव वनकण्टकाः च(श्च)रणव्यधात् च(च्च)रणानां व्यधात् क्षतात् सफलजन्मतां परचरणकर्मकक्षतैः स्वजनसाफल्यं ययुः तथा स्त्रीजनः हरिं मार्गयन् सन् अ(त्र)मुष्य हरेः दौ(दौ)र्लभीं [मुद्रिकां] निरचिनोत् निश्चितवान् ॥१६ ॥

यस्य ते सकलदेहिगोचरां वर्णयन्ति करुणां समे जनाः ।
सत्त्वमीश किंमुपेक्षसे[५] न इत्यारुदन् सुरभिपालकाङ्गनाः ॥१७ ॥

यस्येति । समे सर्वे जनाः । 'अथ समं सर्वम्' इति **अमरः** ॥(३.१.६४) ॥१७ ॥

स्यन्दमाननयनाम्बुभिर्निजान्यार्द्रतां व हृदयान्यलम्भयत् ।
क्रन्दनैर्दशदिगन्तलङ्घिभिः श्रुण्वतां व्रजनितम्बिनीगणः ॥१८ ॥

स्यन्द इ(न्दे)ति । व्रजनितम्बिनीगणः नयनाम्बुभिः निजानि हृदयानीव क्रन्दनैः श्रुण्वतां हृदयानि आ(न्या)र्द्रताम् अ(म)नयन् । हृदयानि वक्षःस्थलानि, **पक्षे**-चेतांसि ॥१८ ॥

---

४. ममो त;
५. किशु (श due to the previous श in °मीश) ;

दीप्यमानविरहानलो महान् बाष्पपूरमसृजन्नतभ्रुवाम् ।
यत्तदम्बु जनितं हविर्भुजेत्याह या विवृणुते स्म तां श्रुतिम् ॥१९ ॥

दीप्यमान इ(ने)ति । नतभ्रुवां दीप्यमानविरहानलः(लो) बाष्पपूरमसृजदिति यत् तत् 'हविर्भुजा अम्बु जनितम् उत्पन्नम्' इति या **श्रुतिः** आह तां विवृणुते स्म । 'अग्नेरापः' इति **श्रुतिः** । [**तै.उप. २.१**] ॥१९ ॥

श्यामरोमलतिकानुषङ्गिणी योषितां नयनवारिसन्ततिः[६] ।
जाह्नवीमशिशिरांशुसम्भवां[७] वाहिनीमुपगतामसस्मरत् ॥२० ॥

श्याम इ(मे)ति । रोमलतिकायमुनयोः साम्यं, नयनवारिसंहतिजाह्नव्योः साम्यम् । श्यामरोमलतिकानुषङ्गिणी नयनवारिसंहतिः यमुनासङ्गतां भागीरथीम् असस्मरत् स्मारयामास ॥२० ॥२१ ॥२२ ॥

दूनतां स्वदयिताजनस्य तां वीक्ष्य जातकरुणो[८] महेश्वरः ।
सर्वसुन्दरमदापहारिणं दर्शयन् स्वमतनोन्मुदं दृशाम् ॥२१ ॥

इन्द्रनीलमणिमेचकत्विषं चित्रवर्णमणिमेखलाञ्चितम् ।
हैमभूषणयुतं सविद्युतं सेन्द्रचापमिव नूतनाम्बुदम् ॥२२ ॥

वस्यमानकनकाम्बरत्विषा दर्शयन्तमटवीं हिरण्मयीम् ।
ईश्वरेण विरहासहिष्णुना भोगिनामिव धृतौत्तरीयकम् ॥२३ ॥

वस्येति । वस् आच्छादने वस्यमानं धार्यमाणं यत् कनकाम्बरं तस्य त्विषा । अटवीं हिरण्मयीं दर्शयन्त[म्] विरहासहिष्णुना भोगिनामीश्वरेण धृतम् औत्तरीयकम् उत्तरीयकर्म येन[९], तमिव । भोगिकनकाम्बरयोः साम्यम् ॥२३ ॥

---

६. P. marginal correction ह changed to त but, the B. scribe without understanding this sign (=) on ह copied it as ह and even the commentator accepts the reading संहतिः obviously not understanding the change effected in the margin. Or, he might have had (possessed) another manuscript having the reading संहतिः on which he commented.

७. भवावाहि (अनुस्वार dropped & jointly written);

८. करुणा;

९. P.1. marginal correction यस्य changed to येन by this sign (=) on the top of the word, as usual.

प्रेयसीघनतरोपगूहनक्लिश्यमाननवमल्लिकास्रजम् ।
हारिणा[१०] भुजयुगेन चोरसा क्लृप्तचन्दनरसेन राजितम् ।।२४ ।।

प्रेयसीति । हारिणा मनोहरेण भुजयुगेन । **पक्षे**-हारवता उरसा राजितम् ।।२४ ।।

धेनुपालतरुणीपयोधरोन्मर्दनाप्तमृगनाभिशोभिना[११] ।
लोहितं करयुगेन वारिजं[१२] खर्वयन्तमलिसम्भृतान्तरम् ।।२५ ।।

धेनुपालेति । मृगनाभिर्मृगमदः, तेन शोभिना करयुगेन अलिसम्भृतान्तरं लोहितं वारिजं खर्वयन्तं तुच्छीकुर्वन्तम् । मृगमदभ्रमरयोः साम्यं, करकमलयोः साम्यम् ।।२५ ।।

आननेन्दु[१३]मधुरस्मितामृतैर्लम्भ्यमानसुखदेवमण्डलम् ।
चर्व्यमाणघनसारवीटिकारञ्जनद्विगुणशोणिमाधरम् ।।२६ ।।

आननमिति । लम्भमानसुखं प्राप्यमाणसुखं, देवमण्डलम् इन्द्रियमण्डलं देवतामण्डलं **च** येन ।।२६ ।।

भर्ममौलिमिहिरातपेच्छया[१४] दीर्घलोचनतटाकनिर्गतौ ।
तद्रुचेव मकरौ पिशङ्गितौ बिभ्रतं मकरहेमकुण्डले ।।२७ ।।

भर्म इति । भर्ममौलिः सुवर्णमुकुट एव मिहिरः सूर्यः, तस्य आ(स्या)तपेच्छया, दीर्घलोचने एव तटाकौ, ताभ्यां निर्गतौ, तद्रुचा सुवर्णमौलिरुचा, पिशङ्गितौ मकराविव मकराकारहेमकुण्डले बिभ्रतम् ।।२७ ।।

छादिते नखसुधाकरांशुभिर्न्यस्यमानमृदुपादपङ्कजम् ।
[१५]वर्त्मनीव वनदेवतागणास्तीर्यमाणमृदुलप्रसूनके ।।२८ ।।

छादित इति । नखसुधाकरांशुभिः छादिते अत एव देवतागणेन आस्तीर्यमाणानि मृदुलप्रसूनकानि यस्मिन् तस्मिन्निव वर्त्मनि न्यस्यमानं मृदुपादपङ्कजं येन, तम् ।।२८ ।।

---

१०. हरिणा;
११. शोभिता;
१२. वारिजें;
१३. आननन्दु;
१४. मोलि....तपच्छया;
१५. वत्म (omits the रेफ) ;

यादृशं जवमुपेत्य वल्लभं प्राप्नुवन्[१६] व्रजमृगीदृशां दृशः ।
तादृशेन तदुपान्तमङ्घ्रयः प्रागधीतगतिमन्दता अपि ॥२९ ॥

यादृशमिति । दृशः यादृशं जवमुपेत्य वल्लभं प्राप्नुवन् तादृशेन जवेन तदुपान्तम् अङ्घ्रयः प्राप्नुवन् । झटिति आगता इत्यर्थः ॥२९ ॥

गाढमाततभुजोपगूह्य[१७] तं काऽपि खेदितपयोधरं हरेः ।
कूणिताक्षमधरं सुधामयं चुम्बति स्म विरराम नामुतः[१८] ॥३० ॥

गाढमिति । काऽपि आततभुजा तं गाढं खेदितपयोधरं यथा [स्यात्] तथा उपगुह्यालिङ्ग्य हरेः अधरं चुम्बति स्म । अमुतः चुम्बनात् न विरराम ॥३० ॥

कांचन व्यवहितैतदंसभूलम्बबाहुरनुमृद्य पाणिना ।[१९]
एक(कै) केन[२०] कुचकुड्मलौ[२१] परेणेश्वरोऽनु जगृहे परां प्रियाम्[२२] ॥३१ ॥

कांचनेति । कांचन स्त्रियं व्यवहितः अनिकटस्थः यो(य) एतस्याः अंसः, तस्य भुवि लम्बमानः बाहुर्यस्य सः । एकैकेन पाणिना कुचकुड्मलौ अनुमृद्य परेण बाहुना परां प्रियां कुचकुड्मलौ अनुमृद्य जगृहे ॥३१ ॥

केवलैरपि विलोकनैः परा दर्शयद्भिरिव भावमान्तरम् ।
प्रेमरूपमरविन्दलोचनो धेनुपालतरुणीरनन्दयत् ॥३२ ॥

केवलैरिति । प्रेमरूपमान्तरं भावं दर्शयद्भिर्विलोकनैः पराः धेनुपालतरुणीः अनन्दयत् ॥३२ ॥

यामुने तदनु सैकते हरेः स्वोत्तरीयमयमासनं शुचि ।
ताभिरारचितमेतदाबभौ श्वेतमध्यग इवाहिपुङ्गवः ॥३३ ॥

यामुने(न) इति । श्वेतं श्वेतदीपं, तन्मध्यगः शेष इव । सैकतस्य श्वेतत्वात् श्वेतद्वीपसाम्यं, आसनस्य शुभ्रत्वात् शेषसाम्यम् ॥३३ ॥

---

१६. प्राप्नुवंन् (अनुस्वार + न्-Marathi influence) ;
१७. गृह्य;
१८. P. marginal gloss– नामुतः = चुम्बनात्;
१९. हिते तदं;
२०. P.&B. एककेन;
२१. कुट्मलौ;
२२. प्रिया;

तच्च तेन रचितोपवेशनं पुण्डरीकमिव बम्भराञ्चितम् ।
आबभौ तमनु ता उपाविशन् तन्मुखेन्दुनिहितात्मदृष्टयः ॥३४ ॥

तदिति। आसनस्य शुभ्रत्वात् पुण्डरीकोपमानं, कृष्णस्य नैल्यात् भ्रमरोपमानम् ॥३४ ॥

त्वत्पदैकशरणा वयं प्रिय त्वां वनेषु मृगयन्त्य आप्नुम ।
येन तावकमनोऽतिकोमलं कर्कशं तदधुनाऽपि मृग्यते ॥३५ ॥

त्वदिति । हे प्रिय, वनेषु मृगयन्त्यः वयं त्वाम् आप्नुम प्राप्ताः स्म । येन कारणेन 'तावकमतिकोमलं मनः कर्कशं जातं' तत्कारणमधुनाऽपि मृग्यते । तदद्यापि न ज्ञातमित्यर्थः ॥३५ ॥

तां[२३] निशम्य दयिताजनोदितां वाचमेष जगतां महेश्वरः ।
तां वनीं विरचयन् द्विचन्द्रिकां व्याजहार दरहासरोचिषा ॥३६ ॥

तामिति । तां वनीं दरहासरोचिषा द्विचन्द्रिकां चन्द्रिकाद्वययुक्तां विरचयन् सन् व्याजहार ॥३६ ॥

विप्रयुक्तमिलितेन यत्सुखं सर्वदा सविधवर्तिना न तत् ।
प्रेयसा मृगदृशां ततोऽस्मि वस्तत्सुखं गमयितुं तिरोहितः ॥३७ ॥

विप्र इति । विप्रयुक्तः वियुक्तः सन् मिलितः, तेन यत्सुखं तत्सुखं सन्निधवर्तिना न भवति । अतः अ(तोऽ)हं तिरोहित इत्यर्थः ॥३७ ।

नित्यसन्निधिगते प्रियान्तरे जायते ध्रुवमरुच्यता नृणाम् ।
कल्पमेकमपि सन्निधिस्थिते नोदयेत दयितारुचिस्त्वयि ॥३८ ॥

नित्यमिति। प्रियान्तरे अन्यत् प्रियं प्रियान्तरे(रं), त्वदतिरिक्तप्रियान्तरे नित्यसन्निधिगते सति नृणामरुच्यता भवति। त्वयि सन्निधिस्थिते सति अरुचिर्नोदयेत् ॥३८ ॥

आन्तरालिकभवद्वियोगजां न व्यथां क्षमितुमीश्वरा[२४] वयम् ।
तेन तत्सुखमभीप्सितं न नः सन्निधिं वितरते सदा प्रभो ॥३९ ॥

---

२३. ता;

२४. P.&B. marginal correction श्महे changed to श्वरा by this sign (=) on the word, i.e. before correction, both the mss. (P&B) read श्महे;

आन्तरालिक इति । त्वद्वियोगकालमारभ्य संयोगकालपर्यन्तं यः आन्तरालिकः मध्यकालभवः यो वियोगः, तज्जातां व्यथाम् । तेन व्यथाऽसहनेन ॥३९ ॥

तं प्रणेमुरिति ताः कृतार्थनास्ता यया समुदतिष्ठिपत् प्रियाः ।
गूढया युगपदेव तुष्टुवे तामसङ्ख्यकरतां निजां हरिः ॥४० ॥

तमिति । यया गूढया असङ्ख्यकरतया ताः प्रियाः समुदतिष्ठिपत् उत्थापयामास तामसङ्ख्यकरतां तुष्टुवे स्तुतवान् । तासां युगपदुत्थापनेनात्मनः अ(नोऽ)-सङ्ख्यकरतां तदा बहु मेने (न) इत्यर्थः ॥४० ॥

ईश्वरोऽथ बहुविग्रहो भवंस्ता नयन् वलयतुल्यपङ्क्तिताम् ।
अन्तरे च निवसन् द्वयोर्द्वयो रासनामविहतिं प्रचक्रमे ॥४१ ॥

ईश्वर इति । बहुविग्रहः बहुकायः सन् । रासनामविहतिः रासनामिका या विहतिर्विहारः क्रीडेति यावत् तां प्रचक्रमे ॥४१ ॥

सा च पङ्क्तिरजयन्महास्रजं चम्पकान्तरितनीलनीरजाम् ।
तत्र ताः[२५] स्वनिकटस्थितात्परं रूपमस्य ददृशुर्न मायिनः ॥४२ ॥

सा चेति । गोपीनां चम्पकसाम्यं कृष्णस्य नीलनीरजसाम्यम् । मायिनः कृष्णस्य स्वनिकटस्थितात् रूपात् परं रूपं न ददृशुः ॥४२ ॥

पूरितं तदनु दर्शनोत्सुकैः साप्सरोभिरमरैर्नभोऽन्तरम्[२६][२७] ।
देवदुन्दुभिरवैरनन्तरं वृष्यमाणकुसुमैः परं ततः ॥४३ ॥

पूरितमिति । प्रथमम् अमरैर्नभोऽन्तरं पूरितम् । अनन्तरं देवदुन्दुभिरवैः पूरितम् । ततःपरं वृष्यमाणकुसुमैःपूरितम् ॥४३ ॥

नृत्तगीतमनधीतमेव यत्तत्र ताः कुशलतां प्रपेदिरे ।
ईश्वरेण य इहानुगृह्यते सोऽनधीत्यपि कलाभिराप्यते ॥४४ ॥

नृत्तगीतमिति । नृत्तगीतम् अनधीतं सत् यत् यस्मात् तत्र नृत्तगीते ताः कुशलतां प्रपेदिरे । तत् तस्मात् यः ईश्वरेण अनुगृह्यते सः कलाभिः स्वयमेव आप्यते ॥४४ ॥

वाद्यजातमपि वाद्यवादकाः क्रीडनेऽत्र परमेश्वरोऽभवत् ।
प्राक्रमन्त तदनु प्रिया हरेर्गीतनृत्तमवधीरिताप्सरः ॥४५ ॥

वाद्यमिति । वाद्यजातं वाद्यवादकाश्च स्वयमेवाभवत् ॥४५ ॥

---

२५. तास्व° (विसर्ग dropped & jointly written);
२६. सास्प° (metathesis);
२७. °मरै नभोऽन्तर;

सर्वविद्हृदयरागवर्जिते रागशून्यहृदयोऽपि स प्रभुः ।
प्रीतिमाप मुखरागतोऽप्यहो भूयसीं सुरभिपालयोषिताम् ॥४६ ॥

सर्वविदिति । हृदयरागवर्जिते हृदयानुरक्तिशून्ये हृदयरक्तिमेति **च** प्रतीयते । रागः अनुरक्तिः । मुखरागतः मुखेन गीयमानात् रागात् मुखरक्तिमातश्च ॥४६ ॥

सादरं यदश्रुणोन्मुनिव्रजस्तच्च गानमधुरत्वहेतुकम् ।
तद्विरागजयशस्तु रक्षितं गीयमानभगवद्गुणोदयैः ॥४७ ॥

सादरमिति । मुनिव्रजः सादरमश्रुणोदिति यत् तत् गानमधुरहेतुमकेव । गानमाधुर्यमेव सादरश्रवणे हेतुः । ननु गानश्रवणेन मनश्चाञ्चल्यात् जितेन्द्रियत्वरूपं यशस्तै[ः] कथं रक्षितमित्याह । गीयमानभगवद्गुणोदयै**र्हेतुभिः** वैराग्यजं **यशो** रक्षितमिति । भगवद्गुणोदयश्रवणस्य वैराग्यस्य भूषास्पदत्वात् तच्छ्रवणेन **यशो** रक्षितमित्यर्थः ॥४७ ॥

तत्सुगीतिमश्रुणोद्यतो वृषा तज्जगाद विरसोऽन्यगीतिषु ।
देवगायनवरं च तुम्बुरुं[२८] गायनेति तदभूत्सगायनः ॥४८ ॥

तदिति । वृषा इन्द्रः यत् यस्मात् सुगीतिमश्रुणोत्, तत् तस्मात् देवगायनं तुम्बरूं-(रुं) गाय न इति न गाय इति 'त्वं गानं मा कुरु' इति जगाद । तस्मात् हेतोः तुम्बरूः(रुः) गायनेति सम्बोधनं बुद्ध्वा सगायनः गायनसहितः अ(तोऽ)भूदिति ॥४८ ॥

प्रत्ययप्रकृतिषु प्रचोदितो यस्य योऽभिनय आत्मना मुनिः ।
ऐक्षताविषयमाश्रुतोदयात्तस्य तं हरिवधूजनैः कृतम् ॥४९ ॥

प्रत्यय इति । यस्य धर्मिणः प्रत्ययप्रकृतिषु प्रचोदितः 'अस्मिन् प्रत्यये अयमभिनयः कार्यः, अस्यां प्रकृत्यामयमभिनयः कार्यः ।' इति आत्मना प्रचोदितः उक्तः अभिनयः । **मुनिः भरतः** आश्रुतोदयात् स्वकृतशास्त्रोदयादारभ्य अविषयं येन केनापि वाचरितं, तस्य धर्मिणः हरिवधूजनैः कृतं तमभिनयम् ऐक्षत्(त) स्वशास्त्रोक्तसदृशमभिनयमपश्यदित्यर्थः ॥४९ ॥

दृश्यमानललिताङ्गहारकं तन्महेशतरुणीकदम्बकम् ।
वायुनेषदिव कम्पितच्छदं शातकुम्भकदलीवनं बभौ ॥५० ॥

दृश्यमिति । 'अङ्गहारोऽङ्गविक्षेपः' इति **अमरः** । [१.७.१६] शातकुम्भ-कदलीवनं सुवर्णकदलीवनम् ॥५० ॥

२८. तेबुरुं;

सन्मृदङ्गनिनदानुवर्तिना नर्तनेन पशुपालयोषितः ।
मेघनादमनु विन्ननर्तना अन्वकुर्वत तदा शिखण्डिनीः ॥५१ ॥

सदिति । मेघनादमनु मेघशब्दं लक्षी(क्ष्यी)कृत्य, विन्नं प्राप्तं नर्तनं याभिस्ताः । 'लब्धं प्राप्तं विन्नं भावितमासादितं च' इति **अमरः** ॥[३.१.१०४] ॥५१ । ५२ ।५३ ॥

नर्तनोच्चलितकिङ्किणीरवैर्वाद्यमानमुरजारवाञ्चितैः ।
योषितामयमवेदि सञ्चयः पञ्चमो धरणिमध्यगोऽम्बुधिः ॥५२ ॥

वीक्ष्य तन्नटनमद्भुताद्भुतं मेनिरे दिविषदो महेशितुः ।
प्रीणनाय बहुरूपतां गता नृत्यतीति नटनाधिदेवता ॥५३ ॥

नृत्तगीतजनिते सुखे उभे भोक्तुकाममुपसीदतां मनः ।
अन्तरेऽकृत मुहुर्गमागमैर्लोचनश्रवणयोर्महापथम् ॥५४ ॥

नृत्तमिति । नृत्तजनितं गीतजनितं च उभे सुखे **कर्म (कर्मणी)** भोक्तुकामम् उपसीदतां तत्र स्थितानां मनः लोचनश्रवणयोरन्तरे मध्ये मुहुर्गमागमैः महापथम् अकृत ॥५४ ॥

श्रान्तिभाजमतिवेलनर्तनात् प्रेयसीगणमवेक्ष्य स प्रभुः ।
नर्तनाद्विरयाम्बभूव तन्नर्तनं[२९] न तु दिदृक्षणाज्जनान्[३०] ॥५५ ॥

श्रान्तिरिति । नर्तनं तु दिदृक्षणात् जनान् न विरयाम्बभूव ॥५५ ॥

स्वोत्तरीयपरिमृष्टतन्मुखस्वेदबिन्दुरथ तन्मुखे हरिः ।
चर्वितार्धघनसारवीटिका[३१]मार्पयत्प्रणयपूर्णमानसः ॥५६ ॥

स्वोत्तरीयमिति । अर्धं चर्विता चर्वितार्धा । घनसारः कर्पूरः, तन्मिश्रिता वीटिका, ताम् ॥५६ ॥

नर्तनाच्चरणयोर्व्यथाऽभवन्मर्दनं तु कृतवानुरोजयोः ।
स प्रियाधरमधूपसेवनान्मत्ततां गत इवामितां हरिः ॥५७ ॥

नर्तनादिति । व्यथामर्दनयोरनैकाधिकरण्यात् मत्ततां प्राप्त **इवेति योजना** ॥५७ ॥

---

२९. तं नर्तनं;
३०. °ज्जनात्;
३१. वीरिकां मां (अनुस्वार retained + सन्धि-Marathi influence)

रतिकामनया यदेष चक्रे भगवांस्तत्प्रतिषेद्धुमङ्गनाभिः ।
चकमे परमन्तरा[32]यभावं यदगान्नर्तनभूः श्रमो महीयान् ॥५८ ॥

रतिरिति । यत् यस्मात् महीयान् नर्तनभूः नर्तनोत्पन्नः श्रमः अन्तरायभावम् अगात्, तत् तस्मात्-यत्तयोर्नित्यसम्बन्धात् । तत् प्रतिषेद्धुमङ्गनाभिः च(श्च)कमे, परं केवलं वाञ्छितं न प्रतिषिद्धमित्यर्थः ॥५८ ॥

अवसितसुरतास्ताः सम्प्रबुध्य प्रभातं
कमलसुरभिगन्धादायिमन्दानिलेन ।
प्रियविरहमशक्ताः सोढु[33]मप्यन्वनाथन्[34]
प्रियतममुपयातुं स्वं निशान्तं नताङ्ग्यः ॥५९ ॥

अवसित इति । अवसितसुरताः समाप्तरतयः ताः स्त्रियः, कमलसुरभिगन्धम् आदत्तेऽसौ कमलसुरभिगन्धादायी यो मन्दानिलः, तेन प्रभातं सम्प्रबुध्य स्वं निशान्तं गृहम् उपयातुं प्रियतमं कृष्णम् अन्वनाथन् याचितवत्यः ॥५९ ॥६० ॥

एवं कान्ताः[35] प्रतिनिशमुपागम्य रम्ये वनेऽस्मिन्
आप्रत्यूषं विहरत मया प्रेमवश्येन सार्धम्[36] ।
इत्याभाष्य प्रमदमतुलं स व्यधात्प्रेयसीनां
दत्तानुज्ञा अथ भगवता स्वस्वगेहं गतास्ताः ॥६० ॥

रजनीषु रथाङ्गनामयोषाजनभुक्तां विरहव्यथां[37] दिनेषु ।
जगृहुर्दिवसेषु ताभिराप्यं प्रियसङ्गं रजनीषु गोपकान्ताः ॥६१ ॥

रजनीष्विति । रजनीषु रथाङ्गयोषाजनभुक्तां विरहव्यथां दिनेषु जगृहुः । दिवसेषु ताभिराप्यं प्रियसङ्गं रजनीषु जगृहुः ॥६१ ॥६२ ॥६३ ॥

इति रानडे-इत्युपनामकश्यामरायाङ्गजविष्णुविरचितायां नीलकण्ठ-कविकृतयादवेन्द्रमहोदयकाव्यस्य टिप्पण्यां सप्तमः सर्गः ॥७ ॥

---

३२. परमेतरां;
३३. साढु;
३४. नाथंन् (अनुस्वार + अनुनासिक-Marathi influence);
३५. काताः;
३६. साधम् (omits the रेफ);
३७. व्यथा (omitsthe अनुस्वार);

यद्धीर्जगज्जातमिवासुरारेस्तनूरखेदाऽभृत शास्त्रजातम् ।
त्रिविक्रमाभिख्यतदात्मजन्मा यः पार्वतीनन्दनतामयासीत् ।।६२ ।।

नीलकण्ठेन तेनास्मिन् यादवेन्द्रमहोदये ।
कृते काव्ये सप्तमश्च सर्गः सम्पूर्णतां गतः ।।६३ ।।[३८]

---

३८. B. adds श्रीकृष्णाय नमः ।

अष्टमः सर्गः

[1]अथाग्रणीः सर्वविदां[2] नारदः कंसमासदत्[3] ।
आप्तकामोऽपि देवानामातन्वन्नभिवाञ्छितम् ॥१ ॥

अथाष्टमः सर्गः । श्रीगणेशाय नमः । अथेति । आसदत् प्राप्तवान् ॥१ ॥

**अवधीरितचण्डांशुसहस्रेणापि तेजसा ।
पुण्यलब्धावलोकानां नृणां नेत्राणि नन्दयन् ॥२ ॥**

अवधीरित इ(ते)ति । धिक्कृतसूर्यसहस्रतेजसाऽपि नेत्राणि नन्दयन् **इति चित्रम्** ॥२ ॥

**आसादयन्त्या निष्पारं परमेश्वरसागरम् ।
विज्ञानगङ्गयोपेतो जङ्गमो हिमवानिव ॥३ ॥**

आसादयन्त्येति । निष्पारं पाररहितं परमेश्वररूपसागरम् आसादं(द)(यं)त्या विज्ञानं विशेषज्ञानरूपया गङ्गया उपेतः जङ्गमः हिमवानिव स्थितः ॥३ ॥

**कृत्वा[4] निजाङ्गसङ्गेन मारुतं पवनक्षमम् ।
पवमानपदं तत्र योगेनापि प्रवर्तयन् ॥४ ॥**

कृत्वेति । पवनं पवित्रीकरणं, तत्र क्षमं कृत्वा । पवते पवित्रीकरोतीति पवमानः -इति **योगेनापि** । पवमानपदं तत्र वायौ प्रवर्तयन् ॥४ ॥

**महतीं करुणां चित्ते वीणां[5] च करपल्लवे ।
श्रवणायोपसन्नानां परानन्दप्रदां वहन् ॥५ ॥**

महतीमिति । महतीं बह्वीं **पक्षे**-महतीसंज्ञकाम् । महती[6] नारदस्यासासीत्' इति **अमरः** । (३.३.६९) । श्रवणाय ब्रह्मोपदेशश्रवणाय । **पक्षे**-श्रवणाय गानश्रवणाय । उपसन्नानां प्राप्तानां परानन्दप्रदाम् ॥५ ॥६ ॥

---

१. P. begins with श्रीकृष्णाय नमः। B. begins with श्रीगणेशाय नमः।
२. °विदान्नन्ना° (अनुस्वार + अनुनासिक)-Marathi influence);
३. °मादसत्, वर्णव्यत्यास-Metathesis;
४. P. कृत्त्वा;
५. वीणीं;
६. The original reading of अमर is वीणाभेदेऽपि महती' (३.३.६९) & is paraphrased by our commentator as महती नारदस्यासीत्।

तं महर्षिमुपायातं[7] भोजराजोऽभ्यपूजयत् ।
अथोत्तमासनासीनो मुनिः स[8] तमवोचत ॥६ ॥

शासता वसुधां राजन् पुण्यवन्तः कृता जनाः ।
भवता हितमत्यन्तं ततस्ते कामयामहे ॥७ ॥

शासतेति । हे राजन्, वसुधां शासता भवता पुणवन्तः(न्तो) जनाः कृताः नाशिताः । 'कृ हिंसायाम्' धातुः । "ततः हेतोः ते अत्यन्तम् अहितं कामयामहे" **इति गूढार्थः** ॥ "भवता जनाः पुण्यवन्तः कृताः, ततः ते अत्यन्तं हितं कामयामहे" **इति बाह्यार्थः** ॥७ ॥८ ॥९ ॥१० ॥

तेन किञ्चिद्द्वयं ब्रूमो[9] भवन्तमवधीयताम् ।
यं[10] ते हन्तारमाचष्टे पुरा वागशरीरिणी ॥८ ॥

तत्पिता जातमात्रं[11] तं नीत्वा नन्दालये[12] न्यधात् ।
आनैषीद् बन्धनागारं सद्योजातां च तत्सुताम् ॥९ ॥

स बालोऽपि बलोपेतांस्तृणावर्तादिदानवान् ।
दिवं प्रस्थापयामास रेणूनिव समीरणः ॥१० ॥

वैमात्रेयोऽस्य यो भ्राता रामो नाम स चेदृशः ।
नोपेक्षणीयौ तावेतौ शूरंमन्यतया त्वया ॥११ ॥

वैमात्रेयेति । शूरमात्मानं मन्यतेऽसौ शूरंमन्यः, तस्य भावस्तत्ता, तया ॥११ ॥१२ ॥

इत्युदीर्य मुनिर्यातस्तदाकर्ण्य महीपतिः ।
मुखेन रोषताम्रेण बालभानुं निराकरोत् ॥१२ ॥

शासनेनेश्वरस्यास्य सदारः शूरनन्दनः ।
निन्ये दुःखमयीं कारां नीचयोनिमिवाघकृत् ॥१३ ॥

शासनेनेति । ईश्वरस्य कंसस्य शासनेन आज्ञया सभार्यः(र्यो) वसुदेवः(वो)

---

७. °यान्ते;
८. सत्तम°
९. P. बुमो
१०. य (omits the अनुस्वार);
११. मात्रे;
१२. वन्दा;

दुःखमयीं कारां निन्ये । यथा ईश्वरस्याज्ञया अघकृत्पुरुषः(षो) दुःखमयीं नीचयोनिं नयन्ति (नीयते) तथेत्यर्थः ॥१३ ॥१४ ॥

अरिष्टकेशिनौ दैत्यावालम्भे वासुदेवयोः ।
आदिश्याक्रूरमाहूय कंस आज्ञामिति व्यधात् ॥१४ ॥

आगामिन्यां चतुर्दश्यां धनुर्यागो भविष्यति ।
नन्दाद्या रामकृष्णौ च तं पश्यन्त्वा[१३]नयेह तान् ॥१५ ॥

आगामिन्यामिति । 'तं यागं पश्यन्तु । इह तान् आनय' इत्याज्ञां व्यधात् **इति पूर्वश्लोकेन सम्बन्धः** ॥१५ ॥

कृष्णो वृषप्रियो मह्यं न द्रु[१४]ह्येद् वृषरूपिणे ।
इतीव वृषरूपः सन्नरिष्टो गोष्ठमाययौ ॥१६ ॥

कृष्ण इति । वृषः धर्मः वृषभः इति **च** प्रतीयते । वृषरूपः धर्मरूपः वृषभरूपश्च ॥१६ ॥

उन्नतस्योच्चशृङ्गस्य तस्यातिधवलद्युतेः ।
हिमाद्रेरिव सान्निध्याद्व्रजावासाश्चकम्पिरे ॥१७ ॥

उन्नतस्येति । हिमाद्रेः सान्निध्यात् शैत्यहेतुना यथा कम्पं प्राप्नुवन्ति तथा भयात् चकम्पिरे । **विशेषणानि उभयत्र योज्यानि** ॥१७ ॥

आसाद्य सन्निधिं विष्णोस्तमयं[१५] प्राजिहीर्षत[१६] ।
असिपुत्रीशि[१७]ताग्राभ्यां शृङ्गाभ्यां दानवाधमः ॥१८ ॥

आसाद्येति । विष्णोः सन्निधिमास्थाय तं विष्णुं प्राजिहीर्षत प्रहर्तुमैच्छत(त्) । असिपुत्री छुरिका, तद्वत् तीक्ष्णाग्राभ्याम् ॥१८ ॥१९ ॥

स तस्य शृङ्गे पाणिभ्यामादाय ज्ञाततन्मनाः ।
निनायाधोमुखीभावं विपर्यासितकन्धरम् ॥१९ ॥

---

१३. श्यत्वा (omitsthe न्);
१४. दृह्येः;
१५. तनयं;
१६. P.marginalgloss प्रहर्तुमैच्छत्;
१७. सिता

अश्वीभूय तदाऽऽयातस्योत्क्रान्ता दानवासवः ।
केशिनो दीपयन् क्रोधं भस्त्रावाता इवानलम् ॥२० ॥

अश्वीति । उत्क्रान्ताः दानवासवः तदा अश्वीभूय आयातस्य केशिनः क्रोधं दीपयन् ॥२० ॥

तेन तद्विमुखीभावं गतेनात्मापकारिणा ।
प्रायो[१८]ज्यथ पदं कृष्णे सौगतेनैव दुर्वचः ॥२१ ॥

तेनेति । तद्वि(द्वि)मुखीभावं कृष्णविमुखीभावं गतेन आत्मनः स्वस्यैवापकारकारिणा तेन कृष्णे पदं सौगतेन बुद्धेन दुर्वचः 'ईश्वरो नास्तीति' वाक्यमिव प्रायोजि प्रयुक्तम् । **विशेषणानि सौगतेऽपि योज्यानि** ॥२१ ॥

तेनेव तेनापि हरेरसम्बधोऽभवत्ततः ।
द[१९]र्ष्टुकामोऽभिमुखतां प्राप कृष्णस्य दानवः ॥२२ ॥

तेनेवेति । तेनेव सौगतवचनेनेव तेनापि दैत्येन हरेः असम्बन्धः अभवत् । सौगतवचनस्य-"इ(ई)श्वरसद्भावेऽपि नास्तीति" वचनस्य-यथा असम्बन्धः, तथाऽस्यापि असम्बन्धः अभवदिति **भावः** ॥२२ ॥२३ ॥

प्रासारयद्भुजं कृष्णो दैत्यस्तं स्वाननेऽग्रहीत् ।
तेन प्रवर्धमानेन रुद्धप्राणो ममार च ॥२३ ॥.

तेन चक्रे व्रजस्थानां साध्वसं मानसाद्बहिः ।
उपसंहतवृद्धिं स्वं करं दैत्याननादथ ॥२४ ॥

तेनेति । यथा दैत्याननात् स्वं करं बहिश्चकार, तथा साध्वसं व्रजस्थानां **मानसात्(द्)** बहिश्चक्रे ॥२४ ॥२५ ॥२६ ॥

अक्रूरो रथमारुह्य प्रतस्थे नन्दगोकुलम् ।
युक्तं हयचतुष्टय्या मारुताधीतरंहसा ॥२५ ॥

श्रुतिस्मृतिमयं यस्य शासनं परमेशितुः ।
अनुष्ठायाऽप्र[२०]मादेन यं साक्षात्कुर्वते चिरात् ॥२६ ॥

---

१८. प्रयो;
१९. P. दंष्टु;
२०. यां प्र;

अहं[२१]दुरीश्वरस्यापि कंसस्याज्ञानुवर्तनः ।
अद्यैव तं महेशानमवलोकेऽद्भुतं महत् ॥२७ ॥

अहमिति । यस्यैव आज्ञायाः अप्रमादेन करणात् यं साक्षात्कुर्वन्ति तमेव दुरीश्वरस्य आज्ञानुवर्तनः अहम् अवलोके साक्षात्करोमीति **अद्भुतम्** । ।२७ ॥२८ ॥

अथवा कंससङ्गान्मां[२२] नेशः स्वं[२३] दर्शयिष्यति ।
यद्दुष्टमवगच्छन्त्यप्यदुष्टं दुष्टसङ्गमात् ॥२८ ॥

कृष्णोऽप्यहो[२४] ममाज्ञत्वमतिः[२५] स्वाज्ञानमूलिका ।
अविन्दन् सकलज्ञत्वं यत्प्रसादेन योगिनः ॥२९ ॥

कृष्णेऽपीति । कृष्णेऽपि ममाज्ञत्वमतिः-"दुष्टसङ्गात् मामपि दुष्टमवगच्छेदिति" मतिः-स्वाज्ञानमूलिका ममाज्ञानहेतुका । कुतः- यत्प्रसादेन योगिनः सकलत्वमविन्दन् । सर्ववेत्ता स कृष्णः मदाशयं ज्ञात्वा मां दुष्टमिति कथमवगच्छेत् । तस्मात् सा मतिः ममाज्ञानमूलिकेति ॥२९ ॥३० ॥

इत्यादि चिन्तयन्मार्गे सुनिमित्तावलोकनात् ।
स[२६] हर्षमतुलं प्राप्य दिनान्ते[२७] गोकुलं ययौ ॥३० ॥

अर्घ्यमाणैर्भगवति पुण्यैरिव महात्मनाम् ।
तदावासमुपायद्भिः प्रविशत्पाण्डुगोधनैः ॥३१ ॥

चतुर्भिर्गोकुलं वर्णयति । अर्घ्यमाणैरिति । भगवति अर्घ्यमाणैः अत एव तदावासं कृष्णावासम् उपायद्भिः महात्मानं पुण्यैरिव स्थितैः प्रविशत्पाण्डुगोधनैर्युक्तम् ॥३१ ॥

अरिष्टगृह्यं मत्वेव वृषभैर्वृषभान्तरम् ।
युयुत्समानैर्नर्दद्भिः[२८] खुरोल्लिखितभूमिभिः ॥३२ ॥

---

२१. दूरी;
२२. गात्मां;
२३. नेश स्वं;(विसर्ग dropped & jointly written-Marathi influence)
२४. कृष्णप्यहे;
२५. मतिस्वा (विसर्ग dropped & jointly written);
२६. प्रहर्ष;
२७. दीनान्ते;
२८. नेदद्भिः(रेफ on द dropped);

अरिष्टमिति । वृषभान्तरम् अरिष्टगृह्यं तन्नामकराक्षसपक्ष्यं मत्वेव युयुत्समानैः योद्धुमिच्छुभिः, अत एव नर्दद्भिः शब्दं कुर्वद्भिः खुरोल्लिखितभूमिभिः वृषभैर्युक्तम् । 'नर्दगर्द शब्दे' इति **धातुपाठोक्तेः** ॥३२ ॥

उद्यम्य पुच्छं गोवत्सैर्लङ्घमानैरितस्ततः ।
पीतक्षीरारब्धमिव[२९] दधानैः पाण्डुतागुणम् ॥३३ ॥

उद्यम्येति । पीतं यत्क्षीरं तेन आरब्धमिव स्थितं पाण्डुतागुणं दधानैः गो(र्गो)वत्सैर्युतम् ॥३३ ॥

निषेवितुमुपायातैरिह सन्तं सदा विधुम् ।
तारागणैरिव[३०] गणैर्गोपालीनामलङ्कृतम् ॥३४ ॥

निषेवितुमिति । इह सदा सन्तं विधुं चन्द्रं विष्णुं **च** । निषेवितुमुपायातैस्तारागणैरिव स्थितैः गोपालीनां गणैः अलङ्कृतम् ॥३४ ॥

मत्वा तदागमं नन्दः प्रत्युद्गम्यानुयुज्य च ।
स्वागतं रामकृष्णाभ्यामानर्ह गृहमानयन् ॥३५ ॥

मत्वेति । रामकृष्णाभ्यां सह प्रत्युद्गम्य स्वागतम् अनुयुज्य च । गृहमानयन् सन् आनर्ह पूजितवान् ॥३५ ॥३६ ॥

कृतातिथ्यं विनीताध्वश्रमं स्वासनमाश्रितम् ।
अक्रूरं व्याजहारेदं सस्मितं गोकुलेश्वरः ॥३६ ॥

अक्रूर हेत्वभूः[३१] स्फीतप्राच्योदीच्यसुकर्मणाम् ।
मम येनातिथीभूय निशान्तं समुपागतः ॥३७ ॥

अक्रूर इति **युग्मम्** । हे अक्रूर, मम प्राच्योदीच्यसुकर्मणां प्राक् उत्तरभाविनां च कर्मणाम् । प्राक्कृतसुकर्मणां हेत्वभूः हेतुः कारणमभूः । जातोऽसि, भाविसुकर्मणां हेतुरनुमापकमभूः । येन सुकर्मणा यस्मिन् चतुराननादारभ्य स्तम्बः सूक्ष्मकीटविशेषः, तत्पर्यन्तं सर्वं जगद्विशति, तं महेशानं निजं स्वान्तम् अवीविशः प्रावेशयत् । एतादृशस्त्वं मम निशान्तं गृहमुपागतः ॥३९ ॥४० ॥४१ (३७ ॥३८) ॥

२९. P. marginal gloss स्थितं;
३०. ताराङ्गणै° (ङ्ग for ग-Marathi influence)
३१. भूस्फी (विसर्ग dropped & jointly written);

त्वं हि यस्मिन्निदं सर्वं जगदाचतुराननात् ।
आस्तम्बान्तं महेशानं निजं स्वान्तमवीविशः ॥३९ ॥(३८) ॥

त्वं तच्चरणराजीवचिन्ताशान्ताखिलस्पृहः ।
कथं प्रावर्तथा अस्मिन्नागमे तन्निगद्यताम् ॥४०(३९) ॥

[३२]आगामिन्यां चतुर्दश्यां धनुर्यागं करिष्यति ।
कंसस्तद्दर्शनाय त्वामाह्वयन् प्रजिघाय माम् ॥४० ॥

कृष्णं च रौहिणेयं च विक्रान्तत्वप्रथां[३३] गतौ ।
उग्रसेनसुतो राजा दिदृक्षामास गोपते ॥४१ ॥

कृष्णमिति । दिदृक्षामास द्रष्टुमैच्छत् ॥४२ ॥४३ ॥(४१ ॥४२) ॥

इत्युक्तवन्तमक्रूरं श्रान्तं विश्रमयन्नयम्[३४] ।
गतोऽन्यतः शशासाथ निजप्रस्थानघोषणाम् ॥४२ ॥

कृष्णोऽथाक्रूरमवदत् प्रलम्बद्विषतोऽन्तिके ।
आवां प्रत्यार्य किं[३५] न्वस्मत्पितरौ समदिक्षताम्[३६] ॥४३ ॥

कृष्ण इति । पितरौ देवकीवसुदेवौ किं समदिक्षतां किं संदिष्टवन्तौ ॥४३ ॥

कथंवृत्तस्तयोरास्ते भोजसन्तानपांसनः ।
युष्मासु च तदेतन्मे यथावदभिधीयताम् ॥४४ ॥

कथमिति । कथंवृत्तं यस्य सः कथंवृत्तः, कथं वर्तनशीलः(ल) आस्ते ॥४४ ॥४५ ॥

युवयोः पितरौ कारां निनाय स दुराशयः ।
पराप्रवेश्यां पूर्वेद्युर्न विद्मः कारणं त्विह ॥४५ ॥

वयं चालब्धशरणास्तस्य छन्दानुवर्तनात् ।
कृच्छ्रेण धारयामोऽसून् ग्रीष्मे जलचरा इव ॥४६ ॥

---

३२. B. omits this verse.
३३. P. Marginal quotation: 'शूरो वीरश्च विक्रान्तः' इति अमरः (२८.७७);
३४. श्रमयंत्र (अनुस्वार + अनुनासिक—Marathi influence);
३५. किन्व (drops the अनुस्वार on कि);
३६. P. marginal gloss समादिष्टवन्तौ;

वयमिति । ग्रीष्मे ग्रीष्मऋतौ यथा जलचराः(रा) जलजन्तवः(वो) जलाल्पत्वात् कृछे(च्छ्रे)ण सङ्कटेन असून् धारयन्ति तथा वयम् असून् धारयामः ॥४६ ॥

इति यद्वान्दिनीसूनुर्भगवन्तमवोचत ।
तत्तस्यावाप फूत्कारभावं क्रोधहविर्भुजः ॥४७ ॥

इतीति । क्रोधहविर्भुजः क्रोधवह्नेः फूत्कारभावम् उद्दीपनकरणत्वमाप ॥४७ ॥

दूराध्वगमनश्रान्त सुप्यतां भूयसी निशा ।
अत्यगादित्युदीर्यैष[३७] स्वं स्वापसदनं ययौ ॥४८ ॥

दूरमिति । हे दूराध्व[ग]मनश्रान्त अक्रूर भूयसी निशा अत्यगात्, सुप्यताम् इति उदीर्य ॥४८ ॥

अथ प्रसृमरा वर्णा हरिप्रस्थानगोचराः ।
गोपीनामविशन् कर्णं दीप्ताङ्गारकणा इव ॥४९ ॥

अथेति । प्रसृमराः प्रसारं प्राप्ताः, हरिप्रस्थानं गोचरं विषयो येषु ते । हरिप्रस्थानविषयाः वर्णाः दीप्ताङ्गारकणा इव गोपीनां कर्णमविशन् । दुःखदायित्वात् अ(द)ग्निकणसाम्यम् ॥४९ ॥

[३८]अतिमात्राविदूनानां तासामर्धकृताः क्रियाः ।
वन्ध्याः प्रवृत्तिविरतेरासंस्तत्कामना[३९] इव ॥५० ॥

अतिमात्रमिति । अतिमात्रमत्यन्तं विदूनानां दुःखितानां तासां गोपीनाम् अर्धकृताः क्रियाः पाकादयः । प्रवृत्तिविरतेः तत्तत्कार्यप्रवृत्तिविरामात् हेतोः, तत्कामना इव तासां कामनाः कृष्णविषयकाभिलाषा इव वन्ध्याः आसन् ॥५० ॥

लम्भयन्त्या परिस्पन्दशून्यतां तां दुरन्तया ।
हेमपाञ्चालिकाभेदाच्चिन्तया विनिवर्तिताः ॥५१ ॥

लम्भयन्त्येति । परिस्पन्दश्चलनात्मको व्यापारस्तच्छून्यतां लम्भयन्त्या प्रापयन्त्या अत एव दुरन्तया चिन्तया, ताः **कर्म**, हेमपाञ्चालिका सुवर्णपुत्रिका, तस्याः भेदात् वि(द्वि)निवर्तिताः चिन्तया निश्चेष्टत्वात् हेमपुत्रिकातुल्यतां प्रापिता इत्यर्थः ॥५१ ॥

---

३७. यै (omits the रेफ);

३८. B. omits this verse;

३९. P. marginal gloss—तासां कृष्णविषयकाभिलाषाः ।;

चक्षुष्मत्तां[४०] कुतो नाम व्यधान्मे चतुराननः ।
अभजं सुन्दरोत्तंसे कृष्णे येनानुरागिताम् ॥५२ ॥

चक्षुष्मत्तामिति । येन चक्षुष्मत्त्वेन सुन्दरश्रेष्ठे कृष्णे अनुरागितामभजम् ॥५२ ॥

[४१]प्राणान्तप्रतिकर्तव्यां ययेमामभजं व्यथाम् ।
इतो हि मथुरां यातो न कृष्णो गोकुलं स्मरेत् ॥५३ ॥

प्राण इति । यथा अनुरागितया प्राणान्तेन प्राणनाशेन प्रतिकर्तव्यां व्यथाम् अभजम् ॥५३ ॥

स्वयं हि वस्तुं तत्स्वान्ते[४२] तद्गताः सर्ववासनाः ।
निर्वासयन्त्यसङ्ख्याता गुणास्तत्पुरयोषिताम्[४३] ॥५४ ॥

गोकुलास्मरणे हेतुमाह स्वयमिति । तत्पुरयोषितां मथुरापुरस्त्रीणाम् असङ्ख्याता गुणाः तत्स्वान्ते कृष्णस्यान्तःकरणे स्वयं वस्तुं तद्गताः कृष्णस्वान्तगता[:] सन्तः सर्ववासनाः कृष्णान्तःकरणस्थाः सर्वसंस्काराः निर्वासयन्ति । वासनाऽभावात् गो(द्गो) कुलं न स्मरेदिति **भावः** ॥५४ ॥

धातर्यदि न मे मृष्यो भवता प्रियसङ्गमः ।
प्राणा अपि प्रियास्तान् मे न वियोजयसे कुतः ॥५५ ॥

धातरिति । हे धातः, भवता त्वया मे मम प्रियसङ्गमः प्रियस्य सङ्गमः न मृष्यो यदि तर्हि प्राणा अपि मे प्रियाः तान् प्राणान् कुतो न वियोजयसे । प्राणवियोजनं कुर्वित्यर्थः ॥५५ ॥५६ ॥५७ ॥५८ ॥५९ ॥

कुतो मे मन्दभाग्यायास्तत्पुण्यं येन तं प्रियम् ।
दृढमालिङ्ग्य चुम्बेयं पुनस्तद्वदनाम्बुजम्[४४] ॥५६ ॥

इत्यादि चिन्तयन्तीभिर्हृदि[४५] दीप्तं स्मरानलम् ।
निर्वापयन्तीभिरिव रुरुदे ताभिरायतम् ॥५७ ॥

---

४०. °ष्मतां (त् omitted);
४१. प्रणा°;
४२. P. तस्त्वान्ते (Metathesis);
४३. °तत्पर°;
४४. °म्बुज (म् dropped);
४५. °भिहृदि (रेफ dropped);

भयं न श्वशुराभ्यां न पत्युर्नो बान्धवान्तरात् ।
तासा[46]मुद्वेलतापानां क्रन्दनारा[47]वमारुधत् ॥५८ ॥

आक्रन्दितस्य महतस्तासां गोपालयोषिताम् ।
यमुनाचक्रवाकीणामाक्रन्दैः प्रतिशब्दितम् ॥५९ ॥

तापोद्रेकासहतया किमु तासां नतभ्रुवाम् ।
निद्रा तस्यां विभावर्यां न ताः सम्प्राप्तुमैहत ॥६० ॥

ताप इति । तापोद्रेकस्यासहतया सोढुमशक्यतया निद्रा ताः **कर्म** सम्प्राप्तुं न ऐहत नैच्छत ॥३० ॥

छेत्ता वियोगिहृद्पद्मान्[48] मत्तश्चन्द्रेन्द्रवारणः ।
[49]वप्रकीडाकृतेऽस्ताद्रिं ययौ [50]कीर्णकरामृतः ॥६१ ॥

छेत्तेति । वियोगिनां हृदयान्येव पद्माः, तान्, छेत्ता नाशकः । चन्द्र एव इन्द्रवारणः ऐरावतः, शुभ्रत्वात् । कीर्णं कररूपम् अमृतं येन । **पक्षे**-कीर्णकरः शुण्डादण्ड[ः], तत्स्थितममृतं जलं येन ॥६१ ॥

तिरोधानमविन्दन्त गगनारण्यचारिणः ।
हरेरागम[51]माज्ञाय ऋक्षव्रातास्तदा भयात् ॥६२ ॥

तिरोधानमिति । हरेः सिंहस्य सूर्यस्य **च**। आगमं ज्ञात्वा ऋक्षव्राताः भल्लूकसमूहाः नक्षत्रसमूहाश्च । भयात् तिरोधानमविन्दन्त । 'नक्षत्रमृक्षं भं तारा' इति **अमरः** ।(१.३.२१) 'ऋक्षाच्छभल्लभल्लूकाः' इति **अमरः** ।(२.५.४) ॥६२ ॥

विदलत्कमलामोदं स्फीतं लोभादुपाहृतम् ।
किरन्नुद्वहनाक्षान्त्या ववौ प्रत्यूषमारुतः ॥६३ ॥

विदलदिति । सामोदः प्रत्यूषमारुतः ववावित्यर्थः ॥६३ ॥६४ ॥

---

४६. मासा;
४७. मारा;
४८. पद्मांन्मत्तःश्चन्द्रे (अनुस्वार + अनुनासिक and विसर्ग & श् both retained-scribal peculiarity);
४९. विप्र;
५०. कीर्णे करा;
५१. रागनमा;

शीतांशुयजमानेन समिद्धारुणपावके।
निजप्रभामयं क्षीरं प्रत्यूषे जुहुवेतराम् ॥६४॥

सुष्वाप पत्या चन्द्रेण रत्या क्लान्तिमिवापिता।
निमीलितेन्दीवरदृक् तदेन्दीवरिणी[५२] वधूः ॥६५॥

सुष्वापेति। इन्दीवरिणी वधूः पत्या चन्द्रेण, रत्या मैथुनेन क्लान्तिमवापितेव प्रापितेव सुष्वाप निमीलनं प्रापेत्यर्थः ॥६५॥

तत्प्राक्काले प्रसृमराः कुमुदोदरकान्तयः।
नेन्दुप्रभा न चेत्तेषु मीलितेषु कुतो न ताः ॥६६॥

तदिति। तत्प्राक्काले कैरवनिमीलनप्राक्काले प्रसृमराः कुमुदोदरकान्तय एव न इन्दुप्रभाः, एवं ने(नो) चेत् तेषु कैरवेषु मिलितेषु सत्सु ता इन्दुप्रभाः कुतो न सन्ति। तस्मात् कुमुदोदरकान्तय एव इन्दुप्रभाभ्रान्तिदायकाः। चन्द्रास्तो जात इत्यर्थः ॥६६॥

उद्यन्तं सूर्ययन्तारं पतगाधीश्वराग्रजम्।
विरावैर्विहगव्राताः स्तुवन्तो मेनिरे जनैः ॥६७॥

उद्यन्तमिति। पतगाधीश्वरः गरुडः, तदा(द)ग्रजं वरुणम्। जनैर्मेनिरे ज्ञाताः। प्रातःकालकृतपक्षिरवः स्तवनरूपेणोत्प्रेक्षितः ॥६७॥

अथोदयाद्रिशिखरं सहस्रांशुरविन्दत।
लोकानां सविता[५३] राजा सिंहासनमिवोन्नम् ॥६८॥

अथेति। सविता प्रेरकः, **उभयत्र समानम्**। 'षू प्रेरणे'। राजा उन्नतं सिंहासनमिव ॥६८॥

उपातिष्ठन्त ते विप्रा येषां राजा निशाकरः।
प्राप्तोदयं तं[५४] श्रीमन्तं ह्युपसर्पन्ति मानवाः ॥६९॥

उपेति। येषां राजा निशाकरश्चन्द्रः, द्विजराजत्वात्, ते विप्राः प्राप्तोदयं तं सूर्यम् उपातिष्ठन्त। हि यस्मात्, मानवाः श्रीमन्तमुपसर्पन्ति। सूर्योऽपि श्रीमान्। प्राप्तोदयमिति **उभयपक्षे**ऽपि योजनीयम् ॥६९॥७०॥

---

५२. वरणी;
५३. P. marginal gloss षू प्रेरणे, प्रेरकः।;
५४. त (अनुस्वार dropped);

तदानीं विहितं कर्म कृतवान् गान्दिनीसुतः ।
स्यन्दनं योजयामास शैलोदग्रं तुरङ्गमैः ॥७० ॥

अथ सन्नह्य गोपाला राजोपायनसम्भृतान् ।
शकटान् वाहयामासुर्बलवद्भद्रयोजितान् ॥७१ ॥

अथेति । बलवन्तः ये भद्राः बलीवर्दाः, तैर्योजितान् शकटान् ॥७१ ॥

द्रष्टुकामैर्व्रजावासैर्निर्यान्तौ रामकेशवौ ।
जनैरनीयत तदा वीथी निरवकाशताम् ॥७२ ॥

द्रष्टुमिति । निर्यान्तौ रामकेशवौ द्रष्टुकामैर्व्रजावासैर्व्रजस्थैर्जनैः वी(र्वी)थी निरवकाशताम् अनीयत ॥७२ ॥

त्वर्यमाणौ प्रयाणाय ततो नन्देन माधवः ।
रामश्चास्पृशतां मूर्ध्ना स्वमातृचरणाम्बुजे ॥७३ ॥

त्वर्यमाणाविति । नन्देन प्रयाणाय त्वर्यमाणौ माधवः रामश्च । मातृचरणाम्बुजे आ(अ) स्पृशताम् ॥७३ ॥७४ ॥

तयोर्यशोदारोहिण्यौ जन्मारभ्यावियोगिनोः ।
वियोक्ष्ये[५५]माणयोस्तापं निर्मर्यादमविन्दताम् ॥७४ ॥

तथाप्यमङ्गलमिति निरुध्याश्रुसमुद्गमम् ।
प्रायुञ्जातां तयोः सर्वा आशिषस्ते गमिष्यतोः ॥७५ ॥

तथापीति । ते यशोदारोहिण्यौ अमङ्गलमिति हेतोः अश्रुसमुद्गमं निरुध्य तयोः रामकृष्णयोः सर्वाः आशिषः प्रायुञ्जातां प्रयुक्तवत्यौ ॥७५ ॥७६ ॥७७ ॥ ७८ ॥७९ ॥

तात द्रुतं निवर्तस्व सुखं मे यदि वाञ्छसि ।
स्रुतस्तन्यावुभे पुत्रावालिङ्गेत्थमवोचताम् ॥७६ ॥

अभ्यनुज्ञातगमनौ मातृभ्यां रामकेशवौ ।
बहिःसदनमागत्य सर्वान् वृद्धान् प्रणेमतुः ॥७७ ॥

---

५५. विक्ष्यौ योक्ष्य° repetition due to the similar following letter;

ततो विरहसन्तापं सन्देशवचनामृतैः ।
शमयामास[५६] गोपीनां भगवन्नूतनाम्बुदः ॥७८ ॥

स्ववियोगासहान्[५७] दूरमनुयातान् व्रजौकसः ।
निवर्तयामास हरिः कृच्छ्रान्मधुरया गिरा ॥७९ ॥

ततः प्रचोदितैरश्वैर्जन्यमानो जवो महान् ।
हरियोग इव न्यास्थद्रथे विष्णुरथाभिधाम्[५८] ॥८० ॥

तत इति। ततः प्रचोदितैरश्वैः र्ज(ज)न्यमानः महान् जवः रथे विष्णुरथाभिधां-विष्णो रथः गरुड-इति अभिधां न्यास्थत् स्थापितवान्। हरियोग इव-यथा हरेः विष्णोः योगः सम्बन्धः रथे विष्णो(ष्णु)रथ इति अभिधां स्थापयति, तथेत्यर्थः ॥८० ॥

दृशो रथं महावेगमनुगन्तुमिवाक्षमाः ।
व्रजभाजां न्यवर्तन्त ततस्तेऽप्याहितव्यथाः ॥८१ ॥

दृश इति । महावेगं रथमनुगन्तुमक्षमा इव व्रजभाजां दृशः(शो) न्यवर्तन्त । ततस्ते अपि आहितव्यथाः सन्तः न्यवर्तन्त ॥८१ ॥

वीक्षमाणैरिवोद्ग्रीवमायान्तं[५९] जवनं रथम् ।
उन्नमद्भिरसङ्ख्यातैस्तरङ्गैर्मण्डितान्तराम् ॥८२ ॥

षड्भिः कालिन्दीं वर्णयन्नाह वीक्षमाणैरिति । अश्वाः स्यन्दनोत्तंसं रथश्रेष्ठं क्षणेन क्षणमात्रेण कालिन्दीमुपानयन् इति **षष्ठश्लोकेऽन्वयः** । तां विशेषयन्नाह-वीक्षमाणैरिति ॥८२ ॥

क्षालनादिव पङ्कानां मज्जतामसितोदकाम् ।
अन्तःप्रविष्टैः कल्येनाप्यलब्धव्यतलह्रदाम्[६०] ॥८३ ॥

क्षालनादिति । मज्जतां स्नातृणां पङ्कानां पापानां कर्दमानामिति [च] प्रतीयते, क्षालनादिव असितोदकां नीलवर्णोदकाम् । **उत्तरार्धेन अगाधामित्यर्थः** ॥८३ ॥

---

५६. P.omits मा;
५७. °सहानूरम°;
५८. धा;
५९. वोद्गीव (रेफ dropped);
६०. P.&B. write as-ह्र-Marathi influence;

प्रवाहसौन्द[६१]र्यमुहुर्दिदृक्षावशगैरिव ।
अप्राप्तपारां[६२] नयनैरपि दूरदृशां नृणाम् ॥८४ ॥

प्रवाह इ(हे)ति । दूरदृशां नृणां प्रवाहसौन्दर्य(र्यं) मुहुर्दिदृक्षावशगैः रि(इ)व नयनैः अप्राप्तपरतीराम् ॥८४ ॥

नानावर्णैरविरलैः सम्फुल्लैः[६३] पद्मकाननैः ।
चित्राम्बरामिव वधूं श्यामसुन्दरविग्रहाम् ॥८५ ॥

नानेति । श्यामः सुन्दरः विग्रहः देहो यस्याः सा, ताम् ॥८५ ॥

उपासितां द्विजवरैर्मन्त्रानिव[६४] कलध्वनीन् ।
आवर्तयद्भिरश्रान्तं परमां[६५] देवतामिव ॥८६ ॥

उपासितामिति । मन्त्रानिव कलध्वनीन् अश्रान्तं निरन्तरमावर्तयद्भिः द्विजवरैर्ब्राह्मणैः पक्षिश्रेष्ठैश्च, उपासितां परमां देवतामिव स्थिताम् । मन्त्रान् अश्रान्तम् आवर्तयद्भिः द्विजवरै[:] ब्राह्मणश्रेष्ठैः उपासितां परमां देवतामिव स्थितां, कलध्वनीन् अश्रान्तम् आवर्तयद्भिः द्विजवरैः पक्षिश्रेष्ठैः उपासिता**मिति वा अन्वयः कार्यः** । ॥८६ ॥८७ ॥

कालिन्दीं[६६] स्यन्दनोत्तंसं क्षणेनाश्वा उपानयन् ।
अथानुज्ञाप्य गोविन्दमक्रूरः[६७] स्नातुमुद्यतः ॥८७ ॥

अवतीर्य स कालिन्द्यां[६८] जपन् मन्त्रान् समाहितः ।
निमज्यान्तर्जलेऽद्राक्षीत्[६९]त्तं रथं यं तटे न्यधात् ॥८८ ॥

अवतीर्येति । यं रथं तटे न्यधात् तं जले अद्राक्षीत् ॥८८ ॥८९ ॥

यं[७०] निमज्य तमुन्मज्य यमुन्मज्य निमज्य तम् ।
पुनः पुनरवेक्ष्यायं विस्मयं परमं ययौ ॥८९ ॥

---

६१. सौंद (अनुनासिक/ अनुस्वार dropped);
६२. पारांत्रयेन (अनुस्वार & अनुनासिक both used-Marathi influence);
६३. सपुल्लैः;
६४. मत्रा (अनुस्वार dropped);
६५. परमादे (अनुस्वार dropped & jointly written);
६६. दी (अनुस्वार dropped);
६७. रस्ना (विसर्ग dropped and jointly written);
६८. द्या (अनुस्वार dropped);
६९. साक्षी;
७०. य (अनुस्वार dropped);

सोऽन्तर्जले दृश्यमानः श्वेतदीपोऽभवत् क्षणात्।
तरङ्गैः प्लाव्यमानान्तो निर्मलैः क्षीरवारिधेः ॥९० ॥

स इति । स रथ एव अन्तर्जले दृश्यमानः सन् क्षणात् क्षीरवारिधेः निर्मलैस्तरङ्गैः अन्तःप्लाव्यमानः प्लाव्यमानान्तो वा श्वेतदीपः अभवत् ॥९० ॥

सोद्यदर्कोदयप्रांशुशृङ्गोपमितमूर्तिभिः ।
दीप्तरत्नैः[७१] फणैरासीदनन्तोऽत्र स्थितो बलः ॥९१ ॥

स इति । अत्र रथे स्थितः बलः बलदेवः, उद्यन् यः अर्कः सूर्यः, तेन सहितानि, उदयः पूर्वपर्वतः, तस्य प्रांशूनि यानि शृङ्गाणि, तैरुपमिता मूर्तिर्येषां, तैः । दीप्तरत्नैः फणैर्युक्तः अनन्तः शेषः आसीत् ॥९१ ॥९२ ॥

तं स्तुवन्तो ददृशिरे दिविजा नतकन्धराः ।
प्रेम्णा बद्धाञ्जलिपुटाः सानन्दाश्रुविलोचनाः ॥९२ ॥

तस्योत्सङ्गे नीलमेघसमानोदर्यविग्रहम्।
मुखचन्द्रप्रसादेन दर्शयन्तमनुग्रहम् ॥९३ ॥

तस्येत्यादिश्लोकनवकेन तत्र स्थितं पुरुषं वर्णयन्नाह । तस्य शेषस्य उत्सङ्गे क्रोडे स्थितं कञ्चित्पुरुषम् ऐक्षिष्ट। महाभागः अ(गोऽ)-क्रूरः(रो) भ्रमापेतेन भ्रमरहितेन चेतसा तं पुरुषं रथस्थितं नन्दात्मजं म(अ)मन्यत **इति नवमेनान्वयः** ॥९३ ॥

मृदुनाऽऽप्रपदीनेन विभान्तं पीतवाससा।
पाण्डुरेणोत्तरीयेण रौक्म्या[७२] च[७३] वनमालया ॥९४ ॥

मृदुनेति। मृदुना आप्रपदीनेन-प्रपदं पादाग्रं, तत्पर्यन्तं प्राप्तेन, पादाग्रलम्बिना-पीतवाससा विभान्तम्। रौक्म्या सुवर्णमय्या वनमालया आपादलम्बिन्या मालया विभान्तम्। 'रुक्मं कार्तस्वरं जाम्बु' इति **अमरः**। (२.९.९५) 'आपादलम्बिनी माला वनमालेति कथ्यते' ॥९४ ॥

रमादृक्शफरा[७४]जीव्यसौन्दर्यामृतसागरम्।
वयसि प्रमदाकान्ते सन्तं षोडशहायने ॥९५ ॥

---

७१. दीपरत्नैः;

७२. रणो;

७३. रौक्मा वचन॰ (वर्णविपर्यय metathesis

७४. शपरा;

रमेति। रमाया दृशावेव शफरौ मत्स्यौ, तयोराजीव्यः सौन्दर्यामृतसागरो यस्य तम्। प्रमदाकान्ते-प्रमदानां कान्तम् इष्टम्, तस्मिन् षोडशहायने षोडशवर्षात्मके वयसि सन्तं स्थितम् ॥९५ ॥

भास्वत्कङ्कणकेयूरकिरीटोदारकुण्डलैः।
अन्यैश्चाभरणैः सूर्यप्रतिबिम्बैरिवार्णवम् ॥९६ ॥

भास्वदिति। सूर्यप्रतिबिम्बैः अर्णवमिव आभरणैर्विराजमानमिति शेषः ॥९६ ॥

शङ्खचक्रगदापद्मसानुप्लवकराम्बुजम्।
संवाह्यमानचरणं सभयप्रणयं श्रिया ॥९७ ॥

शङ्ख इति। सानुप्लवानि ससहायानि कराम्बुजानि यस्य। शङ्खचक्रगदा-पद्मयुक्तकराम्बुजमित्यर्थः। सभयप्रणयं यथा [स्यात्] तथा, श्रिया संवाह्यमानचरणम् ॥९७ ॥

सहस्राधिकभोगीन्द्रफणाविभ्रमदायिना।
पाण्डुरेणातपत्रेण सर्वाधिक्येऽप्यधः कृतम् ॥९८ ॥

सहस्रमिति। अस्य सर्वाधिक्येऽपि आतपत्रेण अधः कृतः अधस्तात् कृतः, तस्य उ(स्यो) परि विराजमानत्वात्, **विरोधः शब्दतः** ॥९८ ॥९९ ॥

शरदिन्दुवलक्षाभ्यां[७५] चलाभ्यां पार्श्वयोर्द्वयोः।
चामराभ्यां विराजन्तं बलाकाभ्यामिवाम्बुदम् ॥९९ ॥

[७६]द्वाःस्थदण्डाहतिप्रोद्यद्धनञ्जयकणत्विषा।
संभिन्नकान्तिमुकुटैर्देवैर्दूरान्नमस्कृतम् ॥१०० ॥

द्वा(द्वाः)स्थ इति। धनञ्जयः अग्निः, तस्य कणकान्त्या। संभिन्नकान्तयः मिश्रितकान्तयः मुकुटा येषां, तैः ॥१०० ॥१०१ ॥

पुरुषं कञ्चिदैक्षिष्ट तं रथस्थममन्यत।
नन्दात्मजं महाभागो भ्रमापेतेन चेतसा ॥१०१ ॥

---

७५. भ्या (अनुस्वार dropped);
७६. P.&B. both write as द्वास्थ dropping the विसर्ग– a scribal peculiarity, B writing स्य & not स्थ;

ब्रह्मादिसुरवर्याणामृषीणां च महात्मनाम् ।
सङ्ख्यातीताननतिप्रेम्णा तस्यैवोद्गायतां गुणान् ॥१०२ ॥

ब्रह्मेति युग्मम्। सः अक्रूरः, तस्य सङ्ख्यातीतान् गुणान् उद्गायतां ब्रह्मादिकसुरवर्याणां देवश्रेष्ठानां महात्मनां ऋषीणां च तारान् उच्चान् ध्वनीन् शुश्राव। तारशब्दनिषेधिनां निषेधं कुर्वतां किङ्कराणां च निर्घोषान् शुश्राव ॥१०२ ॥१०३ ॥

शुश्राव स ध्वनींस्तारान् हरिदन्तातिलङ्घिनः ।
निर्घोषान् किङ्कराणां च तारशब्दनिषेधिनाम् ॥१०३ ॥

तद्दर्शनोदितमहाप्रमदोपजातं
[७७]**बाष्पोपबृंहितकलिन्दसुताम्बुपूरः ।**
बद्धाञ्जलिर्नमितकन्धर ईश्वरं तं
स स्तोतुमारभत पुण्यकृतां वरेण्यः ॥१०४ ॥

तद्दर्शनमिति । बृंहितः अधिकीकृतः कलिन्दसुताम्बुपूरः येन सः ॥१०४ ॥

तुभ्यं नमोऽस्तु भगवन् जगदण्डकोटि-
निर्माणपालनविलोपनशक्तिधाम्ने ।
सर्वङ्कषाऽविलयबोधनिकेतनाय
नित्याऽसमोत्तममुदे करुणार्णवाय ॥१०५ ॥

तुभ्यमिति । सर्वङ्कषः सर्वविषयकः, अविलयः(यो) नाशशून्यः(न्यो) यो बोधः ज्ञानं, तन्निकेतनाय । नास्ति समा उत्तमा च यस्याः सा । नित्या असमोत्तमा मुद्त्(मुत्) यस्य, तस्मै निरतिशयानन्दस्वरूपायेत्यर्थः ॥१०५ ॥

यत्सेवनातिशयलब्धमहाप्रभावाः
सन्तो जगत्यनघतां[७८] **स्मरणान्नयन्ति ।**
येषां मतीरधिवसन्त्यखिलाः पदार्था
धर्मैः समं स्वनिलयैरखिलैः सदैव ॥१०६ ॥

यदिति । यत्सेवनातिशयेन लब्धः महाप्रभावो महत्सामर्थ्यं यैस्ते सन्तः, स्मरणात् यत्स्मरणात् हेतोः जगन्ति **कर्म**, अनघतां निष्पापतां नयन्ति प्रापयन्ति । अखिलाः

७७. पाष्पो (प due to the following प);
७८. घतास्मर (अनुस्वार dropped & jointly written-scribal peculiarity);

पदार्थाः स्वनिलयैः अखिलैः धर्मैः समं सदैव येषां मतीः अधिवसन्ति । ते सन्त **इति सम्बन्धः** ॥१०६ ॥

यं स्वानुचिन्तनकृतो विदधानमाशु
नीरागरोषमनसोऽपि वशीकरोति ।
अन्तर्गतान्यविषयेषु महत्सु रागो
रोषोऽपि तेष्वपकृतामसतां गणेषु ॥१०७ ॥

यमिति । स्वानुचिन्तनकृतः स्वस्यानुचिन्तनकर्तृन् पुरुषान् आशु शीघ्रं नीरागरोषमनसः रागरोषशून्यमनसः विदधानं कुर्वाणमपि यं **कर्म** । अन्तर्गता विस्मृताः अन्यविषयाः भगवदन्यविषयाः यैस्तेषु महत्सु रागः प्रीतिः वशीकरोति । तेषु सत्पुरुषेषु अपकृताम् अपकारकारिणाम्, असतां दुष्टानां गणेषु रोषोऽपि यं वशीकरोति ।

परित्राणाय साधूनां विनाशाय च दुष्कृताम् ।
धर्मसंस्थापनार्थाय सम्भवामि युगे युगे ॥ इति गीतोक्तेः । (४.८)

अन्तर्गतं विस्मृतं स्यात्' इति **अमरः** । [३.१.८६] ।१०७ ॥

सुखं च दुःखान्तमनन्तमिच्छतो
न मेऽस्त्युपायाधिगमो जगत्पते ।
प्रदर्श्य[७९] **तं तस्य निरन्तरायतां**
विधाय दीनं नय मां कृतार्थताम् ॥१०८ ॥

सुखमिति । अनन्तं सुखम् अनन्तं च दुःखान्तं च इच्छतः मे उपायाधिगमः ज्ञानं नास्ति ॥१०८ ॥

इति स्तुतः[८०] **प्रार्थित ईश्वरः क्षणात् ।**
तिरोहितोऽभूदथ गान्दिनीसुतः ।
विधाय कर्तव्यमतीव विस्मितः
सरामकृष्णं त्वरितो रथं ययौ ॥१०९ ॥

इतीति । प्रथमं प्रार्थितः (स्तुतः) पश्चात् प्रार्थितः ॥१०९ ॥११० ॥

---

७९. प्रदश्य (omits the रेफ);
८०. P. स्तुतप्रा° (विसर्ग dropped & jointly written);

कस्माद्विलम्बितमिति ब्रुवतीश्वरे तं
किं वा तवाविदितमित्यभिधाय सोऽथ।
प्राप प्रचोदितहयेन रथेन पूर्वं
नन्दादिकान् गतवतो मथुरोपकण्ठम् ॥११० ॥

मथुरोपवनेऽथ ते निवासं विदधुर्नन्दपुरोगमा अदूरे।
अथ सारथिना नृपाय कृष्णागममावेद्य मुदा गृहं प्रपेदे ॥१११ ॥

मथुरेति। सारथिना नृपाय कृष्णागममावेद्य गृहं प्रपेदे। सारथिर्नृपाय कृष्णागममुक्त्वा स्वगृहं गतवानित्यर्थः ॥१११ ॥११२ ॥

यद्धीर्जगज्जातमिवासुरारेस्तनूरखेदाऽभृत शास्त्रजातम्।
***त्रिविक्रमाभिख्यतदात्मजन्मा यः पार्वतीनन्दनतामयासीत्* ॥११२ ॥**

नीलकण्ठेन तेनास्मिन् यादवेन्द्रमहोदये।
***कृते काव्येऽप्युपनवः सर्गः सम्पूर्णतां गतः* ॥११३ ॥९८ ॥**

नीलकण्ठेनेति। उपनवः नवस्य उप समीपे वर्तमानः उपनवः अष्टम इत्यर्थः ॥११३ ॥

इति रानडे इत्युपनामकशामरायाङ्गजेन विष्णुशर्मणा विरचितायां नीलकण्ठविद्वन्मणिकृतयादवेन्द्रमहोदयकाव्यस्य टिप्पन्याम् अष्टमः सर्गः समाप्तः ॥

नवमः सर्गः

[1]सबलोऽथ महेश्वरोऽपराह्णे सवयस्यो मथुरां विलोकयिष्यन्।
अविशत् समुदग्रहेमसालामभिगुप्तामिव भोजराजधाम्ना ॥१ ॥

अथ नवमः सर्गः । सेति । सबलः बलदेवसहितः महेश्वरः, भोजराजः कंसः, तस्य धाम्ना तेजसा अभिगुप्तामिव, समुदग्रः हेम्नः सालः प्राकारो यस्याः सा, तां मथुराम् अविशत् । 'प्राकारो वरु(र)णः सालः' इति **अमरः** ।(२.२.३) ॥१ ॥

अपहाय फणीन्द्रफूत्कृतीनां दहनैस्तप्ततरं तलस्थमम्भः ।
इतराम्बुचराऽद्रितुङ्गयादस्ततिना खेयवरेण[2] वेष्ट्यमानाम् ॥२ ॥

अपहायेति । अतिनिम्नत्वात् फणीन्द्रफूत्कृतीनां दहनैर्वह्निभिः तप्ततरं तलस्थमम्भः विहाय इतराम्बुनि तलस्थभिन्नाम्बुनि, चरन्तीति चराः, अद्रितुङ्गा यादस्ततिः जलजन्तुपरम्परा यस्मिन् तेन परिखेयवरेण वेष्ट्यमानाम् । -खेयं तु परिखा(खाऽऽ)धार अ(रस्त्व)म्भसां यत्र धारणम् ।' इति **अमरः** । (१.१०.२९) ॥२ ॥

प्रविशन् पुरगोपुरेण मेने स मया यद्बलिनिग्रहाय रूपम् ।
समुदग्रमलम्भि तेन चास्योच्छ्रितहस्तेन दुरासदोऽग्रभागः ॥३ ॥

प्रविशन्निति । पुरगोपुरेण पुरद्वारेण प्रविशन् सः कृष्णः मया बलिनिग्रहाय बलेर्वैरोचनस्य दण्डाय-यत्समुदग्रमुन्नतं रूपम् अलम्भि, उच्छ्रितहस्तेन तेन रूपेणापि अस्य पुरद्वारस्य अग्रभागः दुरासदः दुष्प्रापः इति मेने ॥३ ॥४ ॥

अथ तत्र ददर्श काञ्चनानां विचरत्सुन्दरयोषितां मुरारिः ।
निवहं गगनस्पृशां गृहाणां[3] ससुरस्त्रीकमथास्मरत्सुमेरुम् ॥४ ॥

हयसन्नहनं रवेः क्षुधार्तं भुजगेन्द्रं स्वपटोत्थवातपोतैः ।
स ननन्द विलोक्य नन्दयन्तीः प्रतिसद्मोच्छ्रितहेमवैजयन्तीः[4] ॥५ ॥

हय इति । सः कृष्णः रवेः हयसन्नहनं हयाकर्षकरज्जुरूपं भुजगेन्द्रं स्वपटोत्थवातपोतैः नन्दयन्तीः प्रतिगृहोन्नतपताकाः वीक्ष्य ननन्द ॥५ ॥

---

१ P. begins with श्रीकृष्णाय नमः। B. begins with श्रीगणेशाय नमः।

२. P. marginal quotation 'खेयं तु परिखाधारस्त्वम्भसां यत्र धारणम् ।' इति **अमरः** ।

३. ग्रहाणां-a common mistake of confusing ग्रह with गृह;

४. °द्भोछित° (रेफ dropped);

मनुजानवलोक्य तत्र सर्वान्निजवर्णाश्रमकर्मजागरूकान् ।
इति विस्मितवानहो अमुष्यां शुभशीलाः कथमौग्रसेनिशिष्टाः ॥६ ॥

मनुजानिति । औग्रसेनिः कंसः, तेन शिष्टाः शुभशीलाः कथमिति विस्मितवान् ॥६ ॥

हरिरेवमवेदवेक्ष्य तस्यामपरापेक्षमहाजवैरिवाश्वैः ।
कथमेव समा रवेस्तुरङ्गा मरुता तूलदशां परेण नीताः ॥७ ॥

हरिरिति । हरिः एवम् अवेत् ज्ञातवान् । किं ज्ञातवानित्याकाङ्क्षायामाह-तस्यां नगर्याम् अवेक्ष्य अर्थात् अश्वान् विलोक्य । परेण उपस्थितेन मरुता वायुना ये तूलदशां नीतास्ते रवेस्तुरङ्गमाः, इह स्थितैः, अपरोक्षः साक्षाद्विद्यमानः महाजवो येषु, तैः अश्वैः कथं समाः स्युरेवं ज्ञातवानिति ॥७ ॥

जलधेर्घनपीतशून्यकुक्षेरिव दृश्येन्द्रनिलीनशैलराजेः ।
रथदन्तिगणेन राजवीथ्या भगवान् दिव्यदृशाऽपि नान्तमाप ॥८ ॥

जलधेरिति । भगवान् घनैः पीत अत एव शून्यकुक्षिस्तस्य, अत एव दृश्या इन्द्रभयान्निलीना शैलराजिर्यस्मिन्, तस्य जलधेरिव रथदन्तिगणेन युक्तायाः राजवीथ्याः दिव्यदृशा दिव्यदृष्ट्याऽपि अन्तं पारं नाप, लौकिकदृशा नापेति किं वक्तव्यम् ॥८ ॥९ ॥१० ॥

मणिमौक्तिकहेमरूप्यजालं क्रयिकाणां गलितं करात्प्रमादात् ।
परवित्तपराङ्मुखैः पुरस्थैरहतं सान्द्रमवैक्षि[५] तत्र तेन ॥९ ॥

अवधीरितसुन्दरोत्तमं तं भगवन्तं [६]समुपागतं निशम्य ।
अवलोकनवाञ्छया पुरस्था गृहवातायनमासदन्नताङ्ग्यः ॥१० ॥

वदनैर्विषयैर्दृशां तदीयैः प्रतिसौधं प्रतिमारुतायनं च ।
मिलितैः समुपार्जिता तदानीं युगपत्सम्भवकोटिचन्द्रलक्ष्मीः ॥११ ॥

वदनैरिति । दृशाम् अर्थात् जनदृशां विषयैर्गोचरैः तदीयैर्वदनैः प्रतिसौधं प्रतिवातायनं प्रतिगवाक्षं मिलितैः सद्भिः तदानीं युगपत्सम्भवाः युगपदुत्पन्नाः ये कोटिसङ्ख्याकचन्द्राः तेषां लक्ष्मीः समुपार्जिता ॥११ ॥

---

५. क्षित्तत्र;
६. स्वमु;

अनुषक्तपयोदमेचकाङ्गो नयनेन्दीवरकान्तिभिर्वधूनाम्।
रुरुचे स महानतीव दीर्घैः प्रसृतैः स्वैः किरणैरिवेन्द्रनीलः[७] ॥१२॥

अनुषक्त इति। वधूनां नयनेन्दीवरकान्तिभिः अनुषक्तं पयोदवत् मेचकं नीलमङ्गं यस्य सः कृष्णः प्रसृतैः रवेः किरणैर्युक्तः इन्द्रनील इव रुरुचे ॥१२॥

प्रमदं यमविन्दताङ्गनानां[८] समवायस्तमवेक्ष्य सुन्दराग्रम्।
तदलाभधियाऽथ यं विषादं ननु तावेव तयोर्मिथः समानौ ॥१३॥

प्रमदमिति। तयोः तावेव प्रमदविषादावेव परस्परसमानौ अन्योपमानरहितौ ॥१३॥

अथ राजपथे व्रजन् स यान्तं रजकं[९] कञ्चन धौतवस्त्रवाहम्।
वसनान्यवनिष्ट[१०] तेन चाधिक्षिपता कोपमवापितोऽवधीत्तम्[११] ॥१४॥

अथेति। अवनिष्ट याचितवान् ॥१४॥

धरणीशयनं खले प्रयाते स्वपतीव श्रमतोऽतिभारवाहे।
अनुजीविगणोऽस्य वस्त्रकोशान् परिमुच्यातनुते पलायनं स्म ॥१५॥

धरणीति। श्रमतः श्रमात् हेतोः, स्वपतीव शयनं कुर्वतीव ॥१५॥

जगृहे रुचिराम्बराणि कृष्णो बलभद्रः सुहृदश्च तस्य सर्वे।
अथ कश्चन वायकः सुवस्त्रैर्बलकृष्णावकरोन्मनोज्ञवेषौ ॥१६॥

जगृहे (ह) इति। वायकः तन्तुवायकः ॥१६॥

अथ काऽपि वधूस्त्रिवक्रदेहा नृपयोग्याङ्गविलेपनार्पणेन।
भगवन्तमनुप्रसाद्य तस्मादृजुतां स्वस्य तनोर्मतेरिवाप ॥१७॥

अथेति। तस्मात् भगवतः स्वस्य मतेरिव तनोः ऋजुता (तां) सारल्यमाप ॥१७॥

अथ कश्चन मालिकः सुदामाभिध ईशं परिचस्करे सुमाल्यैः।
स च तत्सदनं धनैरनन्तैः सुतपौत्रादिभिरप्यमोघकामः ॥१८॥

---

७. णैरवे;
८. यमर्विदता;
९. रजकञ्चन (one कं dropped; due to similarity in spelling Haplograpy);
१०. P. marginal gloss: याचितवान्
११. ऽवधीतम् (त् dropped);

अथेति। परिचस्करे अलङ्कृतवान्। सः कृष्णः तत्सदनं धनादिभिः परिचस्करे ॥१८ ॥१९ ॥

सरणावनुयुक्तपौरलोकः सह रामेण स धन्वयागशालाम्।
अविशन्निशितास्त्रयोधगुप्तप्रतिहारामभिभूय रुन्धतस्तान् ॥१९ ॥

स गतोऽन्तरवेक्षितेव चापान्तिकमासाद्य महत्सुपूजितं तत्।
परिगृह्य करे क्षणाद्द्विखण्डं कृतवांस्तेन च रक्षिणोऽक्रुधंस्ते ॥२० ॥

से (स इ)ति। अवेक्षितेव पश्यन्निव। महत् [च] सुपूजितं [च], तेन द्विखण्डकरणेन ते रक्षिणः अक्रुधन्, क्रोधविशिष्टा अभवन् ॥२० ॥

ग्रहणाय वितन्वतां[१२] प्रयत्नं स भटानां निवहं महानुभावः।
परिवारयतां बलश्च वीरः शकलाभ्यां[१३] धनुषोऽहतां क्षणेन ॥२१ ॥

ग्रहणायेति। ग्रहणाय रामकृष्णयोः ग्र(ग्र)हणाय। धनुषः शकलाभ्यां क्षणेन अहतां ताडितवन्तौ ॥२१ ॥

हतशेषभटाः पलाय्य वृत्तं नरपालाय निवेदयाम्बभूवुः।
भगवानपि वासरावसानात् सवयस्यः सबलो निवेशमाप ॥२२ ॥

हत इति। निवेशं गृहम् ॥२२ ॥

श्रुतकार्मुकभङ्गरक्षियोधक्षपणस्योदभवद्य[१४] एष रोषः।
शमितोऽजनि नारदोक्तमर्थं स्मरतो भोजपतेर्भयोदयेन ॥२३ ॥

श्रुतमि(त इ)ति। श्रुतेः(तः) कामुकः (कार्मुकस्य) भृ(भ)ङ्गः रक्षियोधक्षपणे च येन, तस्य भोजपतेः यः रोषः उदभवत् सः (स) नारदोक्तमर्थं स्मरतः त(स्त)स्य तस्य भयोदयेन शमितः अजनि, शान्तोऽभूदित्यर्थः ॥२३ ॥

निखिलं भुवनं प्रतापयन्तं नृपतेजः सवितारमस्ततैक्ष्ण्यम्।
स्वबलेन विधाय भोजराजं भयहेमन्त उदेजयाञ्चकार ॥२४ ॥

निखिलमिति। भयमेव हेमन्तः ऋतुविशेषः, नृपतेज एव सविता सूर्यः तम्। स्वबलेन स्वशक्त्या अस्ततैक्ष्ण्यं विधाय कृत्वा भोजराजम् उदेजयाञ्चकार कम्पयामास ॥२४ ॥

---

१२. वित्तन्वतां;
१३. शलकाभ्यां (metathesis);
१४. दभवयद्य;

अतिवीर्यमहाशनादिदैत्यक्षपणव्याकृतनिस्तुलानुभावः ।
अयमष्टम आत्मजः स्वसुर्मे कमुपायं श्रयतो भवेत्प्रशम्यः ॥२५ ॥

अतीति । मे स्वसुः अयमष्टमः आत्मजः कमुपायं श्रयतः मे मया प्रशम्यः नाश्यः-(श्यो) भवेत् ॥२५ ॥

इति चिन्तयतोऽस्य भोजराजः समये तत्र दृगध्वनीनेमासीत्[१५] ।
अतिरेचितकृष्णभीति सद्योमरणव्यञ्जकदुर्निमित्तजालम् ॥२६ ॥

इतीति । अतिरेचिता वर्धिता कृष्णात् भीतिर्यस्मिन् तत् । एतादृशं दुर्निमित्तजालं दृगध्वनीनमासीत् ॥२६ ॥२७ ॥

स यतो यत ईक्षणानुपातं विदधे भीतमनास्ततस्ततोऽथ ।
ददृशे निशितोद्यतास्त्रै[१६]भीमं वसुदेवात्मजरूपमेव नान्यत् ॥२७ ॥

अतिवृत्य तु भूयसीं त्रियामां नृपतिर्दैववशादलब्ध निद्राम् ।
पुरुषो भयदासि[१७]तोन्नताङ्गो ददृशे[१८] स्वप्नगतोऽतिकृष्णदन्तः ॥२८ ॥

अतीत्य(ति) । दैववशात् निद्राम् अलब्ध प्राप्तः । भयदमसितम् उन्नतमङ्गं यस्य सः ॥२८ ॥

अनु जागरितं नृपेण तस्मिन् समये पद्मवनैरपि प्रबुद्धम् ।
अथ राजसभामुपेत्य मल्लान् नृप आकारितवान् प्रतीतवीर्यान् ॥२९ ॥

अन्विति । अनु स्वप्नमनु नृपेण जागरितम् । तस्मिन् समये पद्मवनैरपि प्रबुद्धं विकसितम् । अनेन निशान्तस्वप्न उक्तः । निशान्तस्वप्नस्यावितथत्वात् ॥२९ ॥

अथ मल्लवरान् शशास सोऽस्मत्पुरतो मल्लरणेन तावदान्तौ ।
वसुदेवसुतौ प्रमापयेतेत्यनुमेने नरपालशासनं तैः ॥३० ॥

अथेति । अस्मत्पुरतः मल्लरणेन मल्लयुद्धेन अदान्तौ अशिक्षितौ वसुदेवसुतौ प्रमापयेत मारयेत इति मल्लान् शशासाऽऽज्ञप्तवान् । तैः न(र्न)रपालशासनमनुमेने अनुमोदितम् ॥३० ॥

---

१५. नना;
१६. स्त्रि;
१७. दसि;
१८. ददृश;

अथ मल्लनियुद्धरङ्गभूमिं परितो निर्मिततुङ्गमञ्चकेषु[१९]।
अतितुङ्गतमे स्थितो दिवं यन् वसतिं काञ्चिदिवाध्युवास कंसः ॥३१ ॥

अथेति । अतितुङ्गतमे मञ्चे स्थितः दिवं यन् प्राप्नुवन् सन् काञ्चित् वसतिम् अध्युवासेव ॥३१ ॥

रणरङ्गभुवं ततश्च मल्ला अभजन्निर्दयवाद्यमानवाद्याम् ।
सकलाः पुरवासिनोऽपि मञ्चान् ययुराकारणमेत्य घोषणाख्यम् ॥३२ ॥

[रण]रङ्गमिति । घोषणाख्यमाकारणम् आह्वानम् एत्य प्राप्य । 'हूतिराकारणाह्वानम्' इति **अमरः** ।(१.६.८) ॥३२ ॥३३ ॥

पशुपालगणैः सहाथ नन्दः समुपागत्य तदाज्ञया प्रणम्य ।
तदुपान्तभुवि क्वचिन्य(न्न्य)षीदन्नयनप्रेरणसूचितोपवेशः[२०] ॥३३ ॥

पृथुगह्वरे[२१]लम्बिकृष्णसर्पं निपतन्निर्झरिणीकमञ्जनाद्रिम् ।
समयन् पृथुहस्ततोन्नतिभ्यामसितिम्ना च मदाम्बुनिर्झरेण[२२] ॥३४ ॥

पृथ्विति । अञ्जनाद्रिं समयन् समीकुर्वन् । कुवलयापीडगजः । पृथुगह्वरलम्बिकृष्णसर्पस्य पृथुहस्तेन शुण्डादडे(ण्डे)न साम्यम् । निर्झरिण्याः मदाम्बुनिर्झरेण साम्यम् । अञ्जनाद्रेः उन्नत्या असितिम्ना च साम्यम् ॥३४ ॥

अनुसृत्य निदेशमौग्रसेनेर्द्विप आधोरणसंप्रणोद्यमानः ।
अजिघृक्षत हन्तुमागतौ द्वार्यथ रङ्गस्य[२३] बलं च वासुदेवम् ॥३५ ॥

अनुसृत्येति । बलं वासुदेवं च हन्तुम् अजिघृक्षत गृहीतुम् ऐ(ऐ) च्छत् ॥३५ ॥

किमरे न रुणत्सि दन्तिनं स्वं न निरुन्त्से यदि हन्यसे सनागः ।
इति कृष्णगिराऽतिरोष्यमाणो बलवत्प्राणुदत द्विपं निषादी ॥३६ ॥

किमरे इति । न निरुन्त्से यदि सनागः नागसहितः(तो) हन्यसे मार्यसे, मयेति

---

१९. निर्मित्त. B. scribe could not understand the sign of deletion of त् from P. hence wrote as त्त;
२०. Both P. & B. have न्य;
२१. B. ह; P. writes as °ह-Marathi influence;
२२. निर्झरण;
२३. रगस्य (अनुस्वार dropped);

शेषः । इति कृष्णगिरा रोष्यमाणः रोषं प्राप्यमाणः(णो) निषादी हस्तिपकः(को) द्विपं बलवत् प्राणुदत प्रेरितवान् ।३६ ॥

अपसृत्य करेण वेष्टिताङ्गो बलिना दन्तिवरेण वासुदेवः ।
धृतदन्त इमं नुनोद पश्चादतिदूरतरं[२४] सकलो विसिष्मियेऽत्र ।।३७ ।।

अपसृत्येति । बलिना दन्तिवरेण वेष्टिताङ्गः वासुदेवः अपसृत्य अपसरणं कृत्वा धृतदन्तः सन् इमं गजं पश्चात् अतिदूरं नुनोद । सकलः जनः(नो) विसिष्मिये विस्मयं प्राप ।।३७ ।।

पुनरस्य जिघांसयाऽऽगतस्य द्विरदस्यैष निपाट्य दन्तयुग्मम् ।
अमुना शिथिलानसून् प्रहारैः शमयन् हस्तिपमप्यथो[२५] अहिंसीत् ।।३८ ।।

पुनरिति । जिघांसया आगतस्य । अमुना दन्तयुग्मोत्पाटनेन शिथिलान् जर्जरितान् असून् प्रहारैः शमयन्, अथो अनन्तरं हस्तिपमपि अहिंसीत् मारितवान् ।।३८ ।।

गजदन्तधरावमू वयस्यैर्न्यविशेतां सह मल्लयुद्धरङ्गम् ।
मनुजस्पृहणीयदर्शनौ तावपि दृष्ट्वा भृशमव्यथिष्ट कंसः ।।३९ ।।

गज इति । वयस्यैः सह न्यविशेतां प्रविष्टौ । कंसः भृशम् अव्यथिष्ट व्यथां प्राप्तः ।।३९ ।।

तनुसङ्गविहीनमप्यवन्तं स नृपश्चेतनमात्मवारबाणम्[२६] ।
यमवेद् बलकेश[२७]वाववादीदथ चाणूर[२८]पदाभिधः स मल्लः ।।४० ।।

तन्विति । नृपः यं तनुसङ्गविहीनमपि अवन्तम् अर्थात् आ(दा)त्मानं रक्षन्तं चेतनम् आत्मवारबाणम् आत्मकवचम् अवेत् सः मल्लः बलकेशवौ अवादीत् उक्तवान् ।।४० ।।४१ ।।

अयि भो भवतोर्नियुद्धदाक्ष्यं श्रुतवानानयदत्र यो दिदृक्षुः ।
तमिमं स्वनियुद्धकौशलेन प्रभुमानन्द्य कृतार्थतां भजेम ।।४१ ।।

---

२४. B. drops तरं & has दूरं;
२५. मप (वर्णव्यत्यास- Metathesis);
२६. वाखरणम्;
२७. drops केश;
२८. चारणूर;

बलिनः स्वयशोहरं भवन्तः कथमिच्छन्त्यबलैः समं [२९]नियुद्धम् ।
इति वादिनमीश्वरं[३०] स मल्लः पुनरप्येवमुवाच[३१] मेति वादीः ॥४२ ॥

बलिन इति । बलिनः भवन्तः यूयं स्वयशोहरम् अबलैः बलरहितैरस्माभिः समं नियुद्धं कथमिच्छन्ति, इति मा वादीः, इत्यवोचत् ॥४२ ॥

न भवानबलस्त्वदग्रजो वा बलवद्दानवभङ्गलब्धवर्णः ।
तदगर्हितमावयोर्नियुद्धं भवतान्मुष्टिकरौहिणेययोश्च ॥४३ ॥

नेति । आवयोः मुष्टिकरौहिणेययोः नियुद्धं भवतात् भवतु ॥४३ ॥

अनुमत्य तयोस्तयोश्च युद्धं समभूदप्य[३२]मरैरदृष्टपूर्वम् ।
परिहृत्य परप्रहारयोगं चरतोर्यत्नवतोः परप्रहारे ॥४४ ॥

अन्विति । अनुमत्य अङ्गीकृत्य स्थितयोः तयोः युद्धं समभूत् ॥४४ ॥

उप[३३]सृत्य मुहुस्तदाऽकृतार्थावपसृप्तौ समविक्रमावुभौ तौ ।
[३४]कटुयाचनिकोक्तिबाधितानां मनसो लोभवतां समावभूताम् ॥४५ ॥

उपेति । मुहुः उपसृत्य तदा अकृतार्थौ अत एवापसृप्तौ । याचकानां कटूक्त्या धर्मोद्यतानां लोभात् हेतोः धर्मानुद्यतानां लोभवतां मनसः समौ अभूताम् ॥४५ ॥

परिरभ्य निपातने प्रयत्नं विदधानावितरेतरस्य शक्त्या ।
इतरेतरकर्मणो निरोधाद्गुणवद्योगमुदाचलाविवास्ताम् ॥४६ ॥

परीति । शक्त्या इतरेतरकर्मणः निरोधात् गुणवतोर्योगः सम्बन्धः, तज्जन्यहर्षेणेव अचलौ आस्ताम् ॥४६ ॥

प्रजहार यदा स लब्धरन्ध्रस्तमयं वा न तदा[३५] तयोर्व्यथाऽभूत् ।
सदृशप्रतियोधलाभजेन प्रमदेनानवकाशितं मनो[३६] यत् ॥४७ ॥

---

२९. समन्नि° (म् changed to न् with which the next word starts- Marathi influence);
३०. वाग्दिन-ग् added to दि like to नि/ति- scribal peculiarity;
३१. °प्येव वाचमेति (मु dropped & jointly written);
३२. भूपप्यम;(प on the analogy of following प);
३३. अप;
३४. कुटु (उ on the analogy of टु);
३५. तदात्तयो (B. scribe could not understand the त् deleted in P. like this त्त);
३६. मना;

प्रजहारेति । लब्धरन्ध्रः लब्धावकाशः अयम् अन्यो वा तं परस्परं प्रजहार । यत् यस्मात् प्रमदेन मनः अनवकाशितं तत् तस्मात् तयोः व्यं(व्य)था नाभूत् ॥४७ ॥

स समं हरिणा न्ययुद्ध यावन्न सुखं तावदपीषदप्यवाप ।
हरितां नयता भयेन सर्वं[३७] नरपालस्तमपि द्विषं हि मेने ॥४८ ॥

स इति । सः नरपालः हरिणा समं यावत् चाणूरः न्ययुद्ध तावदपि ईषदपि सुखं न अवाप । असुखे हेतुमाह-हरिरिति । सर्वं पदार्थमात्रं हरितां विष्णुत्वं नयता भयेन तमपि चाणूरमपि द्विषं शत्रुं मेने । तस्मात्सुखं नावापेत्यर्थः ॥४८ ॥

वयसाऽल्पतयाऽपकर्षमात्मन्यवगत्याप जनो भृशां व्यथां याम् ।
परिदर्शितविक्रमाधिकत्त्वः[३८] परिमार्ष्टुं यतते स्म तां महेशः ॥४९ ॥

वयसेति । परिदर्शितं विक्रमाधिकत्वं येन सः ॥४९ ॥

भगवद्बलवत्प्रहारभग्नावयवस्यापि महाबलस्य तस्य ।
अभवन्न निर्वर्तनोन्मुखत्वं[३९] न यशो मानवता जिहास्यते हि ॥५० ॥

भगवदिति । निवर्तनोन्मुखत्वं नाभवत् । हि यस्मात् मानवता मानिना पुरुषेण यशः न जिहास्यते न हातुमिष्यते ॥५० ॥

परितोषित ईश्वरो नियुद्धक्रतुना दित्सितवान् दिवं परस्मै ।
स पपात हरेः कठोरमुष्टेरभिघातेन दलच्छिरा अथोर्व्याम् ॥५१ ॥

परीति । युद्धक्रतुना परितोषितः ईश्वरः परस्मै शत्रवे दिवं दित्सितवान् दातुमैच्छत् ॥५१ ॥

बलमुष्टिकयोश्च युद्धमेवं चिरकालं समभूद्बलोऽथ रुष्टः ।
अनुयापितवान् स्वमुष्टिघातं परमब्जाक्षहतं तमग्र्यमल्लम्[४०] ॥४२ ॥

बलमिति । रुष्टः बलः परं शत्रुं स्वमुष्टिघातं स्वमुष्ट्या हत्वा तम् अब्जाक्षहतम् अग्र्यमल्लमनु यापितवान् प्रस्थापितवान् ॥४२ ॥

अभजन् शलकूटतोसलाख्या अपि मल्लास्तदवस्थतां नियुध्य ।
नृपतेरसुताभिमानमात्रात् कथमेतेषु यथार्थपञ्चताऽभूत् ॥५३ ॥

अभजन्निति । नृपतेः असुताऽभिमानः-"इमे पञ्च मल्ला मम असवः" इति योऽभिमानः - तन्मात्रात् एतेषु यथार्थपञ्चता मरणं कथमभूदिति ॥५३ ॥५४ ॥

---

३७. सर्वनर° (अनुस्वार dropped and jointly written);
३८. कत्वः;
३९. निववर्त°;
४०. तमब्जैग्र्य °(on the strength of °मब्जा°);

इतरेषु पलायितेषु मल्लेष्वथ वाद्यध्वनिवर्धितां युयुत्साम्।
अभिपूरयितुं बलश्च कृष्णः सवयोभ्यां सह योद्धुमारभेताम्॥५४॥

अथ मन्युगतः शशास कंसो वसुदेवस्य सुतौ पुराद्बहिर्नैः।
कुरुतापधनं च नन्दमेतं वसुदेवं सहदारमालभध्वम्[४१] ॥५५॥

अथेति। नन्दम् अपधनं धनरहितं निर्धनं कुरुत। स्त्रीसहितं वसुदेवम् आलभध्वं मारयध्वम्॥५५॥

इति तत्कठिनोक्तिजातमन्युर्भगवानुत्प्लुत आप कंसमञ्चम्।
असिखेटधरः स आत्मरक्षां विदधानो[४२] विचचार मण्डलानि[४३] ॥५६॥

प्रसभेन निपात्य तत्किरीटं धृतकेशो विनिकृष्य[४४] तुङ्गमञ्चात्।
अधिभूमि निपात्य चोग्रसेनिं निपपातोपरि तस्य दानवारिः॥५७॥

असवो जहिरे न तेन यावद्भगवांस्तं शिथिलासुमुत्तमाङ्गे।
चरणेन खलं जघान तावत् पितृबाधास्मरणोदितोग्रमन्युः॥५८॥

अवलोक्य तथाविधं तमायन्ननुजास्तस्य हि वैरशुद्धिकामाः।
समराय बलार्णवे पतन्तस्त इमेऽङ्गारकणाः क्षणादशाम्यन्॥५९॥

अवेति। वैरशुद्धिकामाः तस्य अनुजाः समराय आयन् आगताः। बल एवार्णवस्तस्मिन् पतन्तः अङ्गारकणा इव अशाम्यन् शान्ताः, बलहस्तेन मृता इत्यर्थः॥५९॥६०॥६१॥६२॥

भगवच्चरणानुषङ्गनष्टांहसि शान्तिं[४५] गत उग्रसेनसूनौ।
कुसुमानि जगत्पताववर्षद्दिविजानीकमवापितप्रमोदम्॥६०॥

ननृतेऽप्सरसां गणेन, गीता दिवि गन्धर्ववरैर्गुणा मुरारेः।
सुरदुन्दुभिताडनोत्थशब्दैर्जगदण्डं परिपूरितं तदाऽऽसीत्॥६१॥

विलपन्त्यवरोधयौवतानि प्रभुराश्वास्य मृतस्य यद्विधेयम्।
तदकारयदुग्रसेन[४६]जानामथ पित्रोरवलोकनेच्छुरासीत्॥६२॥

---

४१. °ध्व (म् dropped);
४२. °धाना;
४३. °ग्नि (नि mostly mis-spelt as ग्नि-scribal trait);
४४. °कृष्णो;
४५. शान्तिगत (अनुस्वार dropped & jointly written);
४६. °संन°;

रचयन्नपनीतबन्धनौ तौ बलभद्रेण सहाच्युतो ननाम।
पितरावभवन्निषेवणान्नावतियातानि वृथा दिनान्यमूनि ॥६३॥

रचयन्निति। पितरौ ननाम। अभवन्निषेवणात् भवन्निषेवणाभावात् नौ आवयोः दि(र्दि)नानि वृथा यातानि गतानि। इमम् अपराधं युवां क्षमेथामिति अवददिति **उत्तरश्लोकेनान्वयः** ॥६३॥

अपराधमिमं युवां क्षमेथा[४७]मवदच्चेत्यथ भो महेश्वर[४८] त्वम्।
इति नार्हसि वक्तुमित्यमुष्य प्रसवित्रीजनकावभाषिषाताम् ॥६४॥

अपराधमिति। अभाषिषाताम् उक्तवन्तौ ॥६४॥

परमेश्वरमायया तिरोऽभूत् परमेशत्वमतिस्तयोः क्षणेन।
परिरभ्य सुतावथ प्रमोदस्रवदास्रस्नपितावमू[४९] व्यधाताम् ॥६५॥

परमेश्वर इति। अमू देवकीवसुदेवौ सुतौ **कर्म,** प्रमोदेनानन्देन स्रवत् यत् आस्रं बाष्पं तेन स्नपितौ व्यधातां कृतवन्तौ ॥६५॥

अधिपं व्यतनोदथोग्रसेनं विषये कंसनिदेशगोचरे सः।
परदेशगतान् भयेन कंसान्मथुरामानयदीश्वरः स्वबन्धून् ॥६६॥

अधीति। कंसनिदेशगोचरे विषये देशे ॥६६॥

व्रजमेति हरिर्नहीति मत्वा व्यथमानो हरिवाक्यवीतशोकः।
व्रजराज उपागमत् सगोपो व्रजमश्रीकमविष्णुसन्निधा[५०]नात् ॥३७॥

व्रजमिति। हरिर्व्रजं न एति इति मत्वा व्यथमानः हरिवाक्यैर्वीतशोकः गतशोकः(को) नन्दः अविष्णुसन्निधानात् विष्णुसन्निधानाऽभावात् अश्रीकं श्रीरहितं व्रजम् उपागमत् ॥३७॥

अथ गार्ग्यमुनीश्वरोपनीतौ सकलज्ञौ ब[५१]लभद्रवासुदेवौ।
उपसेदतुरिष्यमाणविद्याविव सान्दीपनिनामदेशिकेन्द्रम् ॥६८॥

---

४७. °क्षमेताम°;

४८. Joins the two words as महेश्वरत्त्वम्;

४९. °दम्लव°-not clear (illegible);

५०. omits ना;

५१. भल° (on the analogy of भद्र which follows); cf. vs. 93 also;

अथेति । गार्ग्यसंज्ञकमुनीश्वरेण उपनीतौ कृतोपनयनौ, इष्यमाणविद्याविव अभिलष्यमाणविद्याविव सान्दीपिनीनामकं गुरुमुपसेदतुः प्राप्तवन्तौ ॥६८ ॥

सकला अपि तावधीत्य विद्याः[५२] दिवसैः कैश्चिदवोचतां गुरुं तम् ।
भगवन् भवतः समीहितार्थं विरचय्यानृणतामवाप्नुयाव ॥६९ ॥

सकले (ला इ) ति । तौ कैश्चिद्दिवसैः सकलाः विद्याः अधीत्य तं गुरुमवोचताम् । अवाप्नुयाव भजेव ॥६९ ॥७० ॥

स गुरुः "जलधौ मृतोऽस्मदीयस्तनयः षोडशहायनस्तमेनम् ।
यदि जीवितवन्तमर्पयेतं भवतोः[५३] स्यादनृणत्वम्" इत्यवादीत् ॥७० ॥

[५४]गुरुणा विदितस्वशक्तिनैवं गदितौ रामहरी रथेन गत्वा ।
जलधिं तमयाचतां, स [५५]ऊचे "तमहन् पञ्चजनो हि मन्निवासः" ॥७१ ॥

गुरुणेति । मन्निवासः मयि स्थितः पञ्चजनसंज्ञको राक्षसः तं पुत्रम् अहन् मारितवान् ॥७१ ॥

जलधाववगाह्य तं निहत्य स्थितमादाय च कम्बुमस्य कुक्षौ ।
हरिरुत्थितवानथो सरामो भगवान् संयमनीं रथेन भेजे ॥७२ ॥

जलधाविति । तं पञ्चजनं निहत्य हत्वा, संयमनीं यमनगरीम् ॥७२ ॥

विदितागमनेन पूजितौ तौ शमनेनाऽवदतां "गुरोः सुतं नः ।
दिश षोडशहायनं" स ताभ्यां विततारोक्तविधं[५६] निदेशशक्त्या ॥७३ ॥

विदितेति । उक्तविधं षोडशहायनात्मकं विततार । मृतस्य पुनरुज्जीवनदानासम्भवात् कथं दत्तवानित्याशङ्क्याह-निदेशशक्त्येति । भगवदाज्ञाशक्तिरेव पुनरुज्जीवनसमर्था, तया दत्तवानित्यर्थः ॥७३ ॥

गुरवेऽर्पितसूनवेऽथ नत्वा गुरुविश्राणितमाशिषां सहस्रम् ।
अधिगम्य समुद्रवर्षतुल्यं पुरमागत्य निजानानन्दयेताम् ॥७४ ॥

---

५२. BothP.&B.retainedthe विसर्ग (whichshouldhavebeen dropped)consciouslytoemphasizethepluralityoflore:
५३. भवतोस्यां (विसर्ग dropped&jointlywritten);
५४. विरुणा (वि duetothefollowing वि inthenextword);
५५. B.writesas ऊ॑-Marathiinfluence;
५६. °विधनि° (अनुस्वार dropped&jointlywritten)

गुरव इति। समुद्रवर्षतुल्यं निष्फलम्, आशिषामधिगमात् पूर्वमेव, परिपूर्णमनोरथत्वात्। पुरमुपेत्य निजान् स्वकीयान् आनन्दयेताम् ॥७४ ॥७५ ॥७६ ॥

कृतकंसवधं निशम्य कंसश्वशुरः[५७] कृष्णमुदी(दि) ततीव्रमन्युः ।
अरुणन्मथुरामपारसैन्यैर्मगधानामधिपो महाबलोऽथ ॥७५ ॥

भगवान् स्वजनानवन् सरामो बहिरागत्य पुराद्रथाधिरूढः ।
निखिलं विनिहत्य तस्य सैन्यं मगधेशं जगृहे सजीवमेव ॥७६ ॥

कृपया स बलेन मोचितः सन् तपसे निश्चितधीर्न्यवर्ति मित्रैः ।
प्रथमस्य समान् फलेन चक्रे स पुनः षोडशसङ्गरान् सरोषः ॥७७ ॥

कृपयेति । तपसे तपोऽर्थं निश्चितधीः सः मित्रैः न्यवर्ति, तपःसम्पादनादिति शेषः । फलेन प्रथमस्य प्रथमयुद्धस्य समान् ॥७७ ॥

मगधाधिपतौ प्रवर्ध्यमानप्रतिघे[५८]ऽष्टादशसङ्गराय सैन्यम् ।
घटयत्यरुणत् सुरर्षिनुन्नो यवनेशो मथुरां तुरुष्कसैन्यैः ॥७८ ॥

मगध इति । प्रवर्ध्यमाना वृद्धिं प्राप्ता प्रतिघा क्रोधो यस्य सः, तस्मिन्, अष्टादशसङ्गराय सैन्यं घटयति सति । सुरर्षिर्नारदः, तेन नुन्नः प्रेरितः(तो) यवनेशः मथुरामरुणत् रोधितवान् ॥७८ ॥

रिपुरुद्धपुराः पुनः पुनर्नः स्वजना मा स्म भवन् भृशं भयार्ताः ।
इति शौरिरकारयत्पयोधेरधिमध्यं सुरशिल्पिना पुरोद्धम् ॥७९ ॥

रिपुरिति । स्वजनाः पुनः पुनः भृशं भयार्ताः मा स्म भवन् इति बुद्ध्या । पुरोद्धं पुरश्रेष्ठम् । 'प्रकाण्डमुद्धतल्लजौ प्रशस्तवाचकान्यमूनि ।' इति **अमरः** । [१.४.२७] ॥७९ ॥

ककुभामधिपाः प्रभोर्निदेशाद्विभवैस्तां पुरमभ्यपूरयंस्त्वैः (यन्त्स्वैः) ।
प्रथमं त्रिदिवातिशायिनी सा न कथं वा तत उत्तरं तथा स्यात् ॥८० ॥

ककुभामिति । ककुभां दिशाम् । 'दिशस्तु ककुभः' इति **अमरः** । [१.३.१] प्रथमं

---

५७. °रकृ° (विसर्ग dropped & jointly written);
५८. P. marginal quotation प्रतिघा रुट्क्रुधौ स्त्रियाम्(यौ)' इति **अमरः** । [१.७.२६];

विभवपूरणात्पूर्वमेव त्रिदिवातिशायिनी स्वर्गाधिका, ततः उत्तरं विभवपूरणोत्तरं तथा स्वर्गाधिका कथं न स्यात्, अपि तु स्यादेवेत्यर्थः ॥८० ॥

अभिधाऽजनि तस्य यस्य हि द्वार्यकमस्या इति विग्रहः पदं तत् ।
यदयुर्दिविजा अपि प्रवेशेष्विह दौवारिकरोधजन्यदुःखम् ॥८१ ॥

अभिधेति । यस्य पदस्य द्वारि अकं दुःखमस्या इति विग्रहः । तत् पदं तस्य पुरस्य अभिधा अजनि । यत् यस्मात् दिविजाः देवा अपि इह प्रवेशेषु दौवारिकरोधजन्यदुःखम् अयुः प्रापुः ॥८१ ॥

स्वजनं विनिवेश्य तत्र सर्वं निजमायाविभवेन लोकनाथः ।
निरगाद्बलभद्ररक्षिताया मथुराया द्विषमभ्यनायुधः सन् ॥८२ ॥

स्वजनमिति । द्विषमभि शत्रुसम्मुखम् अनायुधः सन् निरगात् ॥८२ ॥

यवनस्तमवेत्य वासुदेवं बहुसङ्ख्यैरथ नारदोक्तचिह्नैः ।
तदुपान्तमुपाजगाम योद्धुं स [५९]पलायिष्ट रणादिवात्तभीतिः ॥८३ ॥

यवन इति । सः कृष्णः इति **चिन्तयित्वेति चतुर्थश्लोकस्थपदेन अन्वयः**, इति विचार्येव आत्तभीतिरिव रणात् पलायिष्ट पलायनं चकार ॥८३ ॥

मदवेक्षणकाम्यया तपस्यन्मुचुकुन्दाख्यनृपः पुरा चिराय ।
इदमद्रिगुहान्तरे शयानः स मया दर्शयता प्रबोधनीयः ॥८४ ॥

मद इ(दि)ति । अयमद्रिः इदमद्रिः, तस्य गुहान्तरे शयानः सः दर्शयता आत्मानं दर्शयता मया प्रबोधनीयः ॥८४ ॥८५ ॥८६ ॥८७ ॥

अमराः प्रति तं पुरा ह्यवोचन्[६०] "शयितं त्वामसमाप्तनिद्रमेव ।
यदि कश्चन बोधयेल्लयं स त्वदवेक्षादहनादुपैष्यती" ति ॥८५ ॥

समरे द्विषतामजय्यभावं वरमाप्नोत्तपसा य [६१]ऊर्जितेन ।
अमुना यवनेन तं प्रबोध्य क्षपयाम्येनमिति स्म चिन्तयित्वा ॥८६ ॥

उदितोऽसि कथं पलायसे भो यदुवंशाभिधशूररत्नखन्याम् ।
निगदन्निति तन्मतानभिज्ञो यवनेशो भगवन्तमन्वधावत् ॥८७ ॥

---

५९. फला॰;
६०. ह्यवोचंन्-(अनुस्वार added-Marathi influence);
६१. B. writes as उ-Marathi influence;
६२. मुच॰ (as also at verse 90);

स निविश्य गुहां गिरेस्तिरोऽभून्[६२]मुचुकुन्दं निजवाससा पिधाय।
यवनोऽप्यनुविश्य तत्र सुप्तं पुरुषं कंसरिपुं विदाञ्चकार ॥८८ ॥

स इति। सः यवनः तत्र गुहान्तरे सुप्तं पुरुषं कंसरिपुं विदाञ्चकार ज्ञातवान् ॥८८ ॥

तमहंश्चरणेन बोधयिष्यन् यवनो जागरितं ततश्च तेन।
यवनं स वियोजितः समाधेरिव शम्भुर्मदनं दृशा ददाह ॥८९ ॥

तमिति। यवनः तं बोधयिष्यन् सन् तं चरणेन अहन् ताडितवान्। ततः तेन जागरितम्। सः यवनं समाधेवि(र्वि)योजितः शम्भुः मदनमिव दृशा ददाह ॥९८ ॥९० ॥९१ ॥

मुचुकुन्दमथ प्रदर्श्य रूपं निजमावेद्य महेशतामपि स्वाम्।
अभिवाञ्छितमर्थमस्य दत्त्वा भगवानद्रिगुहान्तरात्[६३] पराञ्चत् ॥९० ॥

मथुरापुरमेत्य शत्रुसैन्यं सहरामो विनिहत्य तद्धनानि।
वृषमानुषवाहितानि[६४] कृत्वा पुरतो द्वारवतीमभिप्रतस्थे ॥९१ ॥

स बृहद्रथसूनुनाऽर्धमार्गे समगंस्तारचिताभिषेणनेन।
सबलो भगवानथारिसैन्याद्भयमेत्येव पलायितोऽतिदूरम् ॥९२ ॥

स इति। आरचितम् अभिषेणनं शत्रुसम्मुखगमनं येन, तेन, बृहद्रथसूनुना जरासन्धेन सः कृष्णः समगंस्त सङ्गतोऽभूदित्यर्थः ॥९२ ॥

गिरिमारुहतां ततोऽतितुङ्गं बलभद्रश्च हरिश्च मागधस्तौ।
अनुगम्य बलैर्गिरौ निलीनावसमासाद्य ददाह दारुभिस्तम्[६५] ॥९३ ॥

गिरिमिति। गिरौ पर्वते निलीनौ तौ रामकृष्णौ असमासाद्य अलब्ध्वा दारुभिस्तं पर्वतं ददाह ॥९३ ॥

परितो ज्वलितस्य तस्य शृङ्गाद्बहिरग्नेरु[६६]दपप्ततां क्षितौ तौ।
मगधाधिपतिर्मृताववेत्य स्वरिपू सप्रमदः पुरीमगात्स्वाम् ॥९४ ॥

परित इति। तस्य पर्वतस्य शृङ्गात् अग्नेः बहिः उदपप्तताम् उत्पतितौ ॥९४ ॥९५ ॥

---

६३. °हात° (न् dropped);
६४. तागिन (ग्नि for नि-scribal peculiarity);
६५. °स्त (म् dropped);
६६. °रग्रे°;

क्व गतौ बलकेशवौ क्व साऽभून्मथुराऽत्रागमनं कथं[६७] न्वभून्नः ।
इति दुःखितविस्मितान् स्वबन्धून् मुदितांस्तत्पुरमेत्य तौ व्यधाताम् ॥९५ ॥

धात्रा नुन्नो रैवतो नाम राजा प्रादात्कन्यां रेवतीनामिकां स्वाम् ।
रामायाथो रेवतीनायकत्वादप्यौपम्यं प्राप रामः सुधांशोः ॥९६ ॥

धात्रेति । रेवतीनायकत्वात् अपि सुधाशोः औपम्यं प्राप । अपिशब्दात् स्वशरीरधावल्येन पूर्वं चन्द्रसाम्यं प्राप्त इति **ध्वन्यते** ॥९६ ॥९७ ॥९८ ॥

इति रानडे इत्युपनामकशामरायसूनुविष्णुशर्मणा विरचितायां नीलकण्ठकविकृतयादवेन्द्रमहोदयकाव्यस्य टिप्पन्यां नवमः सर्गः समाप्तः ॥९ ॥

यद्धीर्जगज्जातमिवासुरारेस्तनूरखेदाऽभृत शास्त्रजातम् ।
त्रिविक्रमाभिख्यतदात्मजन्मा यः पार्वतीनन्दनतामयासीत् ॥९७ ॥

नीलकण्ठेन तेनास्मिन् यादवेन्द्रमहोदये ।
कृते काव्येऽपि नवमः सर्गः सम्पूर्णतां गतः ॥९८ ॥[६८]

६७. कथन्व॰ (अनुस्वार dropped & jointly written);
६८. P. adds श्रीः; B. adds श्रीकृष्णाय नमः

दशमः सर्गः

[१] विदर्भसंज्ञे विषये बभूव शुभा पुरी कुण्डिन[२]नामधेया ।
तस्यां नृपोऽभूत् किल भीष्मनामा दोषासमानाश्रयसद्गुणौघः ॥१ ॥

श्रीगणेशाय नमः । अथ **दशमसर्गटिप्पनम्** । विदर्भ इति । दोषाणामसमानाश्रयः अनैकाधिकारणवृत्तिः-निर्दोषः इति यावत्-सद्गुणौघो यस्य सः ॥१ ॥

यस्य प्रतापांशुमतोऽपि तापात् सर्वानृतून् ग्रीष्मतया द्विषन्तः ।
अवेदिषुर्वीक्ष्य यशःशशाङ्कं प्रसन्नमन्ये तु शरत्तया तान् ॥२ ॥

यस्येति । द्विषन्तः शत्रवः, यस्य प्रताप एवांशुमान् सूर्यस्तस्य तापात् सर्वान् ऋतून् ग्रीष्मतया अवेदिषुः । अन्ये तु अर्थात् मित्राः[३] (मित्राणि) प्रसन्नं यशःशशाङ्कं वीक्ष्य तान् ऋतून् शरत्तया अवेदिषुः ॥२ ॥

प्रशान्तविक्रान्तरिपोर्वदान्यसङ्ख्यासु पूर्वग्रहणीयनाम्नः ।
विशश्रमुः कोशनिवासमेत्य परं कृपाणा न धनानि यस्य ॥३ ॥

प्रशान्त इति । प्रशान्ताः विक्रान्ताः दारुणा रिपवो यस्य सः, तस्य । कोशः भाण्डागारं खड्गपिधानं **च** ॥३ ॥

द्विजैर्विशुद्धैः परिवारितं यं लक्ष्मीश्चिरं पद्ममिवाध्युवास ।
चिरानुषक्तं कमलाविरोधमुन्मुच्य वाणी च विधेरिवास्यम् ॥४ ॥

द्विजैरिति । **राजपक्षे**-विशुद्धैर्द्विजैः ब्रा(ब्रा)ह्मणैः । **पद्मपक्षे**-विशुद्धैर्द्विजैः हं(हं)सैः । **विधेरास्यपक्षे**-द्विजैः द(द)न्तैः ॥४ ॥

[४] स्वर्णं विसृज्यातिशयेन कीर्तिं शुद्धां वितन्वन् भुवनत्रयेऽपि ।
स्वर्णं विसृज्यासितकीर्तिमुर्व्यां यो भावयन्तं घनमत्यशेत ॥५ ॥

स्वर्णमिति । स्वर्णं सुवर्णं, कीर्तिं यशः । स्वर्णं स्वस्य ऋणं, जलं कीर्तिं पङ्कं [च] ॥५ ॥

---

१. P. begins with श्रीकृष्णाय नमः । B. begins with श्री गणेशाय नमः ।
२. कुण्डन°;
३. Marathi influence (masculine for neuter gender);
४. B. changes the order of abcd to bcda either due to his having another ms. to copy down from or because of his non-attentiveness & negligence.

यस्येक्षणं शास्त्रविनीतबुद्धेः[५] परस्त्रियो नाभजदित्यमिथ्या।
कान्तारभूमीषु निगूढमेव परस्त्रियो वर्तनमाचरन् हि ॥६ ॥

यस्येति। यस्य ईक्षणं परस्त्रियः अन्यस्त्रियः शत्रुस्त्रियश्च। नाभजदिति मिथ्या न, सत्यमित्यर्थः ॥६ ॥

हेमाद्रिमर्थिभ्य इव प्रदास्यंस्तदाश्रितां सर्वशरीरभाजाम्।
एकायनं यः किल दानशौण्डः[६] सर्वामनन्तां स्वभुजे बभार ॥७ ॥

हेमाद्रिरि(मि)ति। हेमाद्रिमर्थिभ्यः याचकेभ्यः प्रदास्यन्निव। तदाश्रितां हेमाद्द्याश्रिताम्। सर्वशरीरभाजाम् एकायनं सर्वामनन्तां पृथ्वीं स्वभुजे बभार ॥७ ॥

यस्मिन्नसन्देहमवेयमानाः सङ्ख्यामतीताः[७] सुगुणा अभूवन्।
सङ्ख्यार्हतां सांशयिका भजन्ते सत्यानृतत्वे जगतीव यस्मात् ॥८ ॥

यस्मिन्निति। यस्मिन् भीष्मके, असन्देहम् निःसंशयम् अवेयमानाः ज्ञायमानाः सुगुणाः शौर्यादयः सङ्ख्यां गणनां विचारणामिति **च** प्रतीयते। अतीताः अभूवन्। यस्मात् सांशयिकाः संशयमापन्नाः पदार्थाः जगति जगद्विषयसत्यानृतत्व इव सङ्ख्यार्हतां विचारणार्हतां गणनार्हतामिति **च** भजन्ते। **केषाञ्चिन्मते**- जगन्मिथ्या, **केषाञ्चिन्मते**-अमिथ्या। जगद्विषयकसत्यानृतत्वे यथा सङ्ख्यार्हतां विचारणार्हतां **[च]** भजतः, तथा सर्वेऽपि सांशयिकाः पदार्थाः(र्था) विचारणार्हतां भजन्ते। एते गुणास्तु असन्देहं ज्ञायमानाः। अत एव सङ्ख्यामतीता इत्यर्थः ॥८ ॥

तस्यात्मजा रुक्मिमुखा अभूवंश्चत्वार एका तनया यविष्ठा।
यां[८] रुक्मिणीति व्यवजह्रिरे[९] स्वा या सोदरी चन्द्रमसः पुरांऽभूत्[१०] ॥९ ॥

[११]सौन्दर्यसौशील्यपुरोगमानामनुत्तमानां गणनातिगानाम्।
तस्या गुणानामनुवर्णनायां कः प्राभवं[१२] नाम भजेत्कवीनाम् ॥१० ॥

सौन्दर्यमिति। प्राभवं सामर्थ्यम् ॥१० ॥

---

५. °बुद्धः;
६. °शौडः(अनुस्वार(ण)dropped);
७. Omitsती;
८. या(अनुस्वारdropped);
९. P.&B. write as ि-ह-Marathi influence;
१०. पूरा;
११. °द°;
१२. प्राभवंभ्नाम;

[१३]शक्रो(क्तो) ऽपि तान् वर्णयितुं न वाञ्छाम्यहं कवीनां[१४] वचसां मृषात्वात्।
मृषागिरं मां यदवेत्य[१५] सत्यान् मद्वर्णितांस्ताननृतानवेयुः ॥११॥

शक्त इति। अहं कवीनां वचसां मृषात्वात् हेतोः तां (= रुक्मिणीं) or तां (= तान्-scribal peculiarity-गुणान्) वर्णयितुं न वाञ्छामि। यत् यस्मात् कवीनां मृषावादित्वात् मां मृषागिरमवेत्य ज्ञात्वा मद्वर्णितान् तान् [सत्यान्] गुणान् अनृतान् अवेयुः इति हेतोः तां (or तान्) न वर्णयामीत्याशयः ॥११॥१२॥

तां कामयामास समस्तकान्तो[१६]ललामभूतां वसुदेवसूनुः।
साऽऽकर्ण्य कृष्णस्य गुणानुदारान् बभूव तस्मिन्निबिडानुरागा ॥१२॥

कृष्णाय देयां सदृशीं तनूजां भीष्मस्य तद्बन्धुजना अवाञ्छन्।
रुक्मी तु मेने किल वश्यतातो देयां स्वसारं दमघोषजाय ॥१३॥

कृष्णायेति। सदृशीम् अर्थात् कृष्णसदृशीम्। वश्यः स्वाधीनः तातो यस्य सः। दमघोषजाय दमघोषपुत्राय शिशुपालायेत्यर्थः ॥१३॥

कृष्णं[१७] द्विषन् यो जगतां जनन्या दुर्भ्रातृकत्वेन चकार योगम्।
जन्मन्यमुष्मिन्नपि सर्वलोकानुद्वेजयन् प्रागिव कालकूटः ॥१४॥

कृष्णमिति। कृष्णं द्विषन् यः सर्वलोकान् उद्वेजयन् प्राग् जन्मनि कालकूट इव अमुष्मिन् जन्मन्यपि जगतां जनन्याः दुर्भ्रातृकत्वेन-दुष्टः भ्राता यस्याः सा दुर्भ्रातृका, तस्याः भावः दुर्भातृकत्वं, तेन-योगं चकार ॥१४॥

छन्दानुवर्ती[१८] तनयस्य भीष्मः सुतां[१९] प्रदास्यन् दमघोषजाय।
चेदीश्वरं भावमवेदयत्स्वं स चानुमेने सदृशेन योगम् ॥१५॥

छन्द इति। भीष्मः चेदीश्वरं शिशुपालं स्वभावं स्वाभिप्रायं कन्यादानरूपम् अवेदयत्। स च शिशुपालः सदृशेन स्वतुल्येन भीष्मेन योगं सम्बन्धम् अनुमेने ॥१५॥

---

१३. Both P.&B. take the word to be शक्र; but P1 rightly takes the word as शक्तः in the प्रतीक of the श्लोक in view of the context;
१४. °ना (drops the अनुस्वार);
१५. यदवत्य सत्या;
१६. °कान्तां ललाम°;
१७. कृष्णद्वि° (अनुस्वार dropped & jointly written);
१८. नन°;
१९. सुतान्प्रदास्यंन् (न् for म् and अनुस्वार & अनुनासिक both used (स्यंन्) - (Marathi influence-scribal peculiarity).

विवाहयोग्ये च बुधैर्मुहूर्ते निर्णीयमानेऽनतिदूरभाजि ।
कृष्णान्तिकं[२०] भीष्मसुता द्विजं[२१] द्रागनन्यभावा गमयाञ्चकार ॥१६ ॥

विवाह इति । गमयाञ्चकार प्रेषितवती ॥१६ ॥१७ ॥

अज्ञातमच्चित्तगतिः सुतस्य छन्दानुवर्ती जनकः प्रभो मे ।
मां दित्सति त्वय्यनुरज्यमानां वीराग्रगामिन्[२२] दमघोषजाय ॥१७ ॥

यन्मे मनः कर्णपथावतीर्णा गुणास्त्वदीया अहरन्नसङ्ख्याः ।
तन्मा वृथा भून्निजविक्रमेण हरस्वं मां विघ्नकृतो निगृह्य ॥१८ ॥

यदिति । ते गुणाः मे मनः अहरन् इति यत् तत् वृथा माऽभूत् ॥१८ ॥

विवाहकालोऽद्यदिनात् परस्मिन्नहन्यष्टमे[२३] पूर्वदिने तु तस्मात् ।
पुराद्बहिर्देवगृहे ममार्च्या स्कन्दप्रसूः[२४] सन्निहितस्तदा स्याः ॥१९ ॥

विवाह इति । स्कन्दप्रसूः गौरी । मम मया अर्च्या पूज्या । तदा तस्मिन् काले, सन्निहितः स्याः भव ॥१९ ॥

इति प्रणामादिपरं विलिख्य भैष्म्यार्पितं लेखमुपाददानः ।
सानुप्लवस्तन्मनसैव विप्रो वेगादभि द्वारवतीं प्रतस्थे ॥२० ॥

इतीति । प्रणामादेः परम् इति पूर्वोक्तं विलिख्य । तस्याः मनसैव सानुप्लवः ससहायः(यो) द्वारवतीं प्रति प्रतस्थे ॥२० ॥२१ ॥२२ ॥

पुरप्रतीहारमुपागतं तं दौवारिकावेदित आदिदेवः ।
अभ्येत्य नीत्वा च निजं निशान्तं सम्पूजयामास[२५] यथाविधानम् ॥२१ ॥

सुखोपविष्टं तपनीयपीठे विनीतमार्गश्रममम्बुजाक्षः ।
तमब्रवीत्त्वामतिथिं दुरापं ब्रह्मन्नवापं बहुजन्मपुण्यैः ॥२२ ॥

---

२०. °न्तिके;

२१. द्विजेन्द्राग°;

२२. बीरा° (व & ब confused for each other - a general tendency of the scribes

२३. P. & B. both write as न्त्य - Marathi influence.

२४. स्कन्धः प्रसूः;

२५. स पूज°;

तं[२६] त्वामभीष्टार्थसमर्पणेन सन्तोषयानीति ममास्ति वाञ्छा।
अतस्तमुत्का[२७](क्त्वा) विदुषां वरेण्य ममाभिलाषः परिपूरणीयः ॥२३॥

तमिति। अतः हेतोः तं वाञ्छितार्थमुक्त्वा ममाभिलाषः परिपूरणीयः ॥२३॥ २४॥२५॥

इति ब्रुवाणे[२८] वसुदेवसूनौ स ब्राह्मणो भीष्मसुतावितीर्णम्।
लेखं प्रदायेदमुवाच, "कृष्ण, भैष्मीपतिस्त्वं भव तन्ममेष्टम्" ॥२४॥

अथ द्विजेन्द्रं बहुमूल्यरत्नधनादिदानेन परं प्रतोष्य।
रथं समारुह्य सहैव तेन सद्यो हरिर्भीष्मपुरीं[२९] प्रतस्थे ॥२५॥

तदुद्यमोत्प्रेक्षितसम्प्रहारः पराक्रमन्यक्कृतकार्तिकेयैः।
पूर्णां सुयोधैर्[३०]ध्वजिनीमपारामादाय रामस्तमनु प्रतस्थे[३१] ॥२६॥

तदिति। तस्य कृष्णस्य उद्यमेन उत्प्रेक्षितः सम्प्रहारो युद्धं [येन] सः। स रामः ध्वजिनीं सेनामादाय तमनु कृष्णमनु प्रतस्थे ॥२६॥

आकारयामास विदर्भराजः कन्याविवाहोत्सवदर्शनाय।
महीपतीनात्मसमानमानान् स्ववैभवन्यञ्चितलोकपालान् ॥२७॥

आकार इति। स्ववैभवेन न्यञ्चिताः तिरस्कृताः(ता) लोकपाला यैः तान् ॥२७॥

विवाहघस्रातिसमीपभावात् प्रेष्या जनास्तत्वरिरे क्रियासु।
स्वस्वानुशिष्टासु विदर्भराजश्चण्डस्य मुक्ताभ्यवहारनिद्राः ॥२८॥

विवाह इति। घस्रः दिनः। चण्डस्य निष्कारणकोपस्य विदर्भराजस्य प्रेष्याः किङ्कराः। स्वस्य स्वस्य अनुशिष्टासु आज्ञप्तासु क्रियासु तत्वरिरे त्वरां चक्रुः ॥२८॥

पुरं तदा लेपनपाण्डुराभिः [३२]सुमृष्टसिक्तामलसर्वमार्गम्।
गृहावलीभिः सितशारदाभ्रैर्व्योमेव सान्द्रैरमलं बभासे ॥२९॥

---

२६. तत्त्वाम°;
२७. Both P.&B. have उत्का (scribal error);
२८. श्रुवाणे;
२९. °पुरी (अनुस्वार dropped);
३०. °दृर्ध्वृ°;
३१. प्रपस्थे (प due to previous प्र-by attraction);
३२. समृ°;

पुरमिति। सुमृष्टाः मार्जिताः, सिक्ताः अत एवामलाः सर्वे मार्गाः यस्मिन् तत्। तत्पुरम् आलेपनपाण्डुराभिः सुधालेपस्य पाण्डुराभिर्गृहपङ्क्तिभिः सान्द्रैः सितशारदाभ्रैः अमलं व्योमेव व(ब)भासे ॥२९॥

मालाविशेषैरधिवीथि बद्धै रम्भाप्रकाण्डैश्च निधीयमानैः।
द्वारो गृहाणामभितो ध्वजैश्च समुच्छ्रितैस्तत्पुरमत्यभासीत्[३३] ॥३०॥

मालेति। अधिवीथि वीथ्यां बद्धैः। गृहाणां द्वारः अभितः द्वारयोरुभयपार्श्वे ॥३०॥

विदर्भराजस्य[३४] गृहोत्तमं तत्सम्पूरितं मङ्गलवस्तुजातैः।
मेने पदं मङ्गलदेवतायास्तदा पुराऽप्यास्पदमिन्दिरायाः ॥३१॥

विदर्भ इति। मङ्गलवस्तुसमूहैः पूरितं तत्पुरं तदा मङ्गलदेवतायाः पदं मेने, जनैरिति शेषः। पुराऽपि इन्दिरायाः रमायाः आस्पदम्। रुक्मिण्याः रमाऽवतारत्वात्। 'रमा मङ्गलदेवता' इति **अमरः**। 'मङ्गलदेवता लक्ष्मीः' ॥३१॥३२॥३३॥

यत्राग्विवाहाच्छुभकर्म कार्यं तत्कारयामास विदर्भराजः।
चेदीश्वरश्चात्मभुवोऽथ भीष्मपुरीं प्रतस्थे स सबन्धुवर्गः ॥३२॥

साल्वश्च बार्हद्रथदन्तवक्त्रौ[३५] विदूरथः पौण्ड्रक एवमाद्याः।
मित्राणि चैद्यस्य हरेर्द्विषन्तो विदर्भराजस्य पुरीमुपायन् ॥३३॥

तेषां पथोऽर्धे मिलतां नृपाणामन्योन्यसंश्लेषजुषो ध्वजिन्यः।
अस्मारयन्मेलनमम्बुधीनां क्षोभं गतानां भुवनान्तकाले ॥३४॥

तेषामिति। पथः मार्गस्य अर्धे मध्ये मिलतां सङ्गतानां तेषां नृपाणाम् अन्योन्यसंश्लेषजुषः ध्वजिन्यः सेनाः(ना) अम्बुधीनां मेलनमस्मारयन् ॥३४॥३५॥३६॥

शैला इवोदग्रतराः शताङ्गा नागास्तदीया इव गण्डशैलाः।
तेषां प्रवाहा इव धावदश्वाः पदातयश्चाप्यरुचन्नमीषाम् ॥३५॥

---

३३. समुच्छिष्ट तैस्तत्पुरमद्य/द्यतासीत्- not clear due to overwritting.
३४. Not clear due to overwriting;
३५. °वक्त्रो°

भेरीरवाः[३६] स्यन्दननेमिघोषा हेषा हयानां द्विपबृंहितानि ।
चक्रुर्भटानामपि सिंहनादाः पुरन्दरस्यापि मनो भयार्तम्[३७] ॥३६ ॥

ते कुण्डिनं येन पथा प्रयाताः स दन्तिदानोदकपङ्कनीलः
पुत्रीभ्रमेणेव विवस्वतोस्त्रैः शोषं[३८] न नीतो बहुवासराणि ॥३७ ॥

त इति । येन पथा ते कुण्डिनं प्रयाताः, दन्तिदानोदकपङ्कनीलः सः पन्था विवस्वता सूर्येण पुत्रीभ्रमेण नैल्यसादृश्यात् यमुनेति भ्रमेण-उस्त्रैः किरणैः ब(र्ब)-हुवासराणि शोषं न नीतः । अत्यन्तं दन्तिदानोदकयुक्त अभूदित्यर्थः ॥३७ ॥

दूतैरवेतागमनोऽथ तेषां बलैः सहाभ्येत्य विदर्भराजः ।
आनीय चैद्यं सुहृदश्च तस्य निवेशयामास गृहोत्तमेषु ॥३८ ॥

दूतैरिति । दूतैः बलैः सह तेषां चैद्यादीनाम् अवेतागमनः ज्ञातागमनः ॥३८ ॥

आकारितान् भूमीपतीन् परांश्च समागतांस्तानिव तत्समानान् ।
सहाग्रजं सध्वजिनीकमेतं कृष्णं च वेलातिगतप्रमोदः ॥३९ ॥

आकारितानिति । एतम् आगतं कृष्णं वेलातिगतप्रमोदः सन् 'गृहोत्तमेषु न्य (नि)-वेशयामासेति **पूर्वश्लोकस्थपदेनान्वयः** ॥३९ ॥

प्रमाददूरोज्झितमानसेन पुरन्दरादप्यधिकश्रियाऽथ ।
भीष्मेण तेषामवनीपतीनां सर्वोपचारा विदधे सपर्या ॥४० ॥

प्रमाद इति । प्रमादेन दूरमुज्झितं मानसं यस्य (सः), तेन, सावधानमनसेत्यर्थः । भीष्मेण सर्वोपचारा सपर्या विदधे कृता ॥४० ॥४१ ॥

तैः संहतैर्भूपतिभिर्विरेजे विदर्भराजस्य पुरं विशालम् ।
पुञ्जीभवद्भिःर्मथनोद्यमेन सुरासुरैस्तीरमिवाम्बुराशेः ॥४१ ॥

अद्यापि नागात्प्रहितो द्विजन्मा मतं न वा तस्य मदिष्टमासीत्[३९] ॥
[४०]सञ्चिन्तयन्तीमिति भीष्मकन्यां प्रियागमोक्त्याऽमदयद्द्विजातिः ॥४२ ॥

---

३६. °रेवा (विसर्ग dropped);
३७. °र्त (म् dropped);
३८. शेषन्न (म् -न्- Marathi influence);
३९. मदिष्टना°;
४०. P.1 rightly takes सञ्चिन्त°, though both P.&B. have सचिन्त° where the अनुस्वार is inadvertantly dropped.

अद्यापीति। मदिष्टं तस्य कृष्णस्य मतम् अनुमतं नासीद्वा इति [४०] सञ्चिन्तयन्तीं भीष्मकन्यां द्विजातिर्ब्राह्मणः कृष्णस्यागमोक्त्या अमदयत् आमोदयामास ॥४२ ॥

अभ्यक्तसुस्नातधृताम्बरोद्धामलङ्कृतामाभरणैरमूल्यैः ।
निर्यापयामास परे द्यवि स्वां भीष्मस्तनूजां गिरिजार्चनाय ॥४३ ॥

अभ्यक्तेति। अभ्यक्ता कृताभ्यङ्गा पश्चात् सुस्नाता। धृतानि अम्बरोद्धानि श्रेष्ठवस्त्राणि यया सा। परे द्यवि परेद्युः। 'परे त्वह्नि परे द्यवि' इति **अमरः**। [३.४.२१] गिरिजार्चनाय निर्वा(र्या)पयामास ॥४३ ॥

विप्राङ्गनाभिः परिवारिता सा सखीसमेता जगदम्बिकायाः ।
अभ्यालयं सञ्चलिता पदाभ्यां सम्भारवाह्योऽनुययुर्नियोज्याः ॥४४ ॥

विप्रा इति। अनु पश्चात् सम्भारवाह्याः अर्थात् पूजोपकरणवाहका नियोज्याः किङ्कराः(रा) ययुः ॥४४ ॥

वि[४१]कीर्णपुष्पप्रकरोऽपि मार्गोऽभविष्यदत्यन्तकठोर एव ।
तस्या न चेत्सा मृदुपादपद्मा कृष्णै[४२]कविन्यस्तमनःप्रवाहा ॥४५ ॥

विकीर्ण इति। मृदुपादपद्मा सा भैष्मी कृष्णैकविन्यस्तमनःप्रवाहा न स्यात् चेत् विकीर्णपुष्पप्रकरोऽपि मार्गः तस्याः अत्यन्तकठोर एवाभविष्यत् ॥४५ ॥

पुरःसरत्काञ्चनवेत्रहस्ता गणे चलन्त्याः पथि राजपुत्र्याः ।
दृशोऽपजह्रु[४३]श्चरणैकसक्ताः शोभां सरोजश्रितबम्भराणाम् ॥४६ ॥

पुर इति। पुरःसरत्काञ्चनहस्तानां गणो यस्मिन् तस्मिन् पथि चलन्त्याः राजपुत्र्याः दृशः चरणैकसक्ताः सत्यः सरोजश्रितभ्रमराणां शोभामपजह्रुः। चरणस्य सरोजोपमानं, दृशः भ्रमरोपमानम् ॥४६ ॥

तस्याः कयाचित्सुकुमारमूर्तेर्महातपत्रेण धृतेन मूर्ध्नि ।
छायां विधायापि कृतेति मेने न सा सुवर्णाभतदङ्गकान्त्या ॥४७ ॥

तस्या इति। तस्याः मूर्ध्नि कयाचित् धृतेन महातपत्रेण छायां विधायापि सा आतपत्रछायाकारिणी सुवर्णसदृशतदङ्गकान्त्या छाया न कृतेति मेने ॥४७ ॥

---

४१. विकर्ण°;

४२. कृष्णौक°;

४३. P. writes as -हुः-Marathi influence. B. strangely spells as जहुः;

निष्कोशतापन्नबिलोद्गताहि[४४]साधर्म्यशातोद्यतमण्डलाग्राः ।
शूरास्तदा राजभटा असङ्ख्यास्तां सर्वतो राजसुतामरक्षन् ।।४८ ।।

निष्कोशतेति । निष्कोशतां प्राप्ताः अत एव बिलोद्गताहितुल्याः शाताः तीक्ष्णाः, उद्यताः मण्डलाग्राः खड्गाः यैस्ते । शूराः राजभटाः सर्वतस्तां राजसुताम् अरक्षन् ।।४८ ।।

नृत्यं वितेनुर्वरवारकान्तास्तस्याः पुरो नाट्यकलाप्रवीणाः ।
तदातनो मङ्गलवाद्यनादः सुधामधः स्वादुतया चकार ।।४९ ।।

नृत्यमिति । वराः श्रेष्ठा, या वारकान्ताः वारनार्यः(र्यो) नृत्यं वितेनुः । तदातनः तत्कालभवः । मङ्गलनाद्यवादः स्वादुतया माधुर्येण सुधामधश्चकार ।।४९ ।।

जनास्तदालोकनमीहमानाः समुन्न[४५]तस्थानमुपाश्रयन्त ।
भ्रमात्तदालोकनतो हि[४६] पुंसां समुन्नतस्थानगतिर्भवित्री[४७] ।।५० ।।

जना इति । हि यस्मात्कारणात् तदालोकनतः तस्याः रुक्मिण्याः आलोकनतः पुंसाम् उन्नतस्थानगतिः उच्चस्थानप्राप्तिः उत्तमपदप्राप्तिश्च । भवित्री भवितुं योग्या, तस्मात्(द्) भ्रमात् तदालोकनोन्नतस्थानप्राप्त्योः साध्यसाधनभावभ्रमात् ज(ज्ज)नाः तदालोकनम् इ(ई)हमानाः सन्तः समुन्नतस्थानमुपाश्रयन्त । लोके फलार्थं साधने **प्रवृत्तेरिति भावः** ।।५० ।।

तां द्रष्टुकामाः सकलाः क्षितीशा हिमाद्रिक[४८]न्यासदनोपकण्ठे ।
रथाधिरूढा रचितप्रतीक्षास्तदागतेश्चै[४९]द्यमुखा अभूवन् ।।५१ ।।

तामिति । तदागतेः तस्याः आगमनस्य रचितप्रतीक्षाः अभूवन् ।।५१ ।।

ददर्श राजन्यगणोऽथ भैष्मीं गौरीगृहोपान्तभुवं प्रयाताम् ।
सौ[५०]न्दर्यसिन्धोर्मथनेन धातुर्जातामिवान्यामरविन्दगेहाम् ।।५२ ।।

---

४४. विलोद्गताही° (व & ब confused for each other-a general tendency of the scribes);
४५. °मुंनत (Marathi influence);
४६. त्वि;
४७. Not clear due to overwriting;
४८. कंन्या (Marathi influence);
४९. °चै° (विसर्ग (श्) dropped);
५०. °द° (न् dropped);

ददर्शेति। धातुः ब्रह्मणः सौन्दर्यसिन्धोर्मथनेन जाताम् अन्यामरविन्दगेहामिव स्थिताम् ॥५२ ॥५३ ॥

आलोहितेनांशुकपल्लवेन संछंन्न[५१]काश्मीरसमानदेहाम्।
आच्छन्नभूयोऽवयवां प्रवालवल्ये(ल्ल्ये) व भान्तीं तपनीयवल्लीम् ॥५३ ॥

मुखेन कण्ठेन विलोचनाभ्यां पद्भ्यां कराभ्यां परिभाविताब्जाम्[५२]।
मध्येन रोमावलिवेणिकाभ्यां वाण्यापकर्ष[५३] हरि[५४]मापयन्तीम् ॥५४ ॥

मुखेनेति। मुखेन परिभावितः अब्जः चन्द्रः, तं (notclear) यया सा, सां (तां ताम्)। कण्ठेन अब्जः शङ्खः, विलोचनाभ्यां पद्भ्यां च कराभ्यां च परिभावितम् अब्जं कमलं यया सा। 'अब्जो धन्वन्तरौ चन्द्रेऽम्बुजे(शङ्खे)ब्जं पद्मशङ्ख(सङ्ख्य)-योः।' इति **हैमः**। [२.६६] मध्येन हरिं सिंहं, रोमावलिवेणिकाभ्यां हरिं सर्पं, वाण्या हरिं शुकम्, अपकर्षम् आपयन्तीं प्रापयन्तीम्। 'हरिर्दिवाकरसमीरयोः' ।[इति **हैमः**। २.४७३]। 'यमवासवसिंहांशुशशाङ्क-कपिवाजिषु। पिङ्गवर्णे हरिद्वर्णे भेकोपेन्द्रशुकाहिषु॥' इति **हैमः** ॥५४ ॥

चन्द्रार्धतः स्वस्य विशेषणेन विशेषकाख्यामनुगच्छदर्थाम्।
सभर्तृकालाञ्छनचित्रकस्य कुर्वत्तदुद्भासितभालदेशाम् ॥५५ ॥

चन्द्र इति। सभर्तृकाणां सौभाग्यवतीनां[५५] लाञ्छनभूतं यच्चित्रकं, तस्य, विशेषयतीति विशेषक इति आख्यां, चन्द्रार्धतः चन्द्रार्धात् सकाशात् स्वस्य भालदेशस्य विशेषणेन व्यावर्तनेन भेदप्रतीतिजने(न)नेन अनुगच्छदर्थं सङ्गतार्थां कुर्वन् कु(कु)र्वतां(ता) तेन तिलकेन उद्भासितः भालदेशो यस्या[ः] सा, ताम् ॥५५ ॥

वर्षाम्बुवाहद्युतिकेशपाशां कर्णार्प्यमाणद्युतिकुण्डलाग्र्याम्।
बिम्बग्रहप्राप्तयशःकपोलां वक्रभ्रुवं भूषितचारुनासाम् ॥५६ ॥

वर्षेति। बिम्बग्रहेण प्रतिबिम्बधारणेन प्राप्तयशसौ कपोलौ यस्याः सा, ताम् ॥५६ ॥

---

५१. संछंन्न (अनुस्वार & न् both used. Marathi influence);
५२. P. marginal quotation- अब्जौ धन्वन्तरौ चन्द्रेऽम्बुजेऽब्जं पद्मशङ्खयोः। 'इति **हैमः**।
५३. °कर्षे;
५४. P. marg. qu. 'यमवासवसिंहांशुभेकोपेन्द्रशुकादिहिषु हरिशब्दः' इति **हैमः**।
५५. Typical Marathi equivalent word used, expressive of his mental inclination;

यो विद्रुमच्छायतया प्रकामं रुच्या हरेर्गोचरतां प्रणीतः ।
तेनाधरेणाऽप्यखिलोत्तरेण कृष्णैकपेयामृतमुद्वहन्तीम् ।।५७ ।।

य इति । यः विद्रुमवत् छाया कान्तिर्यस्य [सः], तस्य भावस्तत्ता, तया । द्रुमच्छायारहितत्वेन च हरेः कृष्णस्य सूर्यस्य **च** । रुच्या अभिलाषेण कान्त्या [च] गोचरतां प्रणीतः । तेन अधरेण अधरोष्ठेन अधरेणापि नीचेनापि अखिलोत्तरेण सर्वोत्कृष्टेन कृष्णैकपेयम् अमृतम् उद्वहन्तीम् ।।५७ ।।

मृणालिकाकोमलबाहुयुग्मामाच्छादयन्तीं[५६] करिकुम्भसाम्यम् ।
हरेर्नखैर्दारणतोऽपि यास्यत् स्तनद्वयं कञ्चुकिपल्लवेन ।।५८ ।।

मृणालिकेति । हरेः सिंहस्य कृष्णस्य **च** नखैर्दारणतोऽपि नखकर्तृकविदारणादपि करिकुम्भसाम्यं यास्यत् कञ्चुमिचं (?) कचु(ञ्चु)कयुक्तं स्तनद्वयं पल्लवेन वस्त्राञ्चलेन आच्छादयन्तीम् ।।५८ ।।

बृहन्नितम्बां[५७] कदलीनिभोरुं सुजानुजङ्घां मृदुलाङ्गुलिभ्याम् ।
नखेन्दुभासाऽप्यधिकप्रभाभ्यां मन्दं चलन्तीं चरणाम्बुजाभ्याम् ।।५९ ।।

बृहदिति । नखान्येव इन्दवश्चन्द्रास्तद्भासाऽपि अधिकप्रभाभ्यां चरणकमलाभ्यां मन्दं चलन्तीम् । चन्द्रकान्त्या कमलस्य मुकुलीभावात् अधिकप्रभाया अभावः । चरणकमलं तु इन्दुभासाऽपि अधिकप्रभमिति, अपेः स्वरसः ।।५९ ।।

यैर्धार्यमाणैरपि रूपशून्या विलोकनीयत्वमवाप्नुयुस्तैः ।
निसर्गसौन्दर्यवदङ्गकत्वान्मोघैरमूल्याभरणैरुपेताम् ।।६० ।।

यैरिति । यैराभरणैः धा(र्धा)र्यमाणैः सद्भिः(द्भी) रूपशून्या अपि विलोकनीयत्वमवाप्नुयुः । तैः नि(र्नि)सर्गसौन्दर्यवदङ्गकत्वात् हेतोः मो(र्मो)घैः निष्फलैः अमूल्याभरणैः उपेताम् ।।६० ।।६१ ।।

सा कृष्णसंदर्शनजातवाञ्छा सर्वत्र सञ्चारितलोचनान्ता ।
विलोक्य कृष्णं श्रुतपूर्वचिह्नमुपान्तभूमौ मुमुदे रथस्थम् ।।६१ ।।

तां पश्यतां पञ्चशरोऽतितीक्ष्णैश्चिच्छेद बाणैर्हृदयानि राज्ञाम् ।
या मातृभावं मम यास्यतीमां पश्यन्त्यमी दुर्मनसेति रोषात् ।।६२ ।।

---

५६. °यन्ती (अनुस्वार dropped);
५७. Not clear due to overwriting;

तामिति । तां पश्यतां राज्ञां हृदयानि मदनबाणविद्धानि अभवन्नित्यर्थः । दुर्मनसा सकामभावेन, मदन[स्य] प्रद्युम्नावतारत्वेन रुक्मिणीपुत्रत्वात् ॥६२ ॥

मय्येव रक्तेयं[५८]मिति भ्रमो यो बभूव राज्ञां स्मरमोहितत्वात् ।

तेष्वन्यहेत्वीरिततद्दृगन्तपातस्तमेव द्रढया[५९]ञ्चकार ॥६३ ॥

मय्येवेति । तेषु राजसु अन्यहेतुना कृष्णदर्शनहेतुना ईरितः यः तद्दृगन्तः तमेव 'मय्येवेयमनुरक्ता' इति भ्रमं द्रढयाञ्चकार ॥६३ ॥

तस्यां सकामानि मनांसि यं यं सङ्कल्पयन्त्यर्थममुं मुखेन ।
उच्चारयन्तोऽतिनिगूह्य[६०]मासन् मूढा हि ते तत्र[६१] जनोपहास्याः ॥६४ ॥

तस्यामिति । मनांसि यं यम् अर्थं सङ्कल्पयन्ति अतिनिगूह्यम् अमुमर्थं मुखेनोच्चारयन्तः ते मूढाः तत्र जनोपहास्याः आसन् ॥६४ ॥

ममैव योग्यां शिशुपाल एनां नार्हत्यसौ साम्प्रतमेव हर्तुम् ।
मयेति दध्युर्लघुमानसास्ते विस्मृत्य तादृक् शिशुपालमैत्रीम् ॥६५ ॥

ममेति । असौ मया हर्तुं योग्या इति लघुमानसास्ते शिशुपालमित्राणि राजानः(नो) दध्युश्चिन्तितवन्तः ॥६५ ॥

रथादवप्लुत्य जिहीर्षया ते तस्याः[६२] स्वसङ्कल्पमयीं[६३] विलोक्य ।
समन्ततस्तामफला निवृत्ता वन्ध्यक्रियत्वाल्लघिमानमापुः ॥६६ ॥

रथादिति । स्वसङ्कल्पमयीं तां समन्ततः सर्वत्र विलोक्य । अफलाः निवृत्ताः वन्ध्यक्रियत्वात् लघिमानं लघुत्वम् आपुः ॥६६ ॥६७ ॥

प्रासादमाविश्य हर प्रियायास्तां पूजयित्वा सकलोपचारैः ।
साऽभ्यर्थयामास, 'तव प्रसादान्मातः पतिः[६४] स्यान्मम वासुदेवः' ॥६७ ॥

---

५८. °द्य°;
५९. द्ध्ढयाञ्चकार (Marathi influence cf. द्ध्ढ केला);
६०. °निगृह्य;
६१. सर्व, P. marginal correction सर्व-तत्र, but, B. retains सर्व only;
६२. तस्यास्व° (विसर्ग dropped & jointly written);
६३. °मयी (अनुस्वार dropped);
६४. पतिस्या° (विसर्ग dropped & jointly written);

'यस्यास्तवेयं जगदुद्भवान्तक्रिया दृगुन्मेषनिमेषकल्पा[६५] ।
सा तेन मे सङ्घटनं प्रियेण यदीच्छसीदं किमु[६६] दुष्करं ते' ॥६८ ॥

यस्या इति । दृगुन्मेषेण जगदुद्भवः, दृङ्निमेषेण जगदन्तः । सा त्वम् ॥६८ ॥

इत्यर्थयित्वा गिरिजां प्रणम्य भैष्मी जरद्विप्रसभर्तृकाश्च ।
तथाऽर्चिताः सन्निधिमत्फलाभिराशीर्भिरासां मुदिता बभूव ॥६९ ॥

इतीति । भैष्मी गिरिजां प्रणम्य तथा अर्चिताः पूजिताः(ता) जरत्यः विप्रसभर्तृकाः प्रणम्य च आसां जरद्विप्रसभर्तृकाणामाशिभिः मुदिता बभूव ॥६९ ॥

पुस्फोर तस्या नयनारविन्दं वामं, तदन्यद्दनुजान्तकस्य ।
तदा तदन्यद्दमघोषसूनोररिष्टमेव[६७] त्रिभिरप्यबोधि ॥७० ॥

पुस्फोर इ(रे)ति । तस्याः रुक्मिण्याः वामं नयनारविन्दं पुस्फोर । दनुजान्तकस्य हरेः तदन्यत् वामा[द]न्यत् दक्षिणम् । दमघोषसूनोः शिशुपालस्य तदन्यत् दक्षिणादन्यत् वामं पुस्फोर । त्रिभिरपि अरिष्टम् अबोधि । रुक्मिणीकृष्णाभ्याम् अरिष्टं शुभं, शिशुपालेन अरिष्टम् अशुभम् ।' अरिष्टं(ष्टे) तु शुभाशुभे' इति **अमरः** ।(३.३.३६) ॥७० ॥

अथाम्बिकाया निलयात्प्रणम्य तां[६८] निर्ययौ राजसुता सहर्षा ।
तदोन्नतात्सा शरदम्बुवाहात् सौदामिनीवोच्चलिता[६९] विरेजे ॥७१ ॥

अथेति । अम्बिकालयस्य सुधाशौभ्रात् शरदम्बुवाहसाम्यं, रुक्मिण्याः गौरवर्णत्वात् तडित्साम्यम् ॥७१ ॥

राजन्यकन्या वसुदेवसूनोः सञ्चारयामास दृशं शताङ्गे ।
साऽऽपादचूडं तमलञ्चकार विकस्वरेन्दीवरमालिकेव ॥७२ ॥

राजन्यमि(न्ये)ति । सा दृक् विकसितेन्दीवरमालिकेव तम् आपादचूडं पादमारभ्य मस्तकपर्यन्तमलञ्चकार ॥७२ ॥

---

६५. दगु;
६६. किमदु°;
६७. P. marginal quotation: 'अरिष्टं तु शुभाशुभे' इति **अमरः** ।
६८. ता (अनुस्वार dropped);
६९. °मिनी°–more commonly used in Marathi/Maharashtra.

कृष्णोऽवतीर्याथ निजाच्छताङ्गादासद्य तामाशु गृहीतपाणिः ।
रथं निनाय स्वममुं[७०] न योग्ययोगानुमत्येव भटा न्यरुन्धन्[७१] ॥७३ ॥

कृष्ण इति । तामासद्य प्राप्य आशु गृहीतहस्तः सन् स्वं रथं निनाय प्रापितवान् । भटाः अमुं कृष्णं योग्ययोगानुमत्येव योग्ययोगाङ्गीकारेणेव न्यरुन्धन् ॥७३ ॥७४ ॥

अथ[७२] ध्वजारूढविहङ्गमेन्द्रः स्वलङ्कृतः काञ्चशैलतुङ्गः ।
महाजवाश्वोऽपि शनैश्चचाल रथो हरेर्द्वारवतीपथेन ॥७४ ॥

कृत्वा तमग्रे बलिनां वरेण्यो रामः[७३] स्वसैन्येन सह प्रतस्थे[७४] ।
अथाविदुश्चैद्यमुखा नृपाला भैष्मीं हृतां मोहितमानसाः प्राक् ॥७५ ॥

कृत्वेति । प्राक् भैष्मीहरणात्पूर्वं मोहितमानसाः अत एव कृष्णप्रस्थानानन्तरं तां भैष्मीं हृतामिति, अविदुः ज्ञातवन्तः ॥७५ ॥

वने हरन् यां कुरुते स्म यस्य जन्मान्तरे यादृशमेव दुःखम् ।
अवाप तस्या हरणेन तस्य तादृक् तदा तद्दमघोषसूनुः ॥७६ ॥

वने (न) इति । दमघोषसूनुः जन्मान्तरे पूर्वस्मिन् जन्मनि वने यां सीतां हरन् सन् यस्य रामस्य यादृशं दुःखं कुरुते स्म तदा तस्मिन् काले तस्य तस्याः हरणेन तत्कर्तृक-तत्कर्मकहरणेन तत् तादृगेव दुःखमवाप ॥७६ ॥

चैद्यं परिम्लानमुखं विलोक्य ततो जरासन्धमुखाः सखायः ।
कृष्णद्विषः सङ्गरदुन्दुभीनां सन्ताडनायामशिषँन्नियोज्यान्[७५] ॥७७ ॥

तद्ध्वानमाकर्ण्य विनिर्गतेन सन्नह्य सैन्येन निजेन भूपाः ।
आगत्य कृष्णं परिवव्रुराशु सह ध्वजिन्या च हलायुधेन ॥७८ ॥

तदिति । भूपाः तत्ध्वा(द्ध्वा)नमाकर्ण्य श्रुत्वा सन्नह्य संन्राहं (सन्नाहं) कृत्वा

---

७०. स्वममुन्र (अनुस्वार turned into अनुनासिक-Marathi influence;)
७१. न्यरुन्धान्;
७२. P. ध्यजा°;
७३. राम (विसर्ग dropped);
७४. प्रतस्थ;
७५. °मशिषंन्रि° (अनुस्वार & अनुनासिक both retained-Marathi influence);

विनिर्गतेन निजेन सैन्येन सहागत्य हलायुधेन ध्वजिन्या सेनया सह कृष्णं परिवव्रुः वेष्टितवन्तः ॥७८ ॥

रे मन्दबुद्धे नवनीतचौर्यसमं विद[७६]न् राजसुतापहारम्।
व्यधाः प्रयोज्या तव मांसवृद्धिस्तस्येव नास्यापि तु मांसकर्तः ॥७९ ॥

रे इति। 'हीनसम्बोधने तु रे' इति **अमरः**।रे मन्दबुद्धे, नवनीतचौर्यसमं राजसुतापहारं विदन् सन् राजसुतापहारं व्यधाः कृतवानसि। तस्येव नवनीतचौर्यस्येव अस्य राजसू(सु)तापहारस्य मांसवृद्धिः न प्रयोज्या अपि तु मांसकर्तः प्रयोज्यः ॥७९ ॥

यद्यर्पयित्वा पुनरेवं तां नो न विन्दसेऽस्मास्ववनम्रभावम्।
स स्याद्विनम्रेषु कृपां हि[७७] कुर्मो द्विषत्स्व[७८]नम्रेषु वयं कृपाणम्॥८० ॥

यदीति। यदि नः अस्मान् ताम् अर्पयित्वा अस्मासु अवनम्रभावं न विन्दसे यदि तर्हि स मांसकर्तः स्यात्। य[तो] हि यस्मात् विनम्रेषु कृपां कुर्मः, अनम्रेषु द्विषत्सु कृपाणं कुर्मः ॥८० ॥

तत्रेत्यवोचन्मगधाधिराजः कृष्णं नृपाणां प्रवरो जरंश्च।
तमेवमूचे वसुदेवसूनुर्मन्दस्मितांशुस्नपिताधरः सन्॥८१ ॥

तत्रेति। मगधाधिराजः जरासन्धः, कृष्णम् इति **पूर्वश्लोकोक्तम्** अवोचत्॥८१ ॥

'द्विषत्स्वनम्रेष्वि'ति पद्यपादेनात्यल्पमुक्तं मगधाधिनाथ।
सर्वाणि यत्सङ्गरसाधनानि मर्य्यर्पयः सप्तदशाजिभग्नः ॥८२ ॥

द्विषदिति। **'द्विषत्स्वनम्रेषु' इति पद्यपादेन श्लोकचतुर्थांशेन** स्वल्पमुक्तं न तु सर्वमुक्तम्। यत् यस्मात् सप्तदशसङ्ग्रामेषु भग्नः पराजितः सन् सर्वाणि सङ्गरसाधनानि कृपाणादीनि मयि अर्पयः अर्पितवानसि। तस्मात् त्वया केवलकृपार्पणम् उक्तं, तदतीवाल्पमित्यर्थः ॥८२ ॥८३ ॥

बार्हद्रथस्तेन तथोच्यमानः क्रुद्धः समीकाय मतिं वितेने।
अथ क्षितीशा इतरेऽथ तेषां सेनाधिनाथा अथ ता[द्]ध्वजिन्यः ॥८३ ॥

---

७६. विदंन् (अनुस्वार + न्-Marathi influence);
७७. वि हिं;
७८. द्विषत्स°;

प्रावर्तत क्षितिभुजां यदुभिर्बलाद्यैः सार्धं रणोऽथ मगधेशपुरःसराणाम्।
तेषां बलैश्च बलभद्रबलस्य यस्य कालत्रयात्परत एव समोऽस्त्य[७९]नीकः ॥८४॥

प्रावर्तत इ(ते)ति। तेषां राज्ञां बलैः साकं बलभद्रबलस्य रणः प्रावर्तत। यस्य रणस्य बलस्य **च** समः अनीकः रणः सेना **च**। कालत्रयात् परत एवास्ति। न तु कालत्रयमध्ये समोऽस्तीत्यर्थः। 'अनीकं रणसैन्ययोः' इति **हैमः** ।[३.२] ॥८४॥

पस्पर्श पूर्वमितरेतरवीरवादो मर्माणि तत्र समरे बलगर्वितानाम्।
पश्चात्तु कुण्डलितकार्मुकनिर्गतेषुधारा द्वयोः पृतनयोश्च मिथो भटानाम् ॥८५॥

पस्पर्श(र्शे)ति। पूर्वं वीरवादः मर्माणि पस्पर्श मर्मस्पृग्भाषणं बभूवेत्यर्थः। पश्चात् कार्मुकनिर्गता इषुधारा बाणपङ्क्तिः पस्पर्श ॥८५॥

रोषारुणानि न[८०]यनानि यथा यथाऽसन्
तालाङ्कतद्रिपुमहीपतिसैनिकानाम्।
स्वारातिरू[८१]क्षवचनेन तथा तथाऽऽसन्
रक्तारुणानि निशितानि तदायुधानि ॥८६॥

रोष इति। तालाङ्कः बलभद्रः। स्वारातिरूक्षवचनेन यथा यथा नयनानि रोषारुणानि आसन् तथा तथा निशितानि अ(आ)युधानि रक्तेन अरुणानि आसन् ॥८६॥

निर्भिद्यमानकवचानि शरैः सिताग्रैः
विद्धान्यतीव भटवीरवपूंष्यमुञ्चन्।
अस्त्राणि नैव विपदा मम हीदमक्षी-
ण्यस्त्रं त्यजन्ति तदहं करवा इतीव ॥८७॥

निर्भिद्येति। सिताग्रैः शरैः विद्धानि अत एव निर्भिद्यमानकवचानि भटवीरवपूंषि **कर्तॄणि**, हि यस्मात् मम विपदा मत्सम्बन्धिविपत्या इदमक्षीणि एतेषां नेत्राणि अस्त्रं

---

७९. P. marginal quotation 'अनीकं रणसैन्ययोः' इति **अमरः**। P.&P1 both quote this passage giving different sources, viz. अमर & हैम respectively, but, it is found in हैम only. It is possible that P. is relying on a faint memory & does not think it necessary to verify.

८०. P. marginal correction: नय changed to वद है B. reads नयनाग्नि (ग्नि for नि scribal peculiarity of B), but, P1 rightly takes नयनानि as it suits the context, hence, retained;

८१. °रुक्ष°;

नैव त्यजन्ति, तत् अस्त्रत्यजनम् अहं करवै अहं कुर्याम् इतीव इति बुद्ध्येव अस्त्राणि अमुञ्चन् ॥८७ ॥

बाणव्यधेन विगलद्रुधिराभिषिक्तैः ।
सर्वाङ्गकैः शुशुभिरे सुभटास्तदानीम् ।
अन्तःप्रदीपनजुषः प्रतिघानलस्य
सन्तापनेन गमिता इव शोणिमानम् ॥८८ ॥

बाण इति । अन्तः अभ्यन्तरे प्रदीपनजुषः प्रदीप्तस्य प्रतिघानलस्य क्रोधानलस्य सन्तापनेन शोणिमानं गमिता इव शुशुभिरे ॥८८ ॥

केचिद्भटाः कुपितशात्रवमण्डलाग्र-
च्छिन्नात्स्वहस्तदक्षिणकरात् पततो गृहीत्वा ।
हस्तेन खड्गमितरेण निशातमाशु
हस्तच्छिदां निचकृतुर्द्विषतां शिरांसि[८२] ॥८९ ॥

केचिदिति । मण्डलाग्रं खड्गः । हस्तच्छिदां द्विषतां शिरांसि निचकृतुः कर्तनं चक्रुः ॥८९ ॥

यावद्भिरावृततनुर्भटसञ्चयोऽभूत्
बाणैः परस्य निशितै रणलब्धवर्णैः ।
आत्ताधिकं स्वमधमर्ण[८३] इवोत्तमर्णं
तं[८४] तावदभ्यधिकबाणगणं निनाय ॥९० ॥

यावदिति । अधमर्णः आत्ताधिकं गृहीतात् अधिकं वृद्धिसहितं स्वं धनम् उत्तमर्णं यथा नयति तथेत्यर्थः ॥९० ॥

अस्पृष्टशात्रवकलेवरमांसमासीत्
शस्त्रं[८५] न किञ्चन तयोरुभयोर्ध्वजिन्योः ।
नैकोऽप्यविद्धतनुतामभजच्छरीरी
तत्सैनिकेषु विधृतोत्तमदंशनोऽपि ॥९१ ॥

अस्पृष्ट इति । विधृतं(त)मुत्तमं दंशनं कवचं येन सः ॥९१ ॥

---

८२. शिरासि (अनुस्वार dropped);

८३. °वर्ण;

८४. ततावदरुभ्य° णनिनाय - (अनुस्वार॰ on त & ण dropped & jointly written); P erases the रु but, B. retains it due possibly to another ms. from which B. was copied down.

८५. शस्त्रन (म् -न् Marathi influence);

आलूनहस्तगजपुङ्गवदेहपातैः
भग्नाः शताङ्गनिवहा धरणौ पतन्तः ।
पार्श्वस्थितं हयपदाति विचूर्णयन्तो
विन्ध्यस्य कुम्भजमृषिं नमतोऽन्वकुर्वन् ॥९२ ॥

आलून इति । गजपतनेन(ना)तिवक्रीभूताः, अत एव पार्श्वस्थितं हयपदाति **कर्म** विचूर्णयन्तः शताङ्गाः कुम्भजम् ऋषिम् अगस्त्यं नमतः विन्ध्यस्य अन्वकुर्वन् अनुकरणं कृतवन्तः ॥९२ ॥

आलूनमस्तकमपि द्विषतां बलेषु
क्षिप्तासि सव्यकरनुन्नचलत्खलीनम् ।
विक्रान्त[८६]सादिनिकुरुम्ब[८७]मरातिखड्ग-
छिन्नोत्तमाङ्गहयपातमनु न्यपप्तत् ॥९३ ॥

आलूनमिति । आलूनमस्तकमपि छिन्नमस्तकमपि द्विषतां बलेषु, क्षिप्तासि क्षिप्तखड्गं, सव्यकरेण नुन्नः चलन् खलीनः येन तत् । एतादृशं, विक्रान्ताः शूराः सादिनः, तेषां निकुरुम्बं समूहः(हम्), अरातिना खड्गेन । छिन्नम् उत्तमाङ्गं यस्य सः, यः(यो) हयः तस्य पातमनु न्यु(न्य)पप्तत् पतितं बभूव । 'शूरो वीरश्च विक्रान्तः' इति **अमरः** । [२.८.७७] ॥९३ ॥

पद्गत्वसंश्रय[८८]तया किल[८९] यैरवाप्या
नापद्गता तदुभयोर्हि मिथो विरोधः ।
तां ताननेष्ट बलवानपरो विरोधः
तेषां[९०] रणे विचरतामसिखेटकाभ्याम् ॥९४ ॥

पदिति । यैः पदातिभिः, पद्भ्यां गच्छतीति पद्गः, पद्गस्य भावः पद्गत्वं, तस्य संश्रयतया, अपद्गता पद्गमनाभावः आपद्गता इति **च** प्रतीयते । नावाप्या न प्राप्या, हि यस्मात्, तयोः पद्गत्वापद्गत्वयोः, मिथः परस्परं विरोधः, तस्मान्नावाप्येति । असिखेटकाभ्यां सह रणे विचरतां तेषां पद्गानां बलवान् अपरः विरोधः विद्वेषः, ताम् आपद्गतां, तान् पद्गान्, अनेष्ट नीतवान्, मारितवानित्यर्थः ॥९४ ॥

---

८६. P. marginal quotation 'शूरो वीरश्च विक्रान्तः' इति **अमरः** ।
८७. °निकुम्बम° (रु dropped);
८८. °सश्र° (अनुस्वार dropped);
८९. P. erases some word completely & writes किल in the right hand margin. After writing ननु, B. changes it to किल in the left hand margin with this (=) sign.
९०. P. marginal gloss पद्गानां;

रक्तापगा दलितकन्धरदन्तिदेह-
मध्ये वहन्त्यहत मेकलकन्यकायाः[११] ।
भां मग्नमालववधूकुचकुङ्कुमेन
शोणाम्भसश्चरितविन्ध्यशिलान्तरायाः ॥९५ ॥

रक्तेति। दलितकन्धरा ये दन्तिदेहाः तेषां मध्ये वहन्ती रक्तापगा मग्नमालववधूकुचकुङ्कुमेन शोणाम्भसः चरितं, विन्ध्यशिलानाम् अन्तरं मध्यो यया सा, तस्याः, मेकलकन्यकायाः नर्मदायाः भां शोभाम् अहत हृतवती ॥९५ ॥

आदाय पाणिचरणादि विलूनगात्र-
खण्डानि तत्र पुनरुत्पतितैरनेकैः ।
कङ्कादिपत्रिनिवहैः[१२] परिपूर्यमाण-
माकाशमन्यरणरङ्ग इवाबभासे ॥९६ ॥

आदायेति । कङ्कादिपत्रिनिवहैः परिपूर्यमाणमाकाशम् अन्यरण[रङ्]गं[ग] इव आबभासे ॥९६ ॥९७ ॥९८ ॥९९ ॥

युद्ध्वैवं चिरमरयः प्रलम्बशत्रोस्तत्सैन्यामितशरवर्षदुःसहत्वात् ।
आतेनुः समरपराङ्मुखाः पलायं स्वानीकैः सह मगधेश्वरादिभूपाः ॥९७ ॥

आसाद्य क्षितिपतयोऽथ दामघोषिं[१३]
तच्छोकं वचनशतैर्निवार्य किञ्चित् ।
प्रस्थाप्य स्वपुरममुं हतावशेषैः
साकं स्वस्वविषयमाप्नुवन्ननीकैः ॥९८ ॥

तदनु हरिविरोधी कुण्डिनं न प्रवेक्ष्या-
म्यहमरिमनिहत्य स्वामलब्ध्वा स्वसारम् ।
इति विरचितसन्धः[१४] कृष्णमासाद्य रुक्मी
समरनिहतसैन्यस्तद्गृहीतो बभूव ॥९९ ॥

---

११. P. marginal quotation 'रेवा तु नर्मदा सोमोद्भवा मेकलकन्यका ।' इति अमरः । [१.१०.३२] B. मेखल°;
१२. निवहैपरि° (विसर्ग dropped & jointly written)·
१३. दामघोषं;
१४. B. inserts the word कृष्णधः between °सन्धः & कृष्ण° which is not at all necessary in the present context as neither the metre nor the meaning requires it. It is influenced by the adjoining words.

तस्यालम्भादथ हलभृता वारितो वासुदेवः
चक्रे भीष्मात्मजमतिरुषास्यासिनोप्तैकपार्श्वम् ।
तन्मुक्तोऽथ द्विषदभिभवाद्दूयमानो निवृत्तो
भैष्मिर्नो[९५]ऽगात्स्वपुरमकरोदान्तमन्यत्र वासम् ॥१०० ॥

तस्येति । तस्य रुक्मिणः आलम्भात् हननात् । अस्य रुक्मिणः असिना खड्गेन उप्तः कृतवपनः एकपार्श्वो यस्य, तं चक्रे । आन्तं मरणपर्यन्तम् अन्यत्र वासमकरोत् ॥१०० ॥

करुणानिधिरीश्वरः स्वदृष्ट्या तदनूज्जीव्य हतान् स्वसैनिकानाम् ।
वपुर[९६]क्षतसंहिताङ्गकं द्राक् रचयं[९७]स्तैर्मुदितैः सह प्रतस्थे ॥१०१ ॥

करुणेति । वपुः अक्षतं क्षतशून्यं संहिताङ्गकं संयोजितावयवं च रचयन् सन् तैः सह प्रतस्थे ॥१०१ ॥१०२ ॥१०३ ॥

रणे विजित्य द्विषतां बलानि भीष्मात्मजामाहृतवन्तमेनम् ।
श्रुत्वोपशल्यं नगरस्य यातं प्रत्युद्ययुर्द्वारवतीनिवासाः ॥१०२ ॥

स उग्रसेनं वसुदेवमन्यान् वृद्धांश्च नत्वा प्रणयाभियातान् ।
यथापुरं स्यन्दनमास्थितः सन् सहैव तैर्द्वारवतीं विवेश ॥१०३ ॥

हृषीकद्वारान्तर्न्यविशत जगद्यत्त[९८]दवसत्
यदीये क्वाप्यंशे ममुरिह जनानां न हृदये ।

यथाऽऽनन्दास्तेषां मधुरशुभवाद्यौ[९९]घनिनदाः
तथा व्याप्ताशेषे वियति विशतीशे निजपुरीम् ॥१०४ ॥

हृषीकमिति । ईशे कृष्णे निजपुरीं विशति सति । हृषीकद्वारा इन्द्रियद्वारेण यत् जगत् अन्तः न्यविशत तत् यदीये क्वापि अंशे प्रदेशे अवसत् । तादृशे अतिविस्तीर्णे जनानां हृदये यथा आनन्दा न ममुः तथा तेषां जनानां मधुरशुभवाद्यौघनिनदाः शब्दाः व्याप्ताशेषे वियति न ममुः । 'हृषीकं विषयीन्द्रियम्' इति **अमरः** । [१.५.८] ' शब्दे निनादनिनदा' इति **अमरः** । [१.६.२२] ॥१०४ ॥

---

९५. °र्नागात्पु°
९६. वपुरक्षित°
९७. चरयद्यस्तैः(वर्णविपर्यय- metathesis);
९८. °द्यत्रद°
९९. °बोद्याद्य° न is not clear due to overwriting.

हरेरतीतोऽभ्युदयः प्रबोधितो महोच्चबन्दिप्रकरोक्तिमालया।
मृषेतरासां समये तदोत्करैस्तथा[100] भविष्यन्नपि स द्विजाशिषाम् ॥१०५॥

हरेरिति। हरेः अतीतः पूर्वकालीनः अभ्युदयः बन्दिप्रकरोक्तिपङ्क्त्या प्रबोधितः कथितः। मृषा[याः] इतराः मृषेतरास्तासां, सत्यानामित्यर्थः। स द्विजाशिषाम् उत्करैः समूहैः भ(र्भ)विष्यन्नपि अभ्युदयः प्रबोधितः ॥१०५॥

तस्याग्रतो नटनमातनिषुः सुवेश्याः[101]
सद्गायनाश्च मधुरं जगुराभिमुख्यम्।
प्राप्याप्सरः स्त्रिय इवेव च नारदाद्याः।
तस्यैव लब्धवसते रविमण्डलान्तः ॥१०६॥

तस्येति। रविमण्डलान्तः रविमण्डलमध्ये लब्धवसतेः तस्यैव तस्य कृष्णस्य आभिमुख्यं प्राप्य अग्रतः अप्सरस्त्रियः इव सुवेश्याः नटनमातनिषुः। नारदाद्या इव सद्गायनाः उत्तमगायकाः मधुरं जगुः गायनं चक्रुः ॥१०६॥

आनीतराजसुतमीश्वरमीक्षमाणाः
प्रासादमारुरुहुरब्जदृशः पुरस्थाः।
तत्र स्थितास्तदुपमा हि तदा सुवर्ण-
पाञ्चालिका अपि जनैः प्रमदाः प्रतीताः ॥१०७॥

आनीत इति। तत्र प्रासादे स्थिताः तदुपमाः स्त्रीतुल्याः सुवर्णपुत्रिका अपि जनैः प्रमदाः प्रतीताः। स्त्रीणां पुत्तलिकानां च भेदं नाज्ञासिषुरिति भावः ॥१०७॥

भीष्मात्मजासुकृतवर्णनवर्णपूर्ण-
रोदो[102]ऽन्तरे पुरसरोजदृ[103]शस्तदानीम्।
कृष्णावलोकसुखविस्मृतमोचनानि
स्मृत्वा हरौ विचकरुः कुसुमानि दैवात् ॥१०८॥

भीष्मे इति (भीष्मेति)। भीष्मात्मजायाः सुकृतवर्णनवर्णैरक्षरैः शब्दैरित्यर्थः। पूर्णं रोदोऽन्तरं पृथ्व्यन्तरीक्षं यस्मिन्, तस्मिन्। तदानीं तस्मिन् काले, पुरसरोजदृशः कृष्णावलोकनसुखेन विस्मृतं मोचनं येषां तानि कुसुमानि दैवात् स्मृत्वा हरौ विचकरुः विकीर्णितवत्यः ॥१०८॥

---

१००. °त्करेस्तथा;
१०१. सवेश्या (विसर्ग dropped);
१०२. °रोदा°;
१०३. °द°;

तैः पौरपद्मनयनाञ्जलिमुक्तपुष्प-
लाजैर्निजोपरि पतद्भिरयं[१०४] तदानीम् ।
गीर्वाणमानवकृताऽवितथप्रशंसा-
वर्णैरिवातिशुचिभिर्भगवान् प्रपेदे ॥१०९ ॥

तैरिति । तदानीं निजोपरि पतद्भिः भगवदुपरि पतद्भिः अतिशुचिभिः तैः पौरपद्मनयनाञ्जलिमुक्तपुष्पलाजैः गीर्वाणमानवकृता अवितथप्रशंसा, तद्वर्णैरिव अयं भगवान् प्रपेदे ॥१०९ ॥

यस्य द्वारे शतमखमुखा द्वारपालैर्निरोधं
नीयन्ते तत्स्वभवनमथाऽऽसाद्य लक्ष्मीसहायः ।
देवक्याद्यं प्रणमति निजं मातृवर्गं स्म[१०५] भक्त्या
न्यग्भूतह्रीभरमथ[१०६] विदर्भेश्वरस्यात्मजाऽपि ॥११० ॥

यस्येति । न्यग्भूतः तिरस्कृतः [१०६]ह्रीभरः लज्जाभरो यस्मिन् कर्मणि यथा [स्यात्] तथा ॥११० ॥

तदनु शुभमुहूर्ते भीष्मराजस्य कन्यां
यदुपतिरुपयेमे स्वानुभावेन लब्धाम् ।
विधिमुखदिविजेन्द्रैरुत्सवं द्रष्टुकामैः
यदुपतिसदनं तत्पूर्णमासीत्तदानीम्[१०७] ॥१११ ॥

तदन्विति । स्वानुभावेन स्वसामर्थ्येन ॥१११ ॥

विभवैर्हि मनोज्ञता महानां विभवा यत्कृपया जनेन लभ्याः ।
न कथं विदधीत नाम तस्या उपयामो जनलोचनप्रमोदम् ॥११२ ॥

विभवैरिति । यैर्विभवैः **करणैः**, महानाम् उत्सवानां मनोज्ञता । 'मह उद्धव उत्सवः' इति **अमरः** ॥[१.७.३८] ते विभवाः जनेन यत्कृपया यस्याः कृपया लभ्याः, तस्याः उपयामः विवाहः(हो) जनलोचनानां प्रमोदं कथं न विदधीत, कथं न कुर्यात्, अपि तु कुर्यादेव ॥११२ ॥

---

१०४. पतद्गि°;
१०५. स्वभक्त्या;
१०६. P.B. & P1 write as -ही- — Marathi influence.
१०७. °त्र° (cf. vs. 104);

विधिवत्पाणौकरणं जगतां जनकेन लोकमातुस्तत् ।
वीक्ष्य प्रजास्तदानीं निर्वेलं[१०८] प्रमद[१०९]माप्नुवंश्चित्रम् ॥११३ ॥

विधिवदिति । जगतां जनकेन लोकमातुः तत् प्रसिद्धं विधिवत् पाणौकरणं पाणिग्रहणं तदानीं प्रजाः जनाः(ना) वीक्ष्य निर्वेलं प्रमोदमाप्नुवन् प्राप्ता **इति चित्रम्** । **चित्रार्थपक्षे**-प्रजाः सन्तानानि । सन्तानकर्तृकपितृमातृविवाहः कर्मकावलोकनासम्भवः, विवाहोत्तरं सन्तानोत्पत्तेः ॥११३ ॥

ऊढ्वा[११०] कृष्णो विदर्भक्षितिपतितनयां सप्त चान्याः, सहस्रा-
[१११]ण्युत्कानां षोडशापि क्षितितनयजयप्राप्तकन्योत्तमानाम् ।
एकैकस्यां तनूजान्[११२] दश दश जनयन्नात्मतुल्यानुभावान्
दुष्टव्रातं निगृह्णन् सुजनसुखकृते लोकनाथो व्यहार्षीत् ॥११४ ॥

ऊढ्वेति । क्षितितनयः नरकासुरः । व्यहार्षीत् विहारमकरोत् ॥११४ ॥

दशरूपधरस्तवप्रभावाहितसारूप्यमिवास्ति सर्गरूपैः ।
दशभिर्निजविग्रहैर्यदेतद्धरिपादाम्बुजयोः समार्पि[११३] काव्यम् ॥११५ ॥

दशेति । यत् दशभिः दशसङ्ख्याकैः सर्गरूपैः निजविग्रहैः निजशरीरैः, दशरूपधरः हरिः, तस्य स्तवप्रभवेन आहितं सारूप्यं येन तत् । तदेतत्काव्यं हरिपादाम्बुजयोः समार्पि समर्पितं, **मयेति शेषः** ॥११५ ॥

श्रीमन्नृसिंहभारत्यभिधानान् देशिकान्नमस्यामि ।
भगवत्पादपुरोगमगुरुमणिमालामणीयते यैस्तान् ॥११६ ॥

श्रीमन्निति । देशिकान् गुरून् । 'गुरौ देश्ये च देशिकः' इति **अमरः** । [३.३.१७] [२७] यैर्देशिकैः भगवत्पादः शङ्कराचार्यः, तत्पुरोगमा तत्पुरःसरा या गुरुमणिमाला तस्यां मणीयते मणिवत् आचर्यते । शङ्कराचार्यशिष्यपरम्परागतानित्यर्थः ॥११६-१२१ ॥

स्वपूर्वजानां[११४] सुगतिप्रदां यो निनाय वाणीं निजमन्ववायम् ।
तपोऽनुभावेन निजेन लोकं भगीरथो देवनदीमिवेमम् ॥११७ ॥

---

१०८. निर्वेदं,(on the analogy of the following प्रमद०);
१०९. द् not clear due to overwriting;
११०. ओढ्वा;
१११. ण्युप्युत्कानां;
११२. °जांन्दश (अनुस्वार + अनुनासिक both used-Marathi influence);
११३. समापि (रेफ dropped);
११४. °जाना (अनुस्वार dropped);

चिद्घनानन्दनाथाख्यं तं नमामि पितामहम्।
अनसूयोपमानां च वेङ्कमाख्यां[115] पितामहीम् ॥११८॥

आकालधर्ममनवाप्तपराभवेन
दुर्दान्तवादिविजयेन कथासु येन।
निष्पादितस्य यशसो जगदेव साक्षि
तं त्र्यम्बकाख्यमहमस्मि नमन् पितृव्यम् ॥११९॥

विद्वद्वरांस्त्रिविक्रमशर्मण आत्मीयपितृचरणान्।
वन्दे सतीवरिष्ठां पार्वत्यभिधां च निजजननीम् ॥१२०॥

गङ्गाधरनामभ्यां[116] न्यायव्याकरणलाभो मे।
याभ्यामभूद्व्रजे तौ कारुण्यनिधी[117] गुरू नित्यम् ॥१२१॥

यद्धीर्जगज्जातमिवासुरारेस्तनूरखेदाऽभृत शास्त्रजातम्।
त्रिविक्रमाभिख्यतदात्मजन्मा यः पार्वतीनन्दनतामयासीत् ॥१२२॥

यद्धीरिति। त्रिविक्रमाभिख्यश्चासौ स च[118] त्रिविक्रमाभिख्यः स त्रिविक्रमाभिख्यः, तस्य आत्मजन्मा पुत्रः ॥१२२ ॥१२३॥

नीलकण्ठेन तेनास्मिन् यादवेन्द्रमहोदये।
कृते काव्येऽपि दशमः सर्गः सम्पूर्णतां गतः ॥१२३॥[119]

इति पुण्यपत्तननिवासिरानडे इत्युपनामकशामरायाङ्गजविष्णुविरचितायां श्रीमद्विद्वन्मणिनीलकण्ठकविवर्यकृत-यादवेन्द्रमहोदयकाव्यस्य टिप्पन्यां दशमः सर्गः समाप्तः ॥

शके १७७१ फाल्गुनासितद्वादश्यां रविवासरे टिप्पनं समाप्तम् ॥

११५. केङ्क (क due to the following क- a case of attraction);
११६. °नामभ्यान्याय° (अनुस्वार dropped & jointly written);
The द्विवचन in नामभ्यां is possibly the result of the द्विवचन in गुरू being foremost in the mind of the poet-since only one गुरु viz. गङ्गाधर, is specifically mentioned. Or is it that his father त्रिविक्रम was also his other teacher?
११७. कारण्य°;
११८. Evidently is is a repetition, committed inadvertently, posibly in a hurry to complete it.
११९. P. adds. श्रीकृष्णाय नमः ॥

ALPHABETICAL INDEX OF VERSES

ALPHABETICAL INDEX OF QUOTATIONS

			या.म.टि.
धर्माः पुण्ययमन्याय°	अमर	३.३.१३९	१.१५
नक्षत्रं ऋक्षं भं तारा	अमर	१.३.२१	८.६२
निकाय्यनिलयालयाः	अमर	२.२.५	४.४७
निकृष्टप्रतिकृष्टार्व°	अमर	३.१.५४	६.४
निर्व्यापारस्थितौ	अमर	३.३.४७	३.५
नुत्तनुन्नास्त°	अमर	३.१.८७	६.३
पङ्कः पापः (पङ्कोऽस्त्री)	मेदिनी	३.२९	२.६४
परित्राणाय साधूनां	भ. गीता	४.८	८.१०७
परे त्वह्नि परे द्यवि	अमर	३.४.२१	१०.४३
पाणिर्निकुब्जः प्रसृतिः	अमर	२.६.८४	३.८३
पीयूषोऽभिनवं पयः	अमर	२.९.५४	३.६
पुरि लुङ् चास्मे	पाणिनि	३.२.१२२	१.२७
पुष्करं खे जलेऽपि च	कोशः	—	५.२१
पुंस्येवान्धुः प्रहिः कूपः	अमर	१.१०.२६	३.११
प्रकाण्डमुद्धतल्लजौ	अमर	१.४.२७(b)	९.७९
प्रतिघः रुट्क्रुधौ	अमर	१.७.२६	९.७८
प्रतिज्ञा (नियमा) श्रव°	अमर	१.५.५.	१.२२
प्रशस्तवाचकान्यमूनि	अमर	१.४.२७(c)	९.७९
प्रश्नोऽनुयोगः पृच्छा च	अमर	१.६.१०	३.३४
प्राकारो वरणः सालः	अमर	२.२.३	३.८५
बले रामो नीलचारु°	अमर	३.३.१४०	४.५१
बुधवृद्धौ पण्डितेऽपि	अमर	३.३.१००	२.६५
भिः सा स्त्री भक्त°	अमर	२.९.४८	२.५९
भुवनं तोयलोकयोः	—	—	६.२४
मङ्गलदेवता लक्ष्मीः	—	—	१०.३१
मन्थनी गर्गरी समे	अमर	२.९.७४	३.२२
मन्थानं मन्दरं कृत्वा	विष्णु पु.	१.९.८४	३.१७
मह उद्धव उत्सवः	अमर	१.७.३८	२.५९; १०.११२

			या.म.टि.
सूतिमासो वैजननः	अमर	२.६.३९	१.५४
स्थायुकोऽधिकृतो	अमर	२.८.७	३.१२
स्फातिर्वृद्धौ	अमर	३.२.९	४.३३
हरिर्दिवाकर॰	हैम	२.४७३	१०.५४
हविर्भुजा अम्बु	—	—	७.१९
हीनसम्बोधने तु रे	—	—	१०.७९
हूतिराकारणाह्वानं	अमर	१.६.८	९.३२
हृषीकं विषयीन्द्रियं	अमर	१.५.८	१०.१०४
हंसकः पादकटकः	अमर	२.६.११०	५.१५